Political Development
in Eastern Europe

edited by
Jan F. Triska
Paul M. Cocks

foreword by
Gabriel Almond

The Praeger Special Studies program—
utilizing the most modern and efficient book
production techniques and a selective
worldwide distribution network—makes
available to the academic, government, and
business communities significant, timely
research in U.S. and international economic, social, and political development.

Political Development in Eastern Europe

PRAEGER SPECIAL STUDIES IN INTERNATIONAL POLITICS AND GOVERNMENT

Praeger Publishers　　　New York　　　London

Library of Congress Cataloging in Publication Data
Main entry under title:

Political development in Eastern Europe.

   (Praeger special studies in international politics
and government)
   Includes index.
   1. Europe, Eastern—Politics and government—
Addresses, essays, lectures. 2. Political participation—
Europe, Eastern—Addresses, essays, lectures.
I. Triska, Jan F., 1922-   II. Cocks, Paul.
JN96.A91P64   320.9'47'085   76-19551
ISBN 0-275-23600-5
ISBN 0-275-89640-4 student ed.

   The editors are grateful to the American Council of Learned
Societies and the Center for Russian and East European Studies at
Stanford University for their financial support. They also wish to
thank Ms. Shannon Salmon for kindly preparing the index.

PRAEGER PUBLISHERS
200 Park Avenue, New York, N.Y. 10017, U.S.A.

Published in the United States of America in 1977
by Praeger Publishers, Inc.

789 038 987654321

Printed in the United States of America

Studies of communism as historical reality have gone through four rather distinct although overlapping stages. In the years after the Bolshevik Revolution roughly in the middle and late 1930s Russian communism was viewed as a dictatorship of a special kind, with its opponents stressing its lawless, despotic characteristics, and its friends stressing its populistic and trusteeship properties.

The term totalitarianism first came into use in the early 1930s and then with reference to Italian fascism. From its very earliest usage it reflected a groping for an adequate description of what seemed to be a new form of polity—one combining the properties of historic tyranny with modern techniques of organization, communication, and coercion. The elaboration of this typological concept occurred in the period from the late 1930s until the 1950s, and it sought to isolate the common properties of Italian fascism, German national socialism, Russian, Eastern European, Chinese, and other national varieties of communism. Hannah Arendt in her *Origins of Totalitarianism*[1] focused on the common characteristics of national socialism and bolshevism, arguing that the extraordinary enhancement of central power and penetrative coerciveness in these regimes was attained through a refusal to make stable delegations of power and functions among the governmental, party, police, and military bureaucracies. Carl J. Friedrich and Zbigniew Brzezinski in the mid-1950s offered a definition of totalitarianism as a highly stable system based on a cluster of six mutually reinforcing features—a single mass party, an official ideology, control over the economy, control over communications processes, the armed forces, and a terroristic police system.[2] Barrington Moore, in an unusually perceptive dynamic analysis of the Soviet Union (1954), presented a latent pluralist model of Communist ideology and politics claiming that traditionalist and technocratic impulses were in conflict with the revolutionary ideological ones and that Soviet development might take a more open form depending on accomplishments, threats, and opportunities in the domestic and international environments.[3] The totalitarian concept was from its very beginning a mixed ideological and analytic concept. Its aptness came to be questioned as Communist reality changed after World War II and particularly after the Yugoslav defection, de-Stalinization and the Eastern European rebellions of the 1950s, and the emergence into the open of the Sino-Soviet conflict.

The third stage of studies of communism was first called national communism and then comparative communism. What both of these concepts sought to capture was the emerging varieties of the Communist experience. While the totalitarianism concept assumed the uniformity of these systems, attributable to the extraordinary transformative capacities of Communist movements, national and comparative communism assumed the vitality and survival of indigenous national and social structural features, and differences in goals and tactics of the leaders of the various Communist countries. Specifying these differences, interpreting their causes, and speculating about future trends were the principal aims of this approach. Beginning with more descriptive studies such as those of Zbigniew Brzezinski and Carl H. Skilling, this approach moved toward more systematic comparison and characterization of ruling and nonruling Communist movements in an international system, reported in the early work of Jan Triska and his associates (1969).[4] Later studies of this kind are reported in Lenard J. Cohen and Jane P. Shapiro (1974) and in Carmelo Mesa-Lago and Carl Beck (1975).[5]

Overlapping with this comparative communism perspective, but becoming increasingly self-conscious in the mid-1960s, was the treatment of Communist phenomena within the more general framework of comparative politics. Pioneering contributions of this kind were Robert Tucker's treatment of communist systems as a variety of "movement regime" and the comparison by Brzezinski and Samuel Huntington of the structure and performance of the United States and the Soviet Union.[6] By the late 1960s this trend was in full swing involving the application of interest group theory to Communist politics in the work of Skilling; participation theory in the work of Jan Triska and Sidney Verba; political culture theory in the work of Robert C. Tucker, Frederick Fleron, and Richard Fagen; organization and administrative theory in the work of Paul Cocks and Aaron Wildavsky; and political development theory in the work of Jan Triska and Paul Johnson.[7]

This last trend toward the assimilation of Communism studies into the comparative politics discipline represents a significant step in the professional maturation of both fields. The introduction of general comparative perspectives in the study of Communist countries illuminated patterns and processes not previously perceived or properly weighted. Perhaps of greater significance has been the feedback from Communism studies to the general field of comparative politics. Our theories of political parties, interest groups, political participation, political recruitment, political culture, policy making, and administrative organization and process have been substantially improved through their having been tested and in some respects found wanting in Communist contexts.

But more important than this has been the contribution of Communism studies to the larger theoretical issues of political change and development. Jan Triska's work from its very beginnings has treated communism as an international system as well as a distinct set of political systems. The political processes and developmental prospects of Communist countries have been and still to a very substantial extent are deeply affected and limited by the fact of membership by the Soviet elite in the internal policy-making coalitions of these countries. Whatever change or "development" takes place in the dependent Communist countries is orchestrated by an external actor operating directly and more or less continuously through the endogenous structures and processes of these countries. This is hardly a novelty among students of international communism, but formulated in general theoretical terms as Triska and Johnson, and now Triska and Cocks have presented it, they have confronted political theorists with the inescapable challenge of dealing with the variety of ways that international and national environments interact one with the other.

The separation of international and comparative studies has never been tenable, but the Communist case presses the weakness of a purely comparative approach to the point at which theoretical creativity becomes unavoidable. It is a tribute to the recent trends in studies of communism, and most particularly to the work of Triska and his associates, that having borrowed from the fund of general frameworks and concepts in comparative theory, they are now repaying this debt with interest by theoretical innovations stemming from the peculiar features of the Communist experience.

An outsider is at a loss to explain the pessimism about Communism studies expressed in one or two of the pieces of the present volume. Surely the last decade has seen an extraordinary production of increasingly rigorous and illuminating work on Communist societies. One factor that has hampered research from the beginning has been the relative inaccessibility of Communist countries to direct field research. That so much has been accomplished despite this difficulty redounds all the more to the credit of the subdiscipline. A second factor must surely be the wave of disillusionment affecting Eastern European studies after the collapse of liberalization in the late 1960s. Expectations of a secular trend toward pluralism, participation, and decentralization have been disappointed, and have contributed to a mood of skepticism about the usefulness of general concepts such as these.

It is true that the first applications of these concepts to Communist countries assumed more isomorphism than was there, but it was only through such assumptions that we began to get a more secure grasp of the peculiar contours of Communist structures and processes. Truth is never won in a single step, and if we take our philosophers of science seriously it may be that we can never win it, but only correct our errors. Popper tells us that progress in scientific work consists in making and correcting our mistakes just as fast as we can. And Pareto with characteristic Latin temperament exhorts us, "Give me fertile error bursting with the seeds of its own correction, and you can keep your sterile truth!"

NOTES

1. Hannah Arendt, *Origins of Totalitarianism* (New York: Harcourt Brace, 1951).

2. Carl J. Friedrich and Zbigniew Brzezinski, *Totalitarian Dictatorship and Autocracy* (Cambridge, Mass.: Harvard University Press, 1956).

3. Barrington Moore, *Terror and Progress USSR* (Cambridge, Mass.: Harvard University Press, 1954).

4. Zbigniew Brzezinski, *The Soviet Bloc* (Cambridge, Mass.: Harvard University Press, 1960); H. Gordon Skilling, *The Government and Politics of Eastern Europe* (Ithaca, N.Y.: Cornell University Press, 1966); Jan Triska, ed., *Communist Party States; Comparative and International Studies* (Indianapolis: Bobbs Merrill, 1969).

5. Lenard J. Cohen and Jane P. Shapiro, *Communist Systems in Comparative Perspective* (Garden City, N.Y.: Anchor, 1974); Carmelo Mesa-Lago and Carl Beck, eds., *Comparative Socialist Systems* (Pittsburgh: University of Pittsburgh, 1975).

6. Robert C. Tucker, "Towards a Comparative Politics of Movement Regimes," *APSR*, June 1961, pp. 281-89; Zbigniew Brzezinski and Samuel Huntington, *Political Power: USA/USSR* (New York: Viking, 1963).

7. H. Gordon Skilling and Franklyn Griffiths, *Interest Groups in Soviet Politics* (Princeton, N.J.: Princeton University Press, 1971); Jan Triska and Ann Barbic, "Evaluating Citizen Performance at the Community Level," unpublished ms., 1974.

Also, Sidney Verba and Goldie Shabad, "Workers Councils and Political Stratification, Jugoslav Experience," unpublished ms., 1975; Robert C. Tucker, "Culture, Political Culture and Communist Society," *Political Science Quarterly*, June 1973, pp. 173-90; Frederic Fleron, "Technology and Communist Culture," in Mesa-Lago and Beck, eds., *Comparative Socialist Systems*, pp. 286-300; Richard Fagen, *The Transformation of Political Culture in Cuba* (Stanford, Calif.: Stanford University Press, 1969); Paul Cocks, "Bureaucracy and Party Control," in Mesa-Lago and Beck, eds., *Comparative Socialist Systems*, pp. 215-48; Aaron Wildavsky, *Comparative Budget-Making* (Boston: Little, Brown, 1975); Jan Triska and Paul Johnson, *Political Development and Political Change in Eastern Europe* (Denver: University of Denver Monograph Series in World Affairs, 1975).

CONTENTS

LIST OF TABLES

LIST OF FIGURES

INTRODUCTION
Jan F. Triska
Paul M. Cocks

The need for new thinking on East European politics has become more and more apparent. Old theories and traditional approaches have proved inadequate in describing and explaining changing realities and the variety of political phenomena that have come to dominate our attention. At the same time, there is a growing need to integrate Communist studies more closely within a broader comparative politics framework. Past experience shows that separate paths of intellectual development tend to produce among both Communist specialists and general comparativists a narrow ethnocentric outlook and deficient culture-bound vision. This book is an attempt to respond to both these needs. Moreover, it is our belief that concepts and analytical tools of the social sciences offer useful insights and perspectives by which we can advance and restructure our knowledge of East European political systems. In short, more effective integration can facilitate and sharpen the style and substance of our rethinking.

To be sure, many models, methods, and metaphors of the social sciences have in recent years been incorporated into and are transforming the whole of our scholarship on Communist systems. Nonetheless, the behavioral revolution in Communist studies is still an "unfinished revolution," uneven in its results and problematical in its course. "A large part of the attempt at theory building has been undertaken primarily with the Soviet system in mind; until recently it had little visible impact on the East European field," notes one authority.[1] Moreover, "the methods and techniques standard to behavioralism are a long way from becoming accepted tools of the field."[2] Indeed, it is the underdevelopment of East European studies in general—the lack of empirical research as well as the absence of theory—that prompted Vernon Aspaturian to declare, "What the field needs is more data and information, not new theories and models."[3]

In many respects, the basic building blocks still do not exist for even modest theory building, let alone for grand designs of comparative analysis. For that matter, glaring evidence also exists of the failings of our general schemes in comparative politics. At a time when comparativists themselves are reexamining the validity and universality of their assumptions and approaches, it would be indeed a sign of cultural lag for Communist specialists to emulate and borrow indiscriminately contemporary social science concepts.[4] Using modern frameworks "does not advance our theoretical knowledge very far," adds Joseph LaPalombara. "It may seriously impede our understanding of how Communist systems work . . . and may even lead us backward in the sense of impeding our ever learning what these systems really are."[5]

Yet even a cursory review of traditional Communist studies shows that a search for more data and information without theories and models is neither productive nor enlightening. Traditional Communist area and country studies have not become means for discovering systematic generalizations and for defining hypotheses; they have become an end in themselves. And they gave students of comparative politics an excellent excuse not to bother with "unsystematic" and "parochial" Communist studies and leave them out of their purview—while paying attention to Latin American, African, West European, East Asian, and other area and country studies. Of course in the process both the Communist systems specialists and the comparative politics generalists were the losers. Neither learned. Description and explanation of politics, based on comparative, systematic empirical analysis of areas and countries, have remained incomplete.

Obviously, our motto must be "to adapt" rather than "to adopt." We feel strongly that what is required in the study of East European politics is both more research and more theorizing. Indeed this volume has been shaped largely with this dual need in mind. While they differ considerably in level of generalization and detail of evidence, all the essays represent creative exercises in theoretical analysis and/or empirical description. They are innovative in presentation as well as in content.

Political development has been chosen as the main focus of the essays for several reasons. First, Western analysis of Communist systems is beginning to emphasize more and more the processes of change in Communist societies. Some of the most innovative, and we think most important, advances in this direction are being made by scholars who are interested in applying and adapting some of the assumptions, approaches, and techniques of modernization theory and political change analysis. Second, perceptions and political research within East European states also are changing. Among Marxist scholars, too, there is movement toward "the change to change." The crises of the 1950s and 1960s have made them increasingly aware of the need to formulate a more adequate theory of political development and political decay in socialist societies. A better understanding of the dynamics of development is sought by Communist elites in part to enable them to adjust more effectively their political structures and processes to the changing conditions and new demands of an increasingly complex world and technological era.

On another level, we wish to stress the role of politics and government in developmental issues and dilemmas. Here we share the concern felt by many students of Communist affairs and voiced recently by Rudolf Tokes, "We must bring back politics into comparative studies by restoring it to its proper place as the central subject of Communist studies."[6] Similarly, LaPalombara notes more generally, "The crying need in comparative political science is to illuminate exactly this sector,"[7] that is, the "black box" aspects of government institutions and processes.

Focusing on developmental concerns, moreover, permits us to illuminate and to clarify the political dynamics in East Europe. A major weakness of the old totalitarian model was its incapacity to change or to resolve developmental problems. The theory of totalitarianism lacked any theory of change. The totalitarian model or syndrome itself amounted to little more than a rigid checklist of supposedly permanent features. One of our principal tasks has been to liberate political analysis of Communist systems from the simplistic and static assumptions that limited it in the past. Again, this is a problem with which our colleagues in comparative politics are still wrestling. Many contemporary behavioral models have been found to be essentially static, not dynamic. For example, a dominant theoretical tendency in comparative politics has taken the form of application of systems theory to the study of politics. Recently, this approach has been increasingly criticized for its basically static, "equilibrium" bias, as unsuitable for the analysis and explanation of political change. Although system-functional theories attempt to deal with change and growth, they tend to be more concerned with and suitable for the explanation of persistence and system maintenance. Accordingly, efforts are now being made to adapt systems theory in a more developmental direction.[8]

Generally speaking, therefore, students of Communist systems as well as those of comparative politics are both beset by many of the same fundamental problems and deficiencies. For far too long, we have tried to overcome these limitations in isolation from each other. Neither field enjoys a monopoly of wisdom and the truth. Each can benefit greatly from closer mutual interaction and intellectual exchange. Each has something to say to the other. Study of political development problems, moreover, provides one of the better subjects in which we can try to enhance our common understanding as well as to test and refine our concepts.

With respect to political development as a subject and a concept, theories and definitions have proliferated like mushrooms after a spring rain, to use a favorite Russian expression. Generally speaking, though, there is substantial if diffuse consensus in the literature that political development is about one or all of three things: increasing equality among individuals with respect to the political system; increasing differentiation of political institutions and structures; and increasing capacity of the political system in relation to its environment.[9] Within this developmental syndrome, concern has recently shifted particularly to the third dimension. Moreover, it is not merely administrative capacity to carry out economic development programs but rather the generalized capacity of government to handle crises, to manage change, and to maintain stability that has become the center of attention.[10] Samuel Huntington, for example, makes the relationship between political participation and political institutionalization the central focus of political change. This relationship determines the stability of the political system.[11] James S. Coleman suggests that political development refers to a special polity capacity:

> It is an integrative, responsive, adaptive, and innovative capacity. It is a capacity not only to overcome the divisions and manage the tensions created by increased differentiation, but to respond to or contain the participatory and distributive demands generated by

the imperatives of equality. It is also a capacity to innovate and manage continuous change.[12]

A creative and not just a survival capacity is the hallmark of a developing polity.[13] Gabriel Almond similarly emphasizes the concept of integrative and mobilization capabilities, their development and transformation. "Political change," he writes, "deals with those transactions between the political system and its environment that affect changes in general system performance, or capabilities that in turn are associated with changes in the performance of system-adaptation functions and conversion functions."[14]

In addition, there has been rising interest in coming to grips with the roles of external influences and foreign participation in national development. Until recently, external factors tended to be completely neglected. Almond, Rostow, Apter, Huntington and all other generalists had treated political systems as if they had no foreign environment. International politics had no effect on domestic politics, and vice versa. There were no linkages. Today, however, efforts are being made to distinguish and describe domestic and international environmental impacts on the politics and processes of development.[15]

Given the growing concern with these topics in the general literature, we have made them the thematic focus around which to organize our discussion of political development in East Europe. Preceding and putting into larger perspective the analyses of institutional development, political participation, and external influences, however, are two broad-gauged essays by Andrzej Korbonski and Paul Johnson (on ideological adaptation and conceptual change). The former attempts to summarize and evaluate Western and East European literature analyzing the process of political change in the region since the mid-1950s. More specifically, Korbonski looks at advances and deficiencies in Western research in the five systemic areas of culture, structure, groups, leadership, and policies as well as in the five developmental challenges and crises of identity, legitimacy, penetration, participation, and distribution, which tend to be faced by most if not all political systems. As regards East European views, he notes growing concern about the impact of scientific and technical progress on the socialist model and about the proper role of the party in postindustrial society.

Closely related but on a more theoretical level, Paul Johnson analyzes the problems of conceptualizing change and attempts by Western scholars to apply modernization theory as an explanation of political change in East European states. By and large, he notes, the theoretical tendency has been to redefine as variables what used to be seen as the essentially static parameters of political life in the region, while the dominant focus has correspondingly shifted from explaining the ways in which the structural setting of politics influenced or determined the pattern of elite conflicts, the making of policy, and the outcomes for society and the world community, toward trying to describe and explain political structure itself. Observing the general neglect in the literature of the whole problem of how to measure system performance, he proposes an analytical framework and modal indicators for measuring change.

Three essays address themselves to the general theme of institutional and organizational development. Paul Cocks examines recent efforts in theory and practice by several East European regimes to refashion and maintain the model of "directed society" for "developed socialism." He traces progress and problems in three areas of administrative retooling: the use of modern analytical techniques in decision making; the search for more flexible organizational structures and effective management systems; and new programs in leadership training and cadre development. Generally speaking, the response of both developed capitalist and socialist governments to the scientific revolution of the mid-twentieth century, he argues, has been basically the same: to try to integrate complexity and manage change through advances in organization and technology.

Ken Jowitt offers us a new analytical framework for viewing political development in European Leninist systems. From this perspective, regime structure may be seen as a set of political-organizational adaptations that emerge in response to specific developmental tasks and strategic political uncertainties (both external and internal). Jowitt identifies three main elite-designated core tasks and stages of development: transformation, consolidation, and inclusion. By the mid-1960s several countries in the region began to shift to an inclusion task orientation. This involved, he explains, attempts to expand the internal boundaries of the regime's political, productive, and decision-making systems, to integrate itself with the nonofficial sectors of society rather than insulate itself from them. Progress toward inclusion has not been without problems and reverses, however. As a result, Jowitt suggests, the 1970s have witnessed the emergence of "amalgam regimes," fragile combinations of conflicting inclusion and mobilization features and responses. A central issue remains the organizational and ideological definition of the Party itself.

The problem of institutional development and elite-mass relations is the subject of Zvi Gitelman's essay. More broadly, he suggests that socialist systems have failed to evolve political institutions as linkages between elites and masses. East European institutions endure and seem stable because they are propped up by power, force, and coercion. Once power is temporarily withdrawn, the stability and persistence of institutions disappear immediately, as evident in Poland in 1956 and in Czechoslovakia in 1968. The basic political problem in the region, he concludes, is "overinstitutionalization," which manifests itself in political constraint, immobilism, and inertia. He illustrates this problem with a detailed analysis of workers' self-management organizations in Poland. These institutions, he shows, became hollow shells through which influence, if it flowed at all, flowed only in a downward direction. In the absence of valued, as well as stable, institutions, elite-mass linkages became weak and tenuous, isolating the Party leadership from the working class and arousing frustration among the workers, who felt unable to communicate with the political elite. Hence, the basis was laid for the December 1970 workers' riots and the fall of the Gomulka regime.

Patterns and problems of political participation in Eastern Europe comprise the central focus of the essays by Jan Triska, Lenard Cohen, and Mary Ellen Fischer. Generally speaking, Western scholars have been reluctant to study political participation in socialist societies for two reasons. First, access to relevant information is difficult. Second, participatory activity has been regarded and dismissed as essentially "pseudo-participation," manipulated and mobilized by government. All three essays not only contribute new and rich empirical data on participation. They also provide new perspectives and argumentation that force us at least to question and qualify, if not change, some of our old assumptions about and interpretations of political participation in socialist regimes.

Reporting on the findings of recent survey research and opinion analysis carried out jointly by Western and East European specialists, Triska discusses citizen involvement in community decision making at the county and district level in Yugoslavia, Romania, Hungary, and Poland. He explores the scope, intensity, structure, and types of citizen participation; analyzes attitudinal factors associated with participation (interest, information, efficacy, and sense of obligation); and compares citizens within and outside various organizational structures. In particular, he looks at how and how much different citizens participate; the difference in citizen participation between functional and other social-political participatory modes; how and how much different nationalities participate in a multinational state; how citizens become deputies; what they think of deputies; how conflicts of interest are handled. From this analysis political participation in Eastern Europe emerges as a multidimensional and mixed phenomenon, encompassing both autonomous and mobilized features; it is a much more complex concept than we have previously assumed and described, one that embodies purposeful activities by citizens to influence, if not to determine, community decisions, especially in specific issue areas.

Whereas Triska examines public opinion and citizen attitudes about political participation, Lenard J. Cohen and Mary Ellen Fischer concentrate on the electoral system and voter behavior in two quite different countries, Yugoslavia and Romania. "The quest to develop institutional structures for the representation and reconciliation of various group interests," Cohen observes, "has been one of the central themes of Yugoslav politics and government." Yugoslav efforts to democratize the electoral system offer, in fact, an excellent case study of the issues and dilemmas involved in the political development of one-party, particularly Communist one-party regimes. In a very detailed analysis of the 1969 elections to legislative assemblies on the republican-provincial level, Cohen discusses the patterns of electoral behavior and voter turnout, especially in relation to political dissent and competition as expressed in the use and consequences of multiple candidacies. The "negative" byproducts of even this limited electoral democracy, however, were apparently too potentially explosive, Cohen suggests, in the regime's view to permit continuation of its short-lived experiment with political competition. Significantly, the new electoral system and constitutional structure established in 1974 in Yugoslavia bear very little resemblance to earlier arrangements.

Mary Ellen Fischer similarly examines recent efforts by the Ceausescu regime in Romania to broaden somewhat the scope of political participation while at the same time preserving the leading position of the single party and its ideology. She devotes special attention to the 1975 national elections and the use, for the first time, of multiple candidates. Drawing upon the small amount of available voting data, personal interviews with election officials, and informal discussions both before and after the elections, she offers some necessarily tentative conclusions about this new election technique and political experiment, much more limited, to be sure, than the Yugoslav example. Like Cohen, Fischer also tries to put these participatory reforms in the broader context of leadership responses and strategies to the political issues and consequences of socioeconomic modernization.

Organizationally, discussion of the impact and role of exogenous variables on East European politics is divided into two sections. The first deals primarily with Soviet influences while the second explores non-Soviet influences. Admittedly, this is a rather arbitrary and artificial separation, since in reality these factors are usually closely related and mutually interdependent. Given the long and strong tendency among Western scholars to view Eastern Europe in a strict dependency relationship with the Soviet Union, as a region relatively isolated and immune from other external forces and stimuli, however, we feel that it is important to make this distinction. We have done so in large part in order to bring out more clearly new dimensions on both sides of the linkages issue.

As regards the "Moscow connection," Kent Brown provides a new perspective on the nature of Soviet-East European relations. Following recent efforts to study more intensively the influence of bargaining, pluralism, and conflict on domestic decision-making processes in socialist regimes, he extends this kind of analysis to the international system and interstate relations. Most policy making in Eastern Europe, he contends, is the result of a process of coalition formation and interaction between domestic and external actors within a particular country's political system. Factions within the Soviet leadership and additional Soviet groups and individuals should be viewed as important participants in the domestic coalition process. Indeed, this cross-national process of coalition formation provides the means by which Soviet influence permeates East European political structures at several levels and on a large variety of issues. Growing internal differentiation and pluralism in the region, Brown concludes, will not necessarily lead to greater independence from Soviet influence. The reverse might hold true. Increasing fragmentation of interests in these countries may force those who hold such interests to become more and more dependent upon Soviet actors and support to achieve the influence and policies they desire.

Bringing to our discussions the perspectives of an economist, Paul Marer examines the prospects for integration in Eastern Europe through the Council for Mutual Economic Assistance. More specifically, he deals with three interrelated topics: (1) the effect of 1973-75 world economic developments (the energy crisis, accelerating inflation, enlargement of the Common Market, and worldwide recession) on East-West trade and on East European economic relations with the USSR; (2) the implications of these developments for CMEA integration; (3) economic and political problems and opportunities that closer integration creates for the USSR and for Eastern Europe. The general thrust of events has been to increase further Eastern Europe's economic dependence on the USSR, raising in the process the cost of noncompliance with Soviet political demands. At the same time, closer cooperation with CMEA in general and with the USSR in particular probably appears more attractive to East European decision makers today, Marer suggests, than when the water of the Western economies were calmer. Nonetheless, the critical factor that will determine the course of CMEA integration, he concludes, is the extent of Soviet commitment to this process.

The aim of Sarah Terry's essay is to take some first and perforce limited steps at building a general analytical framework for evaluating external influences (especially non-Soviet) on political change in Eastern Europe. Admittedly, this is a most difficult task, not only because of a lack of empirical data. We also do not yet adequately understand the dynamics of domestic political behavior and the very political processes whose susceptibility to exogenous influences we are trying to measure. Nonetheless, she begins by establishing a tentative framework, in the form of a checklist or series of questions, for analyzing both sides of the influence equation, that is, the external factors and relevant aspects of the target system. She then applies this framework to selected examples drawn from the East European experience of the past two decades. She ends her discussion with an identification of the external environments and factors that appear most likely to impact upon East European political development in the future. In the final analysis, Terry prudently reminds us, it is still Moscow that determines the admissibility of external influences into the region.

Continuing the discussion of non-Soviet influences, Charles Gati explores the impact of what the West has done vis-a-vis Eastern Europe and how the West is perceived in East European eyes. He takes a critical look at the postwar Western view according to which it would be unrealistic to raise the "non-negotiable" issue of Eastern Europe in a diplomatic setting. He concludes that the underlying theme of our diplomatic approach has been one of underestimated American opportunities and overestimated Soviet determination. The United States has relied almost exclusively, Gati writes, on the economic and cultural instruments of foreign policy, expecting political democratization as a result. The evidence suggests, however, that not even a gradual process of Westernization is taking place in the political realm. There is no necessary linkage between improved economic and cultural contacts on the one hand and political relations on the other. Bridge building without political engagement and ideological confrontation, he contends, is similar to the slogan of "liberation" in that both constitute deception, holding out more hope for liberalization or political pluralism in Eastern Europe than there is reason to expect.

In contrast to the two preceding pieces, which focus more broadly on Eastern Europe as a whole, Bill Zimmerman confines his study of the impact of national-international linkages on internal political development to Yugoslavia. In an innovative presentation, he looks at the domestic social and political consequences of a phenomenon unique to Yugoslavia among Communist countries, namely, the enormous migration of its workers abroad. A conscious policy choice by the Yugoslav regime, the opening of its borders to the out-migration, has had important consequences, which in turn have led to a searching reexamination of the total policy itself. Critiques have come from Croatian nationalists, from the new and old left, and from the neocapitalists. Rather than close the borders, however, the regime has decided largely to use economic rather than administrative measures to encourage the return of the workers.

Much like the Czechoslovak Action Program in 1968, this book has evolved as a "slow-motion happening." Most of the essays were originally presented at the Conference on Political Development in Eastern Europe, held at Stanford University in December 1975. The seventeen scholars who participated in the conference were: Gabriel Almond (Political Science, Stanford); R. V. Burks (History, Wayne State); Paul Cocks (Political Science, Stanford); Melvin Croan (Political Science, Wisconsin); David Finley (Political Science, Colorado); Frederic Fleron (Political Science, SUNY at Buffalo); Charles Gati (Political Science, Columbia); Zvi Gitelman (Political Science, Michigan); Paul Johnson (Political Science, Stanford); Kenneth Jowitt (Political Science, Berkeley); Andrzej Korbonski (Political Science, UCLA); Ivo Lederer (History, Stanford); Gordon Skilling (Political Science, Toronto); Sarah M. Terry (Political Science, Harvard); Jan Triska (Political Science, Stanford); Wayne Vucinich (History, Stanford); William Zimmerman (Political Science, Michigan). This conference was made possible by the cooperative efforts and financial support of the American Council of Learned Societies and Stanford's Center for Russian and East European Studies. Additional essays and redrafts of original studies broadened the scope of the ideas and perspectives originally presented and debated at the conference.

Characteristic of any joint exercise by many scholars with different analytical orientations and intellectual predispositions, this volume has as its hallmark diversity rather than unity of method and view. It does not present a concept or theory of political development in Eastern Europe. Indeed, political development is used loosely and in a variety of ways by most of the authors. In this book we have simply brought together some of the main avenues of ongoing research and analysis dealing with political development in Eastern Europe. It is our hope that these essays will promote new modes of thinking, stimulate further research in the field of political change analysis in Communist studies as well as comparative politics, and raise our general intellectual consciousness.

NOTES

1. Barbara Jancar, "Eastern Europe: Toward a New Paradigm?" *Studies in Comparative Communism* 8, no. 3 (Autumn 1975): 284.

2. Ibid., p. 288.

3. Vernon Aspaturian, "Comment," ibid., p. 302.

4. Ibid., p. 303.

5. See Joseph LaPalombara, "Monoliths or Plural Systems: Through Conceptual Lenses Darkly," *Studies in Comparative Communism* 8, no. 3 (Autumn 1975): 326-27.

6. Rudolf L. Tokes, "Comparative Communism: The Elusive Target," *Studies in Comparative Communism* 8, no. 3 (Autumn 1975): 219.

7. LaPalombara, "Monoliths or Plural Systems," p. 315.

8. See, for example, Gabriel A. Almond, Scott C. Flanagan, and Robert J. Mundt, *Crisis, Choice, and Change* (Boston: Little, Brown, 1973).

9. Lucian W. Pye, *Aspects of Political Development* (Boston: Little, Brown, 1966), pp. 31-48. See also Samuel P. Huntington, "The Change to Change: Modernization, Development, and Politics," *Comparative Politics* 3 (April 1971): 283-322.

10. See the review article by Mark Kesselman, "Order or Movement? The Literature of Political Development as Ideology," *World Politics* (October 1973): 139-54.

11. See Samuel P. Huntington, *Political Order in Changing Societies* (New Haven and London: Yale University Press, 1968), and his essay, "The Change to Change."

12. James S. Coleman, "The Development Syndrome: Differentiation-Equality-Capacity," in *Crises and Sequences in Political Development*, ed. Leonard Binder, et al., (Princeton: Princeton University Press, 1973), pp. 78-79. See also the excellent essay in this same volume by LaPalombara, "Penetration: A Crisis of Government Capacity," pp. 203-33.

13. Coleman, "The Development Syndrome," p. 79.

14. Gabriel A. Almond, *Political Development: Essays in Heuristic Theory* (Boston: Little, Brown, 1970) p. 191.

15. See Robert O. Keohane and Joseph S. Nye, Jr., *Transnational Relations and World Politics* (Cambridge: Harvard University Press, 1972); Samuel P. Huntington. "Transnational Organizations in World Politics," *World Politics* 25 (April 1973): 333-68; Charles Gati, ed., *The Politics of Modernization in Eastern Europe: Testing the Soviet Model* (New York: Praeger Publishers, 1974).

PART

I

IDEOLOGICAL
ADAPTATION AND
CONCEPTUAL CHANGE

1

THE "CHANGE TO CHANGE" IN EASTERN EUROPE

Andrzej Korbonski

INTRODUCTION

A good deal of the Vltava water has passed under the Charles Bridge since H. Gordon Skilling first sounded the clarion call to mend our ways and to revise our thinking about Communist political systems some ten years ago. Although we may argue among ourselves as to who was responsible, and when, for actually signing the death warrant for the totalitarian model, I am prepared to argue that Skilling's appeal to focus our attention on interest group politics in Communist societies probably represented the most important watershed in the history of Soviet and East European studies since the appearance of Carl Friedrich and Zbigniew Brzezinski's totalitarian paradigm.[1] Consequently, Skilling's effort also provides a convenient benchmark for what is intended to be a brief overview and evaluation of Western and Communist literature dealing with the process of political change in Eastern Europe.

Before engaging in this rather formidable task, a few introductory remarks may be in order. First, I have no desire to engage here in definitional or conceptual hairsplitting in an attempt to choose between the notions of modernization, development, and change. Many of my betters devoted considerable energy and time to come up with unambiguous definitions and concepts that would prove useful for analytical, explanatory, and even predictive purposes, yet in my opinion the results proved largely disappointing and only succeeded in adding to the definitional confusion.[2] Instead of following in their footsteps and contributing further to the existing terminological bewilderment, I shall simply view political change as a process or movement, as a result of which various components of the political system become different, altered, modified, transformed, or converted.

Second, I shall deal only with the seven countries of Eastern Europe—
Albania, Bulgaria, Czechoslovakia, Hungary, Poland, Romania, and Yugoslavia—
although I have serious doubt about the propriety or legitimacy of treating all of
them as belonging to a single entity. It may be argued that, apart from being
located in a more or less well-defined geographical region of Europe, the only
other thing that the various countries have in common is the fact that for the
last three decades or so they had been ruled by Communist parties. While this
may have been a necessary and sufficient condition of membership in the Soviet-
dominated bloc of the late 1940s and early 1950s, it is clearly not the case
today. Moreover, it has been suggested more than once that Communist systems
were simply a genus in the family of industrializing or modernizing nations and
that as such they were not essentially different from other non-Communist
regimes bent upon rapid economic development and modernization. In the
words of the chief advocate of this approach, John Kautsky, "Communist phenomena are not distinguished from non-Communist ones by any particular
characteristics,"[3] and if this were true, it would make better sense perhaps to
drop the notion of Eastern Europe in favor of some other configuration the
members of which would show a higher degree of similarity on the basis of other
political, economic, and social criteria.

While personally I have strong sympathy with Kautsky's view, on balance I
am persuaded by Melvin Croan that in the final analysis the fact that the East
European political systems are Communist regimes "has made an enormous difference in the past" and that "it will probably continue to make quite a lot of
difference for the future as long as what is at stake is the 'leading role of the
party,' with all that is implied in practical political terms."[4] Hence, at least for
the purpose of this essay, the Communist party rule can be regarded as providing
the lowest common denominator that enables us to treat Eastern Europe as a
single entity.

Third, I feel that we owe considerable gratitude to the organizers of this
conference for solving one potential headache for us ex ante. I refer here, of
course, to the adoption if not imposition of the Almondian developmental paradigm for the purpose of analyzing the process of change in Communist Europe.
My own belief is that it was a good choice although, as I shall argue below, either
the revised framework postulated by Gabriel Almond in reaction to the criticism
of the original model, or the checklist of key systemic variables subject to
change suggested by Samuel Huntington, might have made our discussion more
focused and realistic.

It is a matter of record that the Almondian approach has been widely
discussed, dissected, praised, condemned, and criticized in the literature,[5] and at
this stage there is no point in summarizing once again the various arguments,
except very briefly. As I see it, the criticism can be roughly divided into two
parts: that dealing with the theoretical underpinnings of the framework—systems
theory and structural functionalism—and that concerned specifically with its

application to the analysis of Communist systems. The former criticism is quite familiar and need not detain us here; the latter is of greater interest and ought to be faced squarely. Thus it appears that the various critics castigated the approach for neglecting the importance of leadership and personality, and for not paying sufficient attention to the influence of external factors (mainly the Soviet Union),[6] for being culture-bound,[7] as well as for generating an "unduly optimistic general theory of political development."[8]

The first two points were well taken. Clearly there was a difference between Stalin and Khrushchev, Rakosi and Kadar, or Novotny and Dubcek, and their respective influences on the political systems. However, as with a number of other concepts, the importance of leadership and personality should not be exaggerated. It was most likely greater in the early stages of the East European political development when it formed an integral part of the totalitarian and post-totalitarian syndromes, but its role today is not as easily ascertained. Although the position of individual leaders is still quite powerful, available personal data provide no significant insights with regard to the character of their influence on politics. The best that can be done is to suggest that, regardless of their family, educational, or professional backgrounds, some East European leaders more than others appeared to be more innovative, skillful, and psychologically more open-minded to a variety of influences and stimuli generated by the process of change or by external factors, as manifested in the behavior differences between Gomulka and Gierek or Ulbricht and Honecker.

The same applies to the impact of Soviet influence on Eastern Europe, which was clearly rigid and overwhelming in scope and depth during the Stalinist period, and which has become somewhat more flexible and unpredictable in the last decade or so. Altogether, estimating and evaluating the impact of Soviet influence on the process of political change in the region presents a problem, especially in recent years. While some scholars claim that the Soviet Union is the only factor affecting the process of change in Eastern Europe, others feel that by now the greatest impetus for change comes from domestic sources, and still others prefer to treat the Soviet presence as an internal rather than an external variable. It ought to be stressed, however, that especially today Eastern Europe is exposed not only to influences radiating from the USSR but also to those emanating from the other Communist countries, the West and the third, and even the fourth, worlds.[9]

Ultimately, the impact and weight of leadership and international environments, neither of which can be easily measured and operationalized, depend on the perception and personal preferences (or idiosyncrasies) of the individual researcher. More often than not there is the strong temptation to explain nearly everything that has been happening in Eastern Europe with reference to either the personality of the leaders or to the influence of Moscow, or both. I submit that, although clearly valid at certain periods in recent East European history, this assumption ignores many interesting internal political and socioeconomic developments occurring spontaneously and autonomously in the various countries. I also am convinced that today it is possible to study the various political and other processes in the region without constantly referring to the "dependence" of the area on the USSR. At the risk of an overgeneralization, this often represents more of an excuse for not doing one's homework than the actual state of affairs in the given countries or in the region as a whole. There is no easy way out of the dilemma. My own personal preference is to analyze the East European developments at two levels: First, by restricting the parameters to the domestic sphere while keeping the hegemonial power of the Soviet Union as a (constant) background condition, and in the second stage by removing the condition of constancy and tracing the impact of the Soviet Union and, for that matter, of other environments and/or universes, on the process of change in the area.

Is the Almondian framework culture-bound and does it reflect an over-optimistic theory of political development? Here again it seems to me that the character and value of a given model, paradigm, framework, or approach lies in the eye of the beholder, and whether a theory is optimistic or pessimistic, ethnocentric or value-neutral, depends on one's perception, training, and ultimate objective in conducting research. In the final analysis, it is largely the matter of what one is trying to show and/or prove. Thus, for example, if it can be shown that recent developments in Eastern Europe resemble those in Western Europe a generation or two ago, an optimist may conclude that East Europe is on the road to establishing a genuine pluralist society whereas a pessimist is likely to point to the continuing presence of Soviet influence, the persisting presence of ideology, and the omnipresent role of the party as proof that nothing has changed. While for one observer the pot may be half-full, for another it is half-empty.

Almond himself was very well aware of the drawbacks of his initial formulation. A few years ago he readily acknowledged the importance of the external (that is, Soviet) influences in analyzing the process of political development in Eastern Europe,[10] and in a more recent revision of his paradigm he emphasized the role played by leadership in developmental causation.[11] Moreover, he also stressed the close connection between the process of development and the individual or collective human decisions, bargains, or choices, some of which, in turn, are rooted in culture and personality.[12]

I fully agree with Huntington that Almond's revised framework was "precisely designed to deal with the problem of change and it was also clearly independent of any particular historical context. . . . [It] could be applied to a primitive stateless tribe, a classical Greek city-state, or to a modern nation-state."[13] Needless to say, it follows that it also was suitable for the study of change in Eastern Europe where the impact of both the leadership and international environment as well as of national political cultures was particularly strong. The approach is also useful since, as suggested by Tucker, "the general theory of modernization has not had a great deal to say on communism as a mode (or modes) of modernization."[14] Moreover, the framework permits us to

study and analyze the process of change without prejudging in advance its ultimate outcome or goal. Hence, in addition to looking at factors causing or
inducing "modernization" and "development," we also are able to consider
influences affecting the process of "political decay" and "dysrhythmic development."[15]

With the Almondian framework as a background, I propose next to survey
the Western and Communist literature on the process of political change in
Eastern Europe, by focusing on the one hand on the five systemic components
suggested by Huntington (culture, structure, groups, leadership, and policies),[16]
and on the other, on the five, by now generally accepted, developmental
challenges or crises—those of identity, legitimacy, penetration, participation, and
distribution.[17]

WESTERN VIEWS

For all practical purposes, Western literature and research on the problem
of change in Eastern Europe are largely confined to the United States. To be
sure, some interesting research results have been achieved in Western Europe,
notably in Great Britain and West Germany, but there is little doubt that the
most innovative and sophisticated work on the subject has been conducted in
the Western hemisphere—the United States and Canada. In Britain, the most
stimulating research on East European developments has been undertaken by a
group of scholars under the leadership of Ghita Ionescu, currently occupying a
chair at the University of Manchester. Several published volumes spawned by the
project testify to the high quality of individual research.[18] Judging from the
surveys of current research on Eastern Europe published regularly in *ABSEES*,[19]
many individual British scholars are presently engaged in studying various
aspects of East European societies but it is my impression that relatively few of
the results eventually get published.

In West Germany, the articles published in the monthly *Osteuropa* reflect
both the traditional German belief in conducting painstakingly detailed descriptive and historical research on different aspects of East European politics, and
nearly total lack of interest in even mild generalizations, not to mention theory
building. Thus, although some German encyclopedic work on individual East
European countries can hardly be improved upon,[20] and although the coverage
of recent and current events in Eastern Europe is also quite comprehensive,[21]
the overall results and accomplishments are not particularly impressive,
especially if one is interested less in facts and more in analysis. The same applies
roughly to France, where the results of research on East European affairs are
usually published in *Revue d'Etudes Comparatives Est-Ouest*, formerly known
simply as *Revue de l'Est*.

This leaves the United States and to some extent Canada, which not surprisingly represent the largest concentration of talent in the field of East European studies and also account for the largest volume of publications. It would be pleasant to report that for once quantity equaled quality but, alas, this has not often been the case. The reason could be found partly in the changing nature of the field and partly in the changing characteristics of the research community.

There is little doubt that from the outset the field of Communist studies in the United States has been strongly policy-oriented and influenced. Thus the period of the cold war and the concomitant emergence of the monolithic Soviet bloc was eventually reflected in the dominant role played in the literature by the totalitarian model, which was assumed to apply not only to the Soviet Union but also to Eastern European countries which were considered as exact albeit smaller copies of the USSR. Therefore, it is not surprising that this state of affairs did not stimulate significant and sophisticated research, and even a quick glance at the bibliographies of books, monographs, and articles published prior to the late 1950s and early 1960s fully confirms the absence of scholarly works dealing with East European politics, in sharp contrast to the research on the Soviet Union which was finally beginning to bear fruit of at least a decade of massive effort in that direction.

To put it simply, there was no reason to study this or that East European country if all that was politically or economically relevant there could have been learned by analyzing the Soviet Union. Thus the intellectual output of the period in question consisted primarily of personal memoirs and reminiscences of escaped anti-Communist leaders, of a variety of cold war articles of little merit, and of occasionally interesting studies of the Communist takeover. Otherwise the box was by and large empty.

Following the upheavals of 1956 there was a growing realization that the Soviet Union and Eastern Europe were not simply two sides of the same coin but that, in fact, the differences between the two began to outweigh the similarities, and that as time went on the gap tended to grow larger, also accompanied by a process of differentiation among individual East European countries. Ultimately this process of fragmentation and change did not escape the attention of Western political scientists, and soon one began to notice the appearance of well-researched monographs dealing with different aspects of East European political and economic systems.

It was at this stage that research on Communist societies was faced with an additional task. The new factor on the scene was the result of the growing dissatisfaction with the methodological and theoretical basis of Communist studies. Above all, it became obvious that the traditional research tool—the "totalitarian model"—was rapidly outliving its usefulness as an analytical and explanatory device. Even the most diehard believers in and defenders of the model had to admit that the Communist systems, especially in Eastern Europe, have been

changing, at least since 1953, and that this process largely invalidated the fundamental assumptions underlying the totalitarian syndrome. The demise of the
latter as a research instrument and its relegation to the realm of abstraction
created a vacuum that had to be filled somehow by students of Communist and
East European affairs, who suddenly· found themselves saddled with a dilemma
of what strategy to employ.

One alternative was to embrace lock, stock, and barrel the "behavioral
revolution," which seemed on the verge of establishing itself as the dominant
research methodology in political science. In practice this meant often an almost
uncritical and wholesale adoption of concepts, models, paradigms, and
approaches developed over the years for the study of advanced industrial societies and, somewhat paradoxically, of the less developed countries. In time, this
led to the birth of a new scholarly subfield—comparative Communism—which
reflected on the one hand the continuing fragmentation and differentiation
within the Communist countries of Europe and Asia, and on the other, the overwhelming urge of Western social scientists to compare, to quantify, and to
operationalize.

Whereas the students of non-Communist systems—both "modern" and
"less developed"—eventually began to realize that they might have gone too far
in their behavioral zeal and decided either to refocus their attention on fundamentals or to achieve a synthesis between the modern and the traditional approaches, many Communist experts have not, thus far, shown an inclination to
do so. There are at least three reasons for it: to begin with, behaviorism
descended upon students of Communist affairs much later than on scholars in
other fields and it is clear that it would take some time before revisionism was
likely to set in.

Second, probably the great majority of Communist specialists have not
had a thorough theoretical and methodological grounding and they have suffered
for some time from an inferiority complex vis-a-vis their more sophisticated
colleagues in other areas. Many students of Eastern Europe were either refugees
or alumni of area studies programs, neither of which managed to supply them
with the intellectual equipment necessary for conducting more than just the conventional descriptive and historical research. While some of them never
succeeded in absorbing the new methodology, others devoted considerable time
and energy to mastering the new research techniques and, having embraced the
"modern" approach and thus achieved intellectual parity with their brethren
specializing in other parts of the world, they have so far shown little desire to go
back to the fundamentals.

Third, after years of trying to attract young scholars of non-East European
origin into the field, which since the end of World War II had been largely dominated by either the refugees or first-generation emigrants, some success was
finally being achieved. However, this meant that many of the younger recruits
entering the field also are offspring of the behavioral revolution and it could be

assumed that at least in the immediate future this particular approach would set the tone and focus of their research.

Yet despite its drawbacks there is no doubt that the behavioral method made a considerable contribution to our knowledge of East European political systems and processes. Perhaps its greatest accomplishment was to bring Communist studies into the mainstream of modern social science analysis by largely removing the heavy historical patina that has for years protected the field from outside interference, and by dismantling to a large extent the Chinese wall of "special expertise," which implied for a long time that while systems other than the Communist could change, develop, or modernize, the Communist societies, being sui generis, had to remain unchanged, being firmly embalmed in the totalitarian, mobilization, or command syndrome.

Returning to the analysis of change in Huntington's five systemic components, it is, I think, fairly obvious that relatively little interesting and solid research had been accomplished in the realm of culture broadly defined. Following the excitement generated by the emergence of revisionism in some East European countries in the late 1950s, there was a long hiatus interrupted only by another wave of revisionist thinking born as a byproduct of the Prague Spring of 1968. Both waves gave birth to several studies, also augmented by the continuing research on ideological deviations and/or innovations in Yugoslavia, probably the only East European country where ideology was still being taken seriously, starting with Milovan Djilas and ending with the *Praxis* group. Under the rubric of revisionism one might also include the analysis of the ideological underpinnings of economic reforms in several countries whose rulers tried with varying degrees of success to square the circle by making the reforms part of the official orthodoxy.[22]

What is perhaps surprising is the absence of research on political culture in Eastern Europe, especially in light of the fact that despite considerable efforts either to destroy or to remake the traditional national cultures, the Communist regimes failed to eradicate them completely. In fact, it might be argued that after the intensive socialization and resocialization campaigns during the Stalinist period, the ruling elites in most countries abandoned for all practical purposes the earlier attempts and in some cases even actively encouraged the revival of the old cultures.

Equally surprising has been the absence of scholarly interest in the problem of nationalism in Eastern Europe, particularly in light of the popularity of this phenomenon in the interwar period. Some of it was probably due to the fact that formerly multinational and multiethnic countries such as Poland, and to some extent Czechoslovakia, became much less so as a result of World War II, but this still does not explain the rather curious situation where with the exception of Yugoslavia, and more recently Czechoslovakia, practically no research on East European nationalism has been conducted by Western scholars.[23]

It is only recently that we have witnessed the revival of scholarly concern for the general topic of Communist political culture in its various manifestations. Here the reasons seem to be, on the one hand, the continued fascination with the notion of comparative communism and the increasing tendency to explain the differences among Communist nations in terms of their respective cultures. The latter attitude has been most strongly articulated by Robert Tucker, who a few years ago suggested that instead of being viewed as a system, communism should be regarded as a "particular form of 'culture'—a political culture."[24] This proposition was warmly seconded by Alfred Meyer, who called for a major research effort to focus on the comparison of Western and Communist political cultures.[25] Thus far, however, with some exceptions,[26] the appeal remained unheeded. This is somewhat puzzling in view of the easily observable impressive staying power of the traditional political cultures, which in some countries have been actively revived with the blessing if not encouragement of the respective regimes.

Turning next to structures, which in this context include political parties, legislatures, executives, and bureaucracies, the scholarly output has been equally unimpressive. To some extent this was clearly due to the lack of interest in Communist institutions such as the legislatures and even executives, whose functions in most East European states consisted essentially of rubberstamping the decisions taken by the party. What is striking, however, is the dearth of solid research monographs dealing with individual East European Communist parties. The existing studies of Post-World War II parties are either dated or incomplete (or both); in addition, some contain errors of fact and interpretation.[27]

Also surprising is the apparent lack of interest in East European bureaucracies despite the seeming popularity of the so-called "bureaucratic model" and of the concepts of "totalitarianism without terror" and "administered society."[28] Perhaps the reason here lies in the belief that the bureaucratic approach works better in theory than in practice, and that while it may apply to the "USSR, Incorporated," its utility for the analysis of the changing East European political systems appears to be limited. At the same time, however, the conventional wisdom view of the Communist bureaucracy, which tended to emphasize its rigidly monolithic and conservative character as the major obstacle to change, was simply not born out by the facts. There is enough evidence to suggest that the East European government and party bureaucracies have been changing either in response to the imperatives of industrialization (that is, via cooptation) or as a result of a generational conflict and pressure from below.[29] Although some interesting work has been done in this particular area, there is clearly much left to be done not only with regard to the bureaucracies but also with respect to the instruments of coercion—police and the military, both of which have been badly neglected by the researchers, especially in the past two decades.

Reference was made at the outset to the intellectual excitement stimulated by Skilling's suggestion to take a close look at the political significance of interest and pressure groups in Communist systems. It appears, however, that due to a curious inertia if not inherent conservatism of the East European specialists, the early interest in utilizing the group theory approach for the study of change in the region evaporated rather quickly and it took several years before serious work on the role of groups in Eastern Europe was resumed.

The long interval between Skilling's initial "call in the wilderness" and the appearance of articles attempting to test his hypotheses in various national contexts cannot be easily explained in view of the fact that the existence of conflicting interests has for some time been formally recognized by the ruling elites in several East European countries who thus acknowledged the bankruptcy of the concept of "solidary society" that has for years provided the philosophical foundation of Communist politics.[30]

On the other hand, the critics of the group conflict approach felt that incipient pluralism in several countries in the region was largely meaningless as a researchable category and that the approach, developed as it were for the study of genuinely pluralistic societies, had little or no validity for Eastern Europe.[31] On the basis of several criteria, no groups existing in any of the East European countries, including Yugoslavia, were said to fulfill the conditions of true pluralism. My personal feeling is that the above view, although formally correct, was too restrictive to be of much value for research purposes, and that a compulsive adherence to rigidly defined categories might prevent us from gaining useful insights into the working of the East European systems. I am thus in considerable sympathy with the suggestion that "in order to push on with serious studies of interest group politics in the Soviet Union we must first rid ourselves of the constricting belief that group theory applies only to groups that operate openly and straightforwardly within a political culture which not only tolerates, but celebrates, pluralism."[32] I further agree with Huntington that "the appeal of interest group analysis to East European theorists is an accurate reflection of the nature of politics in those societies."[33]

What is true for the Soviet Union is obviously even truer for the majority of the East European countries, yet despite what appeared to be a promising target of inquiry, the scholarly output dealing with group behavior in Eastern Europe was next to nil. Thus far, at least, no attempt had been made to replicate for Eastern Europe the pioneering study of Soviet interests edited by H. Gordon Skilling and William Griffiths, and the only research on group politics was focused either on developing a general typology or on analyzing the role of interest groups in some specific policy decisions.[34] Otherwise this was another box that remained largely empty.

Insofar as the leadership variable was concerned, the situation was somewhat better. This was not particularly surprising since scholars had been traditionally fascinated with leaders and personalities. However, the most significant if not the seminal single study was focused not on individual leaders or on succession problems but on the process of transformation in authority patterns in the course of change in Communist political systems, starting with the revolution, moving through the period of system building, and ending with the era of developed Communist systems.[35] Alfred C. Meyer's article undoubtedly provided additional incentive for studying East European elites and individual leaders and for undertaking research on background characteristics of, and turnover in, the ruling Communist bodies and, last but not least, on succession and recruitment problems.

Starting with individual leaders, the few available profiles of such leaders as Dubcek, Gomulka, Tito, and Ulbricht are, by and large, conventional biographies that offer little clue regarding the behavior of the various individuals, especially in times of stress.[36] Thus even today it is well-nigh impossible to explain satisfactorily the apparent change in Gomulka's policy between October 1956 and December 1970, or Dubcek's behavior between January and August 1968, and all we can do is to engage in more or less informed guessing. Two of the most interesting East European leaders—Kadar and Ceausescu—have so far been completely ignored by Western scholars.

The research on the composition, background, and turnover of ruling bodies in the various countries represented one of the most solid accomplishments in the field. In contrast to most other research areas, where results were usually based partly on impressions and partly on intuitions, the work on elites had for the most part the advantage of having some hard data that permitted the testing of some general propositions and even postulating of some hypotheses with respect to changes in age and educational levels of top political leaders or the career patterns of decision makers in different walks of public life.[37]

Perhaps the most disappointing area of research on East European leadership concerned the issue of succession. While the problem of political succession in the Soviet Union attracted considerable attention, the same was hardly true for Eastern Europe, although by 1975 there had been 14 cases of succession at the top level in the region. The recent exhaustive study of succession in Eastern Europe and China, apart from being the only one of its kind, is highly disappointing.[38] It is essentially a descriptive, historical account that makes no effort to consider succession and its consequences as a political event that more often than not has had great impact on the political processes in the various countries. In other words, the question of succession was dealt with in a vacuum although, as suggested earlier, the influence of leadership and especially of its change is now recognized as one of the key elements in the process of political change.[39] Thus, although we were told by Myron Rush where the next leaders were likely to come from, we are still largely in the dark as to the impact of the change in top leadership on the other components of the political system. The fact that a succession crisis in at least one East European country—Yugoslavia—may well cause major reverberations both at home and abroad was largely neglected. Nor was an attempt made to analyze the unique role of the current leader of another

Balkan country—Romania—whose policies clearly affected the process of change in the area.[40]

The final systemic component to be considered, that of policies, was defined by Huntington as representing "the patterns of governmental activity which are consciously designed to affect the distribution of benefits and penalties within the society."[41] This broad category does, in a sense, embrace most if not all of the systemic elements discussed above. This means that a change in any of the other four components—be it culture, structures, groups, or leadership—was bound to be reflected in changing policies.

With the focus on "benefits" and "penalties," one possible way to analyze this particular variable was to study the process of change in the region, starting with the demise of the Stalinist model in the second half of the 1950s. The change that took place affected above all the six basic features of the totalitarian paradigm as elaborated by Friedrich and Brzezinski.[42] As mentioned earlier, some research has been done on at least two of these elements—ideology and the party. It also was pointed out that the area of party-military relations has been nearly completely ignored by Western scholars; the same held largely true for the other two elements—the rule of terror and the party control over mass communications. While the absence of serious research on the role of the military may perhaps be explained by the paucity of data,[43] this cannot justify the overall neglect of the changes in the degree and methods of mass terror and censorship, and of the impact of these changes on the political developments in most East European countries. A good case can be made showing that, after all, it was the arbitrary and indiscriminate use of terror that maintained the Stalinist system intact and that it was Khrushchev's decision to reduce its level and scope that represented the necessary and probably sufficient condition for the far-reaching changes to get under way in a number of countries. Yet, with one possible exception, I am not aware of the existence of any comprehensive discussion of this crucial process; even in the one available study, Eastern Europe is treated largely as an appendix to the Soviet Union.[44]

It may be argued that the same held true for censorship. The impact of the abolition or suspension of censorship on the course of events in Czechoslovakia in the spring of 1968 cannot be exaggerated, and one may go so far as to describe the Prague Spring as "the revolution by mass media." The influence of the partially reduced control over mass media in Hungary and Poland on the events of 1956 also can be documented, and yet, for some reason, no effort has been undertaken thus far to trace in a systematic fashion the impact of the changes in the party monopoly of mass communications on the process of change in the area.

By far the most extensive and sophisticated research concerned the final element of the totalitarian model—that of centrally controlled economy. Here the yeoman's work was performed by the economists, who tended to focus on the question of economic reforms in several East European countries, all of which aimed at reducing the extent of central planning and controls and at introducing some features of market mechanism and managerial autonomy, to the ultimate benefit of large segments of the respective societies. By now the literature on the various aspects of the reforms is quite extensive and the overall level of the discussion is quite impressive.[45]

Perhaps because the early focus of attention was on purely economic features of the reforms, it took Western political scientists a rather long time to analyze the political impact of the changes in the economic systems. This again is not easy to explain since the boundary or borderline between politics and economics in Communist societies has long been recognized as either blurred or nonexistent, and one did not have to be a Marxist to realize the intimate relationship between the two spheres and the inevitable spillover from one into the other. Be that as it may, several years elapsed before publication of the initial efforts analyzing the political rather than purely economic aspects of the reforms; although some progress has been made, much remains to be done, especially with regard to countries that delayed the introduction of major changes in their economies.[46]

Thus far our discussion was confined to a survey of research dealing with changes in the five systemic components treated as discrete independent variables. The underlying implicit assumption was that the process of political change was in a sense a dependent variable and that, caeteris paribus, a change in any individual component was bound to give rise to changes in the system as a whole. However, this procedure provided a restricted and even a distorted picture of the overall process since, after all, things were not equal and the five systemic variables were not independent of each other. This meant that the rate, scope, and direction of change in one component was more than likely to affect the power and content of one or more of the remaining components, thus influencing the rate, direction, and depth of change of the entire system.

It was this changing relationship among different systemic components that attracted probably the greatest interest among Western scholars, many of whom analyzed it in order either to explain the process of change in the past and present or to predict its course in the future. Often the individual researchers focused on one or more of the developmental crises that provided convenient benchmarks for their investigation.

Mention was made earlier of the impact of the behavioral revolution on East European studies. The intellectual ferment manifested itself eventually in a series of research projects focused specifically on the process of change in Communist societies. The role of the catalyst in this case was played by the American Council of Learned Societies (ACLS) Planning Committee for Comparative Communist Studies, which sponsored a series of conferences and workshops examining various aspects of systemic change under communism. By far its best-known product was, of course, the collective volume on *Change in Communist*

Systems, edited by Chalmers Johnson and published in 1970.[47] Another collective work with considerable impact on the direction of research on Communist systems was *Authoritarian Politics in Modern Society*, edited by Samuel P. Huntington and Clement H. Moore and also published in 1970.[48]

Both these studies acted in a sense as trailblazers and provided additional stimulus to the profession, whose members carried forward the work initiated by the contributors to the two volumes. Thus some researchers tried to refine the conceptual framework utilized for the analysis of change in the Communist systems.[49] Others attempted to pin down the key variables responsible for inducing certain specific processes such as liberalization, which occurred in some East European states.[50] Still others utilized, at least partly, the approach developed by Huntington for the study of one-party systems and applied it to Eastern Europe.[51] Probably the most common were the largely descriptive and historical accounts of various political processes in different East European countries, reflecting the fact that specialists in East European affairs were, to use John Armstrong's expression, "taking the historical cure."[52]

Some of the most innovative, perceptive, and stimulating research endeavored to analyze and explain the various systemic challenges and crises. Its success could most likely be attributed to the fact that it was undertaken primarily by the younger generation of East European specialists, well versed in theory and methodology of comparative politics and unencumbered either by their ethnic-national backgrounds and/or cold war ideological baggage. Kenneth Jowitt's study of state and nation building in Romania and his analysis of the various stages in East European modernization[53] as well as Zvi Gitelman's examination of the crisis of authority and legitimacy in the region[54] provided the best illustrations of the new wave reflected in the steady rise in the level of scholarly sophistication of research on Eastern Europe. Other scholars investigated the crises and challenges of participation[55] and distribution,[56] while still others attempted either to measure the degree and extent of change by refining and/or operationalizing the crucial variables[57] or to advance some general propositions or hypotheses regarding the process of political change in the region.[58] Now and then, some less than wise individuals ventured to predict the future path of change in the region with the aid of various analytical frameworks and approaches.[59]

The above highly selective checklist seems to indicate that over the years Western scholarship succeeded in producing a rather impressive body of literature dealing with political change in Eastern Europe, although its quality continued to be uneven. It is also clear that there are still many gaps in our knowledge and many empty or half-full boxes to be filled.

EAST EUROPEAN VIEWS

There are obviously many problems in analyzing East European literature discussing the process of change in the area. To begin with, there is the problem of the region itself, composed of seven countries each at a different level of political and economic development and each speaking a different language. A systematic and comprehensive examination of East European views on the process of change clearly deserves a separate treatment, which cannot be accomplished within the confines of this essay.

Second, there is the problem of the East European literature, the volume and sophistication of which varies sharply from country to country. Neither quantity nor quality appear excessively high, for reasons that are obvious and need not be discussed here. In fact, it is rather surprising that a few years ago there was actually a fair amount of research undertaken in a few East European countries testifying to a more or less genuine revival of interest in the discipline of political science.[60]

In view of the above I decided to confine myself to a very broad and sketchy survey of selected aspects of the process of change in the region that seemed to attract the attention of both the political leaders and social scientists in the various East European countries, including the Soviet Union. The aspects or themes were chosen more or less arbitrarily after a rather perfunctory scanning of Communist journals such as the *World Marxist Review* and *Socialist Thought and Practice*, and translated materials published by the Research Department of Radio Free Europe. This is clearly an unsatisfactory method; the only excuse for even attempting to undertake this task was to find out whether there was any overlap or congruence in research and other concerns between East and West.

Judging by the frequency and level of discussions, two problems in particular seem to have concerned the East Europeans in the past few years: the concept or idea of "developed socialism" and the impact of the "scientific-technical revolution" on Communist societies. Since both these problems were obviously closely interrelated, they often tended to be discussed together.

The examination of both these issues focused essentially on questions already analyzed and discussed in the West, most notably by Richard Lowenthal.[61] In addition to trying to define and fit the concept of developed socialism into the conventional Marxist developmental scheme by putting it somewhere between the stages of socialism and communism, the Soviet and East European ideologues emphasized that the change in the economic substructure induced by the scientific and technological progress did not (and would not) lead to embourgeoisement and convergence but to the creation of a new, higher stage of developed socialism from which the path would lead directly to the establishment of a Communist millenium.[62]

It appears that two yardsticks were used to measure the degree of maturity of socialism in a given country: the percentage socialization of the means of production and the extent of the modern industrial base. Using these criteria, the socialist countries were divided into three groups: those that had completed the process of socialization, but without developing an adequate industrial base (Cuba, Mongolia, and North Vietnam); those that were advanced industrially but were lagging behind in socialization (Poland and Yugoslavia); and those that reached or came close to the ideal of developed socialism, which presumably included the remaining Communist countries in Asia and Europe.[63]

Perhaps the most interesting aspect of the discussions concerned the role of the party in the conditions of an advanced socialist society. Denying the validity of supposedly Western assertions that the importance of the party was likely to decline in the context of the postindustrial state, considerable space was devoted to stressing the fact that, on the contrary, the role of the ruling party would be strengthened to allow it to provide leadership and guidance to an increasingly complex society.[64] To be sure, the party was no longer seen as the traditional Leninist narrow elite of revolutionaries but as the "party of the whole people," yet its leading role in the system was to be upgraded.[65] The same was true for the state, which was not expected to wither away in the foreseeable future but was to remain as strong as ever.[66]

Although the overall picture painted by the official ideologues tended to be rosy, they could not avoid mentioning the continued existence of non-antagonistic contradictions or conflicting interests in their respective societies. While the divergent interests were expected to be eventually reconciled, the amount of attention devoted to this particular issue clearly reflected serious official concern about the persistent if not growing cleavages, especially between the intelligentsia and the working class and between the urban and rural classes.[67] The officially expressed hope was that the scientific and technological progress would erase the differentials in the quality of work performed by the various antagonistic groups, thus eliminating the existing contradictions.

Another widely discussed aspect of developed socialism was "socialist democracy," which emphasized above all equality and participation in political and economic decision making and which condemned excessive bureaucratization of public and private life.[68] Needless to say, the manner and degree of participation was to be coordinated by the party, but here again the discussion mirrored the deep-seated concern of political decision makers worried about the unpredictable consequences of the "scientific-technological revolution."[69] There is little doubt that one of the major worries was the industrial proletariat. Without necessarily subscribing to the old adage about the party creating its own grave diggers, the behavior of the Hungarian and Polish workers in 1956, of the

Czechoslovak working class in 1968, and of the Polish shipyard and dock workers in 1970 testified to the potentially grave repercussions for the various regimes, resulting from workers' dissatisfaction. The privileged status granted to the Hungarian labor unions and the continued coddling of the Polish workers by the Gierek government provided another manifestation of the lingering doubts and insecurity permeating the ruling elite.

The discussion summarized above may be said to have concerned, directly or indirectly, some of the systemic components analyzed in the first part of this essay, such as culture (ideology) and groups (the party). The only other component that was widely debated throughout the region was that of policy, especially that concerned with economic reforms. In this case the East European scholars imitated their Western counterparts by concentrating almost exclusively on purely economic aspects of the reforms. With one or two exceptions, the blueprints of the reforms tended to ignore the impact on the respective political systems; the same was largely true for the official commentaries, which tried to explain the meaning of the contemplated changes to the masses. In Czechoslovakia a special commission composed of party officials, social scientists, and other representatives of public life was formed to examine in a true Marxist fashion the potential impact of the reforms on Czechoslovak politics. To my knowledge the commission met a few times in the mid-1960s and eventually adjourned sine die without issuing a report. There was some discussion of the political aspects of the reforms in East Germany and Hungary, but with the exception of additional authority granted to the Hungarian unions no attempt was made to institutionalize the potential political changes. The significant reforms of governmental structure in Romania (1968) and Poland (1974 and 1975) were due primarily to political rather than economic factors.

In addition to these broad bloc-wide concerns there were some more specific problems that occupied the attention of the elites in the individual East European countries. In some of them such as Hungary and Poland there was a deliberate effort to keep ideological discussion in a low key and to stress instead the economic achievements of the respective regimes. Both countries were engaged in reforming their economies; among other things this included a major expansion of trade with the West, which could possibly arouse the ire of the Soviet Union. For this and other reasons it was clearly preferable from the viewpoint of the Hungarian and Polish leaders to keep a low profile and to pay obligatory lip service to the accepted dogmas while pursuing a pragmatic economic policy.

The major objective of the post-1968 leadership in Czechoslovakia was to erase the scars caused by the Soviet invasion and to come up with a formula that would eradicate the political and some of the economic reforms passed prior to August 1968 by replacing them with a set of rules reflecting the new stage in the country's development. Hence the official views emanating from Prague have been of little interest for our purposes.

While there was no evidence of any major discussion or debates in Bulgaria, long considered the most faithful ally and copy of the Soviet Union, the opposite was clearly true for Romania, whose attempts at the ideological justification of Ceausescu's unorthodox policy proceeded on several fronts at once. Thus, in contrast to the other East European countries, Romania refused to call itself a developed socialist society and insisted on being counted among developing countries.[70] Also, while the other states, including the Soviet Union, subscribed in essence to the doctrine of separation of powers between the party and the state, Romania merged the party-political and government-administrative powers into one at different levels. The official explanation for the move was that greater centralization was necessary to ensure better coordination needed to achieve the ambitious production targets dictated by Romania's plan of a broadfront industrial development.[71]

Ceausescu's drive toward establishment of an almost total personal power also needed to be justified in order to receive approval and recognition from the key strata of Romanian society. According to Kenneth Jowitt, the current Romanian regime resembles that of a "patriarchal-executive" type, which emphasizes authoritarian leadership, welfare, and efficiency.[72] While the latter two objectives are common to all East European countries, Ceausescu's notion of leadership portrays him as "self-disciplined, hard working, tolerant of debate and expert opinion . . . also the concerned father of his people."[73] Moreover, "he appears increasingly convinced that only by developing his personal role to the point where the Party cannot check, divert, or delay his policies can he ensure the successful development of his country."[74] It can be argued that it is in this concept of leadership, akin to the cult of personality, that lies the greatest difference between Romania and the rest of the region and that it also provides at least a partial explanation of the process of change in that country.

The other country where the discussion of the various aspects of political and economic change ranged far and wide was, of course, Yugoslavia. Space does not permit even a brief survey of the different issues that arose in the course of the past decade and only some problems can be mentioned here.

The following passage presents a picture of Yugoslavia seen through official eyes at the beginning of the 1970s:

> Just as bureaucratic and statist tendencies had formerly been the source of numerous difficulties and problems, so have many contradictions now arisen within our self-managing society, because the decentralization we carried out and the economic relations we established led to the disintegration of the economy; and as the new cohesive social forces needed were lacking, working class unity was also impaired to a certain degree. . . . Hence the disruption of class unity, contradictions between the working class of individual regions, enterprises and republics, as well as objective contradictions

within the working class itself. Only one thing was acknowledged as the dominant factor and that was individual interest. . . . While individual and common interests had formerly been coordinated by the state and Party, there was now no other social force to do this in their stead. Self-management was not yet sufficiently developed to be capable of unifying the individual and common interest.[75]

In view of the above it is not surprising that, apart from the post-Tito succession problem reflected in a series of top-level institutional changes decreed in 1971 and 1974, the most interesting was the intensive campaign to bring back ideological purity and organizational discipline to the ruling party, which was formally initiated by the now famous October 1972 letter of President Tito addressed to all members of the League of Communists of Yugoslavia.[76] In recent years the top Yugoslav leaders—Tito, Kardelj, and Dolanc—have been going around the country emphasizing the need to return to the orthodoxy and attacking various disruptive elements.[77] While their main target was "anarcho-liberals," they also condemned the attempts of Stalinist groupings to take advantage of the national conflicts, economic difficulties, and intraparty strife to stage a comeback.[78] It appears that by 1975 the campaign achieved considerable success in restoring a high degree of stability in the Yugoslav party.

The other two major issues that occupied the attention of the Yugoslav policy makers were self-government, which was gradually extended into both the political and economic spheres, and the national conflict that came to a boil in Croatia in 1971.[79] The latter issues had been widely discussed in the West and there is no need to go over it again. The question of expanded self-management was perhaps less visible but obviously given serious attention in Yugoslavia.[80] Ostensibly, the reason for underscoring the importance of further decentralization was to counteract the apparent growing bureaucratization of all walks of life—a theme that echoed similar pronouncements in the early 1950s in response to Stalinist attacks. It can be assumed, however, that the real reason for pushing ahead with increased autonomy was the recognition that national antagonisms as well as class and regional animosities could not be assuaged in any other way. In true dialectical fashion, however, the broader autonomy was to be offset by the greater role to be played by the party.

Reading the statements of Yugoslav leaders, one cannot help being struck by their congruence with the views expressed by other East European elites. Thus Tito's appeals for tighter party control and discipline mirrored the same kind of concern shown by his opposite numbers elsewhere in the region worried about the dilution of party authority and cohesiveness under the impact of growing economic prosperity resulting from the substantial injection of Western technology. The specter of embourgeoisement hung heavy not only over the League of Communists of Yugoslavia but also over large segments of the Yugoslav population, which clearly appreciated the good life as much as the ruling parties and people of most other East European countries. The emphasis on self-government in opposition to excessive bureaucratization echoed similar sentiments expressed by the Poles and the Hungarians, and apparently only the Romanian leadership did not seem to worry too much about these tendencies; but then, Romania saw itself as a developing rather than a developed country, and hence it claimed to be devoid of these problems, at least for the time being.

CONCLUSION

There is little doubt that, as shown by the above survey, the process of political change and its repercussions in Eastern Europe attracted considerable attention in both West and East.

Scholarly inquiry in the West focused either on the change in the individual systemic components or on the process of change in the system as a whole. As such, it was part and parcel of what Huntington called the "change to change," which for the last few years supplied the overarching theme for research in comparative politics. In the case of Eastern Europe, additional impetus was provided by the long overdue demise of the traditional analytical tool—the totalitarian model. Other influences were the growing methodological and theoretical sophistication of the new generation of Western social scientists, and their desire not only to catch up with their counterparts in other geographical areas but also to bring the field of East European studies into the mainstream of Western social science analysis.

As indicated earlier, the results of this research effort appear mixed. To be sure, as anyone who entered the field of East European studies some 20 years ago can testify, the past two decades witnessed a veritable outpouring of books, articles, and other publications, and a graduate student of East European affairs in the mid-1970s is incomparably better off in this respect than his counterpart in the mid-1950s. At the same time, however, there were still considerable gaps in our knowledge of the political processes in the individual countries and in the region as a whole. Indeed, whatever the reasons, it is to some extent paradoxical that we still seem to know more about political development in dozens of countries of Africa, Asia, and Latin America than about the working of the political systems, including change, in the countries located in the heart of Europe.

The quality of research dealing with the various aspects of change in the region also showed considerable improvement; this served to upgrade the field and to bring it to par with other area studies. However, several problems remain to be solved. Thus, in my opinion at least, the new emphasis on the application of rigorous and sophisticated methodology and research techniques, which was responsible for the emergence of several interesting and valuable studies, now and then reached the stage where superficially elaborate frameworks and schemes tended to produce trivial and inconsequential results. Thus some of the East European specialists in their zeal to be more "scientific" appeared almost eager to repeat the errors committed by their opposite numbers in other regions and to lose sight of the one thing they were supposed to be concerned with: politics. Moreover, "one could ask whether the behavioral approach is not as culture-bound as the older legal-institutional or traditional approach it is meant to supplant."[81]

One peculiar characteristic of the state of research in the field of East European studies has been (and is) its uneven rate and level of development. Next to several solid and even exciting studies of the political and socioeconomic aspects of the East European systems, there are some glaring gaps in our knowledge of such basic systemic components as parties, groups, bureaucracies, military establishments, various types of elites, and a host of others. Because of the lack of basic information, a good deal of research on the process of change in the region has been of necessity based on incomplete evidence and forced more often than not to rely on guesswork, impressions, and intuition. Thus one has to agree with John Montias that the most urgent task facing the field is to start testing hypotheses—until now often postulated on a "fragile logical and factual base"—against available hard data.[82]

One possible way out of the dilemma is to put greater emphasis on comparative studies involving Eastern Europe and other parts of the world.[83] This view was expressed by many social scientists whom I polled in January 1974 on behalf of the ACLS-Social Science Research Council (SSRC) Joint Committee on East Europe. It appeared that most respondents felt useful insights could be gained by comparing, for example, stratification processes, mass-elite relations, or leadership recruitment in different geographical settings. It also meant that the majority was not particularly concerned with the propriety of comparing Communist with non-Communist countries; this implied that the adjective Communist was gradually losing its meaning as a distinct systemic characteristic, thus, in a sense, confirming John Kautsky's belief that "Communist regimes are not unique."[84]

Turning to the East European view of change in the region, one is struck by the considerable uncertainty with respect to the future course of events. The frequent denials of the negative effects of the "scientific-technical revolution," the optimistic attitude toward the solution of "nonantagonistic contradictions," and the emphasis on "socialist democracy" testify to basic insecurity on the part of the political decision makers eager to reassure both the elites and the masses about the maintenance and survival of a system faced with the unforeseen and unpredictable consequences of reaching the postindustrial stage. This was clearly the reason for the repeated insistence on the leading role of the party as the only force capable of securing the stability of society by reconciling divergent interests, ensuring participation and democracy, and improving economic performance by taking full advantage of technological progress.

To sum up, it is obvious that for some time now Eastern Europe has been in flux, which has sparked attention and concern in both East and West. In the West the process of change became the primary focus of scholarly inquiry, with the political leaders largely indifferent about the future of the "forgotten region." But in the East it was clearly the major issue of concern for ruling elites worried about their ability to maintain control over the rapidly changing political and economic systems without losing privileged status. Thus, it appears that the process of change in Eastern Europe will remain the object of study and analysis for many years to come.

NOTES

1. H. Gordon Skilling, "Interest Groups and Communist Politics," *World Politics* 18, no. 3 (1966): 435-51.

2. For a recent attempt to clear up some of the confusion, see J. M. Montias, "Modernization in Communist Countries: Some Questions of Methodology," *Studies in Comparative Communism* 5, no. 4 (1972): 413-27.

3. John H. Kautsky, "Comparative Communism Versus Comparative Politics," *Studies in Comparative Communism* 6, nos. 1-2 (1973): 141.

4. Melvin Croan, "Some Constraints on Change in Eastern Europe," *Slavic Review* 33, no. 2 (1974): 242.

5. See Robert T. Holt and John E. Turner, "Crises and Sequences in Collective Theory Development," *The American Political Science Review* 69, no. 3 (1975): 979-94.

6. Gabriel A. Almond, "Toward a Comparative Politics of Eastern Europe," *Studies in Comparative Communism* 4, no. 2 (1971): 76-77.

7. Charles A. Powell, "Structural-Functionalism and the Study of Comparative Communist Systems: Some Caveats," *Studies in Comparative Communism* 4, nos. 3-4 (1971): 58-64.

8. William E. Griffith, "The Pitfalls of the Theory of Modernization," *Slavic Review* 32, no. 2 (1974): 247.

9. See Vernon V. Aspaturian, "The Soviet Impact on Development and Modernization in Eastern Europe," in *The Politics of Modernization in Eastern Europe*, ed. Charles Gati (New York: Praeger Publishers, 1974), pp. 205-55. For a discussion of non-Soviet influences on Eastern Europe, see my "Evaluating External Influences on East European Politics," in *International Politics of Eastern Europe*, ed. Charles Gati (New York: Praeger Publishers, 1976).

10. Almond, "Toward a Comparative Politics of Eastern Europe," pp. 75-76.

11. Almond, "Approaches to Developmental Causation," in *Crisis, Choice and Change*, ed. Gabriel A. Almond, Scott C. Flanagan, and Robert J. Mundt (Boston: Little, Brown, 1973), pp. 17-19.

12. Ibid., pp. 18-21.

13. Samuel P. Huntington, "The Change to Change," *Comparative Politics* 3, no. 3 (1971): 320.

14. Robert C. Tucker, "On the Comparative Study of Communism," *World Politics* 19, no. 2 (1967): 251.

15. Samuel P. Huntington, "Political Development and Political Decay," *World Politics* 17, no. 3 (1965): 386-430; C. S. Whitaker, Jr., "A Dysrhythmic Process of Political Change," *World Politics* 19, no. 2 (1967): 190-217.

16. Huntington, "The Change to Change," p. 316.

17. For an extensive discussion, see Leonard Binder et al., *Crises and Sequences in Political Development* (Princeton: Princeton University Press, 1971).

18. Ghita Ionescu, "The Political Process of the Socialist States in Eastern Europe with Special Regard to Yugoslavia, Poland and Czechoslovakia," Report on a Conference held at Cumberland Lodge, Windsor, England, July 1971. The volumes that have already appeared include Jaroslav Krejci, *Social Change and Stratification in Postwar Czechoslovakia* (London: Macmillan, 1972); Vladimir V. Kusin, *Political Grouping in the Czechoslovak Reform Movement* (London: Macmillan, 1972); David Lane and George Kolankiewicz, eds., *Social Groups in Polish Society* (London: Macmillan, 1973).

19. See British National Association for Soviet and East European Studies, "Information Bulletin" in *ABSEES* Soviet and East European Abstracts Series, vol. 6, no. 3 (1975).

20. For example, Werner Markert, ed., *Jugoslawien* (Koln-Graz: Bohlau Verlag, 1954) and *Polen* (Koln-Graz: Bohlau Verlag, 1959).

21. See, for example, *Berichte* des Bundesinstituts fur ostwissenschaftliche und internationale Studien, which appear several times a year.

22. For an excellent discussion of the East German efforts to incorporate a program of economic reforms into the official ideology, see Thomas A. Baylis, "Economic Reform as Ideology," *Comparative Politics* 3, no. 2 (1971): 211-29.

23. Paul Shoup has been one of the few political scientists interested in the question of East European nationalism after World War II. See his "Communism, Nationalism and the Growth of the Communist Community of Nations," *The American Political Science Review* 56, no. 4 (1962): 886-98, and "The National Question and the Political Systems of Eastern Europe," in *Eastern Europe in the 1970s*, ed. Sylva Sinanian et al. (New York: Praeger, 1972), pp. 121-70.

24. Robert C. Tucker, "Communism and Political Culture," *Newsletter on Comparative Studies of Communism* 4, no. 3 (1971): 3-12.

25. Alfred G. Meyer, "Communist Revolutions and Cultural Change," *Studies in Comparative Communism* 5, no. 4 (1972): 345-70.

26. Kenneth Jowitt, "An Organizational Approach to the Study of Political Culture in Marxist-Leninist Systems," *The American Political Science Review* 68, no. 3 (1974): 1171-91.

27. A good example is M. K. Dziewanowski, *The Communist Party of Poland* (Cambridge, Mass.: Harvard University Press, 1959). See also, Ivan Avakumovic, *History of the Communist Party of Yugoslavia* (Aberdeen: Aberdeen University Press, 1964) and the studies of the Czechoslovak, East German, Hungarian, Polish, and Yugoslav parties in *Communism in Europe*, ed. William E. Griffith (Cambridge: MIT Press), vol. 4 (1964), pp. 19-300 and vol. 2 (1965), pp. 43-276.

28. Carl Beck, "Bureaucracy and Political Development in Eastern Europe," in *Bureaucracy and Political Development*, ed. Joseph LaPalombara (Princeton: Princeton University Press, 1963), pp. 268-300, remains one of the rare attempts to study bureaucratic behavior in Eastern Europe.

29. The standard work on cooptation is Frederic J. Fleron, Jr., "Towards a Reconceptualization of Political Change in the Soviet Union: The Political Leadership System," *Comparative Politics* 1, no. 2 (1969): 228-44. For a discussion of the impact of the generational conflict, see Zygmunt Bauman, "Twenty Years After: The Crisis of Soviet-Type Societies," *Problems of Communism* 20, no. 6 (1971): 45-53.

30. The concept of "solidary society" was first discussed by Gregory Grossman, "The Solidary Society: A Philosophical Issue in Communist Economic Reforms," in *Essays in Socialism and Planning in Honor of Carl Landauer*, ed. Gregory Grossman (Englewood Cliffs, N.J.: Prentice-Hall, 1970), pp. 148-211.

31. Probably the most telling criticism of the application of the group conflict approach to the analysis of Communist societies is that of Andrew Janos in "Group Politics in Communist Society," in *Authoritarian Politics in Modern Society*, ed. Samuel P. Huntington and Clement H. Moore (New York and London: Basic Books, 1970), pp. 437-50.

32. David E. Langsam and David W. Paul, "Soviet Politics and the Group Approach," *Slavic Review* 30, no. 1 (1972): 136-37.

33. Samuel P. Huntington, "Social and Institutional Dynamics of One-Party Systems," in Huntington and Moore, eds., *Authoritarian Politics in Modern Society*, p. 35.

34. Andrzej Korbonski, "Bureaucracy and Interest Groups in Communist Societies: The Case of Czechoslovakia," *Studies in Comparative Communism* 4, no. 1 (1971): 57-79, and H. Gordon Skilling, "Group Conflict and Political Change," in *Change in Communist Systems*, ed. Chalmers Johnson (Stanford: Stanford University Press, 1970). Skilling's propositions were tested recently on selected groups in Hungary and Poland by Jeffrey Porro, "Political Change and the Group Model in Communist Systems: Workers and Writers in Poland and Hungary, 1957-1970," Ph.D. dissertation, University of California at Los Angeles, 1975.

35. Alfred G. Meyer, "Authority in Communist Political Systems," in *Political Leadership in Industrialized Societies*, ed. Lewis J. Edinger (New York: John Wiley, 1967), pp. 84-107. See also his "Legitimacy of Power in East Central Europe," in *Eastern Europe in the 1970s*, ed. Sinanian et al., pp. 45-68.

36. Phyllis Auty, *Tito: A Biography* (Harlow, England: Longmans, 1970); Nicholas Bethell, *Gomulka* (Harmondsworth, England: Pelican, 1962); William Shawcross, *Dubcek* (London: Weidenfeld and Nicolson, 1970); Carole Stern, *Ulbricht* (Cologne: Kiepenheuer and Witsch, 1963).

37. Among the better-known studies are Carl Beck et al., *Comparative Communist Political Leadership* (New York: David McKay, 1973) and *Political Leadership in Eastern Europe and the Soviet Union*, ed. R. Barry Farrell (Chicago: Aldine, 1970). See also *Opinion-Making Elites in Yugoslavia*, ed. Allen H. Barton, Bogdan Denitch, and Charles Kadushin (New York: Praeger Publishers, 1973); Thomas A. Baylis, *Technical Intelligentsia and the East German Elite* (Berkeley and Los Angeles: University of California Press, 1974); Adam Bromke, "La nouvelle elite politique en Pologne," *Revue de l'Est* (Paris) 4, no. 3 (1974): 7-18; Peter C. Lutz, *Parteielite im Wandel* (Cologne and Opladen: Westdeutscher Verlag, 1968).

38. Myron Rush, *How Communist States Change Their Rulers* (Ithaca, N.Y., and London: Cornell University Press, 1974).

39. I discuss this particular problem in "Leadership Succession and Political Change in Eastern Europe," *Studies in Comparative Communism* (forthcoming).

40. The impact of post-Tito succession is ably discussed in William Zimmerman, "The Tito Succession and the Evolution of Yugoslav Politics," *Studies in Comparative Communism* (forthcoming). The recent changes in Romanian leadership and their effect on internal politics are analyzed in Kenneth Jowitt, "Political Innovation in Romania," *Survey*, no. 4 (1974): 132-51.

41. Huntington, "The Change to Change," p. 316.

42. Carl J. Friedrich and Zbigniew K. Brzezinski, *Totalitarian Dictatorship and Autocracy* (New York: Praeger Publishers, 1961), pp. 9-10.

43. One recent exception is Dale R. Herspring, *East German Civil-Military Relations: The Impact of Technology 1949-1972* (New York: Praeger Publishers, 1973).

44. Alexander Dallin and George W. Breslauer, *Political Terror in Communist Systems* (Stanford: Stanford University Press, 1970).

45. For an up-to-date account, see Michael Gamarnikow, "Balance Sheet on Economic Reforms," in *Reorientation and Commercial Relations of the Economies of Eastern*

Europe, compendium of papers submitted to the Joint Economic Committee, 93d Congress, 2d Session (Washington, D.C.: U.S. Government Printing Office, 1974), pp. 164-213.

46. For some attempts, see Andrej Brzeski, "Social Engineering the *Realpolitik* in Communist Economic Reorganization," in *Essays in Socialism and Planning*, ed. Grossman, pp. 148-79; R. V. Burks, "The Political Implications of Economic Reforms," in *Plan and Market*, ed. Morris Bernstein (New Haven and London: Yale University Press, 1973), pp. 373-402; "The Political Hazards of Economic Reform," in *Reorientation and Commercial Relations of the Economies of Eastern Europe*, pp. 51-78; William F. Robinson, *The Pattern of Reform in Hungary* (New York: Praeger Publishers, 1973), passim.

47. Chalmers Johnson, ed., *Change in Communist Systems* (Stanford: Stanford University Press, 1970).

48. Samuel P. Huntington and Clement H. Moore, eds., *Authoritarian Politics in Modern Society* (New York and London: Basic Books, 1970).

49. Paul H. B. Goodwin, "Communist Systems and Modernization: Sources of Political Crises," *Studies in Comparative Communism* 6, nos. 1-2 (1973): 107-34.

50. Andrzej Korbonski, "Comparing Liberalization Processes in Eastern Europe: A Preliminary Analysis," *Comparative Politics* 4, no. 2 (1972): 231-49; "Liberalization in Eastern Europe: A Comparative View," in *Essays on Socialist Systems*, ed. Carl Beck and Carmelo Mesa-Lago (forthcoming).

51. Kenneth Jowitt, "Inclusion and Mobilization in European Leninist Systems," *World Politics* 28, no. 1 (1975): pp. 69-96.

52. John A. Armstrong, "Development Theory: Taking the Historical Cure," *Studies in Comparative Communism* 7, nos. 1-2 (1974): 216-27. Among the recent studies were Charles Gati, "Hungary: The Dynamics of Revolutionary Transformation," Otto Ulc, "Czechoslovakia: The Great Leap Backward," and Trond Gilberg, "Romania: Problems of the Multilaterally Developed Society," all in *The Politics of Modernization in Eastern Europe*, ed. Gati, pp. 51-159; A Ross Johnson, "Yugoslavia: In the Twilight of Tito," *The Washington Papers* 2, no. 16 (1974); H. Gordon Skilling, "Opposition in Communist East Europe" and "Czechoslovakia's Interrupted Revolution," in *Regimes and Oppositions*, ed. Robert A. Dahl (New Haven and London: Yale University Press, 1973), pp. 89-141.

53. Kenneth Jowitt, *Revolutionary Breakthroughs and National Development* (Berkeley and Los Angeles: University of California Press, 1971) and "Modernization and Mobilization in Marxist-Leninist Systems," paper presented a Symposium on the Social Consequences of Modernization in Socialist Countries, Salzburg, Austria, September 1972.

54. Zvi Gitelman, "Beyond Leninism: Political Development in Eastern Europe," *Newsletter on Comparative Studies of Communism* 5, no. 3 (1972): 18-43.

55. Phillip E. Jacob et al., *Values and the Active Community* (New York: Free Press, 1971), passim; Miroslav Disman, "Social Stratification and Civic Participation," paper presented at Conference on New Social Stratification and the Role of Political Elites in East Central Europe, Lawrence, Kansas, April 1973; Jan F. Triska and Ana Barbic, "Evaluating Citizen Performance on Community Level: Does Party Affiliation in Yugoslavia Make the Difference?" unpublished paper, 1975.

56. Andrzej Korbonski, "Political Aspects of Economic Reforms in Eastern Europe," in *Economic Development in the Soviet Union and Eastern Europe*, ed. Z. Fallenbuchl (New York: Praeger Publishers, 1976).

57. Jan F. Triska and Paul M. Johnson, "Political Development and Political Change in Eastern Europe," unpublished paper, 1974.

58. One of the most interesting discussions regarding socioeconomic processes in Eastern Europe took place in 1971 in *Archives Europeennes de Sociologie* (12, no. 1). See Zygmunt Bauman, "Social Dissent in the East European Political System" and Leszek Kolakowski, "A Pleading for Revolution: A Rejoinder to Z. Bauman," in ibid., pp. 25-60.

59. Andrzej Korbonski, "The Prospects for Change in Eastern Europe," *Slavic Review* 33, no. 2 (1974): 219-39.

60. For an account of the growth of East European interest in political science, see David E. Powell and Paul Shoup, "The Emergence of Political Science in Communist Countries," *The American Political Science Review* 64, no. 2 (1970): 572-88.

61. Richard Lowenthal, "Development vs. Utopia in Communist Policy," in *Change in Communist Systems*, ed. Johnson, pp. 33-116. See also, Cyril E. Black, "Marxism and Modernization," *Slavic Review* 29, no. 2 (1970): 182-86.

62. Pyotr Demichev, "Developed Socialism—Stage on the Way to Communism," *World Marxist Review* 16, no. 1 (1973): 10-12, 14; "Characteristics of Developed Socialism," *World Marxist Review* 18, no. 1 (1975): 83-98.

63. Richard Kosolapov, "The Approach to the Study of Developed Socialism," *World Marxist Review* 17, no. 9 (1974): 71.

64. Demichev, "Developed Socialism," pp. 18-21. See also, "The Present-Day Problems of Socialist Democracy and its Perspectives," *World Marxist Review* 18, no. 3 (1975): 101ff.

65. "The Working Class and Its Party in Contemporary Socialist Society," *World Marxist Review* 16, no. 9 (1973): 37-55.

66. "The Socialist State and Democracy," *World Marxist Review* 14, no. 8 (1971): 3-38.

67. "The Working Class and Its Party," pp. 21-36.

68. Imre Pozgay and Bernard Marx, "Marxist Understanding of Social Administration," *World Marxist Review* 16, no. 6 (1973): 21-33 and "The Present-Day Problems of Socialist Democracy," p. 104.

69. "The Scientific-Technical Revolution and Socialism," *World Marxist Review* 15, no. 8 (1972): 5-35 and Werner Krolikowski, "Socialism and the Technological Revolution," *World Marxist Review* 18, no. 9 (1975): 44-51.

70. "Characteristics of Developed Socialism," pp. 84-85.

71. "The Present-Day Problems of Socialist Democracy," pp. 71-72.

72. Jowitt, "An Organizational Approach to the Study of Political Culture in Marxist-Leninist Systems," p. 1190.

73. Ibid.

74. Jowitt, "Political Innovation in Romania," p. 148. See also, Robert R. King, "Nicolae Ceausescu and the Politics of Leadership," *Radio Free Europe Research*, Romania/3, March 29, 1973.

75. Jure Bilic, "The League of Communists and Social Changes in Yugoslavia," *Socialist Thought and Practice*, no. 59 (1973): 25.

76. The content of the Letter is discussed at length in Josip Broz Tito, "We Must Have a Vanguard and United Party," *Socialist Thought and Practice* no. 49 (1972): 6-12.

77. Stane Dolanc, "The Working Class Character of the Struggle for Self-Management," *Socialist Thought and Practice* no. 52 (1973): 44-67; Edvard Kardelj, "Principal Causes and Trends of Constitutional Changes," *Socialist Thought and Practice*, no. 52, pp. 17-20; "Democracy in Socialism and Not Against Socialism," *Socialist Thought and Practice*, no. 5 (1974): 3-33; Josip Broz Tito, "The Surmounting of Problems Depends on Us," *Socialist Thought and Practice*, no. 50 (1973): 93-103.

78. Dolanc, "The Working Class Character of the Struggle for Self-Management," p. 49.

79. For an official Yugoslav view, see "Report on the Situation in the League of Communists of Croatia with Regard to the Outbreak of Nationalism Within its Ranks," *Socialist Thought and Practice* no. 49 (1972): 72-95.

80. See, for example, Josip Broz Tito, "The Struggle for the Further Development of Socialist Self-Management in Our Country and the Role of the LCY," address at the Tenth Congress of the League of Communists of Yugoslavia. *Socialist Thought and Practice* nos. 6-7 (1974): pp. 5-83.

81. Karl W. Ryavec, "Kremlinology or Behavioralism," *Problems of Communism* 22, no. 1 (1973): 84-85.

82. Montias, "Modernization in Communist Countries: Some Questions of Methodology," p. 413.

83. For a pioneering attempt, see Melvin Croan, "Is Mexico the Future of East Europe: Institutional Adaptability and Political Change in Comparative Perspective," in *Authoritarian Politics in Modern Society*, ed. Huntington and Moore, pp. 451-83.

84. Kautsky, "Comparative Communism Versus Comparative Politics," p. 151.

2

MODERNIZATION AS AN EXPLANATION OF POLITICAL CHANGE IN EAST EUROPEAN STATES
Paul M. Johnson

It is by now commonplace to note that many of the intellectual tools used in the past by Western scholars to guide their research and organize their findings on the Communist states of Eastern Europe have come under attack, at least since the 1960s, as inadequate to describe and account for certain highly salient trends and tendencies recently observed in the domestic and international politics of the region. The increasingly heterogeneous patterns of politics that emerged in Eastern Europe and the USSR following the death of Stalin steadily undermined the empirical applicability of the only broad conceptual framework then in wide use—the "ideal type" of the "totalitarian" society.

The erosion of this dominant paradigm by the steady accumulation of anomalous observations led (after some delay) to a widespread search for new organizing concepts by the scholars in the field who were least locked in to the pattern of cold war polemics. That pattern had been much facilitated by the assumptions of the close approximation of these regimes to the totalitarian ideal and of their essential imperviousness to modification through domestic forces.

The initial reaction of many analysts was to attempt to salvage some of the academic investment in the totalitarian model with its careful description of the self-reinforcing mechanisms that served to stabilize and even extend the more exotic traits of "high Stalinism." This was to be accomplished through more precise distinction between the "really essential" defining characteristics of the totalitarian system (now seen as fewer than before) and "contingent" traits whose presence was likely but not essential to the basic configuration. Totalitarian systems, it now appeared, had various subtypes other than the previously recognized fascist and Stalinist variants.

Nevertheless, despite considerable elaboration in terminology, applications of the revised standard version of totalitarianism remained basically the same. They still emphasize the essential durability of the basic differentiating features of Leviathan, despite the possibility of cyclical departure from one-man rule during an interregnum and from blood purges during periods of "consolidation." The task of the Western analyst was still to describe the formidable mechanisms of control that safeguarded the system and to analyze policy making and elite rivalries as primarily determined by the basic structure of the system—"the logic of the totalitarian system" was seen as an adequate explanation of most policy-relevant political behavior.

By the 1960s scholars were catching up with the march of events and elaborated new ideal types to describe what appeared to be emerging in the USSR and Eastern Europe—ideal types that were recognizably distinct from earlier "totalitarian" formulations, although the basic concerns and methodology remained much as before.

Such constructs as Alfred Meyer's bureaucratic model, Robert Tucker's movement regime, Allen Kassof's administered society, and Robert Conquest's ideocratic apparatocracy all directed attention to significant and hitherto insufficiently dramatized features of contemporary Communist politics, and some even facilitated comparison with certain non-Communist regimes.[1] But the fact nevertheless remained that their approaches were still at best the analysis of comparative statics, contrasting the (idealized and abstracted) characteristics of discrete and internally self-maintaining systems, with relatively little effort at the systematic elaboration of the conditions under which actual societies would move toward or away from approximations of the ideal types over time. In effect, the dominant concern did not seem to be with describing and explaining change processes as much as with trying to foresee and delineate the nature of the new equilibrium that was assumed to be just around the corner.

In more recent times a number of scholars in the Eastern European field have been coming to a more dynamic, process-oriented view. Increasingly they are broadening their understanding of their professional role to include the obligation and necessity of more active participation in the construction and verification of theories of political change with more general applicability than was possible within a strict area studies framework. East European studies, like comparative politics generally, is undergoing its own "change to change" in the realm of theoretical problems. This tendency has been most clearly exemplified (and reinforced) by the work of researchers associated with the American Council of Learned Societies' Planning Group on the Comparative Study of Communism and their publication, the *Newsletter on the Comparative Study of Communism.*[2]

If we recognize the question of explaining political change in Eastern Europe as one of the more important items on our professional agenda, it would seem a good idea to clarify just what such an undertaking entails. To explain a specific change, according to the positivists, is at least to specify the conditions under which such changes may be expected to take place, which is to say, to be able to cite general "if . . . then" statements or "laws" from which other statements concerning the characteristics of a particular entity under specified conditions can be deduced with reasonable confidence. A theory of political change would be a set of such general statements, interconnected and noncontradictory, and accompanied by some set of rules for determining whether specific real world occurrences correspond to the categories employed in the general statements. That is, the theoretical categories or descriptions must have operational definitions to link them with observed or observable phenomena. This last is necessary to ensure that the theory is falsifiable. The quality of a theory is evaluated according to some subjectively determined weighting of the competing criteria of accuracy, predictive power, generality, parsimony, causality, policy relevance, normative relevance, and so forth.

Of course there can be no such thing as a theory of change in the abstract, unless one is engaged in the realms of metaphysics and ontology. Change is a relational term and presupposes some specification of what is changing. Whoever constructs a theory of political change must logically begin by identifying the component or components of the political system whose variation (or lack of it) he wishes to explain. Then one proceeds to the identification of other variables whose states or changes are hypothesized to affect (directly or indirectly) the variables of principal concern.

Since the number of attributes of, and relationships within, the political system that could plausibly become significant dependent variables in a theory of political change is limited only by the ingenuity of the researcher in identifying subjectively interesting phenomena, and since independent explanatory variables are not even limited to the "political" aspects of social life, it is clear that we shall be concerned principally with the elaboration of partial rather than general theories of political change for quite some time. Parsimony as well as the practical demands of research dictate that we concentrate on only a few variables at any one time. It therefore behooves us to specify rather carefully the kind of phenomena with which we are most concerned when we speak of political change in Eastern Europe. It is possible that a few master variables can account for a great many important changes, but this should be demonstrated rather than assumed.

What, then, are the substantive political changes of greatest intrinsic interest for scholars in the field of East European politics in recent years? Despite the current tendency to speak disparagingly of the old totalitarian model, it would appear that it indeed identified the dimensions of the Communist political systems that are still the major focus of attention. According to Friedrich and Brzezinski's famous formulation:

> The syndrome, or pattern of interrelated traits, of the totalitarian dictatorship consists of an ideology, a single party typically led by one man, a terroristic police, a communications monopoly and a centrally directed economy.[3]

The principal changes occupying our attention in recent decades have corresponded rather precisely to the negations of these allegedly essential attributes. Specifically, the literature on systemic political change in Eastern Europe has focused on observed, inferred, or anticipated shifts (1) from elite adherence to the strictures of a detailed, dogmatic, programmatic, and messianic ideology to more pragmatic, open-ended, inductive, or secular elite attitudes in policy making; (2) from a one-party system with an autonomous dictator to various styles of collective or oligarchic leadership, and a more active role for other institutional elites in the policy-making process; (3) from a high reliance on terror and physical coercion to greater emphasis on normative and remunerative modes for obtaining compliance; (4) from a univocal, censored, and propagandistic mass media establishment toward greater diversity of published views, less secretiveness in the matter of information dissemination, and even limited policy debate; (5) from rigid ideological/political controls on the military toward more professional autonomy in the interests of technical efficiency and perhaps somewhat greater consideration to military elites in the larger policy-making process; (6) from a centralized command economy to a semicentralized managerial system or perhaps even toward "market socialism."

If we add to this list of changes one more that is not directly suggested by the totalitarian model—the tendency of East European regimes to acquire greater effective autonomy from Soviet influence—we have pretty well summarized the principal subject matter of perhaps 80 percent of the last decade's output of publications on contemporary politics in the region. By and large, we have reacted to the march of events in the post-Stalin period by redefining what used to be seen as the relatively static parameters of political life in East Europe as variables instead. Our theoretical focus has correspondingly tended to shift from explaining the ways in which the structural setting of politics influenced or determined the pattern of elite conflicts, the making of policy, and the outcomes for society and the world community, toward trying to explain, predict, or at least describe political structure itself.

The shift in theoretical focus has been related to the great increase since the mid-1960s in the conscious (or perhaps we should say self-conscious) importation of theoretical frameworks, key concepts, and working hypotheses from the broader disciplines of the social sciences, and especially from the rapidly changing field of comparative politics. There also was a somewhat more grudging, but still substantial, influx of the methodological perspectives and mathematically complex techniques of data manipulation of the so-called behavioral revolution.

Perhaps the most important theoretical notions we have imported from mainstream comparative politics are: (1) the conceptualization of political structure and process in holistic systems-functional terms and (2) the practical identification of structural political change with political development, viewed as a more or less inseparable part of an overarching process of social-cultural modernization and economic development. It is perhaps not too surprising that these borrowings should make their way into the East European field, since these orientations dominated most of the theoretically sophisticated literature in comparative politics throughout the 1960s, reflecting the influence of such figures as Almond, Easton, and Apter. But I would argue that, while the overall impact of these tendencies toward reintegration of East European studies with comparative politics has been positive, there may have been insufficient attention to certain analytical implications in the case of East Europe.

The systems and structural-functional approaches to analyzing and theorizing about politics begin with the assumption that the variable attributes of the system are highly related to each other and that interrelationships maintain certain variables in the system (designated as essential or defining or critical variables) within specified and relatively narrow limits, despite fluctuations in the other variables. That is, excessive variation in one determinant of a critical variable will ordinarily be compensated for by offsetting changes in another element sufficient to restore or maintain the critical variable.

Building a theory within this framework means specifying the essential attributes of the concrete political entity as variables, identifying the factors that determine the presence/absence or the magnitude of these critical variables, and specifying the form of the interrelationships, especially the homeostatic mechanisms that keep the system in its bounds. Models or theories of this type are often criticized as teleological, tautological, and unable to conceptualize or explain systemic change—all of which charges I believe can be successfully countered at the analytical level.[4] But the shortcoming that has not been successfully overcome is the extraordinary practical difficulty of specifying and verifying particular structural-functional or systems theories of political phenomena at the nation-state level. So far as I am aware, no one has ever elaborated a theory that adequately specified the limits of fluctuation of the critical variables and the functional form of the interrelationships in such a way that the researcher could conceivably falsify it in a confrontation with data, even assuming the availability of reliable and valid measures of the theoretical variables. While it seems to me altogether likely that any future broad-gauge verified theory of politics will be system-functional in form, such an achievement is still a long way off; in any case it is much more likely to come about through a process of integrating a number of separately developed partial theories of limited application than through great leaps forward. But if that is the case, systems theory and structural-functionalism become long-range aspirations rather than guides to research. Then the variables and concepts put forward in their name can be regarded as little more than someone's suggestion that these, rather than those, are the most interesting topics for research. Insofar as East European specialists are really primarily interested in explaining the specific types of political changes observed in the post-Stalin era, or in predicting future developments in the area, they are obliged to look very closely indeed at the degree to which borrowed or imported theories have been verified in other contexts. It seems to me that this point has been insufficiently regarded in efforts at theoretically linking post-Stalin developments with modernization and economic development.

The idea that there is a close relationship between economic development and sociocultural modernization on the one hand, and the structural transformation of the political system on the other, is of course a very old one. The particular forms that this general notion has taken in the last 20 years are many, but the various theorists of modernization tend to have a great deal in common. Modernization is seen as a long-term, complex, systemic process involving transformations of truly revolutionary scope; it is believed to affect virtually all areas of human social experience, from the most personal and subjective aspects of cognition and affect to the structure of institutions.

Modernization is about urbanization, secularization, mass education, mass communication, factory production, advancing science and technology, improvement in standards of health and material well-being, large-scale rational-bureaucratic organizations, specialization and differentiation of activities, and so on. All these processes seem to progress more or less together in some very general sense, but we have no adequate theory that specifies the degree to which their historical association was a necessary rather than fortuitous outcome of the unique convergence of several tendencies in modern Europe and its offshoots. Certainly at least some changes seem to have no discernible necessary relationships. Sociologists and economists have not as yet provided us with theories capable of specifying the degree of change in any one dimension necessary to bring about or sustain a given shift on another dimension. Nor can we say whether modernization can continue to progress indefinitely or whether at some point a society becomes fully modern, or even tends to decline.

The relationships between modernization and political change are even more problematic. The early tendency in the political development literature was to concentrate on identifying the political prerequisites of economic development and social modernization in order to provide policy guidance for the leaders of underdeveloped countries. But it was not long before political scientists considerably expanded the concept to include almost every kind of political change that has ever occurred just before, during, or after a period of rapid economic growth or social change. In a heroic effort at synthesis, Lucian Pye attempted to consolidate the political development concept into the three central dimensions of increased equality among individuals in the political system, increased differentiation of political institutions and structures, and increased capacity of the political system with regard to its ability to affect society and the economy, as well as the foreign environment.[5] I would suggest that, when one sets aside the elements of normative prescription as to what a "good" state ought to do, the principal characteristic of political systems most often emphasized in the Western literature on "political development" is really

Pye's third dimension: the enhancement of the capacity of national political organizations to control or regulate social and economic life in accordance with some conception of "the national interest" (defined variously in terms of economic development, military strength, social justice, and so forth). This emphasis is latent in the dominant structural-functional orientation to theorizing about political development, which is methodologically geared to explaining the persistence of essential structures of the political system despire the rapidly changing physical, social, economic, or cultural environment with which it must contend. Essential political structures survive changes (if at all) through processes of adaptation which render role-incumbents more capable of dominating or manipulating the relevant features of the environment. Most of the changes that theorists usually refer to as constituting or exemplifying "political development" (differentiation of political structures, increased levels of national integration, creation of a more rational Weberian bureaucracy, institutionalization of mass political involvement and so on) are so defined because they are viewed as effective means of enhancing the capacity of the political system, or, more concretely, of the nation-state. The writings of Samuel P. Huntington exemplify this emphasis most clearly:

> The most important political distinction among countries concerns not their form of government but their degree of government. The differences between democracy and dictatorship are less than the differences between those countries whose politics embodies consensus, community, legitimacy, organization, effectiveness, stability, and those countries whose politics is deficient in these qualities. Communist totalitarian states and Western liberal states both belong generally in the category of effective rather than debile political systems.[6]

The literature of "political development," insofar as it has any unifying theme at all, represents a body of hypotheses as to what may be the characteristics of political systems that are capable (or most capable) of setting and effectively attaining collective goals in the context of a nation-state whose economy, culture, and society have undergone or are undergoing the processes lumped together under the heading of modernization. Effective performance, and not any particular structural characteristic, is ultimately the test.

One of the great problems with the whole political development literature is, of course, that it is seldom put to the test in a way that would permit falsification, necessitate reformulations and qualifications, and thereby open the way to theoretical advancement. Empirical work in the field has tended to focus upon the differences between the political structures of nation-states at high, medium, and low levels of socioeconomic development rather than upon comparing the performance characteristics of different structural arrangements operating in roughly similar socioeconomic environments. For the most part, the literature reflects this orientation with a noticeable neglect of the problem of how to measure performance, despite the urgings of such theorists as Gabriel Almond.[7]

I have focused at some length on the subject of how mainstream comparative politics has theorized about modernization and political change, and in some respects seems to have gone wrong. I do not wish to minimize the insights that have been developed, and will no doubt in due course find more systematic application in concrete research. But it seems only fair to state that these insights for the most part have not yet been translated into explicit, tested propositions stating strong relationships between characteristics of the modernization/development process and specific kinds of changes in political structure. As things how stand, we cannot explain political change in post-Stalin East Europe by invoking "the theory of modernization" or "the theory of political development."

Nevertheless, there seems to be an increasing tendency to explain these changes by arguments that implicitly assume we do have such verified propositions. I refer, for example, to arguments of the following general form:

Mobilization for development (political structure traits a to z)   (1)
↓
Successful modernization (to some critical level)   (2)
↓
Differentiated complex society and economy   (3)
↓
Diminished effectiveness of political structure traits X, Y, and Z   (4)
↓
Serious decline in system performance   (5)
↓
Elite decision to reform or perish   (6)

Now let me hasten to say that I consider this paradigm of a reform process to be eminently respectable as a sort of orienting framework to begin the study of certain kinds of change in Eastern Europe. Most experts probably have used some variation at one time or another, often with interesting or valuable results. Yet I think it is very important to realize the problems of verification and evidence that are entailed in elevating this to the level of a theory with real explanatory power. How could it be disconfirmed? Few worry very much about the linkage between steps 1 and 2 and between 2 and 3, although economists or sociologists would probably be inclined to quibble a bit, inserting a few qualifications and lots of intervening variables. But the jumps from 3 to 4 to 5, and from 5 to 6, must be considered more problematical by political scientists.

Consider the first linkage (3-4-5), which is the argument that, after the society and economy have reached some higher level of complexity, the persistence of certain political patterns (such as the use of terror as a major control device, or highly centralized economic planning and management) leads to a worsening in system performance. However, to make such an argument falsifiable one must be able to crudely measure the degree of complexity of the society/economy, the presence-absence (or degree) of the alledgedly dysfunctional trait, and the system's level of performance with respect to the relevant outputs and outcomes. Moreover, the argument must specify in some way the range of socioeconomic complexity in which the political trait becomes clearly dysfunctional and the approximate length of time before this is reflected in performance.

It is at this point that it would be nice to have either a deductive theory or an empirical estimation derived from some other set of analogous cases to help make these specifications, but as has been noted, neither presently exists, at least not for the kinds of whole systems at the national level with which we customarily deal. This is a reflection of the still underdeveloped state of the theory of development and modernization, and nicely illustrates the interdependence of area studies and comparative politics.

Linkage 5-6, the process by which a decline in system performance leads to structural change, raises other interesting but difficult questions, and a good deal of concern within the field has been expressed for problems in precisely this area. Here arise questions like: Who are the agents of change? Evolution or revolution? "Transformation or degeneration? The connection between steps 5 and 6 is relatively straightforward for a serious decline in system performance that is uniformly salient to all members of the decision-making group, if all members share the same perceptions as to the cause; in such cases one would expect them to examine the feasibility and costs of change and take appropriate action. In reality, of course, the more common situation is that relevant power holders place different relative importance on the multiple performance indicators that they monitor; they entertain different notions as to the causes of particular difficulties; and they are likely to have strong personal feelings and interests engaged in assessing the relative costs and benefits of various proposed remedies. In this case, decline in one or more area of performance is likely to generate elite conflict, which conditions the ultimate decision and may itself have secondary repercussions for the political structure.

How can these notions be tested in a particular case? Again, one needs to be able to measure system performance in at least those respects relevant to the theory, so as to demonstrate that a decline has indeed occurred. One needs to show that the dimension of performance matters enough to the actors to motivate action, and that at least some actors attribute the decline to the postulated dysfunctional structural trait. If group conflict is to be interpreted within this general framework, as most contemporary commentators on political change in East Europe are interested in doing, then it is very important to identify groups with (or perhaps even define them by) the particular dimensions of systemic performance that are most important to them. One must also pinpoint their perceptions of the nature of the relationship between performance and the attributes of system structure that are in question. Such orientational identification of groups or factions must of course be independently documented, rather than simply assumed.

What if one can demonstrate all this, yet after a reasonable time the performance still remains at a depressed level, no reform has been forthcoming, and the system has not self-destructed? Then one has uncovered an interesting situation in the process of disconforming the last link of the initial theory, and one needs perhaps to reassess the utility of certain pervasive assumptions with which we approach the study of recent political changes in East Europe—assumptions that find their counterparts in the general structural-functional and systems theory orientations to theorizing about politics.

Such a finding would draw more critical attention to the prevalent assumption that system survival in Eastern Europe is so problematic that a study of the mechanisms whereby collapse is precariously staved off can tell us more or less all we need to know about system dynamics. This orientation seems particularly appropriate to highly unstable and poorly institutionalized regimes such as abound in the post-World War II third world and are far from unknown elsewhere. And this may help explain the appeal of such theorizing for comparative politics. The antagonisms of the cold war, and Western revulsion for the anti-liberal and coercive nature of East European regimes, have often found expression in the popular pastime among Western analysts of counting the vultures circling above the system. But it may well be that we tend seriously to underrate the margin for error and the stability of these systems. It may be that what is at stake is often not so much the viability of the system as the direction of its major efforts and to the degree that this turns out to be the case, structural-functional and systems theory frameworks appear increasingly misleading or inapplicable for purposes of explaining political change. Models focusing more explicitly on elite values and the decisional process would tend to come to the fore.

Having discussed the structure and some of the problems of verification in the "political change as adaptation to modernization" approach to theory, I should like to take up the question of just which of the kinds of changes in East Europe, which we identified earlier as major focal points of the literature, seem most ripe for explanation in terms of such a theory.

The type of change process with which analysts have dealt most adequately in terms of the modernization paradigm seems to be the economic reforms of the mid-1960s; indeed, the attractiveness of their efforts in this area may explain much of the interest in applying the approach to other areas as well.[8]

The biggest pluses in this direction are:

1. Rather good measures of economic performance over a substantial

period of time are available (rate of growth of net material product or industrial production, output per worker in industry, balance of trade).

2. The level of economic development attained could be rather adequately specified, given the well-developed technical literature on the subject and its relatively standardized and cross-nationally comparable indicators.

3. The degree of economic centralization was not too difficult to assess roughly, precisely because it tended to be so extreme to begin with, and also because the formalized theories of economics had already defined a number of general decision categories (production function employed, assortment of output, level of wages) whose locus within the economic administration could be determined and used as a basis for measurement.

4. There was abundant evidence that political elites considered the level of economic performance to be extremely important.

5. The writings of East European economists provide evidence that elites were at least made aware of the possibility that overcentralization was at the root of the problem.

And indeed, a casual examination of data on changes in growth rates of net material product in the early 1960s gives at least some support to the theory (see Table 2.1). Czechoslovakia and the GDR, the two most economically developed socialist states, experienced the most striking declines in growth rates and subsequently implemented economic reforms, albeit rather different in content, timing, and degree of elite conflict entailed. The USSR and Bulgaria also suffered significant, although smaller declines in growth rates and also inaugurated rather limited economic reforms—although here it is a little less

TABLE 2.1

Average Annual Rate of Growth of Real Per Capita NMP
(in percent)

Country	1950-60	1960-64
Bulgaria	8.1	5.7
Czechoslovakia	6.5	0.9
German Democratic Republic	8.9	2.4
Hungary	5.7	4.9
Poland	5.6	4.8
Romania	9.0	8.2
USSR	8.3	4.8
Yugoslavia	7.4	7.7

Source: *Compendium of Social Statistics: 1967* (New York: United Nations, 1968).

plausible to attribute the declining growth rates to the advance of modernization and complexity, since Hungary and Poland, which were at rather comparable levels of development, showed only insignificant declines in this period.

On the other hand, Yugoslavia and Hungary constitute rather puzzling cases when considered in terms of the modernization argument. Yugoslavia, the least economically developed of the group, showed a slight improvement in growth rates, yet launched the most thoroughgoing reforms of all in 1965. Hungary, at a relatively advanced level of development, showed only a rather insignificant decline in growth rates, yet in 1965 the Party's Central Committee approved an economic reform package nearly as radical as that which emerged later in Czechoslovakia in the Dubcek period. So it would appear that, while the modernization paradigm accounts nicely for some cases of reform in the economic structure, there also seem to be other mechanisms at work in other cases for similar reforms, which are not adequately captured and need to be accounted for in other ways.

If the modernization paradigm enjoys limited success in accounting for changes in the centralized economic system, what can we say about its present or prospective utility in explaining other kinds of divergences from the totalitarian syndrome? Here the explanation seems to be much more iffy, in large part because of the problems of measurement. In the first place, when we try to talk about changes outside the economic realm, it seems much less plausible to relate them to economic performance because it is not immediately clear that reforms in these areas would powerfully affect the economy for the better. To make such an argument, one has to rely on the positing of intervening relationships that are difficult to demonstrate (although not impossible). It seems likely that dimensions of system performance other than the economic may be much more directly relevant. However, at present we scarcely even have adequate conceptualizations of what these dimensions might be, let alone techniques for measuring them. One approach would be to ask ourselves the question: What do the top decision makers consider when they are trying to determine how well things are going for the system? Answers that come to mind include at least the following: (1) the degree of security from unwelcome foreign influence, intervention, or attacks; (2) the degree of security from civil disorders or popular uprisings; (3) the degree to which social development is proceeding toward an approximation of the ideologically posited ideal of Communist society, including greater equality in the distribution of material goods, educational opportunities, and other amenities; as well as (4) economic development, already mentioned.

(Although it is not normally directly relevant to decision making, it is also useful to know what nonelites look at to evaluate system performance. In that case one might add such additional performance dimensions as responsiveness and opportunities for participation, as well as the degree to which social arrangements are seen to approach whatever other non-Marxist utopias may be subscribed to by sizable numbers. This would seem an important determinant of the system's legitimacy, which in itself might be considered another performance dimension by the elite.)

Plugging the additional performance variables and structural characteristics into the modernization paradigm leads to additional propositions such as the following:

1. At more advanced stages of modernization, "ideological" orientations characteristic of earlier totalitarian periods lead to decline in national autonomy, and/or civil order, and/or social egalitarianism, and/or economic growth.

2. At more advanced stages of development, tight restriction of decision making to a small oligarchy or to a single dictator leads to decline in national autonomy, and/or civil order, and/or social egalitarianism, and/or economic growth.

3. At more advanced stages of development, continued high reliance on coercion and terror leads to decline in national autonomy, and/or civil order, and/or social egalitarianism, and/or economic growth.

4. At more advanced stages of development, continued strict control of the mass media leads to decline in national autonomy, and/or civil order, and/or social egalitarianism, and/or economic growth.

Thus baldly stated, some of the versions of the "modernization leads to structural change" theory appear plausible, others cry out for specification of intervening variables, and still others appear dubious at best. Among the most dubious, on conceptual grounds primarily, are the propositions regarding the strength of ideology. Although one occasionally encounters the "end of ideology" thesis in this form, or something like it, it does not really fit.[9]

When ideology is separated from the policy of relying on coercion and careful central control, what is left is mainly the commitment to egalitarian social policies, plus a set of categories for analyzing long-term social change and a commitment to the support of an international socialist community. It is not at all clear that the genuine conflicts between these commitments and the goal of economic development are exacerbated at higher levels of development. As for the other performance dimensions, it would seem that an ideological stance would be more, rather than less likely to move the society toward greater equality at higher levels of development. Indeed, a case might well be made that such a policy would facilitate rather than hinder the maintenance of civil order, since relative deprivation has been found to be a potent predictor of political violence in other contexts.[10]

It does seem to be historically true that East European elites have tended increasingly to come down on the side of less equality when they perceived a conflict with economic growth. However, this shift of values (if such it is) is rather difficult to attribute to modernization as such—rather, we should perhaps look to such other variables as tenure in office, socioeconomic status, recruitment procedures, and socialization for explanations of this phenomenon.

The marshaling of evidence on all the propositions I have presented is far too large a task to undertake here. Indeed, the portion of the theory that posits modernization as the cause of performance declines may not be testable at all, since the critical level of development remains unspecified; thus, any apparent disconfirmation can be shrugged off by the claim that conclusive confirmation must await further development and "ripening." In this respect, the theory closely resembles the Marxist theses on the inevitable final crises of capitalism, which are quietly rescheduled whenever the patient shows signs of rallying.

Naturally, many are reluctant to give up the modernization aspect of the theory, since it derives its comforting long-range predictions from the presumed inevitability of further socioeconomic modernization in East Europe. However, to me it is the second half of the theory that seems more interesting and potentially fruitful at this stage of the art, and it is really quite separable from the first half.

There is no real reason why the linking of performance to structural change via feedback and adaptation, which is at the core of the system-functional outlook, has to be grafted onto the modernization model. Rather, modernization should be considered only one possible factor influencing the performance of the political system and hence, indirectly, structural change. Increased emphasis on elite evaluations (and secondarily, on mass evaluations) of system performance as a crucial element in the feedback and adaptation mechanism enables us to escape the analytical trap of determinism and to incorporate both environmental changes and value changes by human actors as causal factors in political change.

If one takes this line of analysis, and defers verification of the hypothesized linkage between modernization and the functionality or dysfunctionality of specific political structures, then the main task is to develop techniques for identifying and measuring relevant performance dimensions and for measuring structural changes over time, so as to relate the two classes of variables. One also must get a handle on measuring the relative priorities that elites (and masses) put on the various dimensions of performance. But this cannot be inferred directly from the fact of structural change if such value structures are to help explain the reforms. Content analysis can perhaps supply an adequate solution to this last problem,[11] but it is to the problem in developing the first two measures that I would like to turn now.

First, how are we to measure political structural changes in Eastern Europe? Some changes are relatively easily quantified; for example, changes in career patterns of Politburo or Central Committee members can be gauged by the proportion of members having certain traits or experiences, the rate of turnover, and so on.

Other structural characteristics, such as the degree of control over mass media, necessitate much more impressionistic, or at least subjective measures.

Unfortunately, the latter type of variable seems to outnumber the former. Yet this has not generally deterred scholars from making the kinds of assertions of a descriptive and predictive nature that imply that they have some way of measuring these factors, however crude. In these cases, it seems to me that it would be better to make judgmental estimates explicit in more formalized coding categories than are customarily employed. At least this would leave us able to criticize each other's choices in a systematic fashion, thereby encouraging careful attention to details of evidence and inference and the development of more interpersonally acceptable coding criteria. Only by developing reasonably uniform conventions as to what observations are relevant in determining, for example, whether Poland's economic system today is more or less centralized than Bulgaria's, or whether Poland's economic system in 1968 was more centralized than in 1972, can we hope to say anything meaningful about change. The fact that it is hard to come up with fully valid indicators should not stop us from trying to at least improve the reliability of the judgmental measurements that we nevertheless seem determined to continue making. Whenever possible, of course, it is desirable for each investigator to work with multiple indicators for abstract theoretical concepts.

An example of such a measuring instrument is one that I have developed to monitor change in certain features of economic planning and administration on a year-by-year basis, as well as to make cross-national comparisons. It is based on a number of properties that distinguish the command economy from the idealized model of market socialism. Coding operations require a number of yes-or-no decisions. These codes are then aggregated in a Guttman-type scale. Here is an abbreviated form of the scale:

1. Are charges levied on the enterprise for the use of state capital, or is it supplied substantially without cost?

2. Does the enterprise pay for raw materials supplied?

3. Is managerial income importantly influenced by enterprise profitability?

4. Is the size and composition of the work force substantially at the discretion of the enterprise manager?

5. Is the assortment and quantity of output substantially determined by the enterprise manager?

6. Does the enterprise have substantial discretion in negotiating the price of its output?

7. Is enterprise membership in industrial trusts or combines compulsory or voluntary?

Scores for the various countries of Eastern Europe as of mid-1968 are as follows:

Country	Score
Yugoslavia	7
Hungary	6
Czechoslovakia	6
Bulgaria	4
East Germany	4
USSR	4
Poland	3
Romania	1
Albania	0

In areas of more immediately political concern, the delineation of authority is less explicit and behavior is less well defined by statute and institutional structure than in the case of economic planning and administration. In such areas it therefore may prove more difficult to construct multi-item scales with the same relatively unambiguous crossnational interpretation as the economic reform scale.

Two crucial dimensions of political change that we would wish to monitor are unfortunately among the hardest to measure at the level of whole systems in a way that would permit us to concisely describe variations over time. The problems of group and institutional autonomy, and of meaningful participation in decision making, have been given much discussion in the literature. This is particularly true in the realm of future casting, but also in analysis of contemporary policy making.[12]

Measurement of change in these dimensions has generally been indirect. Milton Lodge has employed content analysis of the specialized media of communications to identify levels of group self-consciousness, external attribution of elite status, and participatory attitudes over time.[13] This approach is useful and revealing, but it may measure changes in degree of control of media content almost as much as changes in the consciousness of specialized groups; at best, it can only be said to manifest psychological predispositions, not behavioral description.

Federick Fleron has approached the problem through analysis of elite recruitment patterns, hypothesizing with great cogency that persons recruited to important party roles after long careers outside party channels are more likely to advocate group interests than those whose careers have focused on advancement through the party apparatus.[14] Fleron's approach makes it possible to show that the relative proportions of "coopted" and "promoted" persons in such bodies as the central committees change systematically over time, and from this one may infer greater input by specialized elites into the decision process.

Still another approach has been the intensively investigated case study of particular major policy decisions, designed to uncover the outcome, insofar as this can be ascertained through careful scrutiny of public statements.[15] Still, inferring changes over time in the pattern of group influence is an extraordinarily difficult proposition, and it seems likely that relatively indirect approaches will have to do until the decision-making process becomes more visible to outside observers. We shall do well to approach the problem simultaneously with many indicators of group participation and influence, placing relatively little weight on findings until they are corroborated using other indicators. In addition to the content analysis of specialized media, and the examination of elite recruitment patterns, we also should note the affiliations of participants in the increasingly common public quasi-debates on policy issues in the mass media; leadership use of special nonparty commissions of experts to draft policy recommendations (frequency and number of policy areas); and similarly relevant but partial measures.

One line of endeavor to which we perhaps should direct more attention is formalization of the judgmental codings that we already make on an ad hoc and implicit basis. For example, Raymond B. Nixon and his associates have attempted crossnational comparisons of the degree of press censorship and control in a large sample of countries for the years 1960-64. Their approach uses panels of experts familiar with the press laws and practices of the various countries to code them along a nine-point judgmental scale, basing judgments not only on close reading of the press over time but also on material gathered by the international press organizations on treatment of foreign correspondents.[16] Within a more limited sample of countries, such as that in East Europe, it should be possible to set up criteria for guiding judgmental coding by well-trained area specialists that would provide meaningful data for longitudinal analysis of change. Such "consensus of experts" scales also would prove useful in estimating the validity of such other, more "objectively based" but indicrect measures as may be devised by other researchers.

The measurement of system performance is the other task of crucial importance in testing the particular kinds of hypotheses suggested earlier. I have already noted that measurement of economic performance is possible by virtue of the labors of economists, although it is an empirical question as to which economic indicators are most salient to the political elites and to various segments of the population in East Europe. Similarly, measuring the success of East European regimes in maintaining public order can be fairly well assessed by examining the incidence of such large-scale public phenomena as riots and protest demonstrations on a year-to-year basis (although it is best to remember that most hypotheses relate political change to changes in level of performance, not the absolute "normal" level of disorder).

Measurement of the two other dimensions of performance I identified earlier—social egalitarianism and national autonomy (national security)—is more difficult. With respect to the measurement of equality, the principal difficulties involve the evident unwillingness of most regimes to make public detailed data on the distribution of income and wealth. The data available are rather fragmentary—when they are available at all.

Probably the most important areas of inequality about which we would like to know would be measured in terms of discrepancies between urban and rural areas, between mental and manual labor, and between different ethnic groups in access to the means of consumption, to education, and to political influence. Possible indicators that are sometimes available as time series include proportion of national income devoted to "collective consumption"; relative wage levels of manual workers, clerical workers, and technical-managerial staff in industry; social origins of students in higher education; social and ethnic composition of the party; presence or absence of privileges granted to elite personnel (special rationing coupons or stores restricted to elites, preferences in housing); and the scope of free social services (is agriculture excluded from the retirement system? free medical care?). Increases in inequality must in some sense represent failures of performance, given the egalitarian aspects of Marxism that are emphasized in legitimation of the regime. They also are likely to exacerbate elite conflict and popular dissent—although it must be admitted that Western analyses have often been rather insensitive to this dynamic.[17]

Measuring system performance on the dimension of national autonomy/national security is perhaps the most difficult of all, except where there are massive failures such as foreign invasions. Nevertheless, most governments constantly evaluate their degree of security, and it seems to be rather important to them. Indeed, Gabriel Almond and his associates, in their study of political change in a wide variety of geographical and historical settings, found that the "military/security" variable was *the* most powerful exogenous variable in explaining system stability and change."[18]

In collaboration with Jan F. Triska, I have tried to deal with the problem of dependence on the USSR as a determinant of institutional deviations from the Soviet pattern regarding "liberalization" in the mid-1960s. In the course of this study I put forward several approaches to measuring national autonomy of East European states.[19] Basically, our measures were of two types. One measure was based on the observed degree of responsiveness of domestic leaders to expressed Soviet wishes in foreign policy and intra-Communist relations. The other types of measure was designed to gauge the "objective" means at hand for the Soviets to exert sanctions for noncompliance—dependence on Soviet trade, dependence on Soviet energy exports, presence/absence of Soviet troops, integration of economic planning with Comecon, elite desire to emulate Soviet models as measured by translations of books from Russian, and so forth. All our measures except the last proved good predictors of domestic differences from the Soviet pattern, and it seems likely that extension of such measures to longitudinal studies of political change would be worthwhile. However, it would be desirable to supplement them with measures of perceived threat from the West, since security in that area is also likely to be crucial in elite evaluation of system performance. Fortunately, research in international relations has developed sophisticated content analysis techniques capable of measuring threat perception with considerable reliability; one example would be the studies of the outbreak of World War I conducted by Robert North and his associates under the auspices of the Stanford Studies of Integration and Conflict. Kjell Goldman recently published time series content analytic data on East-West tension in Europe 1946-70 using similar techniques.[20] Changes in the tension level may well be factors influencing elite perception of system performance.

The last source of indicators relevant in testing the kinds of propositions discussed here is to be found in the recent works of the data bank enthusiasts, as exemplified by such works as the *World Handbook of Political and Social Indicators.*[21] For several years there has been a developing infatuation with generating and storing "events data," coded according to concepts prevalent in the field of quantitative international relations and to a lesser degree designed to test systems-theoretical concepts from comparative politics. A major problem for area studies specialists wishing to avail themselves of these data is the uneven quality of coding; this is due to the fact that most of the coders were not trained area specialists and they were restricted to a small number of sources with rather uneven coverage of events in East Europe. And, of course, the data were evidently intended for a generalist audience interested in making rather broad-gauge comparisons among the most disparate possible range of states; thus, there are obvious problems resulting from efforts to enhance crossnational comparability at the expense of within-system validity of indicators.

Nevertheless, it would seem appropriate that area specialists make a conscious effort to utilize some of these data, which after all represent an enormous expenditure of time and treasure. It is not that they are the best data (they aren't), but it is worth seeing how indicators like "number of purge events" or "number of government sanctions," as coded by the archivists, stack up against our more informed understanding of changes in repression in East Europe. If everything checks out moderately well, we may acquire some handy summary indicators and a bridge to comparative analysis of Communist and non-Communist systems into the bargain. To the extent that such indicators do not adequately represent their theoretical variables in the East European context, we owe it to our colleagues to let them know it.

I began by pointing out that in recent years the concept of "totalitarianism" has largely been replaced as the dominant explanatory framework in East European studies by the concepts of modernization and economic development. These concepts have been (correctly) seen as more suitable for accounting for important changes in these political systems since the death of Stalin. I then sought to delineate the logical structure of common arguments that modernization/development leads to the necessity for political change and to point out some major problems in verifying such a theory; chief among these is the lack of any convincing theoretical mechanism for specifying at what level of modernization various characteristics of the political structure become seriously dysfunctional.

I then suggested that the argument contained the seeds of a more testable systems-theoretic approach if we simply focused upon the portion of the first theory that suggests that the immediate cause of structural change is likely to be a perceived decline in system performance. The decline is attributed to aspects of political structure, said to lead to efforts at adaptation by the decision-making elite. The cause of the decline in performance could be the social/cultural/economic changes associated with modernization, but it could equally well be some other cause entirely, and there is no real need to prejudge that question.

Such an approach has the advantage of generating falsifiable hypotheses. It also makes it possible to avoid the easy trap of economic determinism by leaving open the possibility that value change among the elites or masses could be the cause of structural change (by changing the relative saliency of different performance measures, for example).

I then identified several dimensions of system performance that seemed salient to existing elites in East Europe and employed them to specify hypotheses relating structural change to performance declines over time. I then addressed the question of how to go about measuring both structural change and performance variables in order to test these and similar hypotheses.

Any comprehensive evaluation of this approach must await more systematic empirical research, and other approaches are possible and desirable. But the systematic linking of systemic performance with structural change seems to me a potentially fruitful line of inquiry into political change in East Europe.

NOTES

1. See Alfred G. Meyer, *The Soviet Political System* (New York: Random House, 1965); Robert Tucker, "Toward a Comparative Politics of Movement Regimes," *American Political Science Review* 55, no. 2 (July 1961); Allen Kassof, "The Administered Society: Totalitarianism Without Terror," *World Politics* 16, no. 4 (July 1964); Robert Conquest, *Russia After Khrushchev* (New York: Frederick A. Praeger, 1965).

2. Other noteworthy landmarks in the convergence of East European area studies with "mainstream" political science include Zbigniew Brzezinski and Samuel P. Huntington, *Political Power: USA/USSR* (New York: Viking, 1963); Frederick J. Fleron, Jr., ed., *Communist Studies and the Social Sciences* (Chicago: Rand, McNally, 1969); Chalmers Johnson, ed., *Change in Communist Systems* (Stanford: Stanford University Press, 1970); Roger Kanet, ed., *The Behavioral Revolution and Communist Studies* (New York: Free Press, 1971); Carl Beck et al., *Comparative Communist Political Leadership* (New York: David McKay, 1973).

3. Carl J. Friedrich and Zbigniew K. Brzezinski, *Totalitarian Dictatorship and Autocracy,* 2nd ed. (New York: Frederick A. Praeger, 1966), p. 21.

4. See, for example, Francesca Cancian, "Functional Analysis of Change," *American Sociological Review* 25, no. 6 (1960): 818-26.

5. For a concise catalogue of most of the varied meanings attached to the concept of political development, see Lucian Pye, *Aspects of Political Development* (Boston: Little, Brown, 1966), pp. 31-48.

6. Samuel P Huntington, *Political Order in Changing Societies* (New Haven: Yale University Press, 1968) p. 1.

7. See Gabriel Almond, "Political Development: Analytical and Normative Perspectives," in his volume *Political Development: Essays in Heuristic Theory* (Boston: Little, Brown, 1970), pp. 274-304.

8. For one of the most perceptive and skillfully executed examples, see R. V. Burks, "Technology and Political Change in Eastern Europe," in Johnson, ed., *Change in Communist Systems*, pp. 265-311.

9. See, for example, Richard Lowenthal, "Development vs. Utopia in Communist Policy," in Johnson, ed., *Change in Communist Systems*, pp 50-51.

10. The most impressive of many empirical studies guided by this proposition is Ted Robert Gurr, *Why Men Rebel* (Princeton: Princeton University Press, 1970).

11. The use of the "doctrinal stereotype quotient" by Triska and Finley in their book *Soviet Foreign Policy* (New York: Macmillan, 1968) is suggestive in this regard. An interesting approach to mapping the cognitive aspects of elite subgroups' perceptions of the interrelationships of policy issues and performance characteristics is employed in Tom Fingar, "Issues, Interest Groups and Linkages Between Foreign and Domestic Policy in the Soviet Union," unpublished paper, Stanford University, 1974.

12. See, for example, H. Gordon Skilling and Franklyn Griffiths, eds., *Interest Groups in Soviet Politics* (Princeton: Princeton University Press, 1971).

13. Milton C. Lodge, *Soviet Elite Attitudes Since Stalin* (Columbus, Ohio: Charles E. Merrill, 1969).

14. See Frederick Fleron, "Toward a Reconceptualization of Political Change in the Soviet Union," *Comparative Politics* 1, no. 2 (January 1969): 228-44.

15. For example, Joel J. Schwartz and William R. Keech, "Group Influence and the Policy Process in the Soviet Union," *American Political Science Review* 57, no. 3 (September 1968): 840-51.

16. Raymond B. Nixon, "Freedom in the World's Press," *Journalism Quarterly* 42, no. 1 (Winter 1965).

17. For a relatively comprehensive summary of some of the data available for Eastern Europe and some interesting speculations on the consequences, see Frank Parkin, *Class Inequality and Political Order*, (New York: Praeger Publishers, 1971), with special attention to Chapters 5 and 6. See also Ralf Dahrendorf, *Class and Class Conflict in Industrial Society* (Stanford: Stanford University Press, 1959), esp. Chapters 7 and 8.

18. Gabriel A. Almond, Scott C. Flanagan, and Robert J. Mundt, *Crisis, Choice and Change: Historical Studies of Political Development* (Boston: Little, Brown, 1973), p. 628

19. *Comparing Political Development in East Europe* (Denver: University of Denver Monograph Series in World Affairs, 1976).

20. "East-West Tension in Europe, 1946-1970: A Conceptual Analysis and a Quantitative Description," *World Politics* 26, no. 1 (October 1973): 106-25.

21. Charles Taylor and Michael Hudson, *World Handbook of Political and Social Indicators*, 2nd ed. (New Haven: Yale University Press, 1972).

INSTITUTIONAL
DEVELOPMENT

3

RETOOLING THE DIRECTED SOCIETY: ADMINISTRATIVE MODERNIZATION AND DEVELOPED SOCIALISM
Paul M. Cocks

PASSING OR PURSUIT OF THE DIRECTED SOCIETY

The 1960s had a sobering, if not shattering, effect on minds and models in Communist studies. The image of the directed society, which had long served as the main paradigm for Marxist-Leninist systems, seemed increasingly inadequate as a model of reality and mode of analysis. Indeed, to many Western observers, developments in Eastern Europe, the Soviet Union, and China marked the passing of directed society. Signs of institutional pluralism, group politics, and bureaucratic bargaining became more and more discernible, if not dominant, in the workings of government.

Interest in social engineering and system change subsided as ruling Communist elites struggled anxiously to preserve existing structures and methods. Moreover, their ability to direct and control change either imposed from above or arising spontaneously from below declined substantially. The maintenance of stability, not the management of change, emerged as the main priority. The prevention of political decay, not the promotion of political development, became the chief concern of officialdom. By the end of the decade the dominant mode of advance became "disjointed incrementalism," while the primary means of adaptation and coping assumed the form of bureaucratic "muddling through."[1]

In short, Marxist-Leninist systems in their more modern guise and industrial setting resembled more caricatures of "the mismanaged society" or "the undirected society." Some Western social scientists even began to question more generally the viability of modern forms of authoritarianism in the new technological age. Authoritarian government and politics, they argued, were basically incompatible with a complex, highly developed, industrialized or postindustrial modern society.[2]

Similar perceptions and thoughts about modern socialist society began to weigh heavily upon the minds of Communist elites. For them, too, the 1960s were a period of rude awakening and disillusionment, which forced a rethinking of fundamental assumptions and practices. Dubcek's "counterrevolution" in Czechoslovakia, not to mention Mao's "cultural revolution" in China, made them all too aware of the possibility—indeed, the frightening reality—of political disintegration and decay under socialism. Rule by Khrushchev, Novotny, Gomulka, and Mao revealed the dangers of inept leadership, "harebrained schemes," administrative mismanagement, and institutional devitalization making for political breakdown. Such leadership produced a growing feeling of drift and lack of direction among Communist officialdom generally.

A creeping malaise bordering on a sense of helplessness gripped the ruling establishments as increasingly assertive societies and complex economies, not to mention arbitrary leaders, defied their direction. Indeed, the dream of the administered society rooted in Marxism, especially its Leninist variant, seemed to be vanishing forever. Almost everywhere Communist elites saw power slipping irretrievably from their hands, and with it their hopes for further social engineering and Communist reconstruction.

Gradual realization by East European and Soviet leaders of the possibility of socialist decay was accompanied by mounting awareness of their own backwardness, technological and organizational. Some elite members also came to recognize that the roots of decay and of their own inability to cope effectively with change and complexity lie in part in this technological underdevelopment and the bureaucratic inefficiency that nurtures and sustains it. It was in Czechoslovakia, the most advanced industrial state in East Europe, that the stresses and strains of development began to be felt most keenly. More and more the stagnating Novotny regime was perceived to be a comic paradox. As one Czech explained, the government was as helpless in the handling of absolute power and in running modern society as "a baby with a slide rule."[3] In the eyes of another, the bungling regime was reducing socialism to a "museum piece."[4] Even the present first secretary, Gustav Husak, complained that the political elite had been ruling by "means and methods usual in a kindergarten."[5]

Furthermore, the Czechs were among the first in the bloc to grasp the importance and implications for socialism of the so-called "scientific-technlogical revolution" (STR) sweeping the world. The need to adjust to the changing conditions and new demands posed by the STR, which has become officially the first requirement of developed socialism in the 1970s, was first stressed by a special Czech study team in 1968. In a report, aptly entitled *Civilization at the Crossroads,* they noted that the main internal brake on the STR, felt by socialist countries, was the "insufficient development of the economic structure and of the system of impulses and instruments of management that stem from the essence of [administrative] socialism." Advanced technology and cybernetic models, they declared, provided "the sole possible basis for modern management and planning."[6]

The East Germans, even under Ulbricht, also were quick to recognize and adjust to the "new technological imperative." In fact, they were actually the first to launch a program of rationalization and modernization, one that underlay the GDR's "economic miracle" of the 1960s. By the Seventh Socialist Unity Party (SED) Congress in April 1967, emphasis was placed on "mastering the scientific and technological revolution." This task was to be accomplished in large part by learning and applying the latest analytical techniques and methods of management.[7] The cult of technological change and efficiency, stripped of any liberalizing overtones, received added impetus after the Czech events of 1968 and again after Erich Honecker assumed leadership in 1971.[8] Even in less industrially advanced Bulgaria, at a Central Committee plenum in July 1968, Todor Zhivkov for the first time acknowledged the growing demands placed on management and the need for better forms of organization and government prompted by the STR. He also noted that the STR provided "hitherto unknown scientific and technical means which must be introduced to a maximum in management."[9]

The task of administrative modernization was not really confronted in Poland until after the replacement of Gomulka by Gierek and the coming to power of a more pragmatic and technocratic-oriented ruling group. Nevertheless, even before the December 1970 bread riots and the eruption of worker unrest, the need for change was strongly felt in some official circles. A section of the party apparat itself apparently took the necessity for a technological offensive and breakthrough very seriously indeed. At the November 1969 Polish United Workers' Party (PUWP) Central Committee plenum, a couple of its representatives warned, "We are losing a race against time."[10]

Generally speaking, Soviet leaders were relatively slow in their appreciation of the full impact of the scientific revolution and the role of technology in modern society.[11] It is true that the removal of Khrushchev resulted in the gradual turning of a more technocratic screw in the machinery of power and the wheels of production. But events in Czechoslovakia, it seems, were the real catalytic agent that forced attitudinal and policy change.[12] Within the USSR the scientific community pressed for comprehensive rationalization and modernization. In a letter to party and government leaders in March 1970, Andrei Sakharov and other dissident but concerned scientists admitted frankly that with respect to the computer age, "We are simply living in a different era." They said, "The second industrial revolution came along and now, at the onset of the 'seventies we see that, far from having overtaken America, we are dropping further and further behind." A new style of administrative operations and genuinely scientific methods of management were required, they claimed, in order to restore to Soviet life "a much needed dynamic and creative character."[13]

Among the political elite as well, awareness grew of the need to alter managerial attitudes and techniques. Brezhnev in particular began to speak out and to press, especially after 1970, to accelerate technical progress and to overcome bureaucratic immobilism. In June 1970 he made his statement (which has since become the slogan of the day) that the science of victory in building socialism is in essence the science of management.[14] Again at the Twenty-fourth Party Congress, he strongly accentuated the theme that the USSR was living in a new age. Without mincing words, he said conditions associated with the STR "make new and higher demands on management and do not allow us to be satisfied with existing forms and methods, even when they have served us well in the past."[15]

By the beginning of the 1970s, therefore, signs throughout Eastern Europe and the Soviet Union indicated that "scientific management" would be the new course and that political technocracy would be the new pace of developed socialism in the decade ahead. Underlying this developmental strategy is an explicitly perceived linkage between the problems of modern society and the means of solving them. On the one hand, technical progress generates growing complexity and rapid change, which complicate management of the development process. The STR, on the other hand, also opens up unlimited possibilities through improved managerial and analytical techniques for dealing more effectively with these problems.[16] In short, science and technology are seen not only as a cause of change but also as a response to change, as a means of controlling change. The basic response of the Soviet and East European regimes to the challenge of the STR is, then, to try to integrate and manage complexity through modern organization and technology. Only through administrative modernization can developed socialism be achieved and the directed society maintained. "It is no exaggeration to say," admits one high Soviet official, "that the pace of our advance hinges on organization and capabilities in the system of management."[17] A Bulgarian observer similarly insists, "Life, the struggle for socialism and communism, call for improved management, for a broader introduction of the new methods and instruments of management provided by the scientific and technical revolution."[18]

In many respects, this response is not new. Leninist elites have long respected the power of organization and the use of technology in the pursuit of political goals. Political development under Leninist regimes also was largely organization building. Generally speaking, however, organization and technology have figured most prominently as instruments of policy during the transformation and consolidation stages of socialist development, to borrow Jowitt's terminology.[19] Until recently they were not accorded a central place in the functioning and management of mature socialist society. On the contrary, emphasis on the ultimate withering away of the state and self-administration by the masses led to neglect of state agencies and governmental administration. Subsequently, the crises of the 1960s, especially in Czechoslovakia and Poland, laid bare the growing backwardness, devitalization, and indeed withering of political institutions. They exposed the inability of the bureaucratic infrastructure and political superstructure to control, much less direct, the dynamic processes of development in society and the economy. Only with their belated discovery of the STR in the late 1960s have the ruling elites in the area come to appreciate the potential of modern organization and technology for building and managing developed socialism. The notion of the "organizational weapon" has been given new life and purpose. It needs only to be retooled and tuned to the changing demands of a different developmental stage and technological era.

Similarly, the enhanced desire of the Soviet and East European elites to benefit from Western techniques and experience is not a new theme. Ideological differences with capitalism are no barrier to borrowing advanced capitalist methods if they can be used to improve the functioning of socialist systems and to preserve the power of the governing establishments. Indeed, the ongoing technological competition and ideological struggle between the two social systems internationally demand that the latest gains of Western technology be exploited. Lenin emphasized half a century ago the need to "learn from Europe and America." To overtake and surpass capitalism, Bukharin similarly noted, "It is essential for us, above all, to know what is happening in the sphere of technique in capitalist countries . . . 'whither' the technique of capitalism is going."[20] But the scope of permitted capitalist technique shrunk steadily. From a more general principle of organization and management, it was reduced by the early 1930s to little more than a narrow production method or technical device. In fact, administrative science disappeared in the Soviet Union under Stalin.[21]

Significantly, renewed interest in the broader analytical, managerial, and organizational applications of modern technology and management science underlies the current quest for capitalist technique. It was through the use of more sophisticated planning and management tools, like planning-programming-budgeting, systems analysis, network planning, and scientific forecasting that the United States and West European countries tried to cope more effectively with change and complexity in the 1960s. Such means also were used to overcome growing fragmentation and compartmentalization of government as well as bureaucratic inefficiency and inertia. These ways of improving and rationalizing business and government operations, according to East European and Soviet official observers, have not been without effect. In fact, they are seen as having permitted capitalism to mitigate some of its sharpest contradictions. Greater government regulation of economic and social processes and technocratic trends in management have allowed developed capitalist systems to attain a new degree of stability, even viability.[22] The hope that similar methods also may help developed socialist societies to prevent crises, to solve conflicts, and to maintain stability spurs the campaign for administrative modernization and technology transfer in the 1970s. It is quite ironic, though, that mature socialist states, which pride themselves on their planned and managed character, still feel compelled to learn from developed but still inherently anarchic capitalism about how to overcome pluralism and bureaucratic muddling through.

On a more general level, the accelerated pace of scientific, technological, social, and political change today has increased the problems of managing development, in capitalist and socialist societies alike. Both societies face the need of devising new strategies and instruments to enhance their capability to adapt and cope under modern conditions. Despite underlying differences in political philosophy, organizational approach, and points of emphasis, the rulers in much of Eastern Europe and the USSR are grappling with much the same set of problems and grasping for similar remedies as their American and West European counterparts. That is, the response of both developed capitalist and socialist states (and developing third world countries as well) to the scientific revolution of the mid-twentieth century has been basically the same: to try to integrate complexity and to manage change through advances in organization and technology. Only developed socialism, however, is capable of fully achieving this goal, according to Marxist-Leninist perceptions. In its use of systems techniques of planning and management, capitalism "accepts a system of methods which run counter to its own nature."[23] The inherent disunity and inability of capitalist society to plan on the level of the whole society ultimately doom these methods to failure. Because developed socialism is, in theory at least, supposedly a unified and centrally administered social organism, however, it has the potential capacity to apply modern systems technology successfully.[24]

Since the invasion of Czechoslovakia in 1968, therefore, a determined effort has been mounted, especially in the Soviet Union and the most authoritarian East European regimes (East Germany, Romania, and Bulgaria), to maintain or, more properly speaking, to regain effective management of society. They have not abandoned pursuit of the "directed society," much less rejected the notion of socialism as a consciously directed and centrally administered process. Following the lead of the GDR, they have all launched, in varying degree and thrust, programs for administrative modernization. Rationalization, stripped for the most part of any liberalizing implications (except in Poland and Hungary), has replaced reform as the key slogan of the times. A new kit of more sophisticated analytical aids, managerial techniques, organizational forms, and leadership training programs is in the making. With these more technocratic tools, it is hoped that modern, developed socialism can be built while a directed society is retained. In sum, the craze for scientific management and the chase after computers are quite natural responses for Leninist elites, for whom political manipulation and management of society are deeply engrained.

PLANNING, DECISION MAKING,
AND ANALYTICAL TECHNIQUES

The desire to deal better with problems of uncertainty and choice in an age of growing complexity and rapid change has focused major attention on improvements in planning. A qualitatively higher level of planning and policy analysis is necessary if central planning is to be preserved as a viable instrument and fundamental principle of directed socialist society. "Properly speaking, the ability of society to control its own development," writes a Soviet analyst, "is inseparable from its ability to control the mechanism of decision making. In other words, the process of solving complicated problems must include improvement and corresponding development of the decision-making mechanism."[25]

Accordingly, since the late 1960s there has been deepening interest and research by East European and Russian specialists in the whole area of meta-policy—that is, policy on how to make policy.[26] At the First International Slavic Conference in Banff, Canada, in September 1974, Jan Szczepanski of the Polish Academy of Sciences criticized Western specialists on Eastern Europe for neglecting political processes.[27] To be fair, however, only recently have East European scholars and policy makers themselves begun to take a close and critical look at administrative operations and the policy process in their own countries. Only of late have they discovered the "nerves of government" and become concerned with enhancing organizational effectiveness and the performance of their political systems.

On one level, there has been expanding attention to the role of feedback and information of various kinds in policy making. Particular efforts have been devoted to improving data processing and coping with the information explosion through computers. A broader information base and computerized data-processing capability are needed to support more systematic and comprehensive planning and policy analysis. Hence, work on developing national information systems has been stepped up considerably throughout the area. The 1971-75 plans in all these countries included generous provisions for the establishment of local and regional data banks equipped with computers and transmission systems to be linked to central agencies.[28] To help coordinate bloc efforts in this sphere, an Intergovernmental Commission for Computer Techniques has been set up within Comecon.

Generally speaking, however, these grandiose plans for expanding computer technology in planning and management are not being fulfilled. For that matter, given the backward state of Eastern Europe and the Soviet Union in this sphere, they are simply not technologically feasible, let alone humanly possible.[29] The chairman of the Committee for Science, Technical Progress, and Higher Education in Bulgaria, for example, admitted in February 1974 that the introduction of automated information systems "proved to be a far more complicated and difficult task than many enthusiasts had originally believed." Creation of the necessary psychological setting, aside from the technical aspects, presented "acute and unsolved problems."[30] In Romania, too, computerization is proceeding "at a snail's pace," despite the strong backing of Ceausescu.[31] In the Soviet Union progress in automation also has been slow and difficult. In fact, the cyberneticists and computer cultists, who seem to have held the dominant position among the technocratic modernizers, may be losing ground. More recently, the emphasis on optimization appears to be shifting, perhaps because of the manifold technological obstacles in computerization. The accent is away from information to organization, where the primary obstacles are political rather than technological. But more on this shortly.

Another sphere of growing interest is long-term planning. This is an area in which all the East European regimes, along with the USSR, have been particularly deficient.[32] Belated discovery of the STR, however, has wrought a radical change in their views on the space-time parameters of progress. This has led to rising stress on the need to expand the time horizons of planners from the narrow confines of a single year to a more flexible multiyear framework. With planning on a predominantly annual basis, almost all options are foreclosed by previous commitments. A longer time span enhances opportunities for planning and analysis to have greater impact on future expenditures and opens up more options. More effective long-range planning is needed, above all, to accommodate the kinds of investment allocation decisions and program planning tasks involved in overcoming technological backwardness and structural change.[33] Finally, long-term planning provides a means to surmount the increasing tendency in all these countries to plan incrementally "from the achieved level." Brezhnev and Zhivkov both have intensified their criticism of this bias in planning. Significantly, despite the manifold problems involved in such an exercise, the East Germans, the Russians, the Romanians, the Czechs, and the Bulgarians have all embarked upon drawing up 15-year development plans for the period 1975-90.

Along with stress on long-term planning, there has been burgeoning interest in forecasting and futurological studies. Until the mid-1960s there was little differentiation in approaches to problems of the future. Nor was this seen as an urgent task. Like Western decision makers, however, authorities in Eastern Europe and the USSR have become increasingly aware of the need to anticipate and to evaluate the future impact of science and technology on society, the economy, and the polity. "Such forecasting is essential," say Gvishiani, "if only to prevent some of the negative consequences entailed by scientific and technical progress, or at least to mitigate them."[34] Much as in the West, technological assessment is being promoted as a device to provide planners and leaders with a kind of early warning system, so they are ready and capable of responding more effectively to changing conditions and contingent events. Social forecasting also is designed to facilitate guidance of social processes, to prevent what in official East European terminology are called "shocks," like the Polish workers' riot in 1970. In short, the purpose of forecasting is control over uncertainty. Moreover, it is not uncertainty per se that has brought about the need for forecasting, but the absence of sufficient power to deal with it.

The forecasting movement was greatly accelerated after a symposium on the subject in Moscow in March 1970. At this meeting, attended by deputy planning ministers from all the Comecon states, a decision was taken to establish within Comecon a Scientific Forecasting Association, with headquarters in Moscow. In April 1970 all Comecon members participated in the World Congress of Futurologists in Kyoto, Japan. The same year a special Commission on Forecasting was set up in Bulgaria directly under the Politburo and the premier. The Romanians have been the most enthusiastic, however. A new futurological review, *Viitorul Social* (Social future), was launched in 1972 under the auspices of the Academy of Social and Political Science and the Romanian National Committee on Sociology. That year Bucharest also hosted an international congress on the science of the future.[35]

The key concept that underlies and unites enhanced interest in information theory, decision analysis, long-term planning, and scientific and social forecasting is optimization. If maximization is the motto for extensive economic development of an earlier era of building socialism, then optimization becomes the first requirement of intensive economic growth under developed socialism. Indeed, this is the guiding principle for most of the "new economic systems" of Eastern Europe today. They generally rest on the conviction, Karl Thalheim notes, that "optimization is better than maximization, that the decisive factor therefore is not maximum production results, but the best possible relation between outlay and return, costs and utilization."[36] An optimum or best course implies, moreover, a choice between alternative options, which must be carefully posed and weighed. This requires more critical economic analysis and careful planning in which the elements of risk, uncertainty, and resource constraints play an increasing role.[37]

The need for more systematic and rigorously analytical problem solving has, in turn, prompted the burgeoning systems movement, indeed a systems revolution in the USSR and Eastern Europe. With its accent on formulating goals, devising alternatives, evaluating consequences, and monitoring performance, modern systems analysis is seen as a key tool for improving planning and management. To be sure, a major thrust of systems analysis is on quantification and modern computational technology. Indeed, the assimilation in recent years of quantitative analytic methods and approaches has produced, Alfred Zauberman notes, a "mathematical revolution" in Soviet economics.[38] Similarly, there has developed an expanding arsenal of useful and used managerial techniques and acronyms that resemble PPBS (planning-programing-budgeting system),

PERT (program evaluation review technique), CPM (critical path method), and other systems applied in the United States.[39]

The essence and perceived value of the systems approach, however, lies not on the narrow methodological and technical plane. Rather, it is seen (as in the West) primarily as a cognitive instrument by which to structure and orient both official and public thinking about complex issues, values, and goals.[40] It is a device by which to raise managerial consciousness and to modernize economic thought.

"Taken in its simplest and most general form," two prominent Soviet systems theorists write, "systems analysis actually amounts to the rationalization of intuition in administrative activity, to a search for reasonable ways and means of simplifying complex problems."[41] At the present time, they stress, the systems approach can be regarded not so much as a highly detailed and developed methodology for decision making as a demand for building such a methodology.[42] The systems approach per se does not solve any problems; it merely throws them into a different perspective than is provided by more traditional approaches.[43] Similarly, the development and teaching of analytic techniques are designed not to get in the way of analysis but to nurture systems analytic thinking.

The distinguishing feature of the systems approach is that it insists upon taking an integrated and total view of a problem rather than a fragmented and piecemeal approach. "What interests us," a high Soviet official explains with respect to systems analysis, "is its basic conclusion as to the need for a complex, all-round approach to management and the disclosure of its integrative function." He adds, "This approach makes it possible to see the whole managed system as a complex set of interrelated elements, united by a common aim, to reveal the integral properties of the system, its internal and external links."[44]

Attention is concentrated not so much on the components as on their interrelations and interaction, on the subordination of the parts to the interests of the whole.[45] A key concern is how to combine the elements in order to achieve the optimal solution to a given problem area. Only such an approach, some contend, can prevent complex problems from being dismembered into separate parts or being solved in isolation from other problems.[46]

Broadly speaking, the appeals of the systems approach appear to be threefold. First, it provides a means of promoting better communication among the ruling elites and citizenry. The deficiencies of the system of relying on detailed instructions and direct orders from central authorities to guide and guarantee appropriate administrative behavior have become increasingly apparent. What is required today is an official who can think and act more creatively and with greater initiative under conditions of growing complexity and change. At the same time, a normative structure and steering mechanism is needed to help clarify values, establish rules, set limits, and define boundaries for him. The systems approach and analytic techniques applied through central agencies, such as Gosplan and the State Committee for Science and Technology, create such a more flexible framework whereby the leadership can transmit proper cues and norms to executives at all levels. They thus provide for a system of "indirect centralization," to borrow Michael Ellman's terminology.[47]

On another level, it is also clear that a major problem common to the area is that goals and priorities have become increasingly blurred. Administrative bureaucracies have become fragmented and unresponsive to the views of central authorities. Each individual and social institution takes a narrow and partial view of his role, duties, and interests. Under such conditions it is difficult, if not impossible, to pinpoint responsibility, to enforce discipline, and to monitor performance. Through application of the systems approach the regimes seek to restore a sense of purpose and cohesion to government, to refocus and assert the general interest, and to reorient officialdom to new missions and roles. In contrast to the prevailing system of branch and departmental planning and management, a more "programmed-goals approach" (programmno-tselevoi podkhod) is considered a more suitable means for promoting "management by objectives" and "control by results." Such an approach, above all, facilitates the mobilization of commitment and discipline required to implement policy.[48]

Second, the systems approach permits greater participation and cooperation in planning and management. Underlying this aspect is growing awareness that modern society and the scientific-technological revolution generate a new scale of problems. These are by nature increasingly overlapping, interrelated, and complex. Indeed, throughout the area the need is emphasized for more socioeconomic planning as opposed to strictly economic planning. The major development tasks today are also so-called "interbranch" problems, which cut across departmental interests and branch lines. Accordingly, they require that increasing time and resources be devoted to intergovernmental problem solving and interagency coordination. This is a new class of problems, however, for which integrated solutions are particularly difficult to achieve through the existing fragmented structure, departmental biases, and traditional methods of planning.

Given these constraints, there is mounting stress on the need for more program-type planning and management by objectives for key priority areas. The concept of programming provides a device for integrating and ensuring the fiscal, technical, and human resources that are required to implement major interbranch projects. It facilitates emphasis on a more function-oriented and less department-oriented structure of planning as well as focus on outputs and results as opposed to inputs and items of expenditure accounting.[49] As one of the foremost Soviet exponents of this approach writes, "The program is the transitional link between goals and resources in the plan."[50] As an instrument of cognitive mobilization, systems programming aims at enhancing perceptions of common interests and forming better linkages among different operating agencies and levels engaged in joint activities. Under existing arrangements an organizational climate of mutual suspicion and hostility often predominates so that relatively autonomous ministries and departments compete rather than cooperate with each other.

In view of the larger size of the economy and the number of ministries in the Soviet Union as opposed to Eastern Europe, it is not surprising that the programmed-goals approach has received greatest attention from the Kremlin. Since the Twenty-fourth Party Congress in 1971, official clamor for its use has risen. This movement was given added impetus after the December 1973 Central Committee plenum, which heard a strong attack by Brezhnev against departmental pluralism, parochialism, and incrementalism.[51]

Typically following the Soviet lead, Bulgaria has also expressed mounting interest in program-type planning.[52] Zhivkov, for example, stressed at the December 1972 Central Committee meeting the need for more integrated planning of major interbranch projects and national economic complexes. As part of this new approach, the structure of the State Planning Committee and the branch ministries is being modified. Henceforth, stress will no longer be placed on the branch departments but on "comprehensive teams," which will supposedly effect a more integrated elaboration and fuller balancing of programs.[53] In East Germany, too, there has been increasing attention on "complex assignments" and programs that can facilitate better coordination and interlocking relationships among branches, sectors, and regions.[54]

In general, such program-type planning is designed not to supplant but to supplement the prevailing system of branch and territorial planning. Its application is not being pushed for the economy as a whole but primarily for the key programs and economic complexes that are perceived to be the main links in development strategy for the decade ahead. As one Soviet advocate explains, "Programs do not encompass the entire national economic plan; their purpose is to solve the key structural problems of social and economic development."[55] In the USSR these include the new "virgin lands" program for the Non-Black Earth regions of the RSFSR, building of the Baikal-Amur railway, development of the huge fuel and power complex in Tiumen Province, and construction of a national network of computer centers and information systems to aid in economic planning and management.[56]

Similar complexes in the areas of energy development, machine building, transport, construction, agriculture, petrochemicals, and metallurgy have been singled out in Bulgaria as especially appropriate for more comprehensive planning and programming.[57] Examples of problem areas defined as complex assignments in the GDR range from housing, food, education, and electronic data-processing equipment to environmental protection.[58] It is true that throughout the area efforts have generally been made in recent years to move toward more balanced growth. In the process, however, key goals have become obscured. Priority programs have had to compete for scarce resources with projects of lesser importance. Through more program-type planning and management, therefore, national leaderships hope to preserve and protect what are still perceived as core tasks, the main levers of development. In a sense, then, modern systems approaches reflect more traditional, even Stalinist biases toward development planning.

Enhanced awareness of the complexity of modern problems also carries the possibility of constraints on one-man command and a broadening of participation in decision making. The Romanians have been the most explicit on this score. "The increased complexity of the task of managing makes it imperative to alter the present form of management and to introduce a broad collective management," notes one observer.[59] "Enterprise management can no longer be conceived as the task of a single man," writes another.[60] The solution to contemporary problems involves concerted action and coordinated efforts by many participants. More collegial forms of planning and management facilitate a richer variety of inputs, interests, and skills. As Constantin Cojocaru explains, one of the main purposes of collective leadership is "to create solutions and evaluate the advantages and disadvantages of many solutions in the most complex, most realistic and most comprehensive way over a broader range of criteria."[61]

While not as frank as the Romanians, Russian analysts also note that modern managerial conditions require some modification of traditional authority relations. An expansion of collegial forms of decision making, at least in some issue areas, is perceived as necessary, in part, to check subjectivism and arbitrariness.[62] Broadening of participation can lead, on the one hand, to the inclusion of more specialists and a greater role for technocratic counsel in the decision process. Evidence also suggests that it can facilitate the intrusion, on the other hand, of political authorities, especially party representatives, in planning and management. For the most part, ordinary workers do not appear to be main beneficiaries of expanded participatory patterns anywhere in the area, at least not in terms of any meaningful decision-making capacity.

In addition to improving communication and cooperation, the systems approach also is being championed and applied as a means of promoting learning and leadership adaptability in organizations. The importance of this problem is aptly pointed out by Mel Croan. The two major hallmarks of the Stalinist legacy common to the area, he notes, are the virtually total absence of experience in making critical as distinct from routine decisions and the considerable confusion between role and identity.[63] For the most part, decision making has been a highly intuitive and arbitrary process in which an ad hoc, seat-of-the-pants approach has predominated. The planning process has been unsystematic. Cognitive features have not been made explicit and the bases for decisions have not been recorded. Such an environment impedes learning. It is difficult to reconstruct how decisions were made, to compare results, and to modify goals and programs in light of evolving conditions. In short, it is hard to learn from experience.

The use of systems analytic thinking and techniques amounts to a search for the kind of logic and technology of choice that was deliberately suppressed in the past.[64] The systems approach seeks to make more explicit and rigorous the debate about, and the evaluation of, policy objectives and alternative ways of accomplishing them. It seeks to clarify the critical uncertainties and constraints and to help balance risks against expectations. By providing a conceptual framework and set of formalized procedures for relating means to ends, the systems approach contributes to the learning process. Indeed, the mental exercise and discipline required in the application of systems methods has substantial perceived value.[65]

Finally, it is important to stress that the main impetus behind the systems movement in Eastern Europe and the Soviet Union is official desire to strengthen and modernize the role of the Communist party as the ruling mechanism of government. The spread of systems thinking and analytic techniques is designed to enhance, not to diminish, the party's ability to act as the main integrating and regulating force in society. Traditionally, the party has exercised—indeed, jealously monopolized—two key political functions. First, it is the main decision-making body that sets national goals and priorities. Second, it has primary responsibility for supervising administrative behavior and seeing to it that the governmental machinery implements party policy. In both these areas of policy formulation and performance evaluation, application of the systems approach is deemed particularly relevant and important for raising organizational effectiveness.

More generally, the party also fulfills the role of chief political broker, the agency that mediates the competing claims and special interests of powerful bureaucracies and societal subgroups. The growth of "bureaucratic incrementalism" and "institutional pluralism," according to some Western specialists, has reduced the party to an increasingly passive and indifferent broker. Supposedly, it no longer is interested in actively initiating or able to press forcefully particular policy options, let alone optimal solutions. From this perspective, bureaucratic bargaining has increasingly become a process of give-and-take exchanges in which a suboptimizing strategy is pursued and prevails. Political conflict no longer figures as a major feature, must less problematical element, in the decision process. Underlying this view is an almost deus ex machina faith in the efficacy of the group process and bureaucratic interplay to produce favorable outcomes.[66]

Such an interpretation is not entirely without basis. However, its exponents tend, in this writer's opinion, to overestimate the values and forces of pluralism and to obscure the nature of political culture as well as elite perceptions and motivations in Marxist-Leninist systems. They fail to see or appreciate the conflicting and centralizing forces also at work in these regimes, which seek to impose new limits on group pluralism and incrementalism. The administrative process remains preeminently a political struggle. Nowhere in the area are party agencies expected to be silent arbiters, much less conciliators, of group interests and disputes. On the contrary, they are obliged to focus attention and debate on major objectives, values, and priorities, to assert the primacy of and fight for the general interest over individual and group interests. Indeed, a major aim of the systems movement, it seems, is to enhance the capacity of party agencies at all levels to resolve bureaucratic and social conflicts, to make proper tradeoffs and optimal solutions, and to exercise more effectively their political brokerage functions.

Quite apart from those considerations but equally important, there is another set of purposes for which the systems approach is being promoted in Eastern Europe and the Soviet Union. This concerns its use as a technique not of decision making but rather of image making and morale building. Here the central issue is again leadership adaptability and systemic change.

Moreover, what really counts, as Croan stresses, is that "leadership appears credibly adaptable and cohesive. To the party rank and file, various subelites, and to society as a whole, it should be able to convey a sense of basic agreement on fundamentals."[67]

The spread of systems thinking and techniques facilitates the creation and dissemination of this impression. It helps to convey the notion that the ruling elite and society more broadly manifest coherence of purpose and moral-political unity. Use of the systems approach with its modern terminology and space age methodology also gives the appearance that the leaders are au courant with the times. Indeed, it seems to give them the sophistication for which they have been searching. As Tom Baylis observes with respect to the East German elite, "The new organization men speak the language of the technical revolution, of cybernetics, data processing, and sophisticated uses of mathematics."[68] A new mystique and mythology of omnipotence are in the making. Marxist-Leninist adaptations of modern systems theory help build a new look for administrative socialism, one that can replace the obviously tarnished bureaucratic image and obsolete methods inherited from the past.

ORGANIZATIONAL STRUCTURES AND MANAGEMENT SYSTEMS

Generally speaking, organizational change was not accorded a prominent place in the development strategies of the 1960s. In few of the East European countries did the economic reforms, launched in the middle of the decade, alter the formal organization of industry in any major way. In East Germany, Poland, and the Soviet Union they entailed an administrative streamlining and relatively limited decentralization in which the basic features of the planning and management system remained intact. For the most part, the reforms in these states affected the administrative rules and decision set rather than the formal organizational structure of industry.

In Bulgaria, Czechoslovakia, Hungary, and Yugoslavia the reforms involved varying degrees of more radical decentralization and steps toward the introduction of market socialism. Even here, however, little change occurred in the formal organization of industry.[69] "Indeed, the lack of consideration of formal industrial organization in the reform plans," Pryor points out, "may have been an important source of weakness."[70] The principles and purposes of organization had become, in effect, frozen. This inhibited creative thinking about structure and the development of new approaches to organizational adaptation.

In many respects, promotion of the systems approach as primarily an instrument of cognition and communication can be regarded as a substitute for reorganization. Informal coordination is greatly facilitated when people share the same goals, have the same value preferences, and operate from a common set of assumptions and expectations. When such conditions exist, there is no need for formal restructuring and the creation of more direct coordinating mechanisms to bring diverse elements into harmony in order to accomplish common objectives. A distinguishing feature of all these regimes, however, is their common failure to secure the internalization of administrative goals among officialdom, and of socialist values more generally among the population. Mounting criticism of the persistence of bureaucratic pluralism and departmental parochialism, of individual self-interest and petty bourgeois views, attests to the deficiencies, if not failure, of the systems approach as a cognitive device to raise official and public consciousness and to overcome attitudinal and departmental barriers that impede economic and social progress. Hence, rising stress on the need for structural modernization and organizational change also should be seen, at least in part, as a supplement to and substitute for the development of systems thinking and analytic techniques.

Indeed, the search for more flexible organizational structures and more effective management systems has become a dominating issue throughout most of Eastern Europe and the USSR in the 1970s. In Poland, for example, awareness among the Gierek leadership of the existence of structural "contradictions" and organizational obsolescence led the Politburo of the PUWP in early 1971 to reactivate the work of the party and government commission concerned with modernizing the administrative machinery of the economy and the state.[71] Within the Soviet Union there has been, especially since 1973, greater emphasis on the importance of structural reform and on the need to develop the much neglected field of organizational design. In fact, some argue the mechanism of management should be designed no less carefully than new analytic techniques, information systems, and technology.[72] Criticizing the intransigent scientific establishment in the USSR for "a surplus reserve of stability and even of conservatism," the deputy chairman of the State Committee for Science and Technology has called explicitly for "new, less conservative, more mobile" organizational forms to speed technological progress.[73] In Hungary, too, public and official debates by 1974 began to reflect growing concern for modernization and for more rational organization and management.[74]

Almost everywhere accent has mounted on the importance of technological change and the institutional adjustment needed to accommodate it. With this emerging focus on organizational issues, one Western authority notes, "the question of who gets to set, adjust, monitor and reinforce plan indexes and financial instruments has come to the fore, gradually displacing the issues of marketization or decentralization as the focal point of discussion over systemic economic change within most East European countries."[75]

To phrase the issue somewhat differently, the thrust of the systems approach as an instrument of change in the area of planning and management has broadened to include structure as well as attitude. "Departmental barriers" and "disputes over jurisdictional boundaries" encountered in implementing reforms have illuminated the existence and extent of organizational constraints on change. All too clearly has it been shown that structure influences, if not dictates, process. The complex but highly fragmented administrative structures in these regimes have contributed to the growth of pluralism, bureaucratic bargaining, and incrementalist tendencies in the decision-making process—that is, particularistic forces that the systems approach seeks to counteract and contain.

Modernizing efforts also have revealed that organizational arrangements are not neutral. Much like the administration of public policy in the United States, a choice of organization structure in socialist systems is essentially "a choice of which interest or which value will have preferred access or greater emphasis."[76] Similarly, "organization is one way of expressing national commitment, influencing program directions, and ordering priorities."[77] Coordination, too, is rarely neutral. "To the extent that it results in mutual agreement or a decision on some policy, course of action, or inaction, inevitably it advances some interests at the expense of others or more than others."[78] Cooperation and coordination are simply not the norm between agencies of government in any country, capitalist or socialist. As the Party-Government Commission for Modernization of the Economy and State Administration in Poland found, "Cooperation is still the Achilles' heel of industry."[79] Growing awareness of organizational constraints and of the fact that integration cannot spring forth spontaneously has prompted intensified efforts at systems restructuring.

More specifically, it has become increasingly evident to the ruling elites that organization of government has not kept pace with the substantive nature of the problems it faces. Political development has brought compartmentalization of government and an administrative labyrinth of fragmented and autonomous bureaucratic fiefdoms. Socialist systems have been built along strongly hierarchical lines. Their backbone is the vertical axis. The rigidities of departmentalism have become major blocks to lateral communications and cooperative efforts. These developments have taken place, moreover, at a time when the most critical problems facing society have become highly complex and cut across agency lines. On the organizational side, therefore, the need is increasingly felt for more effective integrating mechanisms that can coordinate interbranch problems and resolve conflicts.[80] Furthermore, there is growing realization in some circles that the essence of management itself also has changed. No longer is it concerned narrowly with production. Modern management, on the contrary, means the management of innovations.[81] Traditional organizational models with their emphasis on hierarchy, routines, processes, and formally prescribed roles, however, also are being criticized for limiting adaptability, innovation, and creativity.

Accordingly, throughout much of the area efforts have been made in the 1970s to recycle, to a certain extent, hierarchical lines of authority and organization, putting stress on horizontal networks for joint action and cooperative activities. The basic building blocks of socialist industry, industrial enterprises, are being reshaped everywhere into larger, more integrated conglomerates. Institutionally, the model of the "industrial association" in various national guises in the region has become ubiquitous. Indeed, one may speak of a new convergence, at least on the organizational plane.[82]

It is also the East Europeans who have taken the initiative in regrouping production units. While production associations were formed in the USSR in the early 1960s, they were not assigned a major role. Only since 1973 has the Soviet leadership pushed strongly to make the association the "enterprise of the future" and the basic unit of production in the economy.[83] Thus, reliance on the marketplace and spontaneity as means to achieve integration and to resolve conflicts has declined substantially, even in Hungary. Again, preference has shifted toward a bureaucratic setting and administrative means to accomplish these ends. On another level, the industrial associations are likened to a multiplant capitalist corporation that has "become the basic unit of production in all advanced industrial countries, thus reflecting the needs of the scientific revolution and of modern technology."[84]

Industrial associations are represented as more viable structures through which to promote modernization and management of industry. According to a leading Soviet official, they provide a means for transforming "awkward external cooperation into harmonious intrafirm cooperation."[85] By integrating more closely research, production, processing, and marketing activities, they facilitate more unified management and better coordination of the production process. While some horizontal integration has taken place across branch lines, the associations aim, for the most part, at closing the production cycle by maximizing vertical integration with respect to a particular branch or product line. Underlying the new structures is organizational aversion to uncertainty and official desire to ensure against supply difficulties.

In general, organizational change may be regarded as having a dual thrust. On the one hand, it seeks to shorten the lines of command and communication that have developed within the system of branch ministries and contribute to its inefficiency and malfunctioning. This is particularly the case in the Soviet Union, where the administrative superstructure is much larger and more complex than in Eastern Europe. On the other hand, structural reform also aims at broadening the scope of related activities within the jurisdiction of managerial authorities in order to enhance their capacity to administer and control programs and policies. In short, it seems the main purpose of restructuring and of "integration," is to preserve and to strengthen, not to weaken, hierarchical principles of command and control on which these systems rest.

The search for more suitable forms of organization and management also has led to growing interest in and experimentation with so-called matrix models of organization and the systems of project management that have evolved in modern Western corporations. Unlike the traditional monocratic organization, which is built along vertical lines, the matrix or mixed organization bifurcates the management system into functional and project roles and structures. It has a formal functional hierarchy for normal routine decision making. Superimposed on this primary authority structure is a secondary authority network, which focuses on accomplishing specific projects. The latter cuts horizontally across vertical functional and departmental lines. Its purpose is to ensure the achievement of common interorganizational objectives through the functional organizations and over their specialized interests.[86] The matrix organization is, above all, a fluid structure. The mixture can lie anywhere between the two extremes of standard functional organization and pure project management. Different types of organization represent varying degrees of authority and responsibility, which are assumed by the project manager and which have been splintered from, or are shared with, the functional manager. The exact shape of the structure is determined by the project-functional interface and by changing task requirements.[87]

The complex organizational dynamics of matrix structures are best explained by the different purposes of project and functional management. The function of the project structure is the reduction of uncertainty, while its purpose is the transformation of a turbulent environment. The task of the functional structure, on the other hand, is the assessment and containment of risk, while its aim is the achievement of stability within the transformed environment.[88] One concentrates on the lateral process of integration; the other focuses on the vertical process of differentiation and technical specialization. The concepts of traditional and project, or systems, management complement each other; they are not two distinct approaches to the executive function. Each form has certain advantages, but none can be considered best for all situations. By incorporating both design principles, the matrix organization tries to capture the best features of each in order to maximize organizational capacity.[89]

Within the Communist world the matrix model has attracted greatest attention in the Soviet Union. Until recently, writes B. Mil'ner, a leading

Russian specialist in management and industrial design, organizational evolution proceeded basically along the path of modifying and improving the line and staff structure of administration. "Since the end of the 1960s," he notes, however, "flexible and dynamic systems of horizontal interfunctional coordination for harmonizing the efforts of individual links oriented to fulfilling concrete tasks have acquired fundamental significance."[90] He continues, "Special place in building modern management systems belongs to [forms] combining vertical and horizontal channels of regulating economic activity."[91]

Georgi Arbatov, director of the Institute for Study of the USA and Canada, similarly emphasizes the need to combine organically functional-line administration with the system of programming and management by objectives.[92] In fact, workers from Arbatov's institute, under the leadership of Mil'ner, have been involved since 1973 in applying principles of matrix organization and project management in the design and operation of selected industrial associations.[93] A matrix scheme of organization is said to be the best embodiment of the "programmed-goals approach." Such a structure provides for the "creation of a special management body with authority to form, coordinate, and regulate all horizontal ties relating to concrete programs and for the redistribution of functions, rights, and responsibilities between new and old organs of administration."[94] Since the matrix organization is designed especially to guide and nurse new products and projects through from start to finish, it is not surprising that its use is being promoted principally in the science-production associations that concentrate on developing and assimilating new technology.[95] Others also have advocated that within certain ministries a special product or project management division should be created. Such a unit could serve as a kind of "curator" for the most important products being produced by associations within the branch.[96]

In general, therefore, the administrative pyramid, which has served as an almost universal management structure and paradigm of rationality, is showing cracks under the strain of development in both capitalist and socialist states. Concerned about organizational innovation and adaptability, modern theorists have aimed at developing structures that can "institutionalize flexibility." Thus, "The name of the game for organizational design has changed from trying to discover the ideal one best way to what is an appropriate design given a discrete set of goals, known material and human resources, a more or less turbulent environment, and captive technologies and programs."[97] Consequently, the trend has been away from an ideal of bureaucratic structures to an array of designs. The most appropriate form for adaptive-organic structures, according to modern management theorists, is not the vertically based, monocratic organization but a matrix or gridlike system that combines and crisscrosses vertical and horizontal channels of authority.

To be sure, this trend toward organization and management by matrix is much stronger in the West than in the East. Indeed, only in the Soviet Union are the initial signs of such a movement visible.[98] Only in Moscow is the idea being broached openly that the matrix structure is "historically appropriate at the contemporary stage of industrial development."[99] Nevertheless, there is considerable dissatisfaction throughout the area with traditional bureaucratic systems and organizations in coping with complexity and change. Growing awareness of the limitations and deficiencies of organization strictly by function and vertical hierarchy is beginning to set in motion forces that seek to change not only existing structures but the principles of organizational design as well. Hence, a variety of variations on the pyramid theme and new shapes for management, at least on a limited scale and in select areas, may be expected to emerge in the future.

While it is certainly premature to discuss the prospects for socialist systems to accommodate matrix schemes of organization, a few general observations seem pertinent. On the one hand, these principles of organization and management are not entirely new. To a certain extent and for some time they have been applied in the Soviet defense industry. More generally, too, the notion of project management fits into a strong tradition of reliance on plenipotentiaries and special organizers vested with central authority to oversee and ramrod through key tasks. Party officials themselves have frequently fulfilled the role of a kind of project leader extraordinary.[100] On the other hand, there are important features of matrix organization that make its widespread application much more of a problematical and fundamentally political issue. The discomfort of dual authority and role conflict permeates the matrix structure and poses grave organizational dilemmas. Indeed, the absence of a single boss and of clearly defined zones of responsibility is singled out as a major disadvantage by Soviet theorists.[101] The tensions inherent in the matrix go basically against the strong accent on unity of command and hierarchical authority that are embodied, indeed enshrined, in the whole concept of "democratic centralism" on which these systems rest. Thus, adoption of the matrix model with its underlying philosophy of management and approach to conflict resolution could substantially alter and upset intraorganizational dynamics and established interorganizational relations. Much like official concern over the use of analytic techniques in decision making, fear that new structural arrangements and management shapes may, in fact, have a disintegrating rather than an integrating effect acts as a powerful constraint on any rapid and radical systemic change.

CADRE DEVELOPMENT AND LEADERSHIP TRAINING

The third major thrust of administrative modernization is the retooling of Communist officialdom and cadre development. Besides decision-making methods and organizational structures, existing managerial skills also are seen to be obsolete. The expanding volume, variety, and complexity of activities that need to be coordinated place growing demands on all levels and kinds of managerial personnel. Indeed, the task of mastering the scientific-technological revolution, it is generally recognized, requires "a leader of a new type."[102] Explains a Hungarian observer: "The old school is no longer adequate because it—understandably—was connected with the old techniques of control." He adds, "All this is not restricted to the economy. It is also applicable to state and party life."[103]

Underlying the call for a new kind of cadre is an understanding of the executive function that stresses, as Kenneth Jowitt notes, leadership rather than command competences.[104] Modernization requires strong integrative leadership, not mere administrative management. For this task a different style and breed of "political manager" is more appropriate than the mentality and methods of the "apparatchik boss," to use Melvin Croan's useful typology of Communist leadership.[105] Here the central issue again relates to capabilities for integration, which lies at the heart of the management function. Integration is not merely unification; it is more than simply bringing diverse social groups and organizations under central control. Integration entails some level of effective commitment and cohesion with respect to accomplishing common objectives. "To manage people," asserts the foremost popularizer of scientific communism in the USSR, "means to inspire loyalty to one's work, to one's place of work, to the people and to the party."[106] Suffice it to say that developments in socialist societies have made increasingly more difficult the direction and motivation of subordinates. Coercion and an arbitrary, aloof leadership style have grown more and more ineffective as means of achieving integration. More subtle forms of social engineering and manipulative skills are needed to generate popular support for official policies and positive cooperation from various strata and interests.[107]

Among the foremost qualities demanded of the modern socialist leader, therefore, is skill in the "art of organizing human talent."[108] V. G. Afanasyev stresses, "He must be a sociologist, with a clear understanding of human relations."[109] This accent on the need for a broad social approach to administration reflects more generally enhanced perception of organization as a social system and of implementation as an inherently social and emotional process. Analytic magic and the power of technique per se are fundamentally incapable of fully solving problems of the "human element" in organization. Awareness of this has led to mounting interest in the sociological and psychological aspects of leadership and organization. Generally speaking, the East Europeans, especially the Poles and Hungarians, have been ahead of the Russians in this regard. Nonetheless, some Soviet scholars are beginning to explore more explicitly the nature of and differences between informal authority and official power, embodied in the concepts of *liderstvo* and *rukovodstvo*, as means of integrating and regulating social processes.[110] Kenneth Jowitt is undoubtedly right when he writes, "The current crises in these systems involve not only power and efficiency but the character of political authority and social relations."[111]

Rejuvenation of the ruling elites is a major problem, perhaps the central problem, for all these regimes. Everywhere political development has led to the entrenchment of an aging bureaucratic establishment that seems to move increasingly by inertia and ineptitude. Events of the last two decades have demonstrated all too clearly the overriding priority and desire among elite members for job security and system stability. Equally important, they have shown that the traditional method of achieving rejuvenation, purge and terror, has become steadily outdated and limited. Whenever a dominant leader, like Khrushchev, tries to ride roughshod over the elite and to use arbitrary, forceful means to alter its composition, he himself is ultimately ousted. Nowhere in Eastern Europe or in the USSR has coercion been a viable instrument in recent years for retooling officialdom.*

Yet the need for rejuvenation and modernization continues to grow in light of the enhanced demands posed by the scientific-technological revolution. Therefore, a general political conclusion has been drawn throughout the area. Since the incumbent elites cannot and should not be removed by coercion, they should be retooled through education. That is, leadership training in scientific management techniques and constant self-improvement have become a surrogate and substitute for the old style of terror and "permanent purge."

The importance of leadership training and retraining has been endorsed from the highest political levels. In the Soviet Union comprehensive study of modern principles of organization and management has been described by a top official as "one of the most important and pressing tasks facing us today."[112] Brezhnev himself has said, "To study the science of management and, if necessary, to learn it anew, becomes the foremost duty of our cadres."[113] Similarly, Ceausescu told the December 1969 plenum of the Romanian Communist Party Central Committee that everyone, including himself, should undergo modern management training. "Otherwise," he observed, "we shall be working without vision, and we shall solve our problems only with great difficulty."[114] More than a year later the Romanian leader again warned, "No one will be promoted in the future, either in production or in political and social life, unless he makes a point of constantly increasing his knowledge, unless he masters all that is new in his field of activity."[115]

Most of the leadership training programs in existence today were begun in the mid-1960s. At that time several East European regimes turned to the Management Development Branch of the International Labor Organization (ILO) for assistance in establishing national management training centers. The ILO had

---

*It is true that, following the Soviet-led occupation of Czechoslovakia in 1968, many supporters of the Prague Spring reform movement were forcefully removed from their posts. The traditional style of purge figured prominently among the "normalization" techniques used to bring the party and society to heel. The promotion of "modernization" was hardly its purpose or effect.

helped set up such a center in Poland in 1960. Accordingly, an Industrial Management Training Center was opened in Bucharest in July 1967 and in Budapest a year later. Progress was much slower in Bulgaria, where only 9 percent of Communist Party members have a higher education and 70 percent do not even have a secondary education. A training center was not completed in Sofia until 1971.[116] ILO collaboration and U.N. funds were not sought by the Kremlin. Nonetheless, a national management institute modeled essentially along the lines of the East European centers was established in Moscow in 1971 under the USSR State Committee for Science and Technology. Generally speaking, all these centers perform the following tasks: to train the very top executive elite in modern methods of management and computer technology; to conduct research on problems of organization and administration; to provide methodological leadership, information services, and overall coordination in the area of management training and development.[117]

Initially, such countries as Bulgaria, Hungary, and Romania tried to concentrate their efforts on training and reschooling cadres without the aid of higher educational institutions, relying mainly on the national management centers.[118] The futility of this approach and attempted "shortcut to modernization" became apparent, however. Hence, steps have been taken in varying degrees throughout the area to enlist the assistance of the universities in management training and research. Indeed, the systems of secondary and higher education are gradually being reformed more broadly and adjusted to the demands of the STR. In addition, under many branch ministries, research institutes, and industrial associations short-term courses and seminars devoted to raising professional qualifications and management instruction have steadily developed in most of these countries. More and more a differentiated approach toward management training is discernible and has contributed to the growth of an extensive and elaborate network of bodies engaged in carrying out a virtual "cultural revolution."

To counteract and contain any narrow technocratic tendencies that may be spawned in the process of management training, measures also have been adopted in almost all the East European countries and the Soviet Union to strengthen and modernize political education and ideological indoctrination of cadres. Not only economic managers and technical specialists but party apparatchiki and government officials as well are being "recycled" and reschooled in modern methods and technology-related matters. In Bulgaria, for example, the Academy for Training Cadres in Social Management was created in January 1970 under the BCP Central Committee. (Actually the Academy was created out of three institutions: the Higher Party School, the Center for Improving Leading Cadres, and the Institute on Organization and Management.) Recently renamed the Academy of Social Sciences and Social Management, it is designed to act as the main directing and coordinating center for the whole system of cadre training for party, Komsomol, and trade union activists. The academy now contains three main divisions: The Higher School of Social Management prepares leading workers through a two-year training program; the Center for Training Senior Cadres provides four to six months of instruction and by 1974 some 80,000 apparatchiki and activists had attended this center or one of its 10 subordinate interdistrict schools; finally, the Institute on Social Management conducts both theoretical and applied research in the area of organization and administration.[119]

Similarly, in Romania the political authorities took steps in February 1971 to extend and intensify the training of party and state cadres. The Stefan Gheorghiu Academy of Social and Political Sciences was reorganized into the Academy for Social-Political Education and the Training of Leading Cadres. Attached directly to the RCP Central Committee, the academy has two main departments. One trains responsible cadres in party and mass organizations; the other trains functionaries in state and economic administration. The training lasts four and two years, respectively. In addition, the number of short-term courses for lower-echelon party activists has been expanded.[120] Indicating enhanced concern by the Gierek leadership over the modernization issue in Poland, the Politburo of the PUWP established the special Management Training Center under the Central Committee in October 1972. The center's task is to oversee the process of raising the qualifications of both the economic managerial bureaucracy and the party apparat.[121] Not surprisingly, political authorities in the Soviet Union probably have taken the keenest interest in training and retraining party and government cadres. Suffice it to say that following the Twenty-third Party Congress an elaborate and extensive network of seminars and refresher courses began to be institutionalized within the system of party schools for this purpose. Between 1967 and 1971 more than 200,000 persons took these retraining courses. Between 1971 and 1974 an additional 180,000 were reschooled.[122]

Despite these efforts, however, dissatisfaction with the state and results of management training continues, if not grows. In Hungary, for example, the Central Committee at the end of 1973 observed that management training still did not measure up to the growing demands of both quality and quantity. The question of "limited capacity" of the entire training system posed the "gravest problem." In all, some 900,000 people, including 9,000 top-level managers, 90,000 middle-level executives, and 800,000 lower-level managers need to be retooled. Meanwhile, the National Management Training Center in Budapest has been able to provide instruction for only 2,800 persons between 1971 and 1974.[123]

The situation in Hungary seems representative of conditions in the other countries as well. Everywhere the goal is to make management training compulsory for all managers with university degrees and five years experience and to have refresher courses every five years. A kind of permanent recycling and retooling process is projected whereby the administrative machinery can be continually tuned to changing requirements of the times. Like the programs for computerization, however, these grandiose plans for management development remain unfulfilled and plagued by problems. Nowhere has a unified and well-coordinated system for retraining and raising qualifications been established. Organizationally and methodologically, these systems remain highly fragmented, predominantly along branch lines. Even in the Soviet Union, it is officially admitted, "This work often is conducted in an unsystematic way; it lacks consequences, a conceptual framework, and purpose."[124] Throughout Eastern Europe and the USSR retraining the "human element" in management has encountered tremendous difficulties and resistance, euphemistically called in official parlance "the psychological barrier." Going through the motions of retraining, moreover, does not automatically yield the desired results. Studies in systems analysis, modern business games, in-basket exercises, and management role playing do not, practice has clearly shown, always change entrenched routines and conditioned reflexes.

Not the least important obstacle to retraining is the underdevelopment of management theory and research. A systematized body of theoretical concepts and guidelines greatly facilitates the training process. Only since the 1960s, however, has management received attention and study as a separate field of knowledge and application. For three decades it was relegated to the dustbin of history as a bourgeois science. Brezhnev gave official support to its rebirth when he noted in April 1970, "Management is becoming a science. This science must be mastered as quickly as possible and as profoundly as possible. It must be studied persistently."[125] Despite progress in establishing management science as a specialized branch of knowledge, there is still considerable confusion throughout the area over its substance.

Initially, the notion seems to have existed that modern principles of organization and management could be borrowed from the West and adapted relatively easily to socialist conditions. Just as ILO assistance was sought in setting up national training centers, many East European and Soviet scholars began to turn to Western theory for ideas around which to build a modern socialist management science. By the early 1970s, however, official warnings mounted over the dangers of "mechanical borrowing." In Hungary, about the same time that economic recentralization and retrenchment became discernible, the party daily pointed out, "To take over the [Western] system lock, stock, and barrel is unreasonable and harmful, and it might lead to serious distortions."[126] Similarly, in the Soviet Union scholars combing Western management literature were criticized for "scooping up a cupful of conceptions, terms, and categories, without any attempt to connect them with our realities."

One observer noted, "A fashion has set in to make a show with a whole mass of words, which when translated into the Russian language prove to be quite trivial." While granting the need to study Western theories, this critic warned against "any attempts at mechanical adoption of some particular organizational idea or method without due consideration of our own experience, of the difference in principle, not only in the social but also in organizational structures, forms, and methods of management in socialist and capitalist countries."[127] In April 1973 a member of the CPSU Politburo voiced similar concerns in the party's theoretical journal.[128] Speaking more broadly about cadre training and management development in the European socialist systems, a Soviet analyst emphasized recently, "It has become clear that simple copying of the experience of other countries, especially capitalist states, is insufficient."[129]

However, the development of a specific socialist science of management, adapted to local conditions, has been very slow and difficult. Writing in April 1973, a leading Soviet official asserted bluntly that such a science was "still in the process of being formed."[130] After much heated debate a national conference held in Moscow in July 1972 was still unable to come up with even a definition of the subject of management science or a formulation of its basic functions.[131] Throughout Eastern Europe and the USSR there is lack of clarity and consensus among management theorists as regards the substance and scope of administration. Policy makers, on the other hand, are dissatisfied and critical of the highly abstract and formalistic character of many management studies. Meanwhile, methodological diversity and terminological ambiguity, which characterize the present state of management theory and research, complicate greatly the organization of studies and the compilation of course materials for retraining cadres. In fact, only recently has a textbook for management education been completed in Hungary.[132] Everywhere problems abound and impede rapid progress.

THE MANAGEMENT OF CHANGE
AND THE ROLE OF THE PARTY

Political developments in Eastern Europe and the USSR suggest that there are at least three major problem areas that affect substantially the prospects for administrative modernization and retooling directed socialist society. These concern the connection between change and conflict, the role of the party in negotiating the transition to developed socialism, and the nature of innovation and adaptation under present conditions.

As regards the first, modernizing efforts have revealed clearly the immobilism of established institutions, the resistance of vested interests, and the intransigence of fixed ideas. That is, change inevitably involves conflict, a struggle between the old and the new. Integration becomes a process of adjustment and change that reduces differences in society to manageable levels of conflict. Recognition of this has led, in fact, to an important reversal of attitude among East European and Soviet theorists toward contradictions in socialist society. Formerly, they were seen as undesirable and detrimental to both system stability

and goal maximization. More recently, however, official writers on developed
socialism have come to stress that contradictions are not only normal and legitimate but indeed desirable and functional. "To deny their existence," wrote a
Bulgarian observer, "means, in fact, to ignore the sources of motion, change, and
development."[133] A Romanian spokesman similarly noted, "Life invalidated
opinions supporting a linear, nonconflicting type of development under socialism."[134] Socialism is now described as "a dynamic society whose continuous
development takes place through the rise and solution of contradictions."[135]
In short, the dialectical process, frozen by command for many years, has been
rediscovered in a socialist context.[136]

Among the contradictions that are said to exist in socialist society, the
struggle between the new and the obsolete assumes central importance. This
struggle, moreover, takes place especially in the process of modernizing administration.[137] Almost everywhere the requirements of economic and social
development have come into contradiction with obsolescent forms and methods
of organization and management.[138] A professor at the Bulgarian Academy of
Social Sciences and Social Management has even called this conflict between the
managed and the system of management the "main contradiction" at the present
stage of development.[139] With the abolition of classes under socialism, the
class struggle retires from the scene as the driving force of history. "But this does
not mean," a prominent Soviet authority argues, "that all contradictions and
struggle disappears." The old is no longer represented by any classes, but it is
upheld by conservative elements.[140] In essence, therefore, the struggle between
the new and the old, between progressive and conservative forces, replaces the
class struggle as the dialectical axis of development for mature socialism. While
these contradictions are generally described as "nonantagonistic," Ceausescu has
admitted that they also may acquire an antagonistic character.[141]

Against this background the "leading role" of the party is being reinter-
preted and given new meaning. Just as the party led and directed the class struggle
during the earlier stages of revolutionary transformation and political consolidation, it is being increasingly thrust into the role of principal political innovator
and manager of the struggle for modernization. As impatience and dissatisfaction
grows among the political authorities over the slow pace of administrative
modernization and bureaucratic obstacles to change, the tendency is to assert a
more activist and interventionist role for party agencies in the implementation
process. This tendency is most discernible, of course, in Romania. There Ceausescu
is directly combining party and state functions and pursuing more intensively a
strategy of "hierarchical unification and organizational compression," to use
Jowitt's apt phraseology.[142] Elsewhere, too, party agencies are intensifying
their efforts and active involvement in promoting economic reconstruction and
administrative modernization.[143] In socialist society, official spokesmen claim,
there is not, nor can there be, any other political organization that is able to

integrate complexity as well as to manage change and conflict generated in the course of modernization.[144]

To a certain extent, recent developments and problems associated with mastering the scientific-technological revolution suggest there may be a parallel in the making with an earlier stage of socialism in the USSR. As the state bureaucracy became hesitant and resistant toward implementing Stalin's policies in the late 1920s and early 1930s, the party apparatus stepped increasingly into the breach as the main driving force behind industrialization. Nearly half a century later, modernizing efforts are again encountering stiff bureaucratic opposition and inertia. Just as they led and engineered the initial revolutionary breakthrough to industrialization, party agencies today also are being called upon to lead and negotiate the STR or the "second industrial revolution." More and more throughout Eastern Europe and the Soviet Union the party machinery is actively pressing the technological offensive and trying to direct the transition to developed socialism or, to use a Western term, the postindustrial society.

As regards the capacity of the ruling parties to fulfill this leadership role under contemporary conditions, the experience of the 1960s suggests that this is most problematic. Indeed, the decade provided two important object lessons. On the one hand, the Communist party almost everywhere appeared more and more as an enervated and inert political force, lagging behind events. Both Mao and Tito, although at opposite extremes of the ideological spectrum, became preoccupied with the problems of the party's declining moral authority and increasing bureaucratic tendencies. The main impetus behind political developments in the mid-1960s was not so much to rescue stagnating economies as to salvage stagnating Communist parties. Fundamentally, the motive force was the spreading malaise and the feeling that the party, previously the source of dynamism and progress, had become a brake, a retarding force on socialist development. It was this specter of backwardness and stagnation in the political sector that ultimately spurred political action in the form of the cultural revolution in China, the Prague Spring in Czechoslovakia, and the purge of Rankovic in Yugoslavia. In all three instances, moreover, the purpose was not to renounce the leading role of the party but to revitalize the party and to restore its moral authority so that it could, in fact, fulfill its claimed leadership role as a creative history-making force.

On the other hand, events also led political authorities to question the efficacy of combining moral and technical leadership functions in the party. In the USSR this view found expression in the reversal by Khrushchev's successors of his policies of merging and confusing party and state tasks. Like the Yugoslavs earlier, the Czech Communist reformers in 1968 came to question the moral capacity of the party to lead society in a postrevolutionary and posttotalitarian direction if it retained significant administrative functions. Mao, on the contrary, came to a similar conclusion but with respect to the ability of the party to serve as a genuinely revolutionary instrument of authoritarian, if not totalitarian, power. All agreed that the primary role of the party should be as an ideological guiding force and that it was the operational role of the party in directing state and economic affairs that prevented it from exercising its true moral role. Involvement of the party in administration led to its acquiring special (bureaucratic) interests of its own that prevented it from acting as a selfless custodian and genuine integrator of society's broad, socialist interests. For the Dubcek reformers and the Yugoslavs, the ultimate solution to check bureaucratic decay and guarantee development of a more democratic form of socialism lay in separating the party from economic management and government administration, divorcing the party from state power. Interestingly, this was remarkably similar to Mao's much more violent remedy to root out the incubus of bureaucracy in China.

For a long time the survival of Communist power and developmental progress were believed to hinge necessarily upon the party having monopolistic and direct control of state and economic power. During the 1960s, however, this view began to change. Success and viability of socialist systems were seen increasingly by members of the ruling elites to depend ultimately upon the party apparatus shedding and redefining its extraparty administrative functions. While there were no radical departures along this line anywhere (except China), the party's grasp, nonetheless, on the administrative levers did gradually loosen and centralized control subsided generally throughout the area.

What we see in the 1970s, significantly, are efforts to reverse, in part at least, the conclusions and practices of the decade before. Almost everywhere, even in Yugoslavia, movement is discernible to strengthen the bases of party rule and to reassert a more activist role for party agencies in the drive for modernization. Without a more interventionist stance and greater supervision over the implementation process, modernization will continue to be frustrated and delayed. At the same time the capacity of socialist regimes to cope effectively with changing conditions and new demands depends significantly on advances in administrative retooling.

Wrestling with the challenge of the scientific-technological revolution, political authorities have become steadily aware of the crux of the party's leadership dilemma: How can the party lead society in the ideological-moral sense if it does not simultaneously have administrative power to enforce its pronouncements? How can the party act as the soul of society without at the same time controlling the body politic or at least the bureaucracy? In a world in which theory without organization and power to enforce it has always been powerless and a source of disunity and disintegration, these questions strike at the heart of socialist polities.

The imperatives of the STR notwithstanding, the overriding desire for stability among the ruling establishments imposes the greatest constraint on any rapid realization of dreams of modernization. The whole theoretical thrust behind the notion of mature socialism stresses, in fact, the evolutionary character of development. Adventurist and voluntarist "great leaps forward" are to be avoided at all cost. Change itself is seen to be no longer the result of a single act (much less a decree) but a dynamic process of improvement and adaptation. Ironically, then, at a time when the task of leadership has once again become system-comprehensive rather than issue-specific,[145] both theory and practice militate against the application of a "systems approach" to the problem of modernization and restructuring.

Indeed, nowhere is a systems approach being effectively implemented, despite all the rhetoric about the need for it. Perhaps Romania comes closest. There Ceausescu has managed to set up, independent of the regular administrative machinery, an array of new party-state bodies to carry out reforms. Little meaningful progress seems to have been made, however. Ceausescu appears rather to have merely added to the bureaucratic crust enveloping the system. In Poland, a party-government Commission for Economic and State Modernization exists. Headed by Politburo member and Central Committee Secretary Jan Szydlak, the commission works closely with the Politburo and Gierek personally. Typical of the Polish pattern, however, the accent is on a guarded, gradual, and piecemeal approach to change.[146]

A comprehensive and well-coordinated program of administrative modernization is particularly absent in the Kremlin. There is no task force on executive reorganization under the Council of Ministers, much less the Politburo. Proposals have been made recently to create a special leadership organ in the form of either a state committee for questions of improving organization and management, or even an authoritative party-state agency for administrative rationalization along the lines of what existed in the 1920s.[147] Nevertheless, leadership over this work remains fragmented and dispersed among numerous organizations. The accent is still on *samoratsionalizatsiia* (self or voluntary rationalization) rather than on arbitrary change imposed from without. Despite enhanced prodding and direct initiatives by party organs, official policy continues more generally to try to promote and integrate administrative improvements through Gosplan and "the plan."

Given this conservative ethos and dominant concern for system maintenance, macrolevel models for comprehensive systemic change have essentially been abandoned in East European socialist states, at least for the foreseeable future. Today the nature of innovation and the dynamics of change revolve increasingly around microlevel or mini models in the form of "experiments." As a prominent Soviet authority on scientific communism explained, "Many questions cannot be decided at once, on a nationwide scale, without preliminary trial, experimentation, and testing on a narrower scale."[148]

Economic and social experiments provide an opportunity to weigh and try out different variants of action and thereby avoid the consequences of hasty and arbitrary decisions about change. Indeed, the number of experiments applying new forms and alternative methods of organization and management has grown considerably throughout the area. N. P. Fedorenko, a Soviet Academician and economist, observed recently that the experiment is no longer "an accidental and sporadic phenomenon" but increasingly "an organic and integral element of socialist management."[149] To be sure, the dominant accent is on stability and continuity. But it is inaccurate to say that there is no change in socialist systems. Society includes, on the contrary, a growing number of pockets of innovation, new kinds of "islands of separateness," coexisting and struggling with the old.

On the political level, therefore, the central question of socialist development in Eastern Europe and the Soviet Union is increasingly not "whither the system?" but "whither the experiment?" The evolution of society more broadly— its predominant organizational shapes and administrative practices—will be determined to a large extent by the fate of individual experiments. That is, the nature and direction of societal change will depend substantially on whether these seeds of innovation are allowed to flower or wilt.

More generally, the focus of bureaucratic politics and the "kto-kogo" struggle is undergoing change. Radical departures from the status quo and grandiose systems engineering are no long viable issues. The bureaucratic struggle and policy debate is revolving more and more around the politics of organization and the management of innovation and experimentation.[150] In another sense, the "experiment" phenomenon may be seen as an additional manifestation of pluralist and incrementalist tendencies in Leninist systems. Taken together, then, all these factors suggest that socialist development in the decade ahead will be "modernization at a snail's pace," to paraphrase Bukharin's slogan from an earlier era of industrialization.

In conclusion, events of the past decade have witnessed intensified efforts—although often begrudgingly made—to adapt socialist systems to the modern age. On the ideological plane, elaboration of the whole concept of developed socialism signifies an attempt to build, really for the first time, a theory of the "directed society" for mature socialism. In the past this was an important ideological void. The problem lies not only in the failure of Marx to depict in any detail the future Communist order but also in his emphasis on the essentially primitive, coercive, and transitional character of the "socialist" phase of development. The dictatorship of the proletariat, especially in its high Stalinist form, does not provide a viable model of a "mature" socialist society. Under Khrushchev little effort was made to elaborate such a model, particularly along the present lines of, essentially, perpetuating the existing system and modernizing the structure of power. On the contrary, the accent in building the future Communist order was under Khrushchev on the withering away of the state superstructure and formal administrative machinery.

That is, theory contained two models, neither of which was appropriate for "developed socialism." There was a model of directed society at an early stage of socialist development when coercion was the dominant means of control. There also was a model of undirected society at the Communist phase of development when self-administration becomes the distinguishing feature of life. In short, a model of "the administered society: totalitarianism without terror" was conspicuously lacking. At a time when such a model has taken shape on the theoretical plane, political and organizational realities in Eastern Europe and the USSR undermine, if not prevent, its actual implementation. As is so often the case in Communist polities, the central issue revolves around *vnedrenie* (introduction) or putting theory into practice.

NOTES

1. Certainly the most eloquent statement of this position is by Jerry Hough. See his articles, "The Bureaucratic Model and the Nature of the Soviet System," *Journal of Comparative Administration* 5, no. 2 (August 1973): 134-67, and "The Soviet System: Petrification or Pluralism?" *Problems of Communism* 21, no. 2 (1972): 25-45.

2. See the volume of essays, edited by Samuel P. Huntington and Clement H. Moore, *Authoritarian Politics in Modern Society* (New York: Basic Books, 1970), especially the piece by Huntington, "Social and Institutional Dynamics of One-Party Systems," pp. 4-5.

3. Ivan Svitak, "With Heads Against the Wall," *Student* (Prague), April 10, 1968, translated in *Studies in Comparative Communism* 1, nos. 1-2 (July/October 1968): 185.

4. Statement by Jan Prochazka, the deputy chairman of the Czechoslovak Writers Association, during an interview on April 25, 1968, with Francois Fejto, referred to in Radio Free Europe, *Czechoslovak Situation Report,* no. 46 (April 26, 1968).

5. Gustav Husak, "An Old Anniversary and New Hopes," *Kulturny zivot,* January 12, 1968, translation in RFE, *Czechoslovak Press Survey,* no. 1999 (January 22, 1968).

6. See Radovan Richta et al., eds., *Civilization at the Crossroads: Social and Human Implications of the Scientific and Technological Revolution* (White Plains, N.Y.: International Arts and Sciences Press, 1969), pp. 101, 236. The research group itself was set up in 1965.

7. Melvin Croan, "After Ulbricht: The End of an Era?" *Survey* 17, no. 2 (Spring 1971): 74-92.

8. See Thomas A. Baylis, "Economic Reform as Ideology: East Germany's New Economic System," *Comparative Politics* 3, no. 2 (January 1971): 211-30. For a more extended discussion of this theme, see his excellent study, *The Technical Intelligentsia and the East German Elite: Legitimacy and Social Change in Mature Communism* (Berkeley: University of California Press, 1974).

9. Referred to by Marko Markov, in "The Scientific and Technical Revolution and the Management of Big Social Systems," in *Science, Technology, Man* (Sofia: Publishing House of the Bulgarian Academy of Sciences, 1973), p. 279.

10. See RFE, *Poland Situation Report*, January 14, 1970, pp. 7, 15. Problems of streamlining the economic management system were being intensively discussed throughout Comecon by the late 1960s. As Radio Warsaw commented on December 15, 1969, "An important problem, and we can observe it clearly in all socialist countries, lies in overcoming old habits, achieving changes in the mentality both of people running the economy and of the workers, technicians, and engineers" (ibid., p. 14).

11. Just as Stalin had underestimated the importance of cybernetics, his successors until recently failed to recognize the potential of the computer and its importance in both production and management. As Wade Holland notes, it was only at the Twenty-fourth Party Congress that major mention of automation and computerization of the economy was

made for the first time. See his comments in *Soviet Cybernetics Review* 1, no. 3 (May 1971): 2.

12. It was probably no accident that the regular police, the Ministry for Preserving Public Order, was reorganized into the new Ministry of Internal Affairs within three months after the Soviet-led invasion of Czechoslovakia. Moreover, a number of measures were adopted at this time that set in motion a major overhaul of the MVD. These aimed at modernizing its structure and technical machinery as well as professionalizing its staff in order to make the whole organization a more effective instrument of surveillance and supervision. On this program and its progress, see *Spravochnik partiinogo rabotnika* (Moscow: Izdatel'stvo Politicheskoi Literatury, 1969), pp. 445-47; N. Shchelokov, "Utverzhdat' sotsialisticheskuiu zakonnost', borot'sia s pravonarusheniiami," *Kommunist Moldavii* 2 (1970): 32-39; *Pravda*, November 10, 1971.

13. Andrei Sakharov, Roy Medvedev, and V. F. Turchin, "Letter of Appeal of Soviet Scientists to Party and Government Leaders of the USSR," March 19, 1970, reprinted in *Survey*, Summer 1970, pp. 160-70.

14. *Pravda,* June 13, 1970.

15. *Pravda,* March 31, 1971. Similar statements have punctuated virtually all of his major speeches since the Twenty-fourth Congress.

16. See Markov, "The Scientific and Technical Revolution and the Management of Big Social Systems," pp. 279, 280, 291; Alexander Akhiezer, "The Scientific and Technological Revolution and Guidance of Social Development," in *The Scientific and Technological Revolution: Social Effects and Prospects* (Moscow, 1972), esp. pp. 168-72.

17. Dzherman Gvishiani, *Organization and Management: A Sociological Analysis of Western Theories* (Moscow, 1972), p. 172.

18. Markov, "The Scientific and Technical Revolution," p. 291.

19. Kenneth Jowitt, "An Organizational Approach to the Study of Political Culture in Marxist-Leninist Systems," *American Political Science Review* 68 (September 1974): 1171-91. See also his essay, "Inclusion and Mobilization in European Leninist Regimes," in this volume.

20. Nikolai I. Bukharin, *Socialist Reconstruction and the Struggle for Technique* (Moscow: Cooperative Publishing Society of Foreign Workers in the USSR, 1932), p. 4.

21. For a discussion of this shrinkage process, see Paul Cocks, "The Rationalization of Party Control," in *Change in Communist Systems*, ed. Chalmers Johnson (Stanford, Cal.: Stanford University Press, 1970), pp. 157-61.

22. See, for example, Hyman Lumer, "Ideological Essence of 'Post-Industrial Society'," *World Marxist Review* (December 1972); Victor Afanasyev, "Scientific Management of Society and Socialist Democracy," ibid. 17, no. 11 (November 1974): 84-93; Tibor Gorog, "The Science of Revolution and Building the New Society," ibid, 12 (December 1974).

23. See the remarks by B. Milner, in *Social Sciences* (Moscow) 5, no. 3 (1971): 178.

24. See V. Afanasyev, *The Scientific Management of Society* (Moscow: Progress Publishers, 1971); "The Scientific-Technical Revolution and Socialism," *World Marxist Review* 15, no. 8 (August 1972): 5-35; O. S. Abbasova, "On the Question of an Integrated Systems Approach to Administration in Socialist Society," in *Nauchnoe upravlenie obshchestvom* (Moscow: Mysl', 1974).

25. Akhiezer, "The Scientific and Technological Revolution," p. 168.

26. See the excellent article on this subject by Erik P. Hoffmann, "Soviet Metapolicy: Information Processing in the Communist Party of the Soviet Union," *Journal of Comparative Administration* 5, no. 2 (August 1973): 200-32.

27. Jan Szczepanski, "Eastern European Studies in the West as Seen from Eastern Europe," *Canadian Slavonic Papers* 16, no. 4 (Winter 1974): 537.

28. See the discussion by Jozef Wilczynski, "Cybernetics, Automation and the Transition to Communism," in *Comparative Socialist Systems: Essays on Politics and Economics,* ed. Carmelo Mesa-Lago and Carl Beck (Pittsburgh: University of Pittsburgh Press, 1975), pp. 397-417.

29. For a discussion of this technology gap and some of the problems associated with overcoming it, see R. V. Burks, "Technology and Political Change in Eastern Europe," in Johnson, ed., *Change in Communist Systems,* pp. 265-312.

30. *Rabotnichesko delo,* February 12, 1974, cited in RFE, *Bulgarian Situation Report,* no. 16 (March 7, 1974).

31. *Romania Libera,* January 26, 1972, cited in RFE, *Romanian Situation Report* no. 8 (February 23, 1972).

32. Jerzy Kleer, "Economic Reforms in the Socialist Countries in the Sixties," *Ekonomista,* no. 1 (1973), translated in *East European Economics* 13, no. 2 (Winter 1974-75): 7.

33. See Paul Cocks, "Science Policy and Soviet Decisionmaking: PPBS Comes to the Kremlin," paper delivered at the 1975 annual meeting of the American Political Science Association.

34. Gvishiani, *Organization and Management,* p. 126.

35. See RFE, *Romanian Situation Report,* no. 2 (January 12, 1972), and *Bulgarian Situation Report,* no. 9 (March 5, 1970).

36. Karl C. Thalheim, "Balance Sheet," in *The New Economic Systems of Eastern Europe,* ed. Hans-Hermann Hohmann, Michael Kaser, and Karl C. Thalheim (Berkeley and Los Angeles: University of California, 1975), p. 556.

37. See Donald V. Schwartz, "The Impact of the Scientific-Technological Revolution on Soviet Administrative Decision-Making," paper delivered at the 1975 annual meeting of the American Political Science Association.

38. Alfred Zauberman, *The Mathematical Revolution in Soviet Economics* (London: Oxford University Press, 1975), p. 1.

39. Robert W. Campbell, "Management Spillovers from Soviet Space and Military Programmes," *Soviet Studies* 23, no. 4 (April 1972): 586-607.

40. Stanislav Vacha, "A Systems Approach to Management of a Socialist Economy," *Politicka Ekonomie* no. 5 (1974), translated in *East European Economics* 13, no. 3 (Spring 1975): 24.

41. I. V. Blauberg and E. G. Iudin, *Stanovlenie i sushchnost' sistemnogo podkhoda* (Moscow: Nauka, 1973), p. 240.

42. Ibid., p. 241. See also I. V. Blauberg, V. N. Sadovskii, and E. G. Iudin, *Sistemnyi podkhod: predposylki, problemy, trudnosti* (Moscow, 1969).

43. E. G. Iudin, "Metodologicheskaia priroda sistemnogo podkhoda," *Sistemnye issledovaniia Ezhegodnik 1973* (Moscow: Nauka, 1973), p. 43.

44. Gvishiani, *Organization and Management,* pp. 140, 142.

45. Ibid., pp. 143-44.

46. O. Deineko, "From the Enterprise to the Ministry," *Pravda,* April 17, 1973.

47. Michael Ellman, *Soviet Planning Today: Proposals for an Optimally Functioning Economic System* (Cambridge: Cambridge University Press, 1971), p. xii.

48. See Kazimierz Sokolowski, "Democratic Centralism in Economic Management," *Nowe Drogi,* December 1971 in RFE, *Polish Press Survey,* no. 2353 (February 2, 1972); A. V. Bachurin, *Planovo-ekonomicheskie metody upravleniia* (Moscow: Ekonomica, 1973), p. 96; Marko Markov, *Sotsializ'm i upravlenie* (Sofia: Partizdat, 1971) and *Subekt't na sotsialnoto upravlenie* (Sofia: Partizdat, 1974).

49. G. Pospelov, "The Systems Approach," *Izvestiia,* March 21, 1974.

50. Academician N. P. Fedorenko in *Ekonomicheskaia gazeta* 2 (January 1974): 12-14.

51. For an excellent discussion of the difficulties of interbranch planning and systems programming in the USSR, see E. V. Kosov and G. Kh. Popov, *Upravlenie mezhotraslevymi nauchno-tekhnicheskimi programmami* (Moscow: Ekonomica, 1972). Studies advocating the systems approach include G. M. Dobrov et al., *Programmno-tselevoi metod upravleniia v nauke* (Moscow: Ekonomica, 1974); M. Ia. Lemeshev and A. I. Panchenko, *Kompleksnye programmy v planirovanii narodnogo khoziaistva* (Moscow: Ekonomica, 1973); Bachurin, *Planovo-ekonomicheskie metody upravleniia* (Moscow: Ekonomica, 1973).

52. See RFE, *Bulgaria Background Report,* no. 3 (March 2, 1973); *Bulgarian Situation Report,* no. 8 (March 28, 1974) and no. 5 (May 29, 1974); *Bulgarian Background Report,* no. 3 (April 19, 1974).

53. R. N. (Bulgarian Unit), "New Planning Approach Adopted by Central Committee Plenum," RFE, *Bulgaria Background Report,* no. 2 (January 15, 1973).

54. See Heinz Sange, "On the Development of Long Range Planning of the GDR National Economy," *Staat und Recht,* August 1974, pp. 1265-75.

55. Fedorenko in *Ekonomicheskaia gazeta,* no. 2 (January 1974).

56. Bachurin, *Planovo-ekonomicheskie metody upravleniia,* pp. 95-97. Also see the review of Kosygin's collected speeches and articles in *Planovoe khoziaistvo,* no. 1 (1975): 11-12.

57. *Rabotnichesko delo,* December 14 and 17, 1972.

58. Sange, "On the Development of Long Range Planning of the GDR National Economy."

59. Nicolae Agachi, "The Caliber of Enterprise Management," *Romania Libera,* September 28, 1966, in RFE, *Romanian Press Survey,* no. 661 (October 12, 1966).

60. L. Petrescu, "The Ability to Make Optimal and the Most Objective Decisions," *Romania Libera,* September 14, 1966, in ibid.

61. Constantin Cojocaru, "The Industrial Central–Optimization of Economic Decision and Action," *Revista Economica,* no. 5 (July 12, 1974): 6-7 in Joint Publications Research Service (JPRS) 62997 (September 18, 1974).

62. See B. Z. Mil'ner, ed., *Organizatsionnye struktury upravleniia proizvodstvom* (Moscow, 1975), pp. 95-106.

63. Croan, "Elites, Leadership and Systemic Change in Eastern Europe," unpublished, p. 7.

64. Zauberman, *The Mathematical Revolution in Soviet Economics,* p. vii.

65. Blauberg and Iudin, *Stanovlenie i sushchnost' sistemnogo podkhoda,* pp. 232-51.

66. See Hough, "The Bureaucratic Model and the Nature of the Soviet System" and "The Soviet System: Petrification or Pluralism?" For a somewhat critical discussion of this approach, see Paul Cocks, "The Policy Process and Bureaucratic Politics," in *Soviet Politics: Studies in Leadership, Policy, and Development,* ed. Paul Cocks, Robert V. Daniels, and Nancy W. Heer (Cambridge: Harvard University Press, forthcoming).

67. Croan, "Elites, Leadership, and Systemic Change in Eastern Europe," pp. 10-11.

68. Baylis, *The Technical Intelligentsia and the East German Elite,* p. 82.

69. Frederic L. Pryor, "Industrial Organization," in Mesa-Lago and Beck, eds., *Comparative Socialist Systems,* pp. 363-64.

70. Ibid., p. 364. See also Hohmann et al., *The New Economic Systems of Eastern Europe,* pp. 4-5.

71. The commission concluded, "There is widespread conviction that the maintenance of the high dynamics of economic growth and elimination of still lingering stresses depends to a large degree on further consistent and comprehensive perfecting of the system of planning and management. There is a close connection between the long-range strategy of socioeconomic development and a modernization of the mechanisms and levers which are used to implement this strategy." See RFE, *Poland Situation Report,* no. 20 (June 1, 1973).

72. See B. Mil'ner, "How Should an Organization Be Designed?" *Izvestiia,* May 13, 1973. These arguments are made even more explicit in the book he has edited, *Organizatsionnye struktury upravleniia proizvodstvom.* See also the important article by G. Arbatov, "Organizational Design for Large-scale Production-Economic Complexes and for the Management of them," *Planovoe Khoziaistvo,* no. 5 (1975): 18, 19, 21. In an obvious criticism of the Soviet computer lobby, Arbatov stated frankly the primacy of organization over information in reform strategy: "At the basis of improving the system of management must lie not techniques of information processing but the organization of administration" (p. 26).

73. D. Gvishiani, "The Scientific and Technological Revolution and Scientific Problems," *Social Sciences* (Moscow) 1, no. 7 (1972): 55-56.

74. William F. Robinson, "Hungary's 11th Party Congress: Climax or Anticlimax?" RFE, *Hungarian Background Report,* no. 48 (March 14, 1975).

75. Henry Schaefer, "The State of Economic Reform in Hungary," RFE, *Hungarian Background Report,* no. 4 (March 23, 1973): 4.

76. Michael D. Reagan, ed., *The Administration of Public Policy* (Glenview, Ill.: Scott, Foresman, 1969), p. 16.

77. Harold Seidman, *Politics, Position and Power: The Dynamics of Federal Reorganization* (New York: Oxford University Press, 1970), p. 14.

78. Ibid., p. 168.

79. "Conditions for Development," *Zycie Warszawy,* April 15, 1972, in RFE, *Polish Press Survey,* no. 2362 (April 25, 1972): 4.

80. Vacha, "A Systems Approach to Management of a Socialist Economy," p. 13; M. I. Piskotin, "The Functions of the Socialist State and the Administrative Apparatus," *Sovetskoe gosudarstvo i pravo,* no. 10 (1972): 3-11; G. V. Atamanchuk, "On the Content of Improving the Apparatus of State Administration," ibid., no. 2 (1975): 62.

81. F. Kutta, "Modifications in the System of Management," *Hospodarske Noviny,* no. 18 (May 3, 1974), in RFE, *Czechoslovak Press Survey,* no. 2520 (May 22, 1974). This view also is expressed by G. Kh. Popov and B. Z. Mil'ner, "Mify i real'nosti menedzhmenta," *Ideologicheskie problemy nauchno-tekhnicheskoi revoliutsii* (Moscow, 1974), pp. 126, 130-32.

82. See Hohmann et al., *The New Economic Systems of Eastern Europe,* p. xii; L. A. Dellin and H. Gross, eds., *Reforms in the Soviet and East European Economies* (Lexington, Mass.: Lexington Books, 1972).

83. See Leon Smolinski, "Towards a Socialist Corporation: Soviet Industrial Reorganization of 1973," *Survey* 20, no. 1 (Winter 1974): 24-35; Alice Gorlin, "The Soviet Economic Associations," *Soviet Studies* 26, no. 1 (January 1974): 3-27.

84. G. Kh. Popov cited in Smolinski, "Towards a Socialist Corporation," p. 30.

85. A. Bachurin, "The Production Association and Technical Progress," *Ekonomicheskaia gazeta,* no. 43 (1970): 5-6.

86. Fremont A. Shull, Jr., *Matrix Structure and Project Authority for Optimizing Organizational Capacity* (Carbondale: Southern Illinois University, School of Business, October 1965); John Stanley Baumgartner, *Project Management* (Homewood, Ill.: Richard D. Irwin, 1963), p. 8.

87. David I. Cleland and William R. King, *Systems Analysis and Project Management* (New York: McGraw Hill, 1968), pp. 172-74.

88. Donald Ralph Kingdom, *Matrix Organization: Managing Information Technologies* (London: Tavistock, 1973), p. 28.

89. See ibid., pp. 47-50, 87-88, 103-07; Cleland and King, *Systems Analysis and Project Management,* pp. 13-15, 178; Chris Argyris, "Today's Problems with Tomorrow's Organizations," in *Management of Change and Conflict: Selected Readings,* ed. John M. Thomas and Warren G. Bennis (Harmondsworth, England: Penguin Books, 1972), p. 184.

90. Mil'ner, *Organizatsionnye struktury upravleniia proizvodstvom,* p. 9.

91. Ibid., p. 7.

92. Arbatov, "Organizational Design for Large-Scale Production-Economic Complexes and for the Management of Them," p. 24.

93. For a detailed discussion of these experiments see Mil'ner, *Organizatsionnye struktury upravleniia proizvodstvom.*

94. Ibid., pp. 108-11; Arbatov, "Organizational Design," p. 24.

95. *Sovershenstvovanie mekhanizma khoziaistvovaniia v usloviiakh razvitogo sotsializma* (Moscow: Ekonomica, 1975), pp. 168-70; D. M. Gvishiani, ed., *Voprosy teorii i praktiki upravleniia i organizatsii nauki* (Moscow, 1975), pp. 14-15.

96. N. G. Kalinin, ed., *Organizatsiia upravleniia v sisteme ministerstva* (Moscow, 1974), pp. 15, 87-88, 302-03.

97. Joseph W. McGuire, ed., *Contemporary Management: Issues and Viewpoints,* p. 146. See also the collection of essays on organizational design and development in James D. Thompson, ed., *Approaches to Organizational Design* (Pittsburgh: University of Pittsburgh Press, 1966).

98. Bulgarian writers on administration, like Marko Markov and Nikola Stefanov, have also expressed interest in the matrix model of organizations.

99. Mil'ner, *Organizatsionnye struktury upravleniia proizvodstvom,* p. 108.

100. See Paul Cocks, "Administrative Rationality, Political Change and the Role of the Party," paper presented at the AAASS Conference on "CPSU Adaptation," Wentworth-by-the-Sea, New Hampshire, May 31-June 1, 1974.

101. See M. M. Kreisberg, *S Sh A: Systemnyi podkhod v upravlenii i pratika promyshlennykh korporatsii* (Moscow: Nauka, 1974), pp. 208-10.

102. See R. Rafailovich, "Podgotovka kadrov novogo tipa kak uslovie realizatsii vozmozhnostei nauchno-tekhnicheskoi revoliutsii (na materialakh PNR)," in *Nauchno-tekhnicheskaia revoliutsiia i preimushchestva sotsializma* (Moscow: Mysl', 1975), pp. 187-204; V. G. Afanasyev, *Nauchno-tekhnicheskaia revoliutsiia, upravlenie, obrazovanie* (Moscow: Politizdat, 1972).

103. L. Rozsa, "Not Managers," *Nepszabadsag,* March 19, 1972, in RFE, *Hungarian Press Survey,* no. 2197 (April 14, 1972).

104. Jowitt, "An Organizational Approach to the Study of Political Culture in Marxist-Leninist Systems," p. 1174.

105. Croan, "Elites, Leadership, and Systemic Change," pp. 26-31.

106. Afansyev, *The Scientific Management of Society,* p. 146.

107. See Donald V. Schwartz, "Recent Soviet Adaptations of Systems Theory to Administrative Theory," *Journal of Comparative Administration* 5, no. 2 (August 1973): 233-64.

108. Rozsa, "Not Managers," pp. 3-4.

109. Afanasyev, *The Scientific Management of Society,* p. 148.

110. See B. D. Parygin, "Rukovodstvo i liderstvo," in *Rukovodstvo i liderstvo (opyt sotsial'no-psikhologicheskogo issledovaniia): Sbornik nauchnykh trudov,* ed. B. D. Parygin (Leningrad: Leningradskii Gosudarstvennyi Pedagogicheskii Institutimeni A. I. Gertsena, 1973), pp. 5-12.

111. Jowitt, "An Organizational Approach to Political Culture in Marxist-Leninist Systems," p. 1176. See also the excellent discussion by Richard Lowenthal, "On 'Established' Communist Party Regimes," *Studies in Comparative Communism* 7, no. 4 (Winter 1974): 335-58.

112. Gvishiani, *Organization and Management,* p. 441.

113. *Pravda,* June 13, 1970.

114. Cited in Harry Trend, "Some Aspects of Current Economic Policies in Rumania," RFE, *Rumanian Situation Report*, no. 6 (March 13, 1970): 68.

115. *Scinteia,* February 13, 1971, cited in Robert R. King, "The Party and the Implications of Technology," RFE, *Rumania Background Report,* no. 110 (March 22, 1971): 17.

116. See Nicholas Hunter, "Training Managers in East Europe," *International Management*, February 1971.

117. R. R. Papaian, "Podgotovka i povyshenie kvalifikatsii kadrov v evropeiskikh sotsialisticheskikh stranakh," in *Kadry upravleniia sotsialisticheskim obshshestvennym proizvodstvom*, ed. G. Kh. Popov and G. A. Dzhavadov (Moscow: Izdatel'stvo Moskovskogo Universiteta, 1974), p. 198.

118. Ibid., p. 192.

119. Papaian, "Podgotovka i povyshenie kvalifikatsii kadrov," p. 197. See the article by Ivan Valov, vice rector of the academy, in *Partien Zhivot*, no. 4 (1974): 22-26, discussed in RFE, *Bulgarian Situation Report*, no. 10 (April 10, 1974).

120. See the RFE, *Rumanian Situation Report*, no. 7 (February 22, 1971) and no. 38 (October 12, 1971).

121. See "Modernization of Management and Administration: A Progress Report," in RFE, *Polish Situation Report*, no. 20 (July 11, 1975): 10.

122. See A. M. Korolev, ed., *Opyt i metodika perepodgotovki partiinykh i sovetskikh kadrov* (Moscow: Mysl', 1975).

123. Gyula Berci, "Managerial Training: Present and Future Reviewed," *Figyelo*, October 2, 1974, translation in JPRS 63448 (November 15, 1974): 10-16.

124. Rodionov, *Opyt i metodika perepodgotovki partiinykh i sovetskikh kadrov*, p. 22.

125. *Pravda,* April 14, 1970.

126. *Nepszabadsag,* March 19, 1972, in RFE, *Hungarian Press Survey,* no. 2197 (April 14, 1972): 3.

127. Fedor Burlatsky, "Hopes and Illusions: The Scientific-Technological Revolution and Management," *Novy mir*, no. 7 (1972).

128. V. Shcherbitskii, "Partiinye organizatsii i sovershenstvovanie upravleniia ekonomikoi," *Kommunist*, no. 6 (1973): 33.

129. Papaian, "Podgotovka i povyshenie kvalifikatsii kadrov," pp. 204-05.

130. V. Lisitsyn, "The Problems of Management and the Plan," *Trud*, April 24, 1973.

131. *Sotsialisticheskii trud,* no. 10 (1972): 27. See also Gvishiani's comments at the conference in ibid, pp. 32-33.

132. Berci, "Managerial Training: Present and Future Reviewed," p. 13.

133. Nikola Trendafilov, "The Dialectics of the New Society," *World Marxist Review* (March 1973): 39.

134. L. Rautu, "The Process of Creating a Multilaterally Developed Socialist Society in Rumania," *Era Socialista*, no. 22 (November 1973), in RFE, *Rumanian Press Survey*, no. 971 (March 15, 1974): 4.

135. Adam Wirth, professor at the Higher Political School under the HSWP Central Committee, in *World Marxist Review* (February 1973): 56.

136. See William F. Robinson, "The Unexpected Revolution," in RFE, *Hungarian Background Report*, no. 2 (March 8, 1972): 5-6.

137. J. Pajestka, "A Discussion on Modernizing Economic Management," *Nowe Drogi*, December 1971, translation in RFE, *Polish Press Survey*, no. 2353 (February 2, 1972): 4.

138. See Grigory Glezerman, "Contradictions under Socialism," *World Marxist Review* 15, no. 3 (March 1972): 110, 112; R. Ronai and S. Karpati, "Basis and Superstructure in the Building of Full Socialism," ibid. 17, no. 1 (January 1974): 54-56.

139. Trendafilov, "The Dialectics of the New Society," p. 43.

140. Grigory Glezerman, *Socialist Society: Scientific Principles of Development* (Moscow: Progress Publishers, 1971), p. 270; Wolfgang Eichorn and Gottfried Stieler, "Source of Progress," *World Marxist Review* (March 1973): 33-38.

141. See Gh. G. Marin, "Instruments to Overcome Economic Contradictions," in *Era Socialista*, no. 1 (1973), in RFE, *Rumanian Press Survey*, no. 941 (February 7, 1973): 2.

142. See his article, "Political Innovation in Rumania," *Survey* 20, no. 4 (Autumn 1974): 132-51. See also *World Marxist Review* (March 1974): 30-31.

143. In Poland the 1974-75 administrative reforms have made the local party secretaries also the chairmen of their respective people's councils. In a move to strengthen central party control over the economy, the Central Committee Secretariat in mid-1971 decided to assume direct patronage over party branches in 163 large enterprises that account for one-fourth of the total industrial work force; *World Marxist Review* 16, no. 9 (September 1973): 52. Similarly, in Bulgaria Central Committee organizers have been appointed to oversee directly the most important state economic concerns. The rights of party organizations in these industrial structures to supervise administrative activity also have been extended; see RFE, *Bulgaria Background Report*, no. 3 (January 22, 1970): 3; "Efforts to Speed Up Modernization Intensified," RFE, *Bulgarian Situation Report*, no. 22 (July 30, 1975). In the USSR, too, primary party organizations in ministries and state committees as well as in research and development institutions have expanded their supervisory activities over management since 1971 in the areas of new technology and administrative modernization; see V. K. Lutsenko, "Deiatel'nost' partii v oblasti sovershenstvovaniia NOT na sovremennom etape," *Voprosy istorii KPSS*, no. 7 (1974): 27-39; Shcherbitskii, "Partiinye organizatsii i sovershenstvovanie upravleniia ekonomikoi"; V. Iagodkin, "Partiinaia zhizn' v nauchnykh kollektivakh," *Kommunist*, no. 11 (1972); V. Staritskii and V. Karetnikov, "Rekonstruktsiia promyshlennykh predpriiatii v usloviiakh nauchno-tekhnicheskoi revoliutsii," ibid., no. 2 (1973): 64-75; "Rukovodstvo ekonomikoi–delo partiinoe, delo politicheskoe," ibid., no. 12 (1975).

144. V. Afanasyev, "Further Improvement of the Management of Soviet Society," *Social Sciences* 3, no. 9 (1972): 79. See also his "V. I. Lenin o nauchnom upravlenii obshchestvom," *Voprosy filosofii*, no. 1 (1974): 24.

145. This is Croan's formulation, as expressed in his "Elites, Leadership, and Systemic Change," p. 20.

146. See the report by Szydlak to the Politburo on July 10, 1974, "From Theory to Practice–Improving the System of Planning and Management," *Zycie Gospodarcze*, July 28, 1974, in RFE, *Polish Press Survey*, no. 2455 (September 23, 1974): 4-12.

147. See *Upravlenie sotsialisticheskim proizvodstvom: Voprosy teorii i praktiki* (Moscow: Ekonomika, 1974), p. 598.

148. Glezerman, *Socialist Society: Scientific Principles of Development*, p. 57.

149. N. P. Fedorenko, "Metodologicheskie problemy sovershenstvovaniia upravleniia ekonomikoi," *Voprosy filosofii*, no. 9 (1974): 14.

150. It is interesting that at the December 1973 plenum of the CPSU Central Committee, Brezhnev particularly emphasized the need to introduce more boldly and rapidly experience gained from various experiments using modern methods. See Lutsenko, "Deiatel'nost' partii b oblasti sovershenstvovaniia NOT na sovremennom etape," p. 36.

4

INCLUSION AND
MOBILIZATION IN
EUROPEAN LENINIST REGIMES

Kenneth Jowitt

DEVELOPMENTAL TASKS, STRATEGIC POLITICAL
UNCERTAINTIES, AND REGIME STRUCTURES

In the history of Leninist regimes* one can identify at least three elite-designated core tasks and stages of development. The first is transformation of the old society; the second is consolidation of the revolutionary regime; the third and current task is inclusion: attempts by the party elite to expand the internal boundaries of the regime's political, productive, and decision-making systems, to integrate itself with the nonofficial (non-*apparatchik*) sectors of society rather than insulate itself from them.

Kenneth Jowitt, "Inclusion and Mobilization in European Leninist Regimes," *World Politics* 28, no. 1 (October 1975): 69-96. © 1975 by Princeton University Press. Reprinted with permission.

I wish to thank Reinhard Bendix, Gregory Grossman, Zygmunt Bauman, Kathy Humphries, and Rebecca Matthews Jowitt for their interest and criticisms.

*The term "Leninist regimes" will be used throughout in a generic sense. Distinctions of a developmental nature will be referred to in terms of specific syndromes of tasks, uncertainties, and structures (transformation, consolidation, and inclusion regimes). Thus, in reference to the period of Stalin's rule in the Soviet Union, the term Leninist regimes does *not* reflect a lack of appreciation of the differences between 1935 and 1925, or between Stalin and Lenin as individual leaders. The term Leninist refers to the existence of an organization-ideology which, although changing in significant respects over time, remains identifiable as a particular type of charismatic institution.

Typically, designation of a core task has two major, related consequences. It specifies a particular locus of political uncertainty and generates a particular regime structure, one that simultaneously reflects the task at hand and the corresponding locus of uncertainty. To expand and illustrate these points: The transformation task refers to a Leninist party's attempt to decisively eliminate the political and military capacity of opposition elites. The defining characteristic of the social and political environment during this period is turbulence. The existence of a highly turbulent environment has very specific political implications for regime organization, power distribution, and consequently, regime-society relations. In such circumstances, Leninist parties are faced with a set of conflicting imperatives within the party and in the party's relations to society. Within the party the imperatives of obedience to central directives and the need for discretion "in the field" compete with one another, while in party-society relations the imperatives of gaining sociopolitical support and controlling that support partially conflict with one another. In short, acting on the task of transformation engenders social and organizational turbulence, which in turn makes it difficult for the regime simply to command support from social groups and obedience at all levels of the party. The need to bargain with "heroic" local cadres and to persuade social strata who are essential in the battle against the class enemy produces a particular type of party organization and regime-society relationship.

With the achievement of a political and military breakthrough, the self-perceived task of a Leninist regime changes from transformation to consolidation. The party's efforts shift to creating the nucleus of a new political system and community in a setting that is designed to prevent existing, "unreconstruc—ted" social and cultural forces from exercising any uncontrolled and undesired influence over the development and definition of the institutions, values, and practices favored by the party. With the adoption of the consolidation task, the locus of political uncertainty shifts. Instead of searching for "risk-taking cadres" and demonstrating a capacity to attract political support, the party elite (or a section thereof) attempts to maximize its insulation from society, to secure the undivided commitment of its cadres by reducing the reference groups for those cadres to one—the party as represented by its leadership. The task of consolidation and the corresponding uncertainty surrounding the issue of cadre insulation bias the distribution of power and the definition of the regime in favor of the individuals and institutions most likely to depersonalize the party's contacts with the society and to maximize obedience within the party.

Just as success with the task of transformation redefines the regime's internal and external environments by creating a less turbulent situation, thereby depriving local cadres and social groups of control over a major locus of uncertainty and power,* so success with consolidation—creation of an articulate

---

*There is no longer a need for the regime to depend on "heroic" local cadres to secure the political support of local social constituencies against the "class enemy";

socialist intelligentsia, elaboration of an industrial base, and the development of military power—has made it increasingly difficult to sustain the rationale for and format of a consolidation regime.

With the achievement of consolidation, these regimes complemented the political-military destruction of traditional elites with the social and economic destruction of traditional institutions; they achieved a decisive breakthrough.* The locus of political uncertainty has shifted once again, reflecting a change in the *sociopolitical* environment and a corresponding attempt by certain components of the party leadership to redefine the regime's core task in light of this change and the party's concern with self-maintenance. The locus of political uncertainty has shifted from protecting the precarious values of a newly established revolutionary regime with charismatic qualities to insuring that the social products of its developmental efforts identify themselves in terms that are consistent with the party's ideological self-image and organizational definition. Uncertainty involves the possibility that the increasing social heterogeneity of socialist society, in the form of an increasing range of articulate social audiences,† might express itself as an articulated plurality of political-ideological definitions.[1] Inclusion is an attempt to prevent that plurality by revising the regime's format and its relationship to society from insulation to integration. The argument to be presented here attempts to explicate this situation, the defining situation for the majority of Leninist regimes. It is hoped that the perspective expressed in the preceding pages will enable students of these regimes to get beyond those analyses that (1) posit a unilinear deradicalization or deutopianization of Leninist regimes,[2] (2) effectively reduce social change in its broadest sense to the proposition that socioeconomic change determines political change,[3] or (3) juxtapose, in a Manichean variant, a series of social social changes that are described as progressive and political responses that, if not "adaptive" in the sense of becoming more liberal, are seen as resulting in "arrested" development.[4]

---

neither is there any longer the disruption that prevented the extension of central party control.

*Revolutionary regimes differ from reformist regimes in their attempts to attack tradition comprehensively at two levels. Reformist regimes are more likely to limit their efforts at social change to changes in elite structure. Revolutionary regimes attack traditional institutions as well as traditional elites. Collectivization in contrast to land reform is a striking instance.

†I would like to suggest the notion of "articulate audiences" in place of both "masses" and "publics" to describe a diverse set of social groups in contemporary Leninist regimes. Unlike masses, these groups are politically knowledgeable and oriented. Consequently they are capable of offering the regime support of a more differentiated and sophisticated character. Unlike publics—i.e., citizens who voluntarily organize themselves around major political issues—these "audiences" are restricted in their political behavior to those roles and actions prescribed by the regime itself.

INCLUSION

The task of inclusion refers to a ruling Leninist party's perception that the major condition for its continued development as an institutionalized charismatic organization is to integrate itself with, rather than insulate itself from, its host society. More specifically, it involves a Leninist party's attempt to devise a new role and set of institutions that allow for a more effective mediation between the status of party *apparatchik* and formal party membership or non-party status. It refers above all to an attempt to expand membership in the regime in a way that allows politically coopted social elites or activists to maintain their social-occupational identity,[5] and the party apparatus to maintain its institutionalized charismatic status. The process of expanding membership has typically included expanding the boundaries of the regime's productive and decision-making systems along with the internal boundaries of the political system itself. The most dramatic instance of the latter phenomenon has been the admission of a wide range of social elites to consultative status in sociopolitical activities.[6] Stable expansion of a political system's membership base indicates a political elite's recognition of the need to respond to previously excluded, distrusted sectors of the population. Such expansion often entails the development of leadership capacities within the regime, which utilize relational skills of persuasion and manipulation in contrast to command capacities largely based on coercion; the latter typify regimes maximizing their insulation from (rather than integration with) their host society.

In the case of Leninist regimes, expansion of the decision-making system has taken the form of placing relatively greater emphasis on the weight of empirical premises (in contrast to ideological assumptions). Such an emphasis creates a more critical, less dogmatic orientation toward problem definition and problem resolution, in part through a greater appreciation of discussion, consultation, and experimentation. Finally, expansion of the productive system in these societies has resulted in placing greater emphasis on merit and procedural criteria. This emphasis indicates a heightened appreciation of formal rationalization as an efficiency- and resource-expanding process. Jointly, these boundary revisions of the political, productive, and decision-making systems reflect a perceived need to gauge and control the complexities of society more accurately, and a basic if not thoroughgoing confidence that past developmental efforts (social, political, and economic) have succeeded in creating a set of strategic groups that can serve as the social basis of a Leninist political community.

However, the adoption of inclusion as a defining or core task presents problems as well as opportunities for a Leninist regime. The opportunities consist primarily of an enhanced ability to control the potential political implications of an emerging set of articulate social audiences. The problems stem from the regime's intention to enhance its legitimacy without sacrificing the charismatic exclusiveness of its official (*apparatchik*) component. Insofar as inclusion becomes a defining task orientation, it adds complexity to the social system. Complexity increases not simply through the arithmetical introduction of more elements (expert consultants), but also through the introduction of elements more resistant to elite fiat and arbitrariness (characteristics of routinized charismatic organizations as well as charismatic leaders). For example, *to the extent* that the party's leadership is committed to a more rational decision-making process, it is constrained by the operation of premises that are empirically grounded. Also, if the party leadership is committed to eliciting rather than commanding the support of different social audiences, it is again constrained— this time by the aspirations and concerns of those elements in the population whose support it desires. In addition, if the party leadership tries to increase productivity by introducing and strengthening formal rules, it is somewhat constrained by their operation.

Throughout the 1950s and early 1960s consolidation was the predominant task orientation for the majority of Leninist regimes. However, beginning in the late 1950s and early 1960s, there is more than adequate evidence that attempts were made within several parties to either modify or redefine the priority of consolidation in favor of inclusion. Modification occurred in North Korea and Bulgaria in 1965-66. Redefinition of task and regime structure occurred in the Soviet Union in the period 1959-61, in Romania between 1965 and 1968, in Yugoslavia and Hungary in 1966, and in Czechoslovakia in 1967-68. There is a crucial difference between the modification and the redefinition of a regime's character. One must distinguish between the introduction of inclusive policies and the creation of a regime structure based on the task of inclusion. When the dominant faction of a party makes the authoritative ideological statement that the issue of "capitalist restoration" has been decisively resolved, and when social reality (both domestically and internationally) is no longer conceived, or related to, in dichotomic terms, it is appropriate to conclude that a change in regime character has occurred. The paradigmatic case is Khrushchev's Soviet regime. The ideological formulations of "state" and "party of the whole people" were announced at party congresses and signified a new structural relationship between regime and society—one of reconciliation versus antagonism, integration versus insulation. Recognition of the third world and the *obshchestvenniki*,* as well as of the intrinsic value of science, signified dramatic

---

Obshchestvenniki are party members who, while active as consultants and even as officeholders in the party organization, are not full-time party apparatus workers. I have attempted to analyze their significance in terms of national development in my paper, "State and National Development in Contemporary Eastern Europe" (unpublished).

and character-defining breaks with the ideological-philosophical-organizational definitions *and* practices of the consolidation period.

However, regardless of whether the outcome was modification or redefinition of regime format, for over a decade the major feature of most Leninist regimes has been the conflict between and accommodation of individuals, policies, ideological formulations, and institutional definitions representing either an inclusion or a consolidation bias. This conflict-accommodation pattern is similar in many ways to the more general conflict-accommodation pattern one discovers between tradition and modernity. Consolidation regimes are obviously not identical with feudal, patrimonial, or tribal sociopolitical orders; however, in some respects they are comparable. It may even be suggested that the congruence between several of the defining premises of a consolidation regime and the defining premises of a traditional peasant society has been one stabilizing factor in many societies that have had consolidation regimes.[7] In examining the conflict-accommodation pattern of consolidation and inclusion policies, institutions, and norms, we are studying a variant of the more general tradition-modernity encounter.

Regime Structures

In ideal-typical terms, regime structure may be viewed as a set of political-organizational adaptations that emerge in response to specific developmental tasks and strategic political uncertainties (both external and internal). Any particular regime structure will reflect the pattern of conflict and accommodation (within a given ruling coalition) among factions with different task priorities.

Regime structure can be analyzed in terms of the organizational, ideological, and policy correlates of a given core task such as consolidation and inclusion. Specification of these correlates should enhance our grasp of the major political uncertainties, conflicting goals, and patterns of conflict and accommodation that characterize contemporary Leninist regimes.

Profile of an Inclusion Regime

To the extent that a Leninist regime shifts its core task from consolidation to inclusion, a series of adaptive changes tend to occur. To begin with, the party develops its corporate character and leading role in opposition to those institutions whose distinctive competence is violence—the security and/or military forces. This institutional shift in influence toward the party as a corporate organization is accompanied by a shift toward oligarchy, away from a neopatrimonial type of leadership. Within the party, the political manager becomes the defining political actor in place of the political bureaucrat. There is a marked change in the social base of the regime as well, with the more professional, skilled, and articulate strata increasing their status vis-a-vis the "new class" of peasant-worker recruited officials. Power is expanded within the regime to allow for a more institutionalized mode of consultation with a variety of social groups. It must be stressed that consultation also occurred during the consolidation period, and consolidation regimes, like inclusion regimes, depend(ed) on social support for their existence (despite a tendency in the literature to assert "society's" nonexistence prior to Stalin's death). However, the mode of consultation in the inclusion regime is distinguished by the regime's willingness and capacity to allow members of particular socio-occupational strata to complement rather than exchange their social and occupational identities with political-organizational responsibilities. For understandable reasons, regimes oriented not to inclusion but rather to consolidation typically define the relationship between socio-occupational status and political-organizational status in mutually exclusive terms. Society and regime are related in a strict hierarchy. A change in status in such a situation does not consist primarily of a change in role, but of a change in identity—a change from nonofficial to official or *apparatchik* status. A structure of this order is predictable in a regime that equates effective political penetration with maximum organizational insulation from social claims. Such a regime will emphasize assimilation to a narrowly defined and exclusive political-ideological status—the quintessential expression of which is the member of the *apparat*.

The radical innovation of inclusion regimes is that, while cooptation remains the sole means of exercising political influence, it is no longer primarily based on the categoric separation and opposition of socio-occupational identity and political-organizational responsibilities in the party.

Consistent with this change, when inclusion becomes the core task, manipulation rather than domination becomes the defining relationship between regime and society. Policy making is expressed more in terms of initiative based on critical scrutiny of problems and less in terms of an indiscriminate emulation of external references and/or dogmatic adherence to past policies. The legislative and representative organs of the state are ideologically and institutionally upgraded. This point warrants some elaboration. The proverbial wisdom is that during the consolidation stage (during Stalin's rule) the state was overwhelmingly powerful. In fact, the security forces were overwhelmingly powerful and in most cases subordinated all other state functions and institutions. During the consolidation period, the state, as a set of institutions and symbols representing the political unity of the whole society, is afforded at best an ambivalent and more often a distinctly inferior status to those state institutions (such as the ministry of interior) whose distinctive competence is vigilance rather than representation.

Inclusion regimes typically upgrade their ideological evaluation of the nation-state. This process is marked by ambivalence and selectivity and differs significantly from the way consolidation regimes deal with the nation-state.

Finally, Leninist inclusion regimes define their international position in terms of a more extensive set of complementary membership groupings. At both the national and international level, inclusion regimes typically adopt a more differentiated and less exclusive view of their political identity.

All of these revisions in regime definition involve a shift away from command, arbitrary, and dogmatic modes of action and organization, and a move toward leadership, procedural, and empirically oriented modes.

The movement to redevelop the integrity of the party as *the* leading political institution may be viewed as an attempt to assert the primacy of an organization whose distinctive competence is sociopolitical rather than coercive, an organization with manipulative and persuasive capacities as well as coercive ones, an organization with a certain claim to social representativeness as well as political and ideological exclusiveness.

The restructuring of the party's leadership from a neopatrimonial to a more oligarchic pattern has typically included a stress on performance, merit criteria, a more rational division of labor at various levels in the party, stricter adherence to scheduled meetings, the regular publication of their results, and in some instances the elaboration of statutes which at least formally guarantee the right of individual dissent within the party.[8] The critical or empirical component of inclusion is evident in the emphasis on collective leadership, which ideally allows for more open inquiry, more diverse sources of information, and more discussion within the leadership echelon. The stress on merit criteria is a development with both procedural and empirical dimensions, given the emphasis on impersonal standards of recruitment and promotion as well as on achievement and observed performance. A measure such as the promulgation of party statutes formally guaranteeing the right of individual dissent within the party simultaneously embodies procedural, empirical, and leadership dimensions, given its (at least formal) specification of legal-rational rights, its support of more open discussion, and its indirect contribution to interaction based more on considerations of reciprocity and less on fear.

The appearance of a new type of cadre, the political manager, is of particular importance. Let us clarify what this cadre's defining features are. We are not suggesting that economic cadres become dominant in Leninist regimes stressing the inclusion task. We should also not confuse the political manager with the technocrat. This confusion is perhaps one of the greatest errors in the literature; namely, the identification of the technocrat as the alternative to the apparatchik.

The managerial political cadre is distinguished by two competences: first, his relatively high level of technical expertise and/or experience and second, and perhaps more important, his manipulative skills in sociopolitical settings. Unlike the technocrat and the apparatchik, the manager is a political actor sensitive to the social-personal dimensions of a situation and possessed of a capacity and

and willingness to manipulate the social and personal dimensions of a situation to achieve his goals. It is this competence, a leadership competence, that distinguishes the political manager from both the command-oriented *apparatchik* and the rule-oriented technocrat. For reasons that will become evident when we discuss the policy-making process in an inclusion regime, political managers tend to complement their leadership orientation with a reliance on empirical and procedural orientations.

The increasing recognition given to the professional skilled stratum in societies ruled by Leninist regimes is a telling indication of the shift from a consolidation to an inclusion orientation. The party's ideological upgrading of the "intelligentsia," the differentiation of wages, and the recruitment patterns of the various parties suggest that for varying periods of time and to different degrees Leninist regimes during the 1960s began to orient themselves to the social products of their own mobilization-industrialization efforts. The new class, with its dogmatic, arbitrary, and command orientation, is no longer the sole sociopolitical stratum that can represent itself as the legitimating base of Leninist regimes. In contrast to the new class, the new articulate, professional-skilled stratum is distinguished by its higher level of training and expertise, its preference for revised authority relations, and its various recognition aspirations. Its preferences seem to lean in the direction of a more rule-ordered system (not necessarily democratic), both as a condition for effective performance and as a guarantee of its status as the indigenous product of the regime's efforts at social-political transformation.

The expansion of power is reflected in a Leninist party's willingness to approach the question of power in a more complex fashion, to differentiate types of power, and to allow different elements in a society to exercise different forms of power. Specifically, the expansion of power refers to the party's willingness to permit a significant degree of functional autonomy or expert autonomy in the performance of specific tasks. This tendency, one that has been noted by a number of analysts, is marked by leadership rather than command orientations inasmuch as it involves the party's recognition, acceptance, and manipulation of skilled strata in the pursuit of regime goals. Its empirical component manifests itself as a greater appreciation of the need for debate and multiple types of information. Finally, the expansion of power contributes to the place of procedural norms in the social system insofar as the expansion of power reflects the party's acceptance of distinct and differentiated areas of competence as well as the scheduled and coordinated discussion of specific topics.

Perhaps the most significant difference between consolidation and inclusion regimes involves the character of authority relations. The shift from a regime-society relationship based on domination to one emphasizing manipulation is a shift from a sociopolitical order based almost exclusively on command and violence to one in which leadership skills of manipulation and persuasion are more significant than in the past. Manipulation, however, is not simply a more economical and clever mode of domination. It allows for a certain measure of recognition and influence to aspiring social strata that have felt relatively deprived of status, influence, and economic well-being. To date, the discussion of manipulation in Leninist regimes has worked with the established sociological paired concept of real and felt influence.[9]

We should elaborate this distinction to suggest that there are at least two forms of real influence and two types of felt influence. Real influence may be exerted over routine and over defining issues, the latter being those that have a direct impact on the overall character of a social-political system.* Felt influence or manipulated participation also may be of two types, one that is characteristic of (but not limited to) consolidation regimes, the other of inclusion regimes. Consolidation regimes engage almost exclusively in symbolic manipulation; the most striking instance is the manipulation of nationalist symbols. Symbolic manipulation indicates the party's perceived need to address imbalances between the regime and society in a context of continuing political distrust and avoidance of commitments to that society. Organizational manipulation, that is, the revitalization of national front organizations, the upgrading of trade unions, and the emergence of peasant unions, is quite a different kind of manipulation. Organizational manipulation not only indicates the regime's recognition of an imbalance, but also allows social elements (professionals) real involvement in routine decisions.

In the policy sphere, regimes oriented to inclusion tend to stress policy initiation more than emulation as the basic premise of policy making. The critical and empirical components of initiation in contrast to emulation as a policy stance are too clear to warrant extended comment here. Consolidation regimes are "traditional" in that major policies tend to become ritualized rather than continually scrutinized—whether the commitment is to machine tractor stations, a reified dichotomic world view, or a dogmatic conception of the party's "leading role."

Policy initiation in turn places a premium on leadership rather than command skills, and on procedural norms rather than political arbitrariness. Policy initiation assumes a degree of discretion by decision-making units. Discretion is an integral component of a decision-making style based on the critical-empirical examination of a problem. However, command orientations emphasize standardization of environments rather than their differentiation. Command orientations

---

*Influence over routine issues must not be confused with influence over insignificant issues. Routine issues may well be significant; they differ from defining issues in the order of significance. The resolution of defining issues has a direct impact on the basic character of the major institutions, values, and/or behaviors that provide a social system with its distinct identity.

also typically emphasize the authority of superior ranks rather than the importance of a particular policy situation or environment. A leadership (rather than command) structure is thus a key element in ensuring the effective operation of a policy-making process marked by policy initiation.

If one views the nation as a decision- or policy-making unit, it is not accidental that independent Communist regimes vociferously demand that international relations within the bloc be based on mutual, reciprocal adjustment among leaders, not on obedience to the commands of one set of leaders—the Soviets. The rationale behind this argument is at least partially that each leader is most familiar with his own policy environment and must have discretion in order to base policy on an adequate (empirical) relationship to that environment. Command structures focus attention on superiors; leadership structures focus attention on problems as well.

Policy initiation also depends on the upgrading of scheduled operations, of formal procedures over political arbitrariness. Formal procedures (contracts) are designed to insure the effective coordination of distinct policy-making units and to minimize any interference with the regular and differentiated analysis of problems and solutions in particular policy-making environments.

All Leninist regimes attending to the task of inclusion through necessity and/or choice tend to upgrade state institutions and symbols that emphasize the representative and unifying quality of the state. The reverse of this is that such regimes typically downgrade those institutions (that is, the ministry of interior) and slogans ("vigilance") that during the consolidation period dominate and subvert all other state institutions and functions.

The state as a set of representative institutions and symbols is downgraded during the consolidation period precisely because the major concern of the party during such a period is to deny the "whole people" representation and legitimation. The nation is precisely what has to be "reconstructed" and denied influence in the process of creating new socialist elites, institutions, and culture during the period of consolidation. The state at this time is upgraded only in one sense: Its monopoly of organized violence is secured and enhanced. When Leninist regimes upgrade the state as a set of institutions and symbols emphasizing representative and reconciliatory functions, it is a sign that in their view the process of consolidation (as defined here) has been decisively effected, with the class enemy not only defeated but replaced by a new, more trustworthy set of social strata deserving ideological and organizational recognition. The upgrading of the state in this manner involves both the symbolic and organizational recognition of "society," and is predicated on a greater incidence of leadership rather than command orientations, and of political integration rather than bureaucratic insulation. In turn, the added stress on more regular meetings of parliament, increased periods of debate, and greater specialization of committees is based on procedural and empirical premises.

Finally, to the extent that Leninist regimes orient themselves to the task of inclusion, they are more likely to demonstrate a positive ideological evaluation of the nation-state. This often involves a more sophisticated and critical attitude toward the country's pre-Leninist history and a more flexible political attitude toward sectors of its national consituency, rather than a "for us or against us" posture. Inclusion-oriented regimes are also likely to define themselves internationally in terms of multiple rather than exclusive membership groupings. The tendency of certain Leninist regimes to define their political identity on the basis of their complementary relationships with different membership groups (the third world, Western Europe, the Warsaw Pact, the United States, or the "world socialist system") reflects a major disposition within such regimes to define themselves by consciously and critically appraising the relationship between their goals, resources, and environments. This disposition may legitimately be interpreted as having an empirical rather than dogmatic character. A critical-empirical posture of this order, one based on complementary memberships, may aptly be called universalistic in contrast to the neotraditional and particularistic definition of political identity adhered to by consolidation regimes. The latter define membership in exclusive terms; that is, to be a member of the socialist bloc means not to consider oneself as a third world or "small" nation. It also must be noted that a Leninist regime's expansion of the criteria and premises for deciding on its posture in the international arena has implications in other realms. The adoption of complementary and diverse memberships favors the development of leadership (rather than command) skills within the party elite—skills that enable the regime to recognize and manage multiple international constituencies. Finally, the perceived need to relate to, but differentiate memberships in different settings (that is, all-European, Warsaw Pact) favors the appreciation of procedural norms such as sovereignty as a device for stabilizing a more complex environment.

One can find a fair amount of illustrative material to support the argument that during the 1960s the majority of Leninist regimes began to shift their priorities in the directions suggested here.

Beginning with the removal of Beria, continuing with the condemnation of the neopatrimonial "cult of the personality" and Khrushchev's upgrading of the party as a corporate institution in the late 1950s, and up to the attacks within the Czechoslovak party in 1967 on Novotny's mode of leadership, the reassertion of the party's corporate integrity has been a visible and politically significant development. The greater emphasis on oligarchic leadership (or, in Leninist terms, collective leadership) was closely related to this reassertion of the party's corporate integrity. Oligarchic leadership has been based on a greater specification of intra-elite responsibilities (one instance was the differentiation of the Executive Committee and Presidium in Romania in the period 1965-74), the rationalization of structure (such as occurred during the mid-1960s in East

Germany and Hungary), the stress on scheduled meetings (a characteristic of both the Gierek and Ceausescu regimes), and an upgrading of the party's regional and local units in regimes as diverse as the Soviet and Yugoslav.

The appearance of political managerial cadres can be documented in a number of regimes. Thomas Baylis and Peter C. Ludz have noted this development in East Germany, and Johnson has pointed out the managerial component in the Polish party and its conflict with the apparatchiki.[10] However, along with Ludz and Baylis, Johnson is disposed to label these cadres as technocrats, thereby possibly obscuring their distinctive political skills and their greater sensitivity to social situations and capacity to manipulate them. The higher level of education among central committee members has been noted by a number of analysts.[11] Data on their operating style are harder to come by. We would suggest, however, that during the 1960s a style of leadership exemplified by Ceausescu, Kadar, and most recently Gierek, appeared in Eastern Europe—one that sharply contrasted with that of leaders like Gomulka, Novotny, Gheorghiu-Dej, Chervenkov, and Stalin. In certain respects the "model" for the political managerial cadre is former U.S. Secretary of Defense McNamara. In an article devoted to McNamara, David Halberstam points to a number of attributes that are also characteristic of the new Leninist political managers.[12] They are rationalists, men who are well trained, authoritarian but still appreciative of the need to receive expert information and to structure situations so as to elicit that information and support. They are "win-oriented," not neutral pragmatists or technocrats. They tend to be sober individuals with a penchant toward the puritanical. They contrast with the rather hedonistic apparatchik new class cadre in the way the modern bourgeoisie analyzed by Weber differed from the traditional capitalist.[13] It is a change from the Berias to the Katushevs, the Stoicas to the Winters.

As for the rise in prominence of the professional and skilled strata, a large number of examples can be provided to illustrate this phenomenon. The Czechoslovak Action Program of the late 1960s, with its stress on the intelligentsia, science,[14] and the need for merit-performance norms, provides a clear instance of one regime's ideological recognition of this stratum. The central places accorded to economic managers and skilled individuals in the economic reform the East Germans promulgated in 1963, and in the New Economic Management of the Hungarians in 1968, are additional instances.[15] The recruitment patterns of the Yugoslav, Polish, Hungarian, and Czech parties in the 1960s provide another illustration of the ascendance of this stratum.[16] In Romania the slogan, *omul potrivit la locul potrivit* ("the right man for the right job"), reflects an increased emphasis on technical qualification and a heightened appreciation of the professional strata created by 25 years of mobilization and industrialization.

Perhaps the most instructive example, however, can be found in the Soviet Union, where during the 1960s there was a struggle over the type of propaganda personnel the regime should employ. It seems that around 1965 "concrete proposals were advanced in the press to replace the traditional agitators with more sophisticated 'politinformators'—that is, information specialists capable of influencing knowledgeable mass audiences."[17] Note the characteristics of the "politinformators." They were drawn not from the ranks of workers and peasants but from the ranks of officials, economic managers, scientists, engineers, agronomists; in short the professional stratum. They specialized in differentiated forms of propaganda. Their skills seemed to be aimed at new types of audiences—audiences that were more articulate, educated, urban, and skilled. Their competence appeared to be based on manipulating select audiences with specialized information rather than haranguing mass audiences with symbolic slogans. According to Unger, they had emerged as a countrywide institution by 1967, and they may now number over 2 million.[18]

As with so many other aspects of the change from consolidation to inclusion, the expansion of power was initiated by Khrushchev with his practice of providing organizational formats for the participation of experts in policy discussions. The attention given to trade unions in Hungary,[19] the increased scope of public debates in the Soviet Union,[20] the creation and revitalization of expert organizations exemplified by the conferences of managers and engineers in Romania,[21] the relative differentiation of social-scientific from strictly ideological studies evident in the growth of sociological institutes throughout most of Eastern Europe—all are instances of a tendency that emerged during the 1960s. It was a movement toward less rigid control and more differentiated appreciation of the social system.

We have already pointed out that the question of manipulation is very complex. It could be argued that all modern societies, regardless of political and ideological orientation, are primarily (although not exclusively) based on manipulative rather than command skills. The nation-state, itself the structural expression of modernity in the political realm, is partially based on the capacity to manipulate the allegiance and identification of millions of people. In this respect, the Leninist regimes' manipulation of society in the postconsolidation period can be seen as a variant of modern manipulation, not as a unique phenomenon. The relative shift from regime domination to regime manipulation of society in Leninist regimes depends on at least two developments: (1) the appearance of urban, educated, and articulate strata that can make a legitimate claim to recognition as integral and trustworthy components of society; (2) at least partial acceptance of this claim by managerial party cadres within the respective regimes. As a mode of control, manipulation indicates the emergence of a more "articulate society" in place of a "silent society," and of a political decision by the regime to organize rather than repress the heterogeneity that characterizes its environment, in order to act effectively on its multiple goals.

Examples of organizational (rather than symbolic) manipulation include periodic visits by the first secretaries of the parties to various areas and constituencies. In this respect, Khrushchev, Gierek, Ceausescu, and Kadar are quite different from Stalin, Gomulka, Gheorghiu-Dej, and Rakosi. A second instance can be found in the proliferation of what are termed representative and collective decision-making units, whether they are agricultural unions, workers' committees, upgraded youth organizations, or nationality organizations. It is not necessary to conclude that the recent attention and emphasis placed on these organizations by Leninist regimes signifies that they are now politically significant in their own right. However, this attention and emphasis do tell us something important about the perceptions of the elites in these regimes—about what new strategies they consider necessary and appropriate. In turn, these strategies indirectly provide us with an insight into the types of social (not just economic) uncertainties these elites see themselves to be facing. The attempt to control society "from within," as opposed to commanding it from an insulated position, is a major change that has character-defining implications for these regimes.

The development of sociology as a legitimate academic pursuit is also indicative of the shift from domination to manipulation. It is not surprising that the manipulation of statistics became a substitute for sociology during the period of consolidation; it was a period during which the regime distrusted the existing society and avoided empirical studies that might challenge its dogmatic beliefs about social reality. With the appearance and recognition of what in certain basic respects are new societies, the reappearance of sociology is not accidental. The system-quantity focus of statistics stands in contrast to the community-quality focus of sociology, a greater concern with the dynamics of social situations. The rise of sociology is a strong indication of the shift in regime tasks, and of significant changes in society and in regime-society relations.[22]

We have suggested that policy initiation is an integral aspect of the shift from consolidation to inclusion. The Romanian emphasis on the right to define internal and external policy independently,[23] the statement in the Czechoslovak Action Program that the "Czechoslovak people will formulate its own attitude toward the fundamental problems of world policy," the criticism that in the past the party had "not taken advantage of all opportunities for active work; it did not take the initiative," the distinguishable initiatives of the Bulgarians in the areas of agriculture and of foreign policy in the Balkans during 1965-66,[24] the Hungarian approach to economic organization, and the Yugoslav approach to the questions of nationality, economic organization, and distribution of political power between 1965 and 1970—all are instances of Leninist regimes engaging in policy initiation rather than emulation, and of a differentiation process within the "world socialist system."

The upgrading of certain state institutions has occurred in a number of countries. We saw the strengthening of the State Council in Romania and Ceausescu's assumption of the role of president of the State Council, the suggestion at the Tenth Congress of the Bulgarian party that a State Council replace the Presidium of the National Assembly and have important executive and legislative functions,[25] the upgrading of the personnel attached to state functions in

Romania, and the somewhat greater role played by legislative organs in most East European nations and the Soviet Union. These changes involved: (1) a regime shift from a "Calvinist" oppositional posture toward society to a "Lutheran" reconciliation posture;[26] (2) a move toward the institutionalization of distinct functions and values; and (3) the tentative construction of a "substitute" public arena distinguishable from both the official and private sectors of the social system.*

Concerning the adoption of a more positive attitude toward the nation-state, one must be careful to observe that during the consolidation period Leninist regimes do not simply forget the nation-state. There are the examples of Stalin's manipulation of Great Russian national feeling and the more recent instances of Gheorghiu-Dej's affair with the "Dacians," Moczar's posture in Poland, the Bulgarian and Albanian emphasis on national history, and Kim Il-sung's attention to nationalism. It is not the manipulation of nationalism that distinguishes (Leninist) inclusion regimes from consolidation regimes; it is the type of nationalism. Consolidation regimes typically manipulate national feelings and symbols in an attempt to generate cohesiveness and support for the regime in the absence of any concrete regime commitments to the society. The result is often the mobilization of traditional ethnic nationalism within the society and the somewhat unintentional adoption of chauvinist postures by the regimes. A prime example is the Gheorghiu-Dej regime in Romania.[27] Inclusion regimes tend to adopt a romantic nationalist rather than an integral or chauvinistic posture. The basis for this is the partial but significant reconciliation of "regime" and "society," and the assertion of party sovereignty vis-a-vis the bloc. Thus, while the move toward party sovereignty may not be initially predicated on nationalist premises (as Galia Golan correctly argues in the case of Czechoslovakia),[28] the assertion of party sovereignty, and more generally the commitment to more empirical premises, lead to a reevaluation and redefinition of the party's various membership groups. Inclusion regimes give some evidence of a balanced and integrated appreciation of the nation-state as a unit marked by continuities

---

*The character and role of publics in national development is a neglected topic in the field of comparative studies, particularly in the study of Leninist systems. The notion of publics and public domain has been bypassed, as has the more general and related focus of national development in the study of Leninist systems, in favor of attention to interest groups and the possibility of multiparty democratic systems. Such attention has in part reflected and in part contributed to the tendency to implicity confuse national development in Leninist systems with movement toward liberal political orders.

and decisive changes. There is support for this argument in the position of the Romanians between 1967 and 1970, and in the Action Program's comments on the nation.[29] One may expect similar tendencies under Gierek.

Finally, the argument that inclusion regimes tend to define their international position in terms of multiple rather than exclusive memberships is clearly demonstrated in the case of nonaligned Yugoslavia in contrast to Bulgaria, Romania in contrast to Albania, and Czechoslovakia under Dubcek in contrast to the same country during Novotny's rule.

It is our argument that at various points during the 1960s the majority of Leninist regimes responded to changes—intended as well as unintended—in the composition of society and regime in a manner distinct from the institutional, ideological, and policy syndrome that characterized them during the 1950s. We are not suggesting that social and political developments within the "world socialist system" inevitably led to the complete defeat of each consolidation regime; to the proportional elaboration of empirical, procedural, and leadership premises in the ideological, institutional, and policy domains of all Leninist regimes; to the appearance of 14 regimes of a uniform political-social character; or to the elimination of all major elements of the preceding regimes. Rather, we see the interaction of consolidation and inclusion forces within Leninist regimes and the societies they rule as a conflict-accommodation process leading to the distinctiveness of each regime and society, much as the interaction of modernity and tradition has historically produced distinctive political, social, cultural, and economic amalgams.

We do not define significant change as complete change. To argue that Leninist regimes significantly changed their character during the 1960s, it is not necessary to posit the removal of all Stalinists any more than it is necessary to posit the complete removal of traditional elements in Japan after 1945 in order to call Japan modern. However, in almost all such regimes issues were raised within the party and problems were presented within society that challenged the existing consolidation format and demanded consideration and adoption of more inclusion-oriented postures and responses. It is important to point out that policy did not always match verbal intent (as in Bulgaria), that development along inclusion lines was not proportional in all domains (as in Romania), that certain regimes emphasized certain developments rather than others (as in Hungary), and that the commitment lasted longer in some countries than in others (Hungary in contrast to Bulgaria). However, such observations do not invalidate the argument that the 1960s witnessed major and relatively widespread changes in the ethos, structure, and policy of many Leninist regimes, in the direction of inclusion. This period was distinguished by the partial but significant replacement of consolidation with inclusion features, plus the development of conflict-accommodation patterns between the two.

INCLUSION AND MOBILIZATION

The most striking development in Leninist regimes in the last seven years or so has been the apparent reversal of the inclusion emphasis that emerged with varying degrees of strength in the 1960s. The pattern is not neat—no neater than the initial shift from consolidation to inclusion—but it is discernible and significant, if thus far inadequately interpreted. Developments in East Germany and Bulgaria in 1967-68, the Husak phenomenon in Czechoslovakia, and the reorientation of the Romanian regime between June 1971 and July 1972 were reactions against the ethos, organization, and policies connected with the adoption of inclusion-oriented policies or inclusion as a core task.[30] How can this apparent reversal be explained, and what is its content?

To begin with, the initial move by Leninist regimes to expand the internal boundaries of their political, productive, and decision-making systems was predicated on the combination of success and failure they had experienced during the consolidation period. However, movement toward or adoption of inclusion as a new core task and political posture revealed additional problems of unsuspected magnitude and raised challenges to the Leninist conception of a socialist political community.

The shift by various regimes to the inclusion task and its correlates strikingly revealed the uneven nature of development that had occurred in the period of "socialist construction." This unevenness was by no means limited to the economic field, but was evident in the social and cultural fields as well. For all the talk in the West of a "postmobilization" period, the continuing impact of industrialization on many of these societies was, if anything, increasing in several senses during the 1960s. First, their social heterogeneity was growing, as working classes with an identity of their own began to crystallize.[31] Second, there was a growth in the whole range of problems associated with geographical and occupational mobility. A third problem involves the crystallization in social-psychological if not social-political terms of the professional and skilled strata, and their desire to become the primary support base of the regime—a development that presaged the replacement of the bifurcation of regime and society based on the "new class" with one based on the professional-skilled class.[32] A fourth problem, the cynicism of youth, became more apparent as a result of sociological studies and remains a highly salient issue and a persistent regime concern.[33] The ideological standing of the working class as well as its social and economic status also emerged as character-defining issues.*

---

*This has been quite evident in Czechoslovakia in the discussions that have been going on since 1967, and in Romania since 1970. One can also find it, not unexpectedly, in consolidation-oriented regimes such as North Korea with its ideological notion of "working-classizing" society, and in Albania.

However, the most dramatic questions have been raised about the organizational and ideological definition of the party itself. The rejection of the consolidation model has not spontaneously provided models of organization and development immediately acceptable to Leninist elites.* Directly connected to the perceived challenge to the party's institutionalized charismatic organization is the concern within these parties that social development not be equated with the emergence of a new political frame of reference that would jeopardize the party's status as the political membership unit in the whole social system. At the international level a related concern is that greater attention to the party's domestic constituency must not jeopardize the existence of some form of international Leninist regime community.

The general response to these problems and challenges has been a reassertion of the mobilizational or charismatic character of Leninist regimes. This reassertion may be seen in part as an attempted elaboration of the expressive dimensions of human behavior evident in the stress on moral incentives, ethical standards, and ideological consciousness.[34] Evidence of such a stress and orientation is by no means evidence of its success. However, such efforts do indicate the continued institutional strength of charismatic orientations within these regimes. But it would be a mistake to conclude at this point that we have adequately defined the reaction of Leninist regimes to the inclusion task and process. What we have established is that this reaction has a mobilization thrust. It would be incorrect to assume that the nature and import of this thrust is identical to the mobilization efforts characterizing these regimes in the late 1940s and early 1950s. Yet, lacking a diversified perspective, many analysts appear to have fallen into this trap.

The chief explanation is that Western analysts of development in these regimes have typically adopted something of a Manichean perspective on the relationship between "regime" and "society." Although the power disparity between the two realms (often discussed as though they were real things) is recognized, there is little (if any) evidence of a multifaceted conception of the term "development" and the process to which it refers.

In place of the assertion that during the consolidation period society had no political impact, we have the new assertion that the party is a stumbling block in the way of future "progress." In certain respects the party is just that. However, that observation does not exhaust or clarify the question of development and developmental patterns in Leninist regimes. Aside from the invitation

---

*In this light the concern expressed by several Leninist regimes to develop studies of leadership, to create a "science of leadership" in order to analyze the dimensions of the leadership task in industrial societies, can be seen as an adaptive (how successful is a question of a different order) response to the uncertainty over what is currently meant by the "leading role of the party."

such formulations offer for the confusion of political preference and analysis, they fail to extend our understanding of what is happening in these regimes.[35] To do so, a more "protestant" and analytical appreciation is called for. Such an approach would view the issues of regime development and social development as reciprocal processes and attempt to define the specifics of each set of dynamics and their relationships. Undifferentiated notions of deradicalization, deutopianization, or "postmobilization" obstruct the efforts of the most qualified scholars. For example in an impressive "devil's advocate" article written several years ago, Jeremy Azrael correctly and succinctly points to the reappearance of mobilization efforts in several regimes.[36] The problem with his argument is that it relies on an undifferentiated pairing of the concepts mobilization/ postmobilization, which he is in one respect opposing. Although he correctly criticizes those who posit the linear deradicalization of Leninist regimes, his conceptual formulation limits him to the assertion that continued political mobilization is still apparent. However, the major point concerning the most recent instances of mobilization is that they are not simply or even primarily the same type of mobilization that was manifest in the transformation or consolidation periods. It is crucial to note that the current mobilization efforts are partially constrained and shaped by the prior efforts and continued commitments to expanding the internal boundaries of the regimes' political, productive, and decision-making systems through greater reliance on empirical, procedural, and leadership premises—in short, by the commitment to the inclusion task.

The current emphasis on mobilization within individual Leninist systems has varied. But even the regimes that made the most limited changes in the direction of inclusion, reacted most strongly against it, and could be expected to limit their understanding of mobilization to that suggested by the Stalinist consolidation model—the Bulgarian and North Korean regimes—have not rejected all the changes that were initiated during the last ten years.[37] If this is true for regimes with the greatest commitment to the task of consolidation, it is even more true of regimes such as the East German, Hungarian, and Soviet. As an example, we refer once more to the issue of the "politinformator" in the Soviet Union: Within a year or two there was a "mobilization" reaction against the "politinformator" in favor of the traditional "agitator"; it did not, however, result in the removal of the "politinformator" but did restore the agitator to a high status position.[38] The point is that we are witnessing the appearance of amalgam-regimes based on selective, tentative, and to varying degrees fragile combinations of inclusion and mobilization.

The developmental and leadership orientations of these regimes reflect a suspicion of strategies that reduce leadership to the tasks of aggregation and coordination and neglect mobilization. Given their continued charismatic bias, one that is organizationally supported, they seek to create party activists and not simply citizens. They are in varying degrees committed to the maintenance of an international regime community as well as to their individual nations; to the deliberate preemption of any potential political arena or role not coterminous with the party organization and party membership; and to a philosophical stand stressing becoming over being, and potential over current performance.

The question to be raised about these regimes is, in what sense do they continue to be radical, mobilizational, or utopian; not, are they or aren't they radical, utopian, or mobilizational. The issue can be stated at the most general level in this way: Are inclusion and mobilization stances antithetical, or can they be seen as conflicting imperatives? Units may be defined as antithetical when the integrity of one is dependent on the subordination of the other.[39] A system made up of antithetical units is not viable until one of them is effectively subordinated to the other, or until they are effectively compartmentalized. Units (i.e., decision-making premises, social forces, or ideological tenets) may be viewed as conflicting imperatives when the integrity of one unit is dependent on the oppositional integrity of the other. An excellent example of the latter is provided by Weber in his discussion of the formal and substantive bases of legal-rational justice;[40] another example would be a functioning two-party system.

The answer requires a developmental perspective. To the extent that groups challenging the fundamental structure of the regime were denied access to resources that might have allowed them to translate their social dissent into political opposition, and to the extent that the regime has created a diverse set of strategic social support groups, such a regime can engage in mobilization without terror and can simultaneously allow for the partial expansion of its internal boundaries in the manner we have spoken of. To say, however, that mobilization and inclusion stances can at certain points in a developmental process stand in a complementary relationship to one another is not to deny the continual conflict between the two stances and underlying premises.[41]

For although mobilization may in some respects be seen as a specific form of the inclusion process—ideally, mobilization expands the number of people, the amount of their time, the extent of their awareness, and their involvement with political tasks—mobilization is based on an approach to tasks that differs radically from that associated with inclusion. The inclusion process is one marked by the methodical consideration and management of tasks. Political mobilization is marked by controlled or elite-directed disruption. Disruption of established routines—social, personal, institutional, and psychological—is the defining element of mobilization. Let us be clear: No value judgment is being made to the effect that inclusion is always and necessarily a "better" regime posture, or that mobilization occupies such a position. It may be that the viability of all regimes (as Jefferson and Mao have suggested) is dependent on some mix of the two.

To return to our immediate concern, the mobilization stance adopted by postconsolidation Leninist regimes has several characteristics that in significant fashion do conflict with those associated with the inclusion task and process. The definitional tendency of Leninist regimes—their attempts to control and specify the substantive dimensions of social developments, not merely the framework within which such developments occur—does pose a challenge to the integrity and effectiveness of formal, procedural norms; the mobilization emphasis on potential and rate poses a challenge to any thorough critical and empirical evaluation of issues and policies; and the charismatic stress on unity poses a challenge to the still fragile collegial orientations and relational competences of these elites. Not only do these stances—mobilization and inclusion—conflict with one another; there is no guarantee that Leninist regimes will effectively combine them. However, that their success is problematic and partial cannot automatically be taken as evidence that they "fall short" of modernity. They do indeed fall short of the liberal variant of modernity.[42] Still, one must consider the possibility that all variants of modernity, including the liberal one, are based on conflicting imperatives and are amalgams with distinctive characters.

All modern societies appear to be based on conflicting imperatives of achievement and equality of performance and potential. In contemporary China, Liu and Mao represent these imperatives; in a different context, Madison and Paine represented them in the early history of American development and modernization.[43] In fact, these two examples demonstrate the importance of recognizing and relating the universal attributes of modernization as well as the specific and distinctive historical expressions that provide them with sociopolitical substance. Viewed from this perspective, different modern or modernizing societies can be perceived both in terms of their similarities and distinctiveness, thereby minimizing the danger of raising one historical variant to the position of the model itself.

It then becomes possible to investigate in what respects certain societies are more modern than others, to compare the variety of problems that characterize different types of modern societies, and to differentiate modern societies in terms of the imperatives they stress and those they tend to neglect. In this light the whole issue of convergence becomes more interesting, complex, and demanding. The focus can shift from a zero-sum perspective that defines development simply in terms of "them" becoming more like "us" or vice versa, to a perspective that appreciates and examines the "unprecedented" but bounded variety of modern amalgams that may emerge and persist. We must be prepared for unprecedented types of modern systems—such as might have emerged from Dubcek's Czechoslovakia.

NOTES

1. For one Leninist regime's attempts to move in this direction see Kenneth Jowitt, "Political Innovation in Romania," *Survey* 93 (Autumn 1974): 132-52.

2. See Robert C. Tucker, "The Deradicalization of Marxist Movements," in *The Marxian Revolutionary Idea* (New York: Norton, 1969), pp. 172-215; Richard Lowenthal, "Development vs. Utopia in Communist Policy," in *Change in Communist Systems*, ed. Chalmers Johnson (Stanford: Stanford University Press, 1970), pp. 33-117.

3. See Samuel P. Huntington, "Social and Institutional Dynamics of One-Party Systems," in *Authoritarian Politics in Modern Society*, ed. Samuel P. Huntington and Clement H. Moore (New York: Basic Books, 1970), pp. 3-48.

4. See Zbigniew Brzezinski, "The Soviet Political System: Transformation or Degeneration?" in *Dilemmas of Change in Soviet Politics,* ed. Brzezinski (New York: Columbia University Press, 1969), pp. 1-35; for a restatement of this thesis, see Zvi Gitelman, "Beyond Leninism, Political Development in Eastern Europe," *Newsletter on Comparative Studies of Communism* 5 (May 1972): 18-44.

5. During the consolidation period, Leninist regimes typically attempt to invidiously distinguish regime supporters from nonsupporters and to socially isolate the former. In short, at the social level as well as in the relations between society and policy, insulation is the major characteristic at this stage of development. Social "elites" are forced to forsake their social-occupational identities in order to share in political status and responsibilities. Inclusion regimes are characterized by attempts to integrate social and political roles. On the "insulative" tendencies of consolidation regimes, see Reinhard Bendix, *Work and Authority in Industry* (New York: John Wiley, 1956), pp. 400-34.

6. On this central point, see Peter C. Ludz, *The Changing Party Elite in East Germany* (Cambridge, Mass.: MIT Press, 1972), pp. 40-42, 126, 185; Alfred G. Meyer, *The Soviet Political System* (New York: Random House, 1965).

7. See Kenneth Jowitt, "An Organizational Approach to the Study of Political Culture in Marxist-Leninist Systems," *American Political Science Review* 68 (September 1974): 1171-91.

8. On the extent of rights of dissent in the Romanian party, see *Statutul Partidului Communist Roman* (Bucharest, 1959), p. 40.

9. See, for example, the interesting article by Thomas Baylis, "East Germany: In Quest of Legitimacy," *Problems of Communism* 21 (March-April 1972): 46-56.

10. Ibid.; Peter C. Ludz, "Continuity and Change Since Ulbricht," *Problems of Communism* 21 (March-April 1972): 56-57. Ludz has provided an excellent and succinct analysis of development in East Germany in *The German Democratic Republic from the Sixties to the Seventies* (Cambridge, Mass.: Occasional Papers in International Affairs, Center for International Affairs, Harvard University, November 1970); see also Ross Johnson, "Poland: End of an Era," *Problems of Communism* 19 (January-February 1970): 28-40.

11. See, for example, Robert H. Donaldson, "The 1971 Soviet Central Committee: An Assessment of the New Elite," *World Politics* 24 (April 1972): 382-409.

12. David Halberstam, "The Programming of Robert McNamara," *Harper's Magazine*, vol. 242 (February 1971): 7-21. The term "model" should not suggest that "managerial" cadres in Leninist regimes consciously have McNamara in mind.

13. For Weber's comparison, see *The Protestant Ethic* (New York: Charles Scribner's Sons, 1958), pp. 69-78.

14. Central Committee of the Communist Party of Czechoslovakia, "The Action Program of the Communist Party of Czechoslovakia," in *Winter in Prague*, ed. Robin Alison Remington (Cambridge: MIT Press, 1969), pp. 88-137.

15. For the East German reform, see Baylis, "East Germany," and "Economic Reform as Ideology: East Germany's New Economic System," *Comparative Politics* 3 (January 1971): 211-31. See also the fine article by Bennet Kovrig, "Decompression in Hungary: Phase Two," in *The Changing Face of Communism in Eastern Europe*, ed. Peter A. Toma (Tucson: University of Arizona Press, 1970), pp. 196-202, for an analysis of the upgrading of economic-managerial personnel that attended the Hungarian reforms.

16. On recruitment patterns during the 1960s, see Frank Parkin, "Class Stratification in Socialist Societies," *British Journal of Sociology* 20 (December 1969): 355-75.

17. Aryeh L. Unger, "Politinformator or Agitator: A Decision Blocked," *Problems of Communism* 19 (September-October 1970): 31.

18. Ibid.

19. See Kovrig, "Decompression"; also Barnabas Racz, "Political Changes in Hungary after the Soviet Invasion of Czechoslovakia," *Slavic Review* 29 (December 1970): 633-51; and in particular William F. Robinson, *The Pattern of Reform in Hungary* (New York: Praeger Publishers, 1973), pp. 238-45, 326-42.

20. See the very perceptive piece by Jerry Hough, "The Soviet System: Petrification or Pluralism?" in *Problems of Communism* 21 (March-April 1972): 25-46.

21. For a report on the meeting of economic managers, see *Scinteia*, February 18, 1972.

22. The rapid and visible rise of sociological studies in Leninist political systems is easily documented. For an interesting analysis of this rise, see Alvin Gouldner, *The Coming Crisis of Western Sociology* (New York: Basic Books, 1970), pp. 447-78.

23. For the Romanian position, see "Statement on the Stand of the Rumanian Workers Party Concerning the Problems of the International Communist and Working Class Movement (April 1964)," in William Griffith, *Sino-Soviet Relations, 1964-1965* (Cambridge, Mass.: MIT Press, 1967), pp. 269-97.

24. See Remington, ed., *Winter in Prague*, pp. 133-34. On Bulgaria, see J. F. Brown, *Bulgaria Under Communist Rule* (New York: Praeger Publishers, 1970), pp. 173-301; Michael Costello, "Bulgaria," in *The Communist States in Disarray 1965-1971*, ed. Adam Bromke and Teresa Rakowska-Harmstone (Minneapolis: University of Minnesota Press, 1972), pp. 135-58; Marin V. Pundeff, "Bulgaria under Zhivkov," in Toma, ed., *The Changing Face of Communism*, pp. 89-121.

25. Costello, "Bulgaria," p. 155.

26. For the comparison of Calvinist and Lutheran attitudes toward man on which this image is based, see chap. 4 of Weber (fn. 20), esp. 137-38.

27. For an analysis of a development of this order, see Kenneth Jowitt, *Revolutionary Breakthroughs and National Development* (Berkeley: University of California Press, 1971), pp. 221-24, 280-82.

28. Galia Golan, "The Road to Reform," *Problems of Communism* 20 (May-June 1971): 11-22.

29. See Miron Constantinescu, "Valorificarea critica a mostenirii culturale," in *Luceafarul*, May 6, 1972; Remington, ed., *Winter in Prague*, pp. 131-32.

30. See Baylis, "East Germany"; Costello, "Bulgaria."

31. As Neal Smelser has pointed out in "Mechanisms of Change and Adjustment to Change," in *Industrialization and Society*, ed. Bert F. Hoselitz and Wilbert E. Moore (Paris: UNESCO, Mouton, 1968), pp. 32-57, the process of differentiation places a premium on effective integrative processes. Social disturbances are often the result of discontinuities between differentiation and integration. One may view the reassertion of a mobilization posture in many Leninist regimes as the party's attempt at an integrative response.

32. On this point, see the discussion in Frank Parkin, *Class Inequality and Political Order* (London: MacGibbon and Kee, 1971), pp. 137-86; on the conflict between workers and managers in Hungary. On the increasing status of managers under the NEM, see Kovrig, "Decompression," and Racz, "Political Changes." The place of China in all this is complex. I would suggest that the cultural revolution was both an attack on the "new class" (against a Stalinist consolidation structure) and an attack on a Soviet-type inclusion structure with its emphasis on "political" integration with a new professional class and exclusion of the mass of the population. China offers the student of Leninist regimes conceptions and definitions of both consolidation and inclusion that differ from those of the Soviets.

33. Kovrig has characterized the contemporary social ethos in Hungary as "collective and intergenerational alienation . . . obsessive materialism and a partial breakdown of traditional morality." "Decompression," p. 208. He notes that young people in Hungary "are reluctant to be transformed into obedient factors of production" (p. 21). There is evidence that young people in Bulgaria, Poland (under Gomulka), Romania, Yugoslavia, and the Soviet Union are estranged in many respects from the structure and ethos of party rule.

34. For example, see the Romanian party's statement on November 4, 1971 (*Scinteia*); the emphasis on ideological preparation in Hungary manifested in county-level "educational directorates" (Racz, "Political Changes," p. 638); the thrust of the Chinese cultural revolution; the emphasis in North Korea on the ideological revolution; the emphasis on *consciencia* in Cuba, and recent developments in Yugoslavia.

35. Gitelman, "Beyond Leninism," is a case in point.

36. Jeremy Azrael, "Varieties of De-Stalinization," in Johnson, ed., *Changes*, pp. 135-53.

37. Although important, the changes in these regimes, particularly the North Korean, were quite limited. See Brown, "Bulgaria"; on North Korea, see Joseph Sang-hoon Chung, "North Korea's Seven Year Plan (1961-1968): Economic Performance and Reforms," *Asian Survey* 7 (June 1972).

38. See Unger, "Politinformator."

39. Thus, at the point of their initial encounter, tradition and modernity are antithetical. They can and do form amalgams, but their viability depends on one or the other establishing a *de jure* or *de facto* superordinate position. As Halpern has argued, "the two things that cannot be combined at all are the best in traditional society and the best in modern society. Indeed before anything significantly traditional can be combined with anything significantly modern, a revolution must first have torn apart the closed system of tradition so that it may not merely add or substitute the new, but become capable of assimilating it." See Manfred Halpern, "The Revolution of Modernization in National and International Society," in *Issues in Comparative Politics*, ed. Robert J. Jackson and Michael B. Stein (New York: St. Martins, 1971), pp. 52; also Jowitt, Part I, esp. n. 5, pp. 63-64.

40. See Reinhard Bendix, *Max Weber: An Intellectual Portrait* (Garden City, N.Y.: Anchor, 1962), pp. 383-416.

41. Here, as in many other basic respects, my conception of development in Leninist regimes differs from that proposed by Huntington, who sees the current stage of development (which he terms "adaption") as one where the conflict between specialists and political generalists is "one between complements" (fn. 7, p. 33). I see the tension between the legal-rational thrusts of inclusion and the sustained charismatic preferences of the apparatus and leadership as much more consequential.

42. See Mark Field, "Soviet Society and Communist Party Controls: A Case of 'Constricted' Development," in *Soviet and Chinese Communism: Similarities and Differences*, ed. Donald W. Treadgold (Seattle: University of Washington Press, 1967), for an analysis that confuses liberal modernity with modernity. In spite of that, Field's analysis of regime-society relationships and developments is very acute. For a more complex appreciation of the character of Soviet development, see J. P. Nettl and Roland Robertson, "Industrialization, Development, or Modernization," *British Journal of Sociology* 17 (September 1966): 274-91.

43. For an excellent and insightful analysis of the conflicting emphases in the American tradition and the character of its resolution, see Norman Jacobson, "Political Science and Political Education," *American Political Science Review* 57 (September 1963): 561-69; for the Mao-Liu conflict, see Franz Schurmann's *Ideology and Organization in Communist China*, rev. ed. (Berkeley: University of California Press, 1968), pp. 501-93, as well as

Benjamin Schwartz's "The Reign of Virtue: Some Broad Perspectives on Leader and Party in the Cultural Revolution," in *Party Leadership and Revolutionary Power in China*, ed. John Wilson Lewis (Cambridge: Cambridge [England] University Press, 1970), pp. 149-70.

5

DEVELOPMENT, INSTITUTIONALIZATION, AND ELITE-MASS RELATIONS IN POLAND

Zvi Gitelman

Elite-mass relations are the essence of politics. How elites and masses relate to each other determines the nature of the political system, its institutions, and its modal behavioral patterns. The most common way of differentiating and comparing political systems is to explicitly or implicitly compare their elite-mass relations, and the analysis of political change within a single system most often revolves around a determination of what has changed in the elite-mass relationship.

Elite-mass relations involve a two-way flow of influence, with masses following the lead of elites and elites acting responsively to mass demands. A crucial difference among political systems is the relative weights of influence flows downward (from elites to masses) and upward (from masses to elites), and the way in which these influences are articulated and transmitted. In general, masses follow the lead of elites because elites have power, authority, the ability to mobilize and demobilize masses through a variety of techniques, or combinations of these attributes.[1] Power may derive from naked coercion, a concentration of talent relevant to the problems and needs of society, or superior organization. Authority is based on the acquiescence by large strata of society that elites have the right to be obeyed and followed for one reason or another (tradition, charisma, legality—that is, rationality, to cite Weber's well-known trinity).

When elites and masses share values, the legitimacy of elite leadership can be established. As Chalmers Johnson points out, "A value structure symbolically legitimates—that is, makes morally acceptable—the particular pattern of interaction and stratification of the members of a social system."[2] Values are given normative expression in rules and laws. When values are no longer widely shared, or when elite and mass values do not coincide, norms will be challenged. "Since they no longer rest on a solid basis of legitimacy in shared values, norms

119

in times of change will be subject to frequent violations, taxing the abilities of authorities to enforce them; and their contents will become a major focus of attention and argument in society."[3] Elites also influence masses through opinion leadership, controlling and setting the agenda of politics, and manipulating mass opinion by various techniques.

Why is the elite ever responsive to the masses? It has been suggested that, if elites resemble masses in their demographic characteristics, they will tend to conceive political issues and preferences similarly, and so there will be a coincidence in political choices and desired policies. It rarely happens that there is close demographic similarity between elites and masses, but even where there is, coincidence of policy preferences does not seem to follow. Norman H. Nie and Sidney Verba found that in the United States, where leaders and ordinary citizens had the same social and economic characteristics, there was no particular tendency for them to share the same views.[4] Moreover, as several studies have shown, socioeconomic background, political attitudes, and political behavior do not correlate very highly. One cannot predict the attitudes of a member of an elite from his socioeconomic characteristics, and one certainly cannot predict behavior from these characteristics.

A second possible explanation of elite responsiveness to masses is that they share not only fundamental values but also specific attitudes and even opinions on discrete issues. This is very unlikely, although some more conservative elements in Eastern Europe claim that this is, indeed, the reality of elite-mass relations in socialist systems. A Romanian scholar claims that a "new feature of public opinion under socialism is its concordance with state power, [to] such a degree that between them collisions have completely disappeared. . . . What insures a concordance, nearly an identity, between socialist public opinion and the activity of party and state, is their common ideological orientation, the conscious adhesion of the whole people to the cause of communist construction."[5] If one accepts this claim, there is no need to empirically test public opinion, since one can assume an identity between articulated elite positions and mass outlooks. However, in socialist countries where empirical research on public opinion has been done, it becomes clear that there is no identity between elite and mass opinion.

A third possibility is that an elite is responsive because it believes it ought to be. It may hold to an ideology that promotes this belief, although it probably becomes increasingly difficult to adhere to this principle as time and different vantage points drive elite and mass perceptions further apart. Leninist ideology consciously rejects this form of responsiveness in its admonition against "tailism." The role of the elite (the "vanguard of the proletariat") is not to follow the lead of the masses, who act spontaneously, but to mold and shape the outlook of the masses, who should follow the elite which acts consciously.

Elite responsiveness may be a consequence of the dependence of elites on masses. In electoral systems, elite dependence on mass support is obvious. But even in systems where elections do not serve the function of changing and choosing leaders, elites must have some modicum of support if they are to carry out their programs, especially if they wish to do so efficiently and effectively. Moreover, lack of support exposes elites to the risk of removal and overthrow.

Finally, elites may be responsive because political organizations link elites and masses. Even where those organizations were originally designed to transmit influence downward, they may come to serve as channels for grievances, demands, and other messages from the masses to the elite. Elites may find it necessary or desirable, if only out of self-interest, to be selectively responsive to mass demands. The linking organizations may be organized interest groups, or organizations such as trade unions and workers' councils. Linkages also can be established by factions and patron-client networks.

Elite-mass relations are conditioned primarily by political culture, ideology, and society's level of development. Kenneth Jowitt has argued that "all Marxist-Leninist regimes are oriented to certain core tasks that are crucial in shaping the organizational character of the regime and its relationship to society." These tasks include transformation, consolidation, and modernization, and in the course of accomplishing them "relations between regime and society are organized along elite designated priorities."[6] Transformation and consolidation involve conflict between the elite and society at large, but modernization "requires a rather significant redefinition of the relationship between regime and society from mutual hostility and avoidance to the regime's selective recognition and managed acceptance of society."[7] This means, among other things, a shift in leadership style, more direct contact with various social groups, and "attempts to elicit social response to and confirmation of policy initiatives before the latter are given official status by the party"[8]—that is, greater account taken of mass policy preferences.

If these assertions are correct, we can assume that political development in socialist societies will involve changes in elite-mass relations in the direction of greater elite responsiveness, or at least a greater concern on the part of the elite to communicate effectively with nonelites. Jowitt suggests that the regime's "selective recognition and managed acceptance of society" mean that the regime is willing to allow "greater functional autonomy in various organizational settings" and that the regime, or elite, engages in "organizational pre-emption of social strata with recognition [of] aspirations or demands."[9] This cautious phrasing is appropriate, for it may well be that institutions in socialist systems generally have not been effective as linkages between elites and masses. They may be perceived as having failed as transmitters of messages upward, and may therefore simultaneously be rendered ineffective as transmitters downward. In fact, it can be argued that socialist systems in Eastern Europe are "overinstitutionalized," and that rather than being a strength and comparative advantage of Communist systems, as Samuel Huntington would have it, institutionalization has become a weakness of such systems as societies have developed.

DEVELOPMENT AND INSTITUTIONALIZATION
IN EASTERN EUROPE

According to Samuel Huntington, "The primary problem of politics is the lag in the development of political institutions behind social and economic change."[10] Modernization brings about a great expansion in political participation, but problems arise when this is not accompanied by a concomitant expansion in the strength of political institutions, thus leading to political decay and disorder. Stability, therefore, varies directly with the ratio between institutionalization and participation. Institutionalization is the process by which organizations and procedures acquire "value and stability."[11] While modernization involves the rationalization of authority, the differentiation of structures, and the expansion of political participation as a result of the expansion of political consciousness and the entry of new social groups into the political arena, development involves "the creation of political institutions sufficiently adaptable, complex, autonomous, and coherent to absorb and to order the participation of these new groups and to promote social and economic change in the society."[12]

East European socialist elites have been successful in achieving political modernization because they have mobilized previously passive social groups and have brought them into the political arena, and they have succeeded in achieving a high level of political involvement, although not necessarily participation, in their societies. However, they have not been as successful in political development because, contrary to Huntington's contention, they have not achieved a high order of institutionalization. Both the participation and the institutionalization that seem to characterize East European politics are to a large extent illusory, masking a lack of political development that manifests itself not only in recurring visible crises but even in daily life. Participation is illusory in the sense that it is of a different order from participation in democratic systems. As Sharlet has pointed out, the Western conception of participation involves efficacy, voluntarism, and responsiveness.[13] The participant believes he is affecting outcomes, he participates because he wants to do so, and he can legitimately see that his participation has some effect, for a response to it is forthcoming. Involvement formally resembles participation in that behavior is the same, but it does not involve a sense of efficacy, it is not spontaneous but is induced or coerced, and it infrequently results in the perception or feeling that some tangible response has been elicited by the involvement. This is not to say that involvement has no purpose, but its purpose is elite-determined. The purpose of elite-induced involvement is socialization, creating a subjective sense of commitment and teaching approved modes of behavior, rather than affecting outcomes. While participation may be said to be transitive in that its primary goal lies outside the act of participation itself, involvement is reflexive since its goal is contained within itself or is the subjective feeling produced by the act itself. Voting in a Western democracy is designed to directly affect the choice of leaders, whereas in a socialist system it has no real impact on this choice but serves the purpose of promoting or reinforcing generalized commitment to the system as a whole. It is an occasion for affirmation of loyalty, not for affecting practical outcomes.

Institutionalization is also at least partially illusory because institutions in socialist systems are channels for involvement, not participation, and therefore fail to become valued either for themselves or for the functions they perform. Socialist systems promote a participatory myth, and expectations are raised that genuine participation is both possible and desirable, and that institutions are the modes through which this participation is to be expressed. However, when it becomes apparent that institutions are frameworks for involvement rather than participation, and that influence and communications flow largely downward through them, institutions decline in value and in importance in the eyes of masses, thereby also weakening their effectiveness in transmitting downward.

Because Huntington's definition of institutionalization includes the attributes of stability and value, he—and others—can easily mistake one for the other. Institutions in Eastern Europe have been remarkably stable—in fact, too stable, as shall be argued. By "valued" Huntington seems to mean valued for their own sake, apart from the concrete benefits they deliver. But this does not mean that they have acquired value. Just because an institution is stable, in the sense that it endures, there is no need to conclude that it is valued or seen as legitimate. "It is obvious that organizations can and do endure for long periods of time through the use or threat of force, manipulation and other such means without necessarily being valued for their own sake."[14] The almost instant melting away of local councils, collective farms, trade union organizations, and party organizations in Hungary, and to a lesser extent Poland, in 1956; the withering away of youth and party organizations in Czechoslovakia in 1968; and the spontaneous creation of workers' councils, political debating societies, journals and newspapers, and even political parties in these countries when the barriers to such spontaneous activity were temporarily lifted, all testify to the underlying fragility of the seemingly stable and enduring institutions of the East European systems.

Moreover, there is considerable evidence that many institutions whose function is to link elites and masses are not valued even in the absence of large-scale social upheaval and political turbulence. The importance of this lies not only in the fact that the institutional linkage between masses and elites is not a very effective one, but also in the conclusion that the stability of the institutions, as well as of the whole system, is superficial. Institutions persist and seem stable because they are propped up by the power, force, and coercion that the regime can mobilize.[15] If power is temporarily withdrawn, the stability and persistence of institutions disappear immediately, for they are not based on an innate sense of value. In fact, the very stability of the institutions may be a barrier to their being valued, if stability is taken to mean lack of change: "The challenges of modernization are such that in order for organizations to be valued, they may be called upon to introduce major innovations, including innovations of a magnitude threatening the stability of the organization. In this sense, if constant innovation indeed characterizes modernization, valuing organizations may indeed mean danger to their stability, while stability may mean that the organization may no longer be valued."[16]

In order to achieve both value and stability it would be necessary to change or completely abolish institutions that no longer can be valued, and hence, in an ultimate sense, are unstable. As the Czechoslovak experience demonstrates, the current generation of Communist leaders may well prefer surface stability, based ultimately on power, to underlying stability based on value, if the latter can be achieved only by upsetting surface stability and risking change in both the institutional forms and behavioral patterns of the system.

There is an analogy to the enterprise director or innovator in Stalin's day: to introduce an innovation that would increase production or save time in the long run would involve a temporary halt or slowdown in production, thus disrupting the system and possibly preventing the accomplishment of the short-run production goal. This would be too high a risk to incur, so the innovation would not be introduced. Similarly, as the Czechoslovaks and Hungarians have discovered, in attempting to infuse value into the system as a whole one runs the risk of destabilizing its institutional superstructure and possibly its very foundations. So one may not be permitted to take this risk, especially since it can reasonably be argued that what will result will not be long-run stability based on value, but continued upheaval. Thus the elite develops an aversion to risk taking and prefers manifest stability in existing institutional arrangements to the latent stability that might be achieved by institutional rearrangement in order that institutions acquire value.

This leads to the conclusion that the political problem in Eastern Europe is not the lack of institutionalization but what Mark Kesselman calls "overinstitutionalization." When institutionalization outstrips, rather than lags behind, participation and mobilization, the process is overinstitutionalization and the outcome is political constraint. "When institutions are better at holding the line than responding to change, political constraint and overinstitutionalization occur."[17] Kesselman argues that Western political systems are characterized by overinstitutionalization because of the past successes of the institutions. These institutions "have outlived their original purposes but refuse to die. . . . If in transitional societies it is easier to destroy old institutions than to build new ones, the problem is reversed in developed polities, where established institutions may be outmoded but still able to withstand challenge."[18]

Perhaps it is success that has made French, and other Western, institutions so resistant to change and unable to adapt to new social and economic challenges. But the stability-rigidity of East European institutions may be as much a result of the exercise or threat of power and some external constraints on innovation (the need to emulate the USSR, and the fear of falling into revisionist error) as it is the result of success in absorbing and channeling participation. In Huntington's conception, Communist systems are politically developed, for they have managed the difficult feat of keeping institutionalization apace with expanding participation. If we apply Kesselman's thesis, we can conclude that Communist systems in Eastern Europe may even be "overdeveloped" because they are "overinstitutionalized," and that they share this problem with non-Communist developed states. In both kinds of polities, inertia, vested interests, and institutions made powerful by elite backing will act to maintain the institutional status quo; in both kinds of polities the 1960s saw attempts, often involving violence, to go outside institutions in order to change the system. However, the Leninist fear of spontaneity, the poorly developed mechanisms for upward flows of opinion (elections, opinion polls, critical and free mass media), and the external constraints imposed by the USSR may make it more difficult for the East European systems to respond and adapt to pressures for change than it is for Western systems to do so.

OVERINSTITUTIONALIZATION AND THE WORKING CLASS IN POLAND

The problems of stability versus value and overinstitutionalization may be illustrated by the case of workers' self-management in Poland, which bears many similarities to developments in Czechoslovakia and Hungary as well. The Polish case is a clear instance of a large social group emerging as a result of economic modernization, being brought into the political arena and mobilized to political consciousness and activity, and then finding political institutions unresponsive to their needs and demands. Because the institutions fail to adapt to the workers, the workers seize opportunities to develop responsive institutions, but the previous institutional structure is restabilized, with a subsequent loss in the institutions' value in the eyes of the working class. This forces the workers to go outside the institutional structure in order to articulate their demands when they perceive their situation as intolerable and amelioration as impossible within the prescribed channels. In turn, this obliges the party elite to confront the dilemma of abandoning institutional stability in order to link up more effectively with the working class, or to maintain the institutional structure and find alternative means of influencing the working class and of channeling working class influence upward to the elite.

The contemporary Polish working class, although heir to a rich labor tradition, is largely a product of the postwar era. The number of industrial workers more than doubled between 1950 and 1970, and in the latter year workers and their families and dependents constituted nearly half the Polish population. This working class has a high proportion of manual workers and of women, and it is a relatively young group with nearly 30 percent of all workers in industry, construction, and related trades being less than 24 years old in 1968.[19] A very high proportion are first-generation workers, having come into the cities and factories from the countryside after the war. Stanislaw Widerszpil found that in 1964 well over half the workers had recently left the countryside and in 1962 only 17 percent of industrial workers had been in that category before the war.[20] The creation of a new working class entailed problems of vocational training, the development of labor discipline and industrial work habits, and the "struggle against the well-known absences during the summer work in the field." In addition there were the obvious urban problems of housing, education, and the overall adjustment of a rural population to the city. The new working class also posed the challenge of political mobilization. As Wlodzimierz Wesolowski puts it, "It is a matter of influencing them in the direction of shaping a true working class sociopolitical attitude, of getting them to understand the meaning of socialist industrialization and the difficulties connected with it."[21]

Over the last 30 years the party has succeeded, of course, in involving the workers to a great extent in Polish political life. By 1971 there were nearly 900,000 workers among the full and candidate members of the party, and they represented 40 percent of the party membership and 13.5 percent of all workers. The proportion of party members is higher in the largest and most important industrial enterprises. The proportion of workers in the party has, in fact, tended to decline over time, as the white-collar elements, in large part recruited from the working class itself, have come to predominate, as they have in other Communist parties.[22] The party aside, trade unions, local government, and a variety of organizations within the enterprise and outside it have been the institutional frameworks developed to promote and to regulate the participation of workers in the social and political life of People's Poland.

Having been taught that the new Poland belonged to the workers, the Polish workers' expectations as to their influence, at least on social and economic matters of direct concern to them, must have been quite high in the late 1940s. These expectations were disappointed under the Stalinist system; this disappointment manifested itself in 1956 workers' demonstrations. In the aftermath of the Poznan riots, attempts were made to close the gap between the participatory myth and the realities of socialist Poland by restoring to the trade unions rights that had never been implemented. By this time, however, this institution had apparently lost the value it undoubtedly once had for the workers. Therefore, "The movement for democratization within the unions was . . . outstripped by the spontaneous formation of workers' councils in some of the larger Warsaw factories. Their formation demonstrated that the workers thought little could be achieved through the discredited trade unions."[23] In November 1956 the government adopted a statute on workers' councils, thereby legalizing what was a fait accompli. The councils were given the right, among others, to approve appointment of factory directors and to recommend their own candidates; to participate in economic planning; and to decide on the distribution of the enterprise's profits. From the very beginning, Gomulka criticized the aspirations of the councils to become political institutions hierarchically arranged, which would have an influence far beyond the enterprises. He insisted on the primacy of the established and officially approved institution, the trade unions, and argued that the role of the councils be confined to improving efficiency and increasing production. Thus, whereas many workers saw the councils as an alternative institution representing the interests of the workers upward—and replacing the unions, which were perceived as "transmission belts" downward—the party leadership insisted that the councils, if they had to exist, were to serve the common goal of increased production, rather than the "narrow" special interests of the working class.

Since the workers' councils had been formed spontaneously, as in Hungary, they did not easily fit into the institutional structure created by the elite. Thus the jurisdictional lines between management, the party organization in the enterprise, the trade unions, and the councils became blurred and a constant source of friction.[24] As a result:

> Within the enterprises the councils were often discredited, because the management and the representatives of the unions and the Party would leave them to make unpopular decisions on their own and only cooperate when the decisions were likely to be generally acceptable. The regime . . . emphasized the relative importance of the trades' unions [sic], since they were more amenable to control, and encouraged the Party committees to exercise influence over the elections to the workers' councils.[25]

The councils were by no means universally popular among the workers, but by December 1957 all of the nearly 300 enterprises having more than 2,000 workers had workers' councils, and half of all enterprises had such councils. The authorities succeeded in undermining the authority and restricting the independence of the councils, and workers soon realized that their high hopes for the councils were to be disappointed.

Articles in *Nowe Drogi* claimed that the workers' councils interfered in the efficient operation of the plant and that the workers were not "mature" enough to administer their own affairs. They openly admitted that the party organization was losing influence to the workers' councils. The councils were criticized for taking up individual complaints and reflecting individual likes and dislikes, and it was concluded that the administration of the enterprise should be in the hands of professionals.[26] It was clear to the workers that the councils were not going to be allowed to continue as they were. Their primary concern became the division of profits, because "on the basis of their experience of the workings of the councils, only those hopes relating to the division of profit had been fully verified . . . whereas the solution of other problems was only in a limited sense within the capabilities of self-management."[27] It was claimed that "The workers' councils have been in existence for eighteen months, time enough to prove that workers' self-government is a broader concept (demanding therefore broader practical expression) than workers' councils."[28] Eventually the councils, instead of being abolished, were coopted into the existing institutional framework, which was slightly adjusted to accommodate them.

In December 1958 the Conference of Workers' Self-Management (KSR) was set up. It includes the councils, the trade unions, the party, the technical organization (STO), and the youth organization. Thus, the councils had been diluted and party control, via the unions and party organizations, was assured. The KSR's primary mission is to increase and improve production; it clearly does not serve to express worker sentiment to nearly the same degree as the workers' councils did before being absorbed into the KSR. As we shall see, the workers were quick to realize the implications of the reorganization. Thus, while the KSR has become a stable institution, in that it has persisted since its creation, it is not highly valued. The workers' councils have lost their standing in the eyes of the workers, who tend to see them as formal but ineffective workers' organizations. As George Kolankiewicz points out, power and influence in the KSR tend to be concentrated in the presidium, and this body tends to be dominated by technical and engineering personnel. "In time, the decision-making body of the workers' councils came to be dominated by persons who maintained that since there was an inherent contradiction between 'professional management' and 'democracy' (and that since in the last analysis the expert was always right) then there was no need for decisions to be taken by a body such as the workers' councils."[29]

Consciousness has won out over spontaneity, and stability was achieved at the expense of value.

THE WORKERS AND THE KSR

There is overwhelming empirical evidence that the workers' councils are not valued institutions. The same is true, perhaps to a lesser extent, for the KSR as a whole. This evidence was available to the party elite in the 1960s, and there were many other indications that workers were alienated from the institutions that purported to represent their interests and that there was a general discontent among the working class. Yet the regime did little to assuage this discontent; when it was forced to confront discontent in December 1970, the regime was toppled.

Several sociological studies point to worker disillusion with the workers' councils and the KSR. Widerszpil, in his comprehensive 1965 study of the composition of the working class, cites a study of over 3,300 manual laborers in state-owned enterprises. It revealed that two-thirds did not know the substance of the last KSR resolutions, with ignorance of KSR affairs especially prevalent among females, less experienced, younger, and less educated workers. Respondents rated the party and trade union as the most active organization in the enterprise; the KSR and workers' councils were seen largely as inactive. When asked which organization had the most authority in the enterprise, 46.3 percent named the union and 25.2 percent named the party; only 8.7 percent named the workers' council and 21.9 percent the KSR. When asked to judge the influence of workers' councils on the affairs of the enterprise, nearly 40 percent said it was small or "not great" and 37.3 percent thought it was great.

Widerszpil concluded that there was an unfortunate tendency for decisions about the enterprises and its workers to be made in the narrow circle of the "big four"—the director, the party secretary, the chairman of the union committee, and the chairman of the workers' council. He said, "Workers' self-management is not only an important link in the system of administration and citizen and socialist control, but also the way to close the gap between the decision-makers and the executors of policy among the workers, and overcoming the major social differences among them"[30] The empirical data indicated that the institutions of workers' self-management were not performing well the functions of linking elites and masses, or workers with other workers.

Several other studies confirm the general tendencies in Widerszpil's data. Maria Jarosz surveyed the workers of a large Krakow cable factory in 1963. More than any other group, manual workers felt that the workers' councils should represent workers' interests, as opposed to those of the plant as a whole or the "national interest." They also favored having most council members come from among the workers, but nearly half the workers thought that engineers and technicians were the most active element in the councils; all groups, including the workers, rated the workers as the least active.[31] Other studies reveal that workers, engineers, technicians, and the administrative employees of the enterprise all believe that the resolutions of self-management bodies have little influence on higher authorities. Over 90 percent of workers and engineers-technicians cited this as the first or second most important factor influencing the effectiveness of self-management. Over two-thirds of workers cited the lack of administration cooperation as the other factor, indicating that workers feel the institutions in which they are involved are not effective vis-a-vis plant administrators and higher echelons.[32] Within the self-management structure, only about 7 percent of those questioned named the workers' council as the organ with most influence.[33]

In 1956 workers placed high hopes in the workers' councils as organs that would articulate and press their interests, but very quickly disillusionment with the councils spread among the workers. After establishment of the KSR, the councils came to be held in very low regard. Jolanta Kulpinska and M. Rokacz surveyed, at different times between 1956 and 1958, the workers in three enterprises reputed to have effective, well-functioning councils. In October 1956 some 97 percent of the workers expressed the opinion that the factory should be managed in the name of the workers, not by the trade union organizations but by the workers' councils. Engineers and technicians were less sanguine about the councils, but two-thirds thought that a workers' council was a good idea. While workers stressed that the main benefit would be higher incomes, engineers and technicians were more inclined to emphasize better factory organization and work conditions. By the spring of 1957 expectations were somewhat disappointed in the light of experience. Workers and engineers-technicians were asked to rate the activity of the workers' council in their enterprise.

	N	Good	Weak	Poor	Don't Know
Factory A					
Workers	348	27.4	49.3	19.0	4.3
Engineers-technicians	66	47.6	30.1	8.0	14.3
Factory B					
Workers	144	50.7	34.0	8.3	7.0
Engineers-technicians	20	23.8	52.4	–	23.8
Factory C					
Workers	129	21.7	53.9	23.2	1.2
Engineers-technicians	36	19.4	52.8	25.0	2.8

When probed as to their low ratings of workers' councils, workers gave such explanations as "because they don't have the complete right as a council to disagree with the management and central authority," or "because the workers' council usually only supports suggestions given from above."[34]

By February 1958 opinion about the workers' councils among both workers and engineers-technicians had become more negative. When asked to evaluate the activities of the councils, the factory employees answered as follows (coded responses):

Factory	N	Positive	Average	Negative	Indifferent*
A	328	16.5%	38.7	23.8	21.0
B	139	12.2	20.3	40.1	27.4
C	196	3.6	14.3	56.1	26.0

*Includes "don't know" and "not interested."

This time, only among the workers of one factory did higher income emerge as the most important benefit of the workers' councils. Overall, the workers rated control over management and administration as the councils' most important task, whereas the technical personnel stressed interpersonal relations. It must be pointed out that a good part of the decline in the councils' standing among the workers apparently is attributable to the councils themselves and not to any deliberate attempts by the regime to stifle them. As one worker put it, "I feel that the workers' council has not accomplished a thing, unless you consider the quick promotion of the chairman of the council an accomplishment." Another said, "There is too much favoritism in the council. Meetings are held without the knowledge of the work crew. various premiums are divided up among their friends. The council does not direct the management, but the management directs the council." A feeling expressed with increasing frequency was, "The council in this structure is not our representative but a privileged group."[35]

After absorption into the KSR, the councils fell considerably in the estimation of workers. Aleksander Owieczko surveyed over 1,100 workers and over 300 engineers and technicians in four large enterprises. Over 60 percent of the workers and over 70 percent of the technical employees asserted that the "self-government" (KSR) had not increased the influence of employees on factory matters.[36] Even members of the KSR, who generally thought that appropriate conditions existed for self-government, did not feel the KSR had much influence in important factory matters. Nearly half said that its influence was insignificant, and 7 percent said it had no influence at all, though 39 percent claimed it had great influence.[37] Half or more of the members of the enterprise party organization and the workers' council felt that KSR influence in important matters was insignificant, and two-thirds of both workers and technical personnel said that they had no possibility of influencing the decisions of the workers' councils within the KSR. This points to the widespread feeling that the putative representatives of the work crews were acting independently and were not responsive to their nominal consituency.

The feeling that the KSR had been bureaucratized and coopted into management was frequently expressed.[38] While on this question there were no significant differences among party and non-party members, young or older workers, or more and less educated ones, those who were generally more satisfied with work conditions also tended to feel that they could influence KSR decisions. Overall, there were strong feelings that the rank and file was inefficacious, that the first and final effort to be responsive to the work crews occurred around election times, and that the work crew was ignored in KSR decisions. "The workers' council does not inform the workers. . . . Everything takes place behind the workers' backs. . . . No one asks me about anything; Only a small group has any influence. . . . KSR representatives do not inform or associate with the workers."[39] Even among worker members of the KSR, only 44 percent claimed that work crew opinions were taken into consideration in decision making, although two-thirds of the technical employees who were KSR members felt that opinions were taken into account.[40]

An examination of the composition of the various bodies in the self-government apparatus reveals that workers are best represented at the lower levels, and at the higher levels party members and technical personnel dominate. In the four enterprises surveyed by Owieczko, the distribution of workers, party members, and technical personnel was as follows (in percent):[41]

	Workers' Councils	KSR	Workers' Council Presidia
Workers	59.8	57.7	40.0
Engineers-technicians	32.2	34.0	42.5
Party members	45.9	55.2	67.5

The proportion of party members increases with the importance of the organization, and the proportion of workers declines. In all four enterprises the percentage of workers in the presidia was lower than in the workers' council or the KSR as a whole. It is striking that, the more active an employee is in some aspect of factory life, the more likely he is to feel that the self-government acts without regard to workers' opinions and feelings. Therefore, it is among the people most familiar with the internal operations of the enterprise that one finds stronger feelings that self-governing bodies are unresponsive. Owieczko found two major criticisms of self-government: that workers did not influence decisions and that activities of the self-government organs were "oriented primarily 'upwards'—their direction was toward the needs and purposes of the directors."[42]

Moreover, workers were concerned primarily not with the comanagement function of the KSR but rather with its function as a representative of their particular interests, a function it performed inadequately. They were looking for an institution representing their interests; instead they found another transmission belt. Therefore, it was not surprising to find that since 1956 interest in the workers' councils, and then the KSR, had declined and that there was widespread ignorance of the activities of the KSR, even where there were more positive evaluations of KSR activity. This conclusion fits well with the finding that KSR agendas were set exclusively by the enterprise director in most cases, and that many workers felt that the KSR was a tool of the administration.

Workers advocated that more blue-collar employees serve on self-government organs and that they be chosen for their responsiveness to the work crews and independence of the directorate. But engineers and technicians expressed skepticism about workers' abilities to deal with the enterprise management and saw the workers as concerned only with their narrow interests and insufficiently educated to deliberate about the general affairs of the enterprise.

Whatever the merits of these different outlooks, it is clear that the workers did not perceive the self-government organs as representing their interests; workers saw them merely as channels for the communication of decisions downward. When asked to construct a hierarchy of matters actually dealt with by worker self-government, workers rated labor discipline first and determining production plans second. Increasing control of the work crew over the administration was ranked at the very bottom of the list.[43] Moreover, when referring to involvement in production planning, workers have in mind establishing the limitations of such plans and affecting the conditions under which they will be fulfilled, rather than improving production at whatever cost to the labor force.

Some research done in Poland provides insights into the relative standing of the various organizations in the enterprise. Several studies have investigated the prestige and perceived power of the organizations, as well as the degree of trust accorded to them. Owieczko investigated both trust as well as perceived power (figures are percentages):

Organization	Which organization enjoys the trust of the work crew?		In matters important to the work crew, which has the most to say?	
	Crew members	KSR members	Crew members	KSR members
Workers' council	14.1	14.8	11.1	17.0
Party committee	22.3	29.5	32.1	37.5
Trade union	45.1	54.5	16.9	25.0
Directorate	13.5	9.1	40.6	40.9

The directorate and the party are thus seen as having the most power but the trade union is most trusted, with both the workers' council and management enjoying very little trust.[44] The same kind of ranking was found in a study in Bialystok, with even more power attributed to the party and even less to the workers' councils.[45] The question of trust was examined, controlling for party membership.[46] The figures are percentage responses to the question: Which organization enjoys the most trust among the work crews?

	Workers		Engineers-Technicians	
	Party members	Non-Party	Party members	Non-Party
Workers' council	8.5	15.9	9.6	9.0
Party committee	50.0	18.0	50.0	28.0
Trade union	37.3	45.1	28.7	43.8
Directorate	4.9	15.7	18.7	21.2

It is not surprising that the party enjoys most trust among its own members, although one wonders why only half the party members name the party organization as the most trusted. What is striking is that the party and management enjoy more trust, even among non-party members, among the engineers and technicians than among the workers. Engineers and technicians seem to identify more with management and the party, and workers tend to see the party and management as on the same side, sitting across the table from them.

As regards influence and power, both party and non-party workers and engineers-technicians rated the party and management as most influential. Curiously, while workers in the party rated the party ahead of management, and workers who were not in the party put management ahead of the party, among the technical personnel both party members and non-party people rated management as more influential than the party.[47] Still, both workers and technical personnel exhibited tendencies to turn, not to any of the organizations, but to their immediate supervisors with complaints or perceived injustice.[48]

Writing after worker discontent had erupted in violent and dramatic fashion at the end of 1970, Zbigniew Maciag pointed to the gap that had existed between the "theoretical and normative" attributes of the worker organizations and their actual functioning. Until 1967, he claimed, there was an awareness of the inconsistency between theory and practice in self-management, since many studies demonstrating this had been published. After 1967, however, the topic faded from consciousness at the very time that the self-government institutions became even less responsive to the working class.[49] Maciag cites the familiar problems of unclear jurisdiction, dependence on the cooperation of the enterprise director to implement any decisions taken by self-government, domination by the presidium, the management monopoly of agenda setting, and the lack of enforcement powers for the self-managing bodies. These rendered self-management pretty much a sham; and it is the informal groups formed in the enterprise that exercise effective power. "The existence of this informal structure indicates that the legally established structural forms are not, from the perspective of realistic practical operation, entirely functional."[50]

Maciag also noted a tendency for the development of an enterprise elite, even among the workers, who played multiple roles and became increasingly removed from the problems and interests of the rank and file. In the larger enterprises the workers' council is most often composed of representatives of the departmental councils, that is, the subunits of the council on the departmental (oddzial) level of the enterprise. These representatives take greater interest in enterprise council activities than in their departmental council. The same individuals are usually KSR members, and this multiplicity of roles turns these activists into enterprise politicians who have little time for or interest in the rank and file they are supposed to represent. This tendency toward professionalization of the representative function obviously reduces even further the responsiveness of enterprise organizations to workers.

The key organization in the enterprise is the party committee. The significance of the other organizations depends directly on the extent to which the party operates through them. The party committees in the 1960s tended to ignore the work crews, and this diminished the party's effectiveness with the rank and file. The party's activity became "unidirectional and one-sided."[51] Trade unions also were said to ignore workers' interests and to concentrate on implementing the programs and requests of the management. Unions were said to be busying themselves with organizing canteens and cafeterias, planning and arranging summer vacations, and supplying workers with fruit, potatoes, and Christmas trees![52] Production plans, nominally to be approved and evaluated by the KSR, were sent to the enterprise too late to alter, so KSR ratification became an embarrassing farce. In general, "since the majority [of KSR members] are employed in management and are persons holding permanent positions in the sociopolitical organizations, their activity is identified in the minds of the work crew with the activity of the administration and generates a belief that their interests are not being represented."[53]

ELITE-MASS RELATIONS AND THE CRISIS OF 1970

Sociological research had documented what was common knowledge in Poland of the 1960s—that the trade unions, workers' councils, and KSR were hollow shells through which influence, if it flowed at all, flowed downward only. The events of late 1970 demonstrated that the party, too, was an institution that had power but lacked authority. Whereas the party may have been perceived as effective and powerful, it was not seen as responsive and representative. Thus, there were institutions not valued by the working mass, although all had manifested outward stability. In the absence of valued, as well as stable, institutions, elite-mass linkages became weak and tenuous. The party leadership was isolated from the working class and the workers felt unable to communicate with the political elite that was making the economic and social decisions to determine their standard of living. Accumulated resentments and frustrations were brought to the surface by the sudden, drastic price increases in late 1970, which acted as a catalyst spurring the working class in the Baltic areas, and later in other parts of the country, to take to the streets in protest.

Analyzing the events of December 1970, the influential weekly *Polityka* commented, "the events which took place in December were proof" that the ties between the working class and the party "have been seriously strained." It called for a mechanism to be created to prevent the dissolution of these ties.[54]

In February 1971 the Party Central Committee held its eighth plenum and discussed the recent events and leadership changes. It acknowledged that the demonstrations and riots "were simply the culminating point of a steadily growing process whereby the bond linking the workers' class and the party—

especially the latter's central authorities—was weakened. The fact that effective steps designed to reverse this harmful process could be taken only in the tragic circumstance of a political crisis and street riots proves that some serious errors must have found their way into the methods used in guiding the party and the socialist community."[55]

To be more specific, it demonstrated that there was no officially sanctioned institution through which the working class could communicate effectively with the political elite. The party itself had become ineffective for "There was . . . no climate suitable for an open, serious, and perceptive discussion inside the party of the symptoms attesting to the disrupted ties between the policy of the party and the masses."[56] Therefore, what was needed was

> a change of method and style in running the party and state, and, above all, concerning the problem of strengthening the ties between the party and the working class. . . . The crisis of confidence pervaded interparty relations on several levels: the basic mass of party members, subjected, on the one side, to the pressure of the worsening moods, and on the other side to the political decisions made by the leading authorities, about whose rightness it was not fully convinced, was losing arguments indispensable for maintaining its ideological defensive spirit. The crisis of confidence was constantly widening the rift between the aktif and the party apparatus on the one hand, and the leading authorities on the other.[57]

Thus, there was an elite-mass crisis not only between the party and the population but even within the party itself. The leadership was unresponsive to the party rank and file, which was in daily contact with the non-party masses. In early 1971 there were many complaints by members of party cells in factories that their reports of workers' grievances and complaints had never reached the higher echelons or were ignored; the party leadership admitted this to be true. As one speaker said in a party meeting in a textile plant, "There was information, all right . . . only there was no response. We submitted suggestions, demands, but no one deigned to answer." Another pointed out the "Comrade Piechocki was speaking about the lack of contact between the former CC [Central Committee] and the masses. . . . But there is no need to look that far. No one deigned [to] come to our electoral conference, not even from the district level."[58]

Two fundamental strategies were proposed to close the elite-mass gap. The first was to "overhaul the state machinery," that is, to change the institutional structures linking masses and elites; the second was to change the "manner of ruling,"[59] or political style of leadership.

While many pointed out that the change in leadership would not be sufficient to guarantee the necessary changes in elite-mass relations,[60] overall it seems that the strategy of the Gierek regime has been to leave the instiutional structure pretty much as it was, at least in regard to the working class, and to emphasize changes in leadership style. Discussing the changes wrought by the new leadership, only in passing did Politburo member Stefan Olszowski mention "the problem of having representative bodies function more effectively"; he concentrated on the "style and methods of work," mainly direct consultations with party members at different levels and with workers in large, important plants. He mentioned the "informal visits" of Politburo members, including Gierek, to plants and factories and to the countryside. He said, "Experience shows that many matters can be solved by direct action on the spot. It is not always necessary to draw up new laws and regulations." He did cite the flow of information between the citizenry and party leadership as a crucial problem, commenting that "inappropriate methods of selecting the data that should flow from the top downward are still being used, and there is still the danger that misinformation will flow from the bottom to the top." While he stated, "We must create institutions that will guarantee proper selection and a proper flow of information," Olszowski noted that "these are very difficult matters"; he could not suggest a specific way of ensuring this flow except to say that "I can only say—a special one."[61] A fundamental reform of existing institutions, or the creation of new ones, was not mentioned.

One practice instituted by the present leadership illustrates its preference for avoiding major institutional changes, and for bypassing institutions with informal and semiformal means. In addition to the much publicized visits to enterprises by Gierek and other leading party officials, 164 major plants—accounting for about a quarter of the industrial labor force, of party members employed in industry, and of industrial output—were selected as "bastions of socialism." These enterprises have great influence on the "sociopsychological climate" of the communities in which they are located, and are thus politically strategic. A Central Committee lecturer is assigned to each enterprise and is obliged to consult directly with party activists and workers there. The lecturer meets with a group of 150 to 200 enterprise employees, replies to questions, and takes down proposals and suggestions. He is supposed to report in detail to the Central Committee. There is supposed to be a detailed and prompt reply to these proposals, issued by the relevant officials. Moreover, other steps have been taken to improve two-way communication between the enterprise and the political leadership. Factory party committees now get the same information as secretaries at the next highest level; there are annual seminars where trade union and factory party officials meet with party and government officials, who explain policy and discuss proposed legislation; members of the Politburo address several enterprise meetings every month; Central Committee members belong to factory party organizations.[62]

How effective these innovations will be, and whether the populist, consultative style of the Gierek regime will be an adequate substitute for institutional change, remains to be seen. There are many indications that the changes are perceived as cosmetic, and that consumer discontent is once again rising, as the improvement in the consumer's lot in 1971 and thereafter begins to slow down while expectations continue to rise. Surveying the changes made under Gierek, Vincent Chrypinski concludes that his strategy may not work in the long run:

> More than efficient authoritarianism and psychic stimuli, Poland needs a basic reform of the centralized bureaucratic system of government. It is not enough to introduce technical rearrangements of the economy, or to admit more people to sharing the symbols of authority. Real reform requires a break with old authoritarian tendencies and the acceptance of a genuine democratic participation with individuals convinced of their influence on the decision makers.[63]

There is little evidence that such reform is in the offing. On the other hand, the government's hasty retreat in the summer of 1976 from announced price rises, following workers' riots, showed that the fundamental problem remains.

CONCLUSION

The Polish case illustrates that institutions designed to link elites and masses and facilitate communication between them tend to be very stable in socialist systems, and capable of surviving mass upheaval and leadership changes. It also shows that this stability is not necessarily based on these institutions being valued.

Institutional stability derives from inertia and the reluctance of the political leadership to admit that institutions have been ineffective for reasons other than the malfeasance of the individuals connected with them. The basic structure, it is maintained, is sound and need not be thoroughly revamped. What has to be changed is the activity and attitudes of people involved in these institutions. Clearly, there are powerful vested interests with a stake in the survival of present institutional arrangements. Management undoubtedly finds subservient workers' organizations much to its liking, and workers do not feel that the institutions are amenable to reform or to being made effective in representing their interests. Rather than run the risk of upsetting the status quo and opening the way to unanticipated and undesirable changes in the fundamental nature of the elite-mass relationship, which must remain basically authoritarian if the nature of the Leninist system is to be preserved, the elite chooses to try to improve the workings of the existing institutions and, if need be, circumvent them by adopting dramatic, highly visible ways of increasing elite-mass contacts. Some Polish observers privately express the view that even though the institutions discussed here serve no useful function, the regime is afraid that abolishing them would arouse worker opposition since they would perceive such a step as a further reduction of their autonomy and power.

A leadership that is challenged by competitors from within the party, and further constrained by the Soviet Union's supervision, will naturally choose the more conservative strategy of controlling spontaneous forces, rather than giving them their head. The Leninist reflex of insisting on control even at high costs continues to be a natural one for the leadership. Those who would experiment with allowing spontaneous forces to shape political life, as the Czechoslovaks did in 1968, run very high risks.

Overinstitutionalization is not a problem limited to Leninist regimes. It also has manifested itself in Western democracies, especially in the 1960s. Overinstitutionalization may be a problem endemic to all developed societies, irrespective of the regime or the type of system.

What, then, are the differences between developed Communist and non-Communist regimes? They seem to lie in the way that the problem of over-institutionalization is dealt with. In Communist regimes it is much more difficult for social action to take place outside approved institutions. Social movements, "counter institutions," and public organizations, all of which provide alternatives to and critiques of institutions in the West, cannot legitimately form in Communist systems. This means that dissatisfaction with institutions can be expressed only by abandonment, such as nonparticipation or formalistic involvement, or by an attempt to completely overthrow them. Reform from within, which really comes about as a result of pressure from without, is an unlikely possibility. The capacity of Communist institutions for incremental self-renewal is limited; drastic, nonincremental strategies are more effective, when they can be pursued, in bringing about institutional change.

Theoretically, it should be easier to accomplish wholesale, fundamental institutional change in Communist systems if the party decides to do so, for it disposes of a greater concentration of power than political leadership in the West. Present at all levels of all hierarchies, the party should find it easier than a Western executive to confront vested interests and to dismantle, create, and rearrange existing institutions and organizations.

But Khrushchev's experience, and that of Czechoslovak, Polish, and Hungarian reformers does not support this hypothesis. Institutions are able to mount effective resistance against campaigns to reform or abolish them, and some institutions—the party, collective farms, trade unions—seem untouchable. A leader such as Gierek, who cannot be sure that he enjoys wide support among strategic elites, is undoubtedly wise to choose to circumvent, rather than to displace, existing institutions.

A second important difference between Western and Communist systems is that the former are not constrained in attempting institutional reforms by the kind of outside force that the USSR represents in Eastern Europe. There is no need to anticipate outsiders' reactions, and the risks of external intervention are small, although the United States did intervene in other countries to promote or prevent systemic change.

Their commitment to consciousness means that socialist systems have an ideologically based bias against responsiveness and a suspicion of spontaneity. As a result, leaders see institutions as molding reality rather than reflecting it. Certainly from Stalin's day on, the institutional superstructure has been regarded not as the reflection of social and economic realities, but as the molder of those realities. Jerzy Wiatr expresses this very clearly:

> As to the power structure, it is a significant and characteristic feature of socialist construction that this structure is by no means a direct reflection of the class and stratum structure. . . . A distinctive feature of Poland's social structure at its present stage of development is its mixed and transitional character. . . . This applies primarily to the class, stratum and socio-occupational structures and not to the power structure. . . . Politics is the main lever of structural change in the period we live in. It enables . . . the implementation of socialist transformation. For these transformations do not occur spontaneously, by way of the accumulation of quantitative changes. On the contrary: they are the result of the conscious implementation of policy, and they can only take effect under the condition of the conscious and consistent realization of socialist politics.[64]

The power structure is the elite operating through the institutions it has constructed as instruments for the implementation of its program of social and economic transformation. Institutions are creatures of the elite and serve its purposes. Even their putative function of channeling messages to the elite from the nonelites is also designed, primarily, not to directly serve the interests of the nonelites but to better inform the elite as to moods, desires, and anticipated reactions of the nonelites, so that elite policy, determined almost exclusively by the elite itself, can be better implemented. The point is not necessarily to be more responsive to the masses, but to be more knowledgeable about the masses so that they can be made more responsive to elites.

Ultimately, institutions are only concrete manifestations of the larger system. When institutions are not valued, this may be either because of some characteristics specific to them, or because they are identified with the whole system, which is not valued. Whether the lack of value characterizing East European institutions reflects inadequacies in the institutions themselves or disenchantment with the entire system of which the institutions are a part is an important, but open, question.

NOTES

1. This discussion of elite-mass relations owes much to Robert D. Putnam, *The Comparative Study of Political Elites* (Englewood Cliffs, N.J.: Prentice-Hall, 1976), Chapter 6.

2. Chalmers Johnson, *Revolutionary Change* (Boston: Little, Brown, 1966), p. 13.

3. Ibid., p. 43.

4. Sidney Verba and Norman H. Nie, *Participation in America* (New York: Harper and Row, 1972), p. 330.

5. Mihail Ralea, "Success in Socialist Society," *Rumanian Journal of Sociology* 1 (1962): 42-43.

6. Kenneth Jowitt, "An Organizational Approach to the Study of Political Culture in Marxist-Leninist Systems," *American Political Science Review* 63, no. 3 (September 1974): 1173-75.

7. Ibid., p. 1174.

8. Ibid., n. 15.

9. Ibid., n. 16.

10. Samuel Huntington, *Political Order in Changing Societies* (New Haven: Yale University Press, 1968), p. 5.

11. Ibid., p. 12.

12. Ibid., pp. 93, 266.

13. Robert Sharlet, "Concept Formation in Political Science and Communist Studies: Conceptualizing Political Participation," *Canadian Slavic Studies* 1, no. 4 (Winter 1967): 640-41.

14. Mark Kesselman, "Overinstitutionalization and Political Constraint: The Case of France," *Comparative Politics* 2, no. 1 (October 1970): 25.

15. Gabriel Ben-Dor, "Institutionalization and Political Development: A Conceptual and Theoretical Analysis," *Comparative Studies in Society and History* 17, no. 3 (July 1975): 312.

16. Ibid., p. 313.

17. Kesselman, "Overinstitutionalization," p. 24.

18. Ibid., pp. 24, 44.

19. Maria Jarosinska and Jolanta Kulpinska, "Transformation of the Working Class in People's Poland," in *Transformation of the Social Structure in the USSR and Poland* (Moscow-Warsaw, 1974), p. 137.

20. Stanislaw Widerszpil, "Tendencje zmian w skladzie klasy robotniczej w uprzemyslowionych spoleczenstwach kapitalistycznych i w Polsce Ludowej," *Studia Socjologiczne* 1 (1964): 47. See also his "Sociology and Problems of the Working Class," *World Marxist Review* 16, no. 10 (October 1973).

21. Wlodzimierz Wesolowski, "Changes in the Class Structure in Poland," in *Empirical Sociology in Poland*, ed. Jan Szczepanski (Warsaw, 1966), p. 14. For a discussion of other problems, see Jarosinska and Kulpinska, "Transformation," p. 138.

22. See Widerszpil "Sociology"; George Kolankiewicz, "The Working Class," in *Social Groups in Polish Society,* eds. David Lane and George Kolankiewicz (New York: Columbia University Press, 1973), pp. 91-92, 97.

23. Ibid., p. 102.

24 "The relationships between the workers' council, trade union, and Party were not always appropriately formulated. there was an attempt to set the council in opposition to

the factory council [trade union] and the factory [Party] committee. In certain enterprises there was opposition to the workers' council, its activity was weakened, or the council was dissolved." J. Balcerek and L. Gilejko, "Aktualne problemy samorzadu robotniczego w Polsce," *Nowe Drogi*, September 1958, p. 20.

25. Richard Hiscocks, *Poland: Bridge for the Abyss?* (New York: Oxford University Press, 1963), p. 280.

26. See Jozef Balcerek and Maria Borowska, "Zaloga a rada robotnicza," *Nowe Drogi*, February 1958.

27. Maria Hirszowicz and W. Morawski, *Z badan nad spolecznym uczestnictwiem w organizacji przemyslowej* (Warsaw, 1967), pp. 34-36, quoted in Kolankiewicz, "The Working Class," p. 114.

28. Jozef Kofman, "Worker Self-Government," *Polish Perspectives*, nos. 3-4 (July-August 1958): 16. See his more extensive "Na marginesie diskusji nad projektem ustawy o samorzadzie robotniczym," *Nowe Drogi*, August 1958.

29. Kolankiewicz, "The Working Class," p. 119; based on research by Polish sociologists. One of them, Wlodzimierz Brus, writes, "The purpose of this complicated organisational network was obvious: to outnumber the workers' council, which was the only body elected by the workforce and was deprived of any higher-level superstructure, by the party and union authorities, who were subordinate to hierarchically constructed apparatuses and completely dependent on them—politically, materially, and disciplinarily." See *Socialist Ownership and Political Systems* (London: Routledge and Kegan Paul, 1975), p. 156.

30. Stanislaw Widerszpil, *Sklad Polskiej klasy robotniczej* (Warsaw: PWN, 1965), pp. 3-327.

31. Maria Jarosz, *Samorzad robotniczy w przedsiebiorstwie przemyslowym* (Warsaw: PWE, 1967), pp. 225, 212, 215.

32. Zygmunt Rybicki, "Plant Disputes and Their Settlement in a Socialist System," *Polish Round Table Yearbook IV, 1970-71* (Warsaw: Ossolineum, 1972), p. 112.

33. Ibid., p. 114.

34. J. Kulpinska and M. Rokacz, "Rada robotnicza w opinii zalogi," *Nowe Drogi*, August 1958, p. 74.

35. Ibid., p. 85.

36. Aleksander Owieczko, "Samorzad robotniczy w przedsiebiorstwie przemyslowym a zaloga," *Studia Socjologiczno-Polityczne* 22 (1967): 14.

37. Calculated on the basis of data presented in ibid., Table 4, p. 16.

38. Ibid., p. 18.

39. Ibid., p. 21.

40. Ibid., p. 26. In 1962, in the country as a whole, workers constituted 69 percent of worker council members, and in 1963, 68 percent. In the KSR in 1964 they constituted about two-thirds of the membership. Ibid., p. 28, n. 6.

41. Based on data in ibid., Table 14, p. 29.

42. Ibid., p. 33.

43. Engineers and technicians ranked the distribution of bonuses and premiums first, determining production plans second, and control over administration seventh. Aleksander Owieczko, "Dzialalnosci i struktura samorzadu robotniczego w opinii zalog fabrycznych" *Studia Socjologiczne* 3 (1966): 67. It is worth noting that, when asked what the hierarchy of self-government concerns should be, only 6.4 percent of the workers cited control of administration, but 14.7 percent of workers in the KSR cited this. The most frequent citation by workers involved pay and working conditions, and 18 percent said they did not know what the KSR should be concerned with. Ibid., p. 71.

44. Owieczko, "Dzialalnosc," p. 79. The patterns are similar for engineers and technicians, although they are less trusting of the union and more trusting of the party. They

also attribute less influence to the union and council, seeing influence as resting almost exclusively in the hands of the party and management.

In the light of the events of 1956 and 1970, it is obvious that trade unions are valued only relative to other organizations, and that they too have proved an inadequate instrument for articulating workers' needs.

45. Ibid., p. 79, n. 11.

46. Ibid., p. 82.

47. Ibid., p. 83.

48. Ibid., p. 84.

49. Zbigniew Maciag, "Funkcjonowanie organizacji spolecznopolitycznych w przedsiebiorstwie (samorzad robotniczy)," *4 Zeszyty Naukowy UJ* (Krakow), 1972, p. 147.

50. Ibid., p. 158.

51. Maciag, part two, ("Organizacja partyjna, zwiazkowa, i mlodziezowa"), *5 Zeszyty Naukowy UJ* (Krakow), 1973, p. 113.

52. Ibid., p. 116.

53. Ibid., p. 127.

54. *Polityka*, January 2, 1971. Quotations from the press are from Radio Free Europe press translations.

55. *Nowe Drogi* (special issue, undated), RFE *Polish Press Survey,* no. 2313, p. 8.

56. Ibid., p. 14.

57. Ibid., p. 1.

58. *Glos Koszalinski*, February 20, 1971.

59. See, for example, *Zycie Warszawy*, January 8, 1971.

60. As some university students put it, "The departure of several persons from the highest leadership does not settle everything. Things have gone badly in this country: the sejm has not been a parliament, the government has not governed, the labor unions have been a 'holiday and Sunday tourism office,' youth organizations have been an obedient tool, and committees and plenums have served only to pass on decisions from above." *Student,* March 1971.

61. Interview with the editor of *Polityka*, September 25, 1971.

62. See "Poland: Bastions of Socialism," *World Marxist Review* 17, no. 10 (October 1974).

63. Vincent C. Chrypinski, "Political Change Under Gierek," in *Gierek's Poland*, ed. Adam Bromke and John W. Strong (New York: Praeger Publishers, 1973), p. 51.

64. Jerzy Wiatr, "Political Effects of Changes in the Social Structure," *Polish Round Table Yearbook V, 1972-73* (Warsaw: Ossolineum, 1973), pp. 64, 65, 66.

PART

III

**POLITICAL
PARTICIPATION**

CITIZEN PARTICIPATION IN COMMUNITY DECISIONS IN YUGOSLAVIA, ROMANIA, HUNGARY, AND POLAND

Jan F. Triska

There is substantial if diffuse consensus in the literature that political participation grows with political development: the more developed the political community, the greater the participation of citizens in the community decisions. The social changes associated with political development create: (1) a socio-psychological environment conducive for political participation and (2) governmental need for at least some citizen participation in the decisional process. At the same time, however, participation tends to become more diffuse: As government becomes more complex and technical, decision-making units grow larger and decisional gravity shifts from lower to higher levels. As a result, while the participation of citizens goes up, probably together with the increase in influence of the citizenry on governmental decisions, the relative influence of any single citizen goes down.[1]

Some political systems value citizen participation; others do not. Developing countries tend to place little value on political participation because it is inefficient—central decisions are often delayed, some programs are compromised, and some goals are sacrificed—and may adversely affect governmental effectiveness. Participation also may promote inequality and retard growth.

On the other hand, democrats and Marxists alike place high value on citizen participation. If "the Jacksonian idea that every citizen is capable of discharging the normal functions of government is a peculiarly American one in the modern world," as Samuel Huntington and Joan Nelson argue,[2] then the Lenin idea of every cook being able to master the skills of a public administrator is the activist persuasion in the Communist world: "All the working masses without exception must be gradually induced to take part in the work of state administration," stated the 1919 program of the All-Russian Communist Party (Bolsheviks).[3] Both political systems have perceived citizen participation as an important input in their respective political processes as well as an essential instrumentality of political development and modernization. The developed socialist society, just like the developed capitalist society, requires processes and institutions that set goals and choose means to respond to and to solve social issues. To reflect the distribution of preferences in an advanced society, community decisions need to absorb citizen views; an advanced socialist society can ignore and disregard this problem only to its peril. In fact, "this need . . . is much greater in socialist countries where it is a question of vital importance for political life as a whole."*

Developed socialism, said to be the product of the scientific-technological revolution, requires "active enlistment of the toilers in participation in governmental affairs and in sociopolitical activities." And the party supports citizen participation: "Each Soviet man has the guaranteed opportunity to take part in the discussion and decision of important problems on national, republican, oblast, city, or raion scale. Besides that, in their work collectives, the Soviet people daily decide a multitude of questions connected with the administration of their enterprises, institutions, and organizations."[5]

The Marxist causal model of socialist development ("the highest type of democracy") is in fact very similar to the "liberal model of development" of Huntington and Nelson: Greater socioeconomic equality (brought about by the revolution) leads to greater participation and greater political stability, which in turn leads to rapid socioeconomic development. The Marxist model of socialist development is as follows:

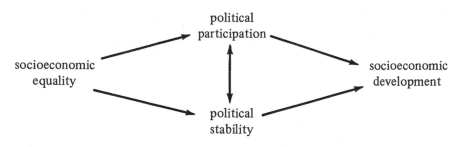

---

*Najdan Pasic, the leading Yugoslav political sociologist, put it this way: "The further a society has gone along the road of socialist development, the more developed the process of socialization of its economic and political life, the greater is its need for modernization of political institutions and the discovery of new forms of active participation by individuals and groups in the democratic process of political decision making. . . . As the process of technological socialization of production and the closely related socio-economic integration advanced, it became increasingly clear that the classic system of general political representation did not suffice to provide a real reflection of differing social interests to facilitate real and adequate participation by particular social groups in the process of political decision making. . . . This need for political modernization in keeping with the demands of profoundly altered socio-economic realities is much greater in socialist countries where it is a question of vital importance for political life as a whole."[4]

In turn, the Marxist model of capitalist decay is similar to Huntington's technocratic model: Socioeconomic development in capitalist systems leads to increase in social and economic inequality, decrease in political stability, and increase in political participation, which results in participation explosion, that is, social revolution.[6] The Marxist model of the doomed capitalist development or the capitalist decay is as follows:

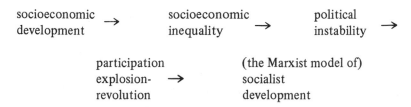

socioeconomic development $\rightarrow$ socioeconomic inequality $\rightarrow$ political instability $\rightarrow$

participation explosion- $\rightarrow$ (the Marxist model of) socialist development

Until recently, Western political scientists have been reluctant to study political participation in Eastern Europe and the USSR for two reasons. First, they found access to relevant information difficult, if not impossible; second, they considered political participation in the socialist countries largely ceremonial, government-sponsored and supportive, manipulative and mobilized, and thus not worthy of their attention.[7] If citizens participate in elaborate charades of support for the government and of solidarity with its values and goals, without any possibility of influencing political decisions, why should one study such pseudo-participation? And if citizens are denied the institutions of a competitive political system, how can they possibly engage in genuine participation in the first place?[8]

More recently, however, some scholars studying East European politics have found that coupling their research interests and activities with East European colleagues often made access easier. They discovered that, with tact and sensitivity, they could engage in political science research in Eastern Europe, sometimes even in field research and, in a few cases, in survey research and similar forms of broad empirical investigation. It appears that, with the end of the cold war, some East European countries became more hospitable to serious political science research than they were before. I do not mean to overstate the case; things change. But I would argue that overall access to information and data tends to be a little easier now in Eastern Europe than it was in the past.

With reference to manipulative participation, the distinction between mobilized and autonomous participation may not always be as simple as it seems. The real intent and motivation of a political participant or a group of participants may not always be easy to fathom: "How does one compare the Soviet citizen, proud of his country and his party, who casts his vote in a single-ballot election, with the American voter, moved by a sense of civic duty and perhaps by partisan loyalty, who casts his ballot for a state official virtually guaranteed of reelection (despite the opposition)?"[9] Moreover, participatory activity, originally motivated by coercion, may become voluntary and supportive of the system in the process, as when a political participant undergoes a change of heart. And the mobilized action may be indistinguishable from an autonomous activity and their outcomes may be similar or the same.[10]

My preference would be to maintain a distinction between autonomous and mobilized participation when possible. But I agree with Huntington and Nelson that virtually all political systems include a mix of mobilized and autonomous participation. "The mix varies from one system to another, and changes over time in any particular system. We are dealing with matters of degree not only at the level of individual actions but also at the level of political systems."[11] Mobilized and autonomous participation are not dichotomous variables but form a spectrum. The dividing line between the two is often arbitrary.[12] As D. Richard Little points out, "much of the impetus for political participation arises . . . as a result of mobilization by a variety of institutional and social agencies" in both political systems, democratic as well as Communist. While mobilization in the Soviet Union is more "overt, intense, and heavily promoted" by the party and the government, it is "more subtle and decentralized . . . through organizational and social influences" in the United States. In both political systems citizens have free choice of whether to become involved in politics or not; the only difference is that "choices are more serious and significant to the individual citizen" in Communist countries and more casual in democracies.[13]

In addition, as Jerry Hough argues, the impact of citizen participation on political decisions—the political influence citizens exercise—either directly on given decisions or indirectly via public discussion on public policy, is a question mark.[14] We don't really know whether citizens in the United States have more influence over public decisions than citizens in East Europe because we don't know how to find out, how to determine it. As yet, we have no tools for measuring, let alone for comparing the respective impact and influence. We can compare the input, the actual citizen participation, but not the results: "The idealistic notion that participation is only significant when it results in direct influence on national policy formulation bears little relevance to the actual role of mass publics either in democracies or in nondemocratic systems."[15]

For most of us, political participation has a deep-seated ideological connotation. We think of it in terms of its origin and context in Western liberal democracy. "Stripped of its ideological content, the concept appears in a simpler and more useful form . . . as the involvement of individual citizens in collective political activities related to the functions performed by the formal institutions of the political system."[16]

The several studies discussed in this essay explore issues that do not impinge, at least not directly, on the question of mobilized versus autonomous participation. Instead, they address themselves to such problems as the processes that bring citizens into community activity, the issues on which they focus that activity, and the response of community leaders to the citizen activity. They explore the scope, intensity, channels, and structures of political participation, and investigate types of citizen activities as well as relationships among resulting political acts. In particular, they ask how and how much different citizens participate (Triska and Barbic); the difference in citizen participation between functional (workers' councils) and other sociopolitical participatory modes (Verba and Shabad); how and how much different nationalities participate in a multinational state (Barbic); how citizens become deputies (Nelson); what citizens think of their deputies (Dzieciolowska and Zawadzki); how conflicts of interests are handled (Szego); and how conflicts of interests are resolved (Wroblewski and Zawadzki). All the studies treat political participation as a multidimensional phenomenon, a complex concept embodying activities carried out by citizens with a view to influencing community decisions. And they all investigate citizen participation on the community and communal (county, district) level.

BACKGROUND

To learn about political participation in socialist systems of Eastern Europe, we invited interested colleagues in Yugoslavia, Czechoslovakia, and Hungary in 1968 to meet with us with a view to launching a study of political participation in those three countries. For that purpose, several Yugoslav social scientists helped us to prepare a pilot study of political participation, which they pretested in Slovenia and which we in turn discussed with the Czechoslovak and Hungarian colleagues at a conference in Bled in 1969. Unfortunately, the project could not be carried out in Czechoslovakia; in Hungary the study was undertaken—and is now completed—but only one study is available as yet. In Yugoslavia, the Slovenian social scientists formed an all-Yugoslav team that redesigned the original questionnaire and administered it to a cross-section sample of the citizenry and local leaders in Serbia, Croatia, Slovenia, and Macedonia. Next came processing of the data for analysis. The major issues we wanted to analyze were the amount of participation in Yugoslavia, the kinds of citizen activity, the relationship of those activities to political attitudes, and the demographic correlates of these activities (sex, age, education). The data also were run so as to allow comparisons among the republics. By now, four studies based on the Yugoslav data have been completed. They are described below.

In addition, we have offered the completed research instruments and the studies based on them to our Polish colleagues engaged in a study of local councils, as well as to an American student of local politics in Romania. Although both followed their own research designs, they incorporated parts of our questionnaire in their research. The results of their studies are reported below as well.

YUGOSLAVIA

Yugoslavia is a fertile research site for students of political participation in Eastern Europe. A one-party system aiming at socialist transformation via widespread sociopolitical activity of its citizens, Yugoslavia has led other socialist countries in the development of participatory institutions such as workers' councils, councils of producers, economic cooperatives, self-managing interest communities, and other organizations of self-management. This is why we felt, at the outset, that Yugoslavia may be an ideal starting point.

We now have four studies all based on the same Yugoslav data: "Women in Sociopolitical Life" by Ana Barbic; an unfinished essay, "Political Participation of Citizens in Four Republics: Unity Versus Diversity," also by Ana Barbic; "Workers' Councils and Political Stratification," by Sidney Verba and Goldie Shabad; and "Evaluating Citizen Performance on the Community Level: Does Party Affiliation Make a Difference?" by Jan Triska and Ana Barbic.

Women

Sociopolitical participation in Yugoslavia is still predominantly the domain of men, concluded Ana Barbic in "Women in Sociopolitical Life." Moreover, as

TABLE 6.1

Citizen Participation in Yugoslavia: Men and Women (in percent)

	Men	Women	Total	N
Commune self-management (assembly or council— elective office)	7	1	4	133
Local community council (elective)	11	1	7	197
Nominating committees (elective)	15	3	9	274
Social contacting	17	5	11	332
Workers' self-management (elective)	29	10	20	598
Citizens' meetings	63	26	44	1,327
Pre-electoral voters' meetings	62	27	45	1,341
Local community actions	64	43	56	1,681
N	1,563	1,431	−	2,994

Source: Compiled by the author.

TABLE 6.2

Participation of Men and Women in Four Yugoslav Republics
(in percent)

	Croatia		Macedonia		Slovenia		Serbia	
	M	F	M	F	M	F	M	F
Commune self-management	9	2	8	1	10	1	7	2
Local community council	9	1	10	1	14	1	12	2
Nominating committees	10	2	14	2	18	5	17	3
Social contacting	22	6	19	4	13	6	16	3
Workers' self-management	26	9	30	4	35	14	29	10
Citizens' meetings	62	36	59	16	57	30	62	22
Pre-electoral voters meetings	63	23	59	15	63	41	61	24
Local community actions	57	39	54	31	69	59	71	50
Total	352	344	280	151	256	320	675	616

Source: Compiled by the author.

Table 6.1 shows, the more difficult, limited, removed, initiative-requiring, time-consuming, and involved the activity, the less do women participate, and vice versa. (Proportionately, men display the same pattern.) The closer the activity to the community decision making, the more the men predominate.

Just as there are differences in political participation of citizens among the several Yugoslav republics, Ana Barbic expected to find that there would be differences in women's participation: The more economically developed the republic (with Mid-European cultural-historical tradition), she hypothesized, the smaller the difference in political participation between the sexes. In the less-developed republics (with Muslim-Turkish tradition), she assumed, women would participate less. Table 6.2, however, confirmed the hypothesis only partially. In political participation, the difference between the sexes is statistically significant in all the republics and in all the political activities.

It is not that different cultural-historical traditions have no influence on the political activities of women. Rather, it is that only a small number of women have succeeded in overcoming the barriers of tradition and male domination. Federal and republican legislation stipulating complete equality among the sexes and full inclusion of women in the country's socioeconomic and political life have not succeeded as yet in altering the deeply rooted modes of thinking of the past. The socialist political culture in Yugoslavia is still essentially male-oriented and male-dominated. What is important, however, is that women activists participate in politics largely independently of their political

TABLE 6.3

Citizen Participation in Four Yugoslav Republics
(in percent)

	Croatia	Macedonia	Slovenia	Serbia	Total %	Total N
Elective sector						
Commune self-management (assembly or council)	5	5	5	4	4	133
Local community council	5	7	7	7	7	197
Nominating committees	6	10	11	10	9	274
Workers' self-management	17	21	23	20	20	598
Communal sector						
Social contacting	14	13	9	9	11	332
Citizens' meetings	49	44	42	43	44	1,327
Pre-electoral voters' meetings	48	43	45	48	45	1,341
Local community actions	48	46	63	61	56	1,671
N	695	432	576	1,291		2,994

Source: Compiled by the author.

views, information, and interests. Compared to men activists, they score much lower on all these three attitudinal variables. This probably expresses the women activists' motivation and their willingness, determination, and readiness to make the effort to get personally involved in public life. In the process, they hope to help to change the Yugoslav political culture in favor of women.

For the present, public activity is still men's domain in Yugoslavia. Economic dependence of wives on their husbands does not help matters. "Only planned social action can do away with domination of men among women," concluded Ana Barbic. "Socialist social relations and socialist society can be built only with complete participation of women in all activities of sociopolitical life."

Political Unity Versus National Diversity

New participatory institutions have been applied in a relatively uniform way across a wide range of different cultures in Yugoslavia. Citizens of the eight constituent units—six republics and two autonomous provinces—differ in ethnic composition, culture, language, religion, and historical experience as well as in levels of economic development. To what extent do the common sociopolitical institutions differ when established in different republics? Do different citizens participate differently? How much is participation shaped by the common political system, and how much is it shaped by the varying historical-cultural traditions?

In her paper "Political Participation of Citizens in Four Yugoslav Republics: Unity versus Diversity," Ana Barbic seeks to answer these questions.

First, as Table 6.3 shows, many people participate in "easy" activities and few in "difficult" ones in all four republics. There is no difference here. If the political activities are divided between elective modes (commune self-management—assembly or council; local self-management—community council; workers councils; and nominating committees) and communal modes (social contacting; citizens' meetings; pre-electoral voters' meetings; and local community actions), however, then the first group, the elective sector, displays participatory similarities across the four republics while the second group, the communal sector, displays differences from republic to republic. This is probably because the common Yugoslav sociopolitical order reaches the elective sector but not the communal sector. Here citizen participation differs, and the differences depend on particular modes of activity (for example, more Slovenes and Serbs participate in local actions than Croats and Macedonians, but more Croats and Macedonians contact officials on community problems than Slovenes and Serbs). No particular pattern, however, can be observed.

Barbic argues that the participatory differences in the communal sector should not simply and solely be attributed to the remains of cultural-historical traditions among Yugoslav nations and nationalities. These differences should also be sought in socioeconomic characteristics of local communities and in individual characteristics of the citizens. For this reason, Barbic turns next to the League of Communists (14 percent of the population) as the leading ideological-political force, and the Socialist Alliance of the Working People (40 percent of the population) as the main organizer of citizen political activities.

The differences among republics are most prominent among citizens who are members of neither the league nor the alliance (six out of the eight modes of participation). However, the fact that the Slovenes and the Serbs, on the one hand, and the Croats and the Macedonians, on the other hand, display similar participatory patterns suggests to Barbic that the cultural-historical tradition does not influence political participation of citizens; the participatory patterns split squarely both the mid-European and the Muslim-Turkish tradition down the middle.

The differences among republics with respect to political participation are less pronounced among members of the Socialist Alliance (five out of six modes of participation). Serbian Alliance members are most active, Croatian members

TABLE 6.4

Regression on the Variable Communal Factor

Variable	Correlation Coefficient	Partial Correlation Coefficient	Beta	Level of Significance
POLORGM	.31	.20	.20	.00000
EDRESP	.22	.13	.16	.00000
AGEGRP	.02	.06	.05	.00199
SEX	−.42	−.33	−.33	.00000
INCOME	.09	.03	.03	.18008
ECONDVLT	−.02	.03	.03	.11658
AGRICINH	.04	−.00	.00	.88789
INHABTS	−.09	−.07	−.09	.00004
URBNRURL	−.09	−.09	−.14	.00000

Note: delta = 25662; F = 114.45800; level of significance = .00000; POLORGM: member of political organization; EDRESP: respondent's education; AGEGRP: age of respondent; SEX: sex of respondent; INCOME: family's monthly income; ECONDVLT: economic development of the community; AGRICINH: number of inhabitants in agriculture; INHABTS: number of inhabitants of community; URBNRURL: urban-rural composition of community.

Source: Compiled by the author.

TABLE 6.5

Regression on the Variable Elective Factor

Variable	Correlation Coefficient	Partial Correlation Coefficient	Beta	Level of Significance
POLORGM	.63	.57	.58	.00000
EDRESP	.30	.11	.12	.00000
AGEGRP	.05	.11	.09	.00000
SEX	-.29	-.14	-.11	.00000
INCOME	.20	.01	.01	.47777
ECONDVLT	-.00	-.01	-.01	.51546
AGRICINH	-.03	-.00	-.00	.82608
INHABTS	.03	-.03	-.03	.09173
URBNRURL	.05	-.07	-.09	.00015

delta = .44132   F = 261.90262   level of significance = .00000
Source: Compiled by the author.

least active, and Slovenian and Macedonian members are in between. The respective republican leaderships of the alliance should probably be credited—or debited—for this outcome.

The members of the league are the highest participants in all four republics. They differ significantly only in two participatory modes: citizens meetings and local community actions. (In these activities, the Serbian league members lead, followed by Croatian, Slovenian, and Macedonian members, in that order.) It thus appears that, while the national league leadership succeeded in activating its membership throughout different republics, it failed to activate the unorganized citizenry and, to a large extent, the alliance membership as well.

Which citizens participate most in which activities in the four republics? Ana Barbic found that in all four republics, participation in communal sector activities correlates significantly with sex (men) and membership in the league (and also to a limited extent in the alliance). Education plays a significant role in Serbia, Slovenia, and Croatia, but not in Macedonia. Age is important in Slovenia, and income in Croatia. Communal activities are more pronounced in rural communities in Slovenia and Croatia, and in small (mixed) communities in Croatia and Serbia. More economically developed communities display more communal activities only in Serbia (see Table 6.4).

As to the more homogeneous elective sector, the pattern is similar. Membership in the league, and also in the alliance, is significant for citizen political participation. It is followed by sex, education, age, and degree of urbanization of the community, in that order (see Table 6.5).

Thirty-odd years seems a short time period to build a state out of many separate nations and nationalities. The Yugoslav leadership has done well, especially via the League of the Communists. But there is still a great deal to be done. Ana Barbic concludes: "[Past] traditions still represent obstacles to [full], equal participation of citizens in sociopolitical life of their communities . . . . [Especially] working classes are not sufficiently politically active. But, as one of the positive achievements of the Yugoslav political system . . . income is not a significant parameter of sociopolitical status."

Workers' Councils

Does the establishment of direct participatory channels in decentralized socioeconomic and political institutions—such as the workers' councils—help to solve the citizen participation problem? Sidney Verba and Goldie Shabad in their study of "Workers' Councils and Political Stratification" focus their attention on this issue. Are the workers' councils real participatory channels open to all the working population, or are they dominated by the League of the Communists, by a technocratic elite, or both?

Of all the various participatory mechanisms available to a citizen in his community, the workers' council is the one most distinctive of Yugoslavia's socioeconomic organizations and of its ideology of functional decentralization and self-government. Verba and Shabad found that participation in workers' councils is a fairly widespread activity: 20 percent of all citizens in the sample reported having been at one time or another a member of a workers' council. Indeed, if the sample is limited to the work force in the socialist sector only, 40 percent of all workers have been members of workers' councils—an impressive number. In this sense, workers' councils do provide participatory opportunities for a wider proportion of the population than would be possible if self-governing bodies were limited exclusively to the political arena.

Who are the workers' council members? The candidate members must be employed in the socialist sector to be eligible for membership. In that pool, however, the more skilled and better educated workers—those who have status within the context of the work place—have a much greater chance of becoming council members than the rest. Unskilled workers are underrepresented; skilled workers are overrepresented; and white-collar workers with high levels of education are the most overrepresented of all occupational categories. The bias in favor of males is greater in political self-government activities than in workers' councils. (Still, there are 68 percent of men and only 32 percent of women employed in the socialist sector.) Members of the League of the Communists are more likely to be elected to workers' councils than nonmembers; this is a reflection of the fact that league members tend to be more skilled and better educated workers. However, both blue- and white-collar workers with high levels of skill or education do not need to be league members to have access to membership on workers' councils; they certainly are not locked out. This situation contrasts with other forms of political participation where league membership is more important, Verba and Shabad conclude. In this sense, workers' councils add a new and important dimension to political participation in Yugoslavia.

In a brief appendix, Verba and Shabad also looked separately at the four republics—Slovenia, Croatia, Serbia, and Macedonia. They found that the patterns of citizen participation on workers' councils were remarkably similar in all four. That the authors found such similarity and uniformity despite major national, cultural, and economic differences suggests to them that the superimposition of uniform political institutions on such a diverse country as Yugoslavia has been quite successful.

The Communists, the Alliance Members, and the Rest of the Citizens

Who are the best Yugoslav citizens? The constitution, the program of the League of the Communists, and the statutes of the Socialist Alliance prescribe what the citizen civic behavior and attitudes should be. In their study "Evaluating Citizen Performance on the Community Level," Jan Triska and Ana Barbic sought to find out what the citizen civic virtues in fact are, how they compare to the codified norms in the three official documents, and how the three citizen groups—the Communists, the alliance members, and the rest—stack up against each other.

The data confirmed by and large the official prescriptions. The league members were found to lead the rest of the citizens in every civic attitudinal and behavioral category examined. They displayed the highest interest in and were best informed about politics, knew more political leaders than the other citizens, thought highly of citizen political efficacy, were better satisfied with government performance than other citizens, and participated more in community politics in every single category than the rest of the legitimate voters. The alliance members, on the other hand, although not as good citizens as the Communists, surpassed the unorganized citizens in every single category. In fact, in the aggregate, the alliance members appeared to stand almost exactly in the middle between the league members and the rest of the citizens who occupied the broad base of the Yugoslav pyramid (see Tables 6.6 and 6.7).

Triska and Barbic found that the league members are thus the most politically aware, active, and influential citizens in Yugoslavia. Not all of them, however, show equal civic virtue. While over one-third of the Communists are outstanding citizens who closely resemble the official norms—they are young/middle-aged, well educated, well paid, male white-collar employees living mostly in cities with high immigration rates—almost one-third are in the low/zero category, and the rest (one-third) are in the middle-medium range.

TABLE 6.6

Attitudinal Comparison of League Members, Alliance Members, and Others
(in percent)

	League Members	Alliance Members	Others	Total	N
Political awareness ("moderate" and "high")					
Political interest	69	38	16	32	1,566
Knowing political leaders	63	28	10	25	1,204
Political information	84	52	28	36	2,231
Citizen efficacy ("high")					
Citizen influence on government	44	32	21	29	1,404
Self-management as a channel of influence					
At working place	32	19	11	17	832
At communal level	26	15	9	14	679
At republic and federal levels	21	13	7	12	565
Citizens' own political influence	9	3	1	3	154
Citizen participation					
Commune self-management (assembly or council)	17	5	1	4	216
Local community council	20	7	2	6	320
Nominating committees	23	12	3	9	443
Social contacting	28	12	5	11	544
Workers' self-management	53	23	7	20	967
Citizens' meetings (always attends)	29	15	6	13	637
Pre-electoral voters' meetings (attends and nominates)	44	18	16	16	203
Local community actions (participates and offers ideas)	39	19	7	16	798
Satisfaction with government performance ("very good")					
Republican and federal government	25	14	9	13	647
Commune government	8	4	3	4	209

Source: Compiled by the author.

TABLE 6.7

Citizens Who Score High/Very High

	Total		League Members		Alliance Members		Others	
	%	N	%	N	%	N	%	N
Civic awareness								
Political interest	32	1,566	69	482	38	734	16	350
Political information	19	944	54	378	22	422	6	144
Knowing political leaders	25	1,204	62	442	28	536	10	226
Citizen efficacy								
General citizen influence								
on government	29	1,404	44	313	32	618	21	413
One's own influence	3	154	9	65	3	64	1	25
Self-management as								
influential channel								
At work place	17	832	32	222	19	364	11	246
At commune	14	679	26	185	15	293	9	201
At republic, federation	12	565	21	148	13	250	7	167
Participation								
Communal social								
self-management	4	216	17	116	5	89	1	11
Local community								
social self-management	7	320	20	139	7	14	2	40
Nominating committees	9	443	23	160	12	225	3	58
Social contacting	8	381	22	158	8	151	3	72
Workers' self-management	20	967	53	368	23	446	7	153
Pre-electoral								
voters' meetings	16	803	44	313	18	358	6	132
Citizens' meetings	13	637	29	206	15	294	6	137
Community actions	16	798	39	237	19	362	7	163
Citizen evaluation of:								
Communal government	4	209	8	55	4	80	5	74
Republican and federal	13	674	25	177	14	269	9	201

Source: Compiled by the author.

Similar variations may be found within the alliance, as well as among the unorganized citizens. But these two groups show a reverse pattern. Less than one-fifth of the alliance members score high, about one-fourth score medium, and over half score low. The unorganized citizens follow this pattern as well. The alliance members, however, excel over the unorganized citizens: While the alliance members score well over the high and the medium of the totals, the rest of the citizens rank below them.

Triska and Barbic conclude that, as far as citizen performance on the community level is concerned, party affiliation is an important key to quality citizenship. But it is not the only key. Education is important as well (while income is less so). And non-league members are certainly not locked out from Yugoslav public life. In fact, speaking in terms of absolute numbers rather than proportionately, there are often twice or even three times as many non-league members who are as fine citizens as the outstanding members of the league.

ROMANIA

Who Are the Local Deputies?

Daniel Nelson, in his paper "Citizen Participation in Romania: The People's Council Deputy," sought to know how and why citizens become activists in Romania; who they are; how they get selected for public functions; and what relationships there are between the local deputies and the citizens. He interviewed a sample of 250 members of local people's councils as well as other community elites in four Romanian counties—Timisoara, Cluj, Brasov, and Iasi. (Romania has 39 counties; they are subdivided into communes, cities, and towns.) The four counties are geographically separated and display contrasting socioeconomic levels and rates of development.

Nelson found that most deputies are party members. They are selected, screened, and nominated by the Socialist Unity Front, a coalition of all mass organizations in Romania (like its counterpart in Yugoslavia, the Socialist Alliance). The candidate must not only be a distinguished citizen in civic and political terms but must fit into the community "quota" as well. This is a device, enforced throughout the country, to ensure that the composition of people's councils reflects the composition of their constituencies. Ethnic background and occupation come first, but age and sex also play a role. Thus, there may be a need for a local deputy who would be an outstanding young female blacksmith of Hungarian descent.

How do citizens become deputies? Nelson divided all deputies into three groups: the local elite, the "needed," and the "fillers." The local elite, a few deputies among many, are the local citizens with high party and state positions— party secretaries, secretaries and vice presidents of councils. The "needed" form a much larger group. They are the articulate, the educated, the expert, and the loyal—the heads of departments of the local state bureaucracy, school administrators, presidents of local courts, directors of local banking and finance institutions, supervisors of health and sanitation districts, doctors. "The fillers" legitimize people's councils through the representation of a broad popular base— a function of governments everywhere. The party is overrepresented in people's councils by seven or eight to one, as is higher education (3 or 4 to 1).

Deputies are not paid salaries, but they view the position as a genuine increase in their sociopolitical status, recognition of their accomplishments, and an honor. Moreover, they often get preferential treatment in housing, at food stores, in admission to higher education, in jobs.

As in Yugoslavia, political participation in Romania is not uniform. In their political backgrounds, the deputies differ from county to county. Neither their political activities nor their entrance into the party displays a uniform pattern. And the manner in which diversity occurs is often coincidental, in Nelson's opinion, with the levels of development/modernization of their counties. Politicization occurs earliest in the most developed/modernized counties and corresponds to early party membership. But coincidental as it is, more rapid socioeconomic development probably fosters social mobilization in functional nonparty activities.

Similarly, with reference to deputies' interaction with their constituency, Nelson suspects that citizens in less developed/modernized counties are more public-minded than citizens in more developed/modernized areas. In the former case, citizens tend to be more people and community-oriented and involved than in the latter case.

Still, localities go about their business stressing different local ways and means to meet local needs or to reach local goals: citizens' committees in Brasov and Cluj, personal deputy encounters in Iasi and Timis, mass media in Brasov, and education in Iasi and Timis (see Table 6.8).

This suggests to Nelson that the measures designed by the party to bring about socioeconomic development—such as the nonparty activities of deputies in low socioeconomic regions—may exceed the party's capacity to control them. He concludes that diversity in political participation exists in Romania in spite of procedural uniformity and quota-type recruitment of prospective members of people's councils. The nature of this diversity implies to Nelson a possible relationship between the rate of socioeconomic development and the degree to which deputies—and citizens—identify with the party. The higher the rate, the less the identification with the party.

TABLE 6.8

Nature of Problems Raised by Citizens, Summarized
(percentages weighted)

Category	Timis Actual N	Timis Percent Total	Cluj Actual N	Cluj Percent Total	Brasov Actual N	Brasov Percent Total	Iasi Actual N	Iasi Percent Total
A	19	33.4	21.5	29.7	32.5	46.8	33	32.5
B	14	57.5	20.5	63.3	16	44.2	25.5	54.6
C	2	4.6	2.5	1.4	1.5	9.0	3.5	7.6
D	2	4.6	2	5.1	—	—	2	5.4
E	—	—	.5	.4	—	—	—	—

A Proposals of a general or public character.
B Proposals of a personal character.
C Claims and complaints of a general or public character.
D Claims and complaints of a personal character.
E Other.
Source: Compiled by the author.

HUNGARY

Are local interests different in different communities? And if they are, as they must be, how are the differences aggregated and reconciled when they clash at the county level? In her empirical analysis of the relationship between interest structures and the decision-making process in three Hungarian counties (Baranya, Heves, and Gyor-Sopron) entitled "Local Public Administration, Representative Institutions, and Interest Relations," Andrea Szego interviewed in 1972 a representative sample of 1,746 county and district deputies, district and county employees, and citizens at large.

Local community (village, settlement) interests are represented by deputies elected by the local population to district councils and by district deputies appointed to county councils. It is at the county level that the differing local interests must be articulated, conflicts among them reconciled, and the local interests integrated with the interests of the county as a whole. How is this done?

Szego asked county councils' deputies in the sample, first, whether local communities have independent interests and, if they do, who mediates conflicts among these interests. Second was a more neutral question, whether local communities have independent and special interests, but of the kind that do not conflict.

The answers were astounding. Of the respondents, 37 percent claimed that local communities have no independent or special interests, and 48 percent admitted the existence of differing local interests, but only of the nonconflictual type—an absurdity in itself, in Szego's view. In other words, 85 percent of the respondents did not regard local interests, which they presumably represented at the county level, as independent interests subject to interest integration. This finding is in sharp contrast with the response to the same questions by the county employees and officials: 90 percent of them agreed that different localities have independent and conflicting interests. (Of the deputies who admitted that there were conflicting interests, 7 percent claimed that this was due to local interests clashing with other local interests. Some 1 percent attributed the conflict to the interests clash between local and county levels. And 3 percent admitted occasional conflicts of interests between local communities and counties.)

Zones are areas with different levels of development and supply. They are larger than local communities, and their interests are different from local communities. Zonal differentiation is socioeconomic and functional, while local community differentiation is geographical and political. And yet, 26 percent of the county council deputies denied the existence of special zonal interests. On the other hand, only 9 percent of the county council employees and officers thought that there were no special zonal interests.

Assuming that the most typical form of conflict of interests is an open disagreement of deputies with others on issues discussed, Szego asked county deputies whether they ever openly disagreed with others. Some 97 percent stated that they have never done so, and 91 percent answered they had never openly disagreed with county council's employees and officials. (But only 14 percent said that they had not expressed views conflicting with those of officers of the county councils—presidents, vice-presidents, secretaries.) From these answers, Szego deduces that the forum where interest articulation, conflict, and integration takes place is not the session of the county council but the couloirs in the background where deputies discuss problems of their constituencies and caucus—among themselves, with the professional county bureaucrats, and with the officers of the councils. This assumption was strengthened by the deputies' response to a question concerning consultations prior to their speeches in the council. Of the deputies sampled, 31 percent indicated that they had consulted other deputies before addressing the council, while 28 percent called on "influential personalities" in the county prior to their speeches. (But 43 percent of council deputies had never taken the council floor, and 64 percent had never used the form of interpellation or putting questions to the president of the council.)

Andrea Szego concluded that the professional district and county bureaucrats, familiar with the socioeconomic and political problems of the county on a working basis, recognized the existence of independent and special interests, articulated them, and helped to reconcile conflicts among them as a matter of course. The local deputies, on the other hand, regarded the existence of and conflicts among independent interests as negative phenomena—or believed that others did: 56 percent of the respondents said that they considered conflicts of interests as definitely harmful socially, 6 percent as definitely useful, and 32 percent as useful "under certain conditions." (Given the attractiveness of "medium answers," this is a low rate, according to Szego.) To the local professionals, then, conflicts of interests are part of the routine; to the local deputies, they are socially detrimental. They must be taken care of quietly, without fanfare. They certainly should not be advertised.

POLAND

In the past 15 years, in addition to the research described below, three major empirical studies of citizen participation in community decisions were conducted in Poland. The first concerned primarily the degree of autonomy of local decision makers, that is, deputies in the local people's councils.[17] The second inquiry consisted of a systematic analysis of 52 case studies of local decisions from 16 towns of various sizes, concerning conflicts among interacting local interests. The conflicting interests were typically both horizontal—local social groups with differing demands and grievances—and vertical—higher government and party organs.[18] The third research study was an inquiry into the working of the principle of "democratic centralism" on the local level. The local decision makers apparently found it easier to integrate various local interests than the intervening hierarchy of vertical interests.[19]

Conflict of Interests

All three studies thus focused on a problem neglected, for obvious reasons, in the past: conflicts of interests. Although Jerzy Wroblewski and Sylwester Zawadzki point out (in their paper on "Citizen Participation in Decision-Making Process of Local Government") that the conflict is "not based on class antagonism," they admit that "one cannot exclude such possibility." In any case, the studies do recognize and identify groups within the Polish society according to their various and sometimes conflicting interests.

First, there are conflicts of interests within the so-called social sector. This sector or factor consists of unorganized citizens with their local and individual needs, wishes, opinions, and grievances; social self-government bodies such as action committees, house committees, and settlement committees, which represent collective interests of their members for better child care, housing, water supply, and roads; local trade union organizations with their economic, social, cultural, and organizational functions, which may lobby, say, for housing for members in a particular factory or for increased pensions for retired railroad employees. The United Workers (Communist) Party is "the dominant [local] political power"; the Front of National Unity has a "relatively less influence" than the party; and the people's councils with their permanent commissions are the organs both of state on a local level as well as of local self-government. The party supposedly sees to it that both state and local interests are properly aggregated in the decisions of people's councils.

The Polish constitution lays emphasis on popular participation in decision making. It regulates extensively the role of individuals, social groups, and people's councils as initiators in the decision-making process. And yet, the constitution does not touch upon the party. "The discrepancy between the role of the Polish United Workers Party and the lack of its reflection in the constitutional provisions is now discussed in Poland and the need for institutionalization is being aired," the two authors maintain. Indeed, the party influences the local decision-making process in three ways: In general, by determining major trends in people's council activities; in particular, by voicing local party organization views on concrete issues; and through individual party members serving on the people's councils. In addition, the party shapes public opinion through its own activities as well as through trade unions, the Front of National Unity, and various social committees. The party thus plays a decisive role in local decision making—and yet, its role is entirely extraconstitutional.

The second sector, the so-called professional and administrative factor, (which may include scientific, technological, and cultural interests) tends to conflict with the social factor.[20] While the social factor approaches problems from the point of view of social needs, the administrative factor treats problems in terms of material resources and financial means. The social factor formulates demands and initiatives as expressions of social needs; the administrative factor, on the other hand, assigns importance to hierarchical structures and prevailing laws. The social factor tends to neglect technical realities; the administrative factor emphasizes them, sometimes out of proportion. And while the social factor has the capacity of grasping the whole decisional problem, however complicated, the administrative factor favors only a narrow and often partial departmental view. This is why confrontation of the two factors leads to problems.

Given the multiple, complex conflict of interests on the local level, within as well as between sectors, and recognizing the need for conflict-solving formulas, the authors recommend introduction of three major criteria, into local decision making: political (satisfaction of material, social and cultural needs of citizens); praxeological (opting for optimal effects with minimal costs); and social (taking into account complicated and long-term consequences of decisions as well as local public opinion concerning the issues to be decided).

Citizens and Their Deputies

In a longitudinal study of local government ("The [1973] Reform of Local Government in Poland in the Eyes of the Population"), Stefania Dzieciolowska and Sylwestern Zawadzki report on a survey research project conducted in 1965 and again in 1973 (and in part also in 1974) as to the changes in citizen perception of the local representative organs.

The 1965 nationwide study was conducted by Polish Radio and Television Center for Public Opinion Research. The 1973 (and 1974) study was performed by the Polish Academy of Sciences, Institute of Legal Studies, with the author's assistance. The late 1973 survey was conducted almost a year after a nationwide local government reform on January 1, 1973. The reform was designed to modernize all levels of government; to strengthen the representative organs especially at the local level; to make rural administration more efficient (reducing the local rural administrative units or *gromadas* from 4,672 to 2,381, making them almost twice as large in area and averaging some 8,000 inhabitants each); to provide the local units, the people's councils, with all the prerequisites for social, economic, and cultural satisfaction of citizens by transferring many functions from districts to localities; and to increase the educational levels of deputies.

Of course, the deputies assessed the changes in the involvement and activities of people's councils far more positively than the citizens did. Still, the no opinion column was high (see Table 6.9).

TABLE 6.9

Deputies' Assessment of Changes in Institutions of Community Representation
(in percent)

	Positive Changes	No Change	No Opinion
Activity of new people's councils' sessions	48.1	13.3	38.6
Importance of new people's councils' resolutions compared with that of *gromadas* people's councils' resolutions	53.7	14.7	31.6
Importance of people's councils as organs of self-government	52.3	26.9	20.8
Role of standing committees of people's councils	43.5	27.5	29.0

Source: Compiled by the author.

The authors wanted to know what the citizens thought about the performance of their local people's councils, about the role the people's councils played, and about the relationships between the deputies and the constituents. Are the people's councils efficient? Are they effective? Are they responsive to constituent needs? And in particular, did citizens change their views on these issues between 1965 and 1973 (and 1974)?

To start with, the researchers wanted to know how local officials treat the citizens: Are they friendly? Do they get results? Table 6.10 shows that improvement over time has been considerable, especially in the rural areas. The 1973 reform appears to have been successful in this respect in the short run.

How active are the local deputies? Do they do everything they properly should? Do they take their responsibility seriously, more so than in the past? Table 6.11 shows that the citizens thought they did. The very high proportion of citizens with no opinion is explained by the author as follows: The average citizen is less familiar with the deputies' total involvement and activities than he or she is with their administrative activities; and the two-year period since the reform, during which only several sessions of the people's councils had taken place, was too short a time span for citizen evaluation.

Again, while many citizens thought that their deputies exercised definite and increasing influence on public affairs, many others could not tell (see Table 6.12).

Like the Yugoslav questionnaire, the Polish survey instrument included questions on citizens contacting the deputies. To probe the role, responsiveness,

TABLE 6.10

Treatment of Citizens by Local Officials
(in percent)

	Rural Areas			Urban Areas		
	1965 (N = 924)	1973 (N = 914)	1974 (N = 451)	1965 (N = 926)	1973 (N = 997)	1974 (N = 529)
Friendly	56	67	89	41	54	73
Unfriendly or indifferent	34	25	8	50	39	25
No opinion	10	8	3	9	7	2
Rapid and efficient	45	57	85	31	44	73
Slow and inefficient	32	34	10	50	45	20
No opinion	23	9	5	19	11	7
Results						
Generally positive	53	69	87	42	50	76
Generally negative	9	13	7	22	25	14
No opinion	37	18	6	35	25	10

Source: Compiled by the author.

TABLE 6.11

Public View of Deputies' Activities, 1974 Compared with 1973
(in percent)

	Rural Districts		Towns
	1973 (N = 914)	1974 (N = 451)	1974 (N = 529)
Increased	13.7	23.8	20.4
No change	30.5	27.9	18.3
Decreased	9.4	2.9	2.1
No opinion	46.6	45.4	49.2

Source: Compiled by the author.

TABLE 6.12

Public Assessment of Influence Exerted by Deputies
in Their Area of Responsibility
(in percent)

	Rural Districts		Towns
	1973 (N = 914)	1974 (N = 451)	1974 (N = 529)
Great	24	34	30
Small	37	28	19
Very small or none	16	6	6
Hard to tell	23	32	45

Source: Compiled by the author.

standing, and prestige of the deputies, citizens were asked to give names of as many deputies as they could; their assessments of those deputies; the number of contacts they had had with those deputies, either in person or on committees; what issues they brought to the attention of those deputies; and what ideal deputies should be like.

Compared with the Yugoslav studies, the results were striking. While 46 percent of the citizens in towns and cities knew at least one deputy's name

TABLE 6.13

Citizen Assessment of Deputies' Activities in 1969-73
(in percent)

	Towns (N = 455)	Rural Districts (N = 734)
Very good, very active	13.3	9.3
Fairly good, did his best	41.8	38.3
Rather passive, did not exert himself	15.6	27.5
Completely passive	11.0	12.6
Hard to tell	18.3	13.3

Source: Compiled by the author.

on their people's council, 80 percent of citizens did in the rural communities. Apparently, strong social ties between constituents and their representatives exist in the countryside. Deputies are well known and sought after. And they are probably subject to stricter social supervision than in the cities, where they tend to be more anonymous. This is confirmed by data on citizen evaluation of the deputies' activities: The constituents know their deputies well and they are critical. They probably make greater demands on their deputies and are not always realistic (see Table 6.13).

TABLE 6.14

Citizen Contact with Deputies
(in percent)

Frequency of Contacts During Year Preceding Investigation	Towns		Rural Districts	
	1973 (N = 997)	1965 (N = 926)	1973 (N = 914)	1965 (N = 924)
None	64.7	70.8	46.3	54.2
Once	15.8	13.2	17.5	13.8
Several times	13.3	11.2	24.0	17.8
Many times	6.1	3.8	12.1	10.8
No information given	0.1	12.	0.1	3.4

Source: Compiled by the author.

This finding is supported by Table 6.14. In 1965 and in 1973 the rural constituents led the urban constituents in contacting their deputies. Moreover, the contacting increased more for rural than for urban constituents. As to concrete citizen demands, submitted to deputies at citizen-deputies meeting, the data favor somewhat (1 to 4 percentage points) the more responsive and efficient urban deputies. Well over half the citizens in the sample reported that their stated needs were only partially fulfilled.

What are these needs? Table 6.15 indicates the needs and the citizens' demands. Significant changes occurred over the eight-year period. In 1965 the

TABLE 6.15

Citizen Needs and Demands
(in percent)

	Towns		Rural Districts	
	1973 (N = 997)	1965 (N = 926)	1973 (N = 914)	1965 (N = 924)
Consumer goods	30.2	29.9	20.5	8.5
Housing: new	28.7	36.5	10.2	7.6
Cleanliness and esthetic aspects of towns and villages	20.0	21.2	5.7	4.8
Development of sports and culture	15.0	24.6	15.8	29.1
Communications	13.1	15.1	7.8	5.2
Street and local road building and repairs	9.8	13.8	33.3	46.1
Community facilities	9.6	15.8	17.3	11.8
Development of services	8.7	6.2	5.5	4.6
Improvement in the work of citizen militia	8.7	10.4	3.8	—
Development of education and child care	7.9	16.9	10.8	24.3
Improvement of local administrative work	6.0	26.6	4.6	26.3
Housing: repairs and maintenance	5.1	9.5	1.2	no data
Development of health services	4.5	7.6	7.2	8.5
Employment	2.0	7.1	0.8	—
Activation of local industries	0.8	5.1	0.3	—
Activation of agriculture	0.2	—	20.2	31.5
Supply of machinery and tools for agriculture	0.1	—	5.1	0.8
Electrification of the countryside	—	—	0.4	9.8
No opinion	9.3	5.4	13.3	4.2

Source: Compiled by the author.

TABLE 6.16

Public View of Characteristics Desirable in a Deputy
(in percent)

	Towns		Rural Districts	
	1973 (N = 997)	1965 (N = 926)	1973 (N = 914)	1965 (N = 924)
Honesty, reliability	52.5	55.9	46.3	53.2
Initiative, energy	48.8	27.6	37.6	36.1
Familiarity with problems of his area	42.8	44.2	52.2	52.7
Experience in life, wisdom	30.0	29.0	24.8	25.7
Experience in social work	27.3	27.6	34.7	36.6
Civic courage, ability to uphold his point of view	22.2	21.5	22.0	18.1
Ability to deal with people	17.0	30.0	22.4	27.6
Standard of education	14.2	23.8	12.2	22.1
Kindness	9.2	15.7	9.1	14.2

Note: Each respondent could specify up to three characteristics.
Source: Compiled by the author.

citizens in towns and cities wanted more housing, greater availability of consumer goods, improvement in local administration, more sports and culture, and
greater cleanliness in streets and public facilities, in that order. But in 1973 they
wanted development of services (and consumer goods, housing, public cleanliness, and sports and culture), but felt that public administration had improved
considerably. The rural population, on the other hand, in 1965 most wanted
new or better streets and roads, more public attention to agriculture, more
sports and culture, better local administration, and more and better schools and
kindergartens. In 1973, while their needs stayed with better roads, agricultural
improvement, and more sports and culture, their priorities shifted from local
administration, education, and child care to consumer goods and community
facilities—sports, culture, entertainment. In both urban and rural sectors the rate
of change in demands in the eight-year period was considerable, and the shift
suggests socioeconomic development and a higher standard of living, especially
in the rural sector.

Finally, Table 6.16 stipulates what a model deputy should be. The rural
population had not much changed its views from 1965 to 1973. Familiarity with
the problems of constituents, and personal honesty and reliability, remained
high. Experience, energy, and iniative came next, followed by such personal

qualities as wisdom, courage, and ability to get along with people. Clearly, the wise, prudent, knowledgeable local activist was the 1973 model in the countryside. In the urban areas, the change over time has been more pronounced. The citizen concern with social problems demanding resolution tended to result in a composite deputy who might be less familiar with his constituents but would be energetic, full of initiative, resourceful, honest, and familiar with the community problems.

Overall, the data show that in the public view the people's councils improved between 1965 and 1973 (1974), in some respects considerably, both in urban and rural areas. The local deputies tend to be viewed as better educated, more responsive, more active, and more influential. Still, the difference between town and country is pronounced. Provincial and land-oriented, the rural society tends to lag behind the highly organized urban society. Politically, the rural representative system still tends to resemble a traditional patronage-based polity. The emphasis is on localism—the deputies' familiarity with people, their conditions and problems; relations are highly personal. In cities, on the other hand, relations are impersonal, functional, and problem-oriented. It is almost a matter of two different cultures, and the study shows it well. An important reason for the 1973 reform was to cope with this dualism on the local level; the data show that, in this respect, the reform has not been entirely successful.

CONCLUSION

This report offers introductory and still fragmentary evidence that there is citizen participation in community decisions in Eastern Europe. The nature, scope, intensity, and channels of such participation are indeed affected by ideological, cultural, and structural constraints. As compared with citizen participation elsewhere, however, constraints are similar, as are attitudes and attributes of citizens that affect participation.[21]

The several conclusions advanced in the studies summarized above may be put forward as hypotheses for testing in other developed socialist systems. They include the following major findings:

1. Organizational (party) affiliation determines how and how much citizens participate in community decisions. Such affiliation, however, is not the only determinant of participation; education (skill) is significant as well. Income, on the other hand, plays a lesser (and different) role than in nonsocialist countries (Yugoslavia, Romania, Hungary, Poland).

2. In spite of superimposed political uniformity, diversity exists in Yugoslavia, Hungary, Romania, and Poland. While elective (political, functional) participation tends to be uniformly politicized in Yugoslavia, communal (socioeconomic) activities display great diversity. In Romania, a high rate of

socioeconomic development and change tends to make for greater concern with local (community) issues than with national matters. In Poland the national dichotomy between town (modern) and country (traditional) still seems to persist. And in Hungary diverse local interests tend to be reconciled at the county level.

3. It appears that, the more developed the socialist system, the greater the citizen participation, the more ambitious the aspirations and demands of the citizens on the political system, and the better educated, more active, and more responsive the local officials (in Poland).

4. With the slight exception of workers' councils, public activity is still a man's domain. Such citizen attributes as age and occupation, and the level of community development, are much more important for political participation than sex (in Yugoslavia, and probably in Poland, Hungary, and Yugoslavia as well).

5. As different groups have different interests, conflicts of interests arise. Such conflicts may or may not originate in class antagonism, but they need to be reconciled. In Hungary public employees, the professional bureaucracy, engage in interest reconciliation openly and as a matter of course. Elected representatives, on the other hand, consider conflicts of interests socially harmful, to be dealt with behind closed doors. In Poland it is recommended that, in the absence of legal provisions, an overall institutional conflict-solving formula and mechanism be devised to introduce rational, efficient, and legitimate reconciliation of conflicts of interests.

This is but a beginning. We plan to continue to pursue the study of political participation in Eastern Europe because we believe that developed socialist systems have been adapting to the basic requirements of political development and adopting institutions of interest articulation. Without citizen participation in community decisions, we are persuaded, these polities would not be able to advance on their respective developmental paths and would in fact risk economic, social, and political decay.

NOTES

1. Sidney Verba and Norman Nie, *Participation in America* (New York: Harper and Row, 1972), Introduction.

2. Samuel P. Huntington and Joan M. Nelson, "Socio-Economic Change and Political Participation," Report to the Civic Participation Division of the Agency for International Development (Cambridge, Mass.: Harvard University, unpublished, 1973), Chapter 6, p. 7.

3. Text in Jan F. Triska, ed., *Soviet Communism: Programs and Rules* (San Francisco: Chandler, 1962), p. 138.

4. Najdan Pasic, "Socialism and Modernization of Politics," *International Political Science Association Roundtable,* September 16-20, 1968, p. 1, p. 4, cited in Zvi Gitelman,

"Beyond Leninism: Political Development in Eastern Europe," *Center of International Studies* (occasional papers), Pittsburgh, Pa., October 1971, pp. 8, 10.

5. E. M. Chekharin and D. A. Kerimov, "Sotsialisticheskaia demokratiia na sovremennom etape kommunisticheskogo stroitel'stva," in *XXIV s'ezd ob ukreplenii sovetskogo gosudarstva i razvitii sotsialisticheskoi demokratii*, ed. D. A. Kerimov (Moscow: Mysl', 1973), p. 12. Cited in Jerry F. Hough, "Political Participation in the Soviet Union," unpublished paper, 1975. Hough argues that there has been sharp increase in citizen participation in the USSR in the last 10 years.

6. Huntington and Nelson, *Socio-Economic Change,* Chapter 3, p. 6.

7. On the lack of authentic participation in socialist systems, see Zvi Gitelman, "Beyond Leninism," p. 16; and Robert S. Sharlet, "Concept Formation in Political Science and Communist Studies: Conceptualizing Political Participation," *Canadian Slavic Studies* 1, no. 4 (Winter 1967): 640-49. (In Gitelman's view, Sharlet "has demonstrated the irrelevance to Communist systems of Western concepts of participation by identifying the defining characteristics of participation as efficacy, voluntarism and responsiveness, none of which are typical of political participation in Communist systems. Efficacy, involving the belief by an individual that his political behavior may affect governmental decisions, is submerged under the doctrine of the collective and group primacy. Responsiveness to citizen demands is relatively low in Communist systems, especially in regard to non-local issues. Voluntarism is seriously impeded by the Party's distrust of any spontaneous activity.") See also Zbigniew Brzezinski and Samuel P. Huntington, *Political Power: USA/USSR* (New York: Viking, 1964), p. 93.

8. Myron Weiner, "Political Participation: Crisis of the Political Process," in Leonard Binder et al., *Crises and Sequences in Political Development* (Princeton: Princeton University Press, 1971), p. 164.

9. Huntington and Nelson, *Socio-Economic Change,* Chapter 2, p. 7.

10. Ibid., p. 8.

11. Ibid., p. 7.

12. Ibid.

13. D. Richard Little, "Political Participation in the U.S. and the U.S.S.R.: A Conceptual Analysis," *Comparative Political Studies* 8, no. 4 (1976): 451-60.

14. Hough, "Political Participation," p. 25. Also, see William R. Schonfeld, "The Meaning of Democratic Participation," *World Politics* 28, no. 1 (October 1975): 138-41; Verba and Nie, *Participation in America,* p. 300.

15. Little, "Political Participation," p. 453.

16. Ibid., p. 454.

17. W. Sokolewica and S. Zawadzki, "The Results of Research Concerning Resolutions of People's Councils and Their Presidia," *Problemy Rad Narodovych* 3 (1965), in Polish.

18. J. Wroblewski, ed., "Determinants and Decisional Processes of Urban People's Councils," *Problemy Rad Narodovych* 30 (1974), in Polish.

19. J. Tarkowski, *Comparative Study of Political Systems of [two Polish] Districts, Pultusk and Wadowice* (Warsaw: Polish Academy of Sciences, 1971) in Polish.

20. The social-administrative factor dichotomy is narrower than Huntington's citizens-political professionals dyad. See Huntington and Nelson, *Socio-Economic Change,* Chapter 2, p. 2.

21. For comparison, see Alex Inkeles, "Participant Citizenship in Six Developing Countries," *APSR* 63, no. 4 (1969): 1120-41 (Argentina, Chile, East Pakistan, India, Nigeria, and Israel).

POLITICAL PARTICIPATION, COMPETITION, AND DISSENT IN YUGOSLAVIA: A REPORT OF RESEARCH ON ELECTORAL BEHAVIOR

Lenard J. Cohen

Can the political leaders of one-party states cope with the pluralizing consequences of their own modernization programs? In recent years that question has been the source of considerable discussion among social scientists. A central issue in the discussion has centered upon the capacity of various one-party states to satisfy pressures for the political participation of the new groups and interests that result from the rapid economic and social transformation of society. While the existence of such pressures is widely acknowledged, views differ regarding the probable impact of modernization on one-party states. Some authors anticipate movement toward a more open and pluralistic political system, if not a fully "democratic" one. Others foresee the continuation or strengthening of barriers to political participation in order to preserve the dominant position of the single party. However, most observers agree that any policy adopted by the leaders of one-party states in the face of demands for expanded and more significant group involvement in politics is likely to be fraught with difficulties. A sustained effort to disregard or contain the political activity of various groups may promote serious antiregime dissent and subversion, as well as deprive the governing elite of badly needed resources for economic development (expertise, information, popular support).

Alternatively, measures to broaden the opportunities for the expression of different group preferences and ideas can have a dangerous multiplier effect that, if unchecked, may seriously undermine and eventually eliminate the control of the single-party elite. "Repression or explosion," Robert Dahl has observed, is the dilemma of all "mixed regimes," that is, political systems "with broad citizenship but limits on public contestation, particularly on the right to form opposition parties."[1]

Yugoslavia during the past two and one-half decades provides a good example of a mixed regime. Beginning in the early 1950s, as part of the general reorganization in the wake of the rift with the Soviet Union, the Yugoslav leadership began to experiment with various institutional reforms designed to broaden the scope of political participation while at the same time preserving the "leading" position of the single party (renamed the League of Yugoslav Communists in 1952) and its ideology. Among the East European Communist states, the Yugoslav case represents the earliest and certainly the most ambitious attempt to confront the political consequences of modernization. Indeed, the quest to develop institutional structures for the representation and reconciliation of various group interests has been one of the central themes of Yugoslav politics and government.

This essay focuses on one particular aspect of the Yugoslav experience, the electoral system, which in contrast to various other major features of development in that country (workers' self-management, local government, ethnic relations) has received only marginal attention from foreign observers.[2] As will be more apparent from the discussion that follows, this study is motivated by the belief that the Yugoslav effort to "democratize" the electoral system offers an excellent case study to examine various issues concerning the political development of one-party, and particularly Communist-party regimes.[3]

In order to place this study in context, the first section briefly sketches the changing role of elections and voting during successive phases of Yugoslav political development. Given the exceedingly complex and fluid character of Yugoslav electoral institutions, we will intentionally avoid a descriptive presentation of structural changes, concentrating instead on the general "functions" of elections and voting in relation to the broader context of Yugoslav politics. The subsequent portions report the preliminary findings of a research project on electoral behavior using aggregate voting data from the 1969 elections to legislative assemblies on the republican-provincial level of the Yugoslav federation.

YUGOSLAV ELECTIONS IN TRANSITION

Yugoslav postwar political development can usefully be divided into four periods: (1) the period of "administrative socialism" from roughly 1945 to 1952; (2) the "transitional period" or "new system" from 1953 to 1962 marked by the introduction of workers' self-management; (3) a period of liberalizing political and economic reforms from 1963 to 1971; and (4) an attempt from late 1971 through 1976 to revive the regimes' initial revolutionary elan and unity, as well as to retard the growth of internal political opposition through a return to greater party control.

The character and functions of elections in Yugoslavia closely reflect broader changes in each successive period of development. The elections held during the first period were modeled closely on the Soviet (Stalinist) system, with special allowance for particular Yugoslav features. Voting was officially regarded as an act of acclamation rather than choice, an exercise to mobilize popular support and symbolically enhance the legitimacy of the new regime. The first postwar election, in November 1945, took place just a little over a year and a half after Tito's partisan forces entered Belgrade. Although the Communist Party was firmly in control of the country and had considerable popular support, the government was formally a coalition between the Communists, representatives of the royal government-in-exile, and several prewar political parties. Sizable pockets of opposition to the new regime still existed in parts of the country, as a result of the vicious civil war that had gone on parallel to the resistance struggle against the Axis powers. The voters were asked to support a single list of candidates under the label of the Communist-organized People's Front and pledged to support its program. As there was no alternative to the front, the election was actually a plebiscite. Citizens could vote against the front by dropping their ballots in the so-called "box without a list" (*kutija bez liste*), popularly referred to as the "black box" or the "widow" because it bore the name of no political party. Passive opposition could be expressed by abstaining entirely. Given the controls and coercive sanctions wielded by the Communist Party during this period, active electoral opposition to the new regime was a high-risk enterprise. The regime regarded the 88.7 percent turnout as an overwhelming victory, although under the circumstances the large number of people who either voted against the front (9.5 percent of the voters), or abstained (11.3 percent of the eligible citizens) was surprisingly high. An official history of the period provides a glimpse of the atmosphere during the elections:

> The elections of November 11th were transformed into a national holiday and a united demonstration of support for the program of the People's Front and the Republic. Voting began in the morning hours so that some polling places were finished before noon. The very ill arrived at the polling places with the help of their relatives or members of the People's Front. Voting became a patriotic duty. The whole day activists of the People's Front carrying banners and slogans moved through the streets of the cities and villages in processions. National dances, slogans, and songs of young people contributed to a holiday atmosphere. . . . Loudspeakers were installed in the cities to announce the results of voting in the election. . . . The national celebration didn't conclude until late in the evening. The next day there were tumultuous demonstrations at all voting places as a spontaneous expression of the people's enthusiasm because of the great electoral victory.[4]

The reorganization of the entire political and economic system during the early 1950s had a marked influence on the theory and practice of Yugoslav elections. The most significant changes in the context of this essay were: (1) a decrease in overt intimidation and force by the regime to influence voter participation; (2) provisions for increased citizen participation in the nomination and slating of candidates; and (3) the introduction of plural-candidate contests for legislative elections in a limited number of districts. Despite the significance of the above changes, elections in this period were still officially regarded as performing a primarily legitimizing function and great stress was placed on the importance of voting as a civic duty. One foreign observer of the 1953 election campaign noted that "the chief problem of the government running the elections under the new system was to make them as free and democratic as possible in form, while at the same time, insuring that the 'right' results were obtained."[5] Yugoslav analysts pointed with pride to the decrease, compared to 1945, in the number of "opposition" or dissenting votes (ballots placed in the "box without a list" in 1945 and 1950, "invalid ballots" beginning in 1953), as well as the number of voters who completely abstained (see Figure 7.1).[6]

Although a complete analysis of voting behavior during this period is outside our present scope, it appears that Yugoslav elections were beginning a slow process of transition from what Jerzy Wiatr has called "safe elections" to "consent elections." Consent elections, according to Wiatr, do not provide the voter with a choice between competing parties for power, but:

> (1) he is personally free to express his acceptance or disapproval of a governmental policy with the assumption that his vote would have some meaning for the future policy; (2) he can influence the selection of the members of representative bodies both in negative and positive ways (by voting against some and/or for some other candidates). The consent elections do not decide who will rule the country but they influence the way in which the country will be ruled.[7]

It can be argued, of course, that while the regime dispensed with the heavy-handed methods used earlier, elections throughout the period between 1953 and 1963 were "safe" in the sense that the Yugoslav Communists did not permit any competition from other parties. They did, however, allow the population some modicum of choice, as well as the right to withhold or offer consent to the regime without fear of the severe sanctions formerly employed. Vestiges of the past persisted to be sure but, as Thomas Hammond observed in a suggestive study of the 1953 elections, a large portion of the population took advantage of the new atmosphere to register indifference or opposition to the regime. Adding together abstentions (nonvoters) and invalid votes (votes against the candidate or candidates, and ballots incorrectly marked) to construct a rough measure of voter nonconformism, Hammond drew attention to districts where electoral "opposition" ran as high as 43.3 percent (Djakovo, Croatia) and as low as 3.3 percent (Mlavski, Serbia). Cross-regional comparisons of opposition revealed a high of 21.7 percent in Vojvodina (an autonomous province within Serbia) to a

FIGURE 7.1

Abstention (Nonvoters) and Dissent (Invalid Votes) in Yugoslav Federal Elections, 1945-69

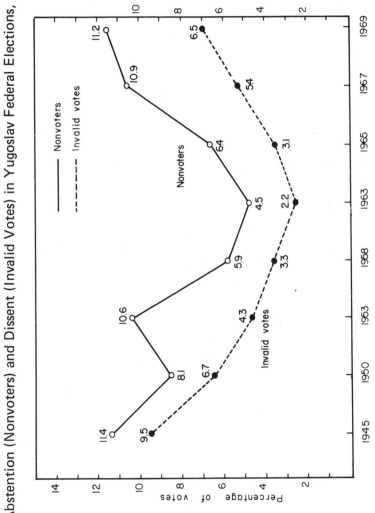

Source: Documentation Service of the Federal Assembly (Belgrade).

low of 9.7 percent in Montenegro. Hammond's study suggested that although the electoral system in Yugoslavia was far from fully "democratic," an analysis of voting data under the more liberalized conditions introduced in 1953 might reveal some interesting patterns of political behavior among regions and over time.[8]

The major impetus to the further democratization of the electoral system in this period was the changing role of the Yugoslav Communist Party in the political process. The reorganization of the party beginning in 1952 from a command-oriented revolutionary movement into an "ideological-guiding force" (reflected in its new designation as the League of Yugoslav Communists) opened the way for the emergence of a more pluralistic political system. One beneficiary of this trend toward the diffusion of political influence was the parliamentary system, which gradually became a more important factor in political decision making. The removal of the league from operational control over broad areas of social and economic activity made the structure of legislative assemblies a focal point for the active consideration of matters previously handled exclusively by the party apparatus. Once the political influence and status of the parliamentary system grew in significance, the composition of legislative bodies and consequently the character of elections naturally assumed greater importance.[9]

The real takeoff stage of parliamentary and electoral development followed the adoption of a new constitutional system in 1963. Theoretically grounded on the principles of constitutionalism and legality (*ustavnosti i zakonitost*), the new system was directed toward the institutionalization of political power within a framework of legal norms. The process of institutionalization (or what some observers have termed "disinstitutionalization" and "reinstitutionalization")[10] included the revitalization of certain democratic measures initiated ten years earlier, as well as several innovations in the political structure and process. The most important measures were: (1) the establishment of an autonomous Constitutional Court to adjudicate a variety of different disputes and safeguard basic legal rights; (2) the creation of multichamber legislative assemblies incorporating a mixture of popular, ethnoregional, and functional representation; (3) the mandatory "rotation" of legislators and civil servants by means of a limitation on the length of time for holding office in order to "deprofessionalize" public service and increase opportunities for citizen participation in political decision making. The intention of these and other changes was both to limit the concentration of political power and to broaden the scope of political participation.

It is also in this period after 1963 that one finds Yugoslav party leaders and scholars endorsing the view that conflicts stemming from divergent economic and social interests are a normal feature of socialist development.[11] Once the plurality of group interests was recognized as a legitimate topic of discussion, it was a short step to the question of how such interests might be politically expressed and satisfied. "The essential aspect of political pluralism," wrote a prominent Yugoslav writer, "is the institutionalization of pluralism."[12] One alternative, the development of a multiparty system, was clearly unacceptable to the regime even if, as some Yugoslav commentators suggested at the time, the parties were all socialist.[13] In the opinion of the Yugoslav leadership, however, the absence of competing parties did not rule out the existence of "socialist alternatives." Such alternatives, it was alleged, could vary from different preferences regarding:

> concrete measures and means, to concrete ideological political principles. But, they do not deny the sociopolitical premises of the socialist society, and are based on the interests, concepts, and the will of the working people, being applied to the methods, means, forms, and tempo for achieving a policy which stems from the society and serves it. . . . These alternatives confront one another but are not opposed to each other, they are open to discussion (*dijalogicne*) but not conflicting, they are in a certain sense friendly and not hostile to each other. No one is a priori a greater marxist and socialist if he accepts one of them.[14]

Yugoslav authors proposed a number of channels and arenas through which socialist alternatives might be expressed. These included the various territorial units that comprise the federal structure of the country, the multicameral organization of legislative assemblies, competition between different self-managing enterprises, as well as different sociopolitical and professional organizations. Sounding more Madisonian than Marxian, many Yugoslav constitutional specialists even suggested that the supremacy of "assembly government" in their country did not preclude a healthy separation or "division of powers" among relatively autonomous legislative, executive, and judicial branches of the governmental structure.[15]

It was at this juncture in the mid 1960s that increasing attention focused on the electoral system as another acceptable and reasonably manageable site for the institutionalization of socialist alternatives. In June 1965 the Socialist Alliance (the successor of the People's Front and the mass sociopolitical organization with direct responsibility for the organization of legislative elections in Yugoslavia) passed a resolution urging more extensive use of plural-candidate electoral contests for legislative assemblies: "under present conditions the nomination of several candidates is an expression of the creative possibilities for broader selection of people who can perform public functions in sociopolitical life. It is the right of people to nominate one or more candidates. The essence of democracy isn't in the number of candidates but in respecting the right of citizens to directly express their suggestions and to select candidates throughout the entire electoral process."[16] In October 1966 Edward Kardelj, the principal architect of Yugoslav governmental reforms, and at that time president of the

Federal Assembly, was even more emphatic when speaking to a national symposium of political functionaries and academic specialists called specifically to discuss the electoral system. Kardelj observed:

> It seems to me that we are still arguing a great deal about whether it is better to have one or more candidates. Everyone knows that it is better to have more candidates than one, to have more freedom in the process of nomination, etc. The essential question is, however, what conditions do we need to create so that we really can secure a more or less uninterrupted process of growth, and so to speak, the quantitative accumulation of those conditions which allow the development of our society to unfold without difficult convulsions, explosions, and various anti-democratic tendencies?[17]

As pointed out above, plural-candidate electoral contests within the single-party Yugoslav framework had already taken place during the 1950s, although on a very limited scale and exclusively on the local (communal) and regional (republican-provincial) levels. In 1963 and 1965, under the new constitutional system, there were no plural-candidate contests on the federal level and only a few on the republican-provincial level. More choice was offered in elections for communal assemblies, but even at that level a report of a Socialist Alliance indicated that "several candidates for one mandate occurred in an insignificant number of electoral districts. And where several candidates were proposed, many withdrew for fear of not being elected, or at the suggestion of the political leadership."[18]

The gradual impact of the 1963 constitutional reform, together with the economic reforms of 1965, the purge of the secret police in July 1966, and renewed efforts to "divorce the party from power," all converged to provide the necessary momentum for further changes in the electoral system. In the election of 1967, for the first time there were plural-candidate races for seats to the Federal Assembly, and also a considerable increase in the number of contested elections for republican and provincial assemblies (see Table 7.1).

In the general political atmosphere prevailing at the time, the advent of widespread plural-candidacies, along with the serious effort to broaden citizen participation in the nomination process, opened a new if only short-lived phase in Yugoslav electoral development. A transition from the completely safe elections of the early postrevolutionary period to consent elections was now clearly evident. The regime was still attempting (as the above remarks by Kardelj indicate) to walk the fine line between electoral choice, with its risks to single-party dominance, and socialist order, with the attendant dangers of excessive central control along Soviet lines. The tilt in 1967, however, was toward more choice, and both Yugoslav and foreign observers interpreted the change as a hopeful omen of future political development.[19]

TABLE 7.1

The Legislative Recruitment Filter

	Number of Seats	Total Candidates Proposed at Voters' Meetings	Total Candidates Nominated	Total Candidates Slated by Electoral Commissions	Total Candidates Listed on Final Popular Ballot*
Federal elections					
1963	120	158	142	120	120
1965	58	378	305	64	58
1967	60	565	455	97	81
Republican/provincial elections					
1963	650	797	753	650	650
1965	325	1,334	1,141	482	360
1967	325	1,764	1,533	1,749	429

*After (s)election by communal assemblies.
Source: Predstavnicka tela drustveno-politickih zajednica: izbori i sastav (Belgrade: Savezni zavod za statistiku, 1964, 1965, 1967), nos. 296, 372, 491.

The hesitancy with which the regime approached any injection of genuine competition in the political process was illustrated by the reaction to the results of the 1967 election. Utilizing the newly liberalized nomination process, individuals in a number of electoral districts were able to get proposed, nominated, and even elected without the support of, and sometimes in direct opposition to, the local and/or federal party leadership. It is noteworthy that these so-called "private candidates" were not anti-Communists or non-Communists, but in most cases popular Communist war heroes with a large enough local following to be elected without official backing. Ironically, most of these maverick candidates were either members or supporters of the conservative political wing in the party (league), a group that had opposed the recent series of economic and political reforms, including the liberalization of the electoral system. It appeared that the electoral system, as one of a growing number of centers for political influence, offered itself to those best equipped to use it, irrespective of their underlying commitment to democratic norms.[20]

Reacting to the surprises of the 1967 elections as well as to other manifestations of unmanaged political pressure from "below" such as the student rebellion in June 1968, the party leaders quickly attempted to regain control over events. In preparation for the 1969 legislative elections a new law gave the Socialist Alliance greater leeway to influence the nomination and composition of candidates and made it more difficult for nonofficial or unorganized political forces to get their candidates on the ballot. In effect, the threshold of recruitment for legislative elites, which had never been open very wide, was again narrowed, although as the 1969 election was to demonstrate it was still large enough to permit a small number of officially unacceptable candidates to get a foot in the door. As in 1967, there were cases involving the appearance of "private candidates" who had not received local party sponsorship. In several instances, candidates and their supporters crossed the boundary of what the regime regarded as tolerable conflict among socialist alternatives and engaged in a so-called "struggle for power." It was officially alleged that these practices sometimes aroused unsavory remnants of bourgeois pluralism such as "canvassing" (kortestvo—campaigning by means of group-oriented appeals and attacks on fellow candidates) and cheap "demagogy" (electoral promises). Despite these "negative" consequences, the Yugoslav regime claimed, with considerable justification, that the elections of 1967 and 1969 were more democratic than those held during the preceding periods. The gradual increase throughout the 1960s in the number of citizens who either abstained from voting or invalidated their ballots (see Figure 7.1), a phenomenon that certainly would be troubling to other Communist regimes, was officially attributed by the Yugoslavs to the more tolerant political atmosphere and the elimination of "plebiscitarian" elections. It was now officially acknowledged that "electoral alchemy" had been responsible for the high rate of voter turnout and the absense of conflicts in earlier years.[21]

The dilemma of the mixed regime, however, persisted to confront the Yugoslav leadership. As one observer noted, the central problem was how to reconcile "a commitment to more participation and more choice among 'socialist alternatives' with their continued unwillingness, when the chips are down, to leave it to the voters. . . . to choose freely and make 'mistakes' even among communists representing various points of view within the party."[22]

In 1974 the Yugoslav regime's penchant for institutional reorganization and improvization (a central and too often neglected component of the elite political culture) reasserted itself. The entire constitutional structure, including the method of electing legislative assemblies, was once again completely altered. The specific provisions of the new constitutional structure partially reflected earlier difficulties encountered with the operation of governmental institutions, as well as the regime's intent to push ahead with the organization of the state according to the principles of self-management. Equally important as motivating factors for the design and spirit of the changes introduced in 1974 were several serious issues facing the party leadership. These included continued difficulties with the "national problem" preparation for the trouble expected to accompany Tito's ultimate departure from power, factionalism within the League of Communists, internal dissent, and foreign subversion. The effort to deal with these problems began with Tito's purge of nationalists in 1971, and has been continued in a wide variety of measures through 1976.

With regard to the electoral system established in 1974, the new structure bore very little resemblance to earlier arrangements. Inspired by Marx's endorsement of the political structure adapted by the short-lived Paris Commune of 1871, the newest Yugoslav electoral and legislative procedures are designed to eliminate the remaining "vestiges" of "classical bourgeois parliamentary democracy," which allegedly characterized preceding elections. The complex and novel electoral mechanism introduced in 1974 is based on the "delegate principle" whereby each tier of the assembly system (federal, republican-provincial, and communal) is composed of delegates elected by legislative bodies on the lower levels of the structure. The entire system emanates, at the bottom of the structure, from delegations elected by citizens in the individual "self-managed" enterprises, organizations, and communities that comprise the basic electoral constituencies.[23] Although a systematic analysis of the new electoral mechanism in operation for the first time in April 1974 is outside the scope of this report, it appeared similar, at least in practice, to a much earlier phase of Yugoslav Communist political development, namely, closely controlled or "safe" elections aimed at the symbolic legitimation of the regime through the near perfect mobilization of all eligible voters. Following the practice officially endorsed during the preceding decade, the new electoral system did provide some element of choice for the voter, with the number of candidates in excess of the number of delegates to be elected. The competitive features of the electoral process in 1974, however, were severely restricted by a political climate far less tolerant of divergent opinions than during the period from 1965 to 1971, and by the determination of the regime to exercise greater "guidance" over candidate selection according to "precisely established and socially negotiated criteria."[24] The electoral process aside, however, it was premature in 1976 to draw any firm conclusions regarding the ability of the new legislative structure to genuinely enhance democratic participation, as claimed by its designers.

The above discussion of elections in Yugoslavia is intended to offer an overview of Yugoslav electoral development within the context of general political changes. Although the most interesting period of Yugoslav electoral history from 1963 to 1969 has been frequently noted and described by foreign observers, there have been no attempts to utilize the extensive and highly accessible body of empirical material produced during that period for the systematic analysis of political behavior. It is our belief that, irrespective of one's judgment regarding the degree of genuine choice and participation provided in Yugoslav elections over the past decade, the nature of the experience offers an extremely fertile area for political research. This is especially true of the rich and relatively untouched storehouse of data on such areas of electoral behavior as voter participation, electoral dissent, and patterns of political competition. Moreover, the probable elimination of this type of information on voting behavior in the future, owing to the regime's decision to completely reorganize the electoral system (a decision that also, unfortunately for political inquiry, limits comparability between earlier and current elections), only increases the importance of retrospective electoral research. The following section of the study presents a framework for the analysis of voting behavior in Yugoslavia and a preliminary analysis of the 1969 elections.

THE ANALYTICAL FRAMEWORK

The Sample and Units of Analysis

The data for this study are drawn from officially published reports of the results of the April 1969 elections for seats to the republican and provincial legislative assemblies in Yugoslavia.[25] The study is limited to electoral contests for the republican chamber or provincial chamber of the assembly in each of the republics and provinces, that is, the one chamber in each of the multicameral legislative bodies that was directly elected on the basis of population In 1969 the remainder of the chambers (collectively referred to as the chambers of working communities) in each assembly were elected on the basis of functional or producer representation from the various "self-managed" sectors of Yugoslav society (the economy, education, health) and are not included in this study.

The decision to concentrate on the republican and provincial level of the Yugoslav federation was made primarily to increase the size of the sample for analysis. On the federal level in 1969 there were only 120 seats to the popularly and directly elected "sociopolitical chamber" of the Federal Assembly. Of these, only 49 were plural-candidate races, or a relatively small number in each region of the country. By focusing on elections for the republican and provincial assemblies, each having a popular and reelected chamber of its own, it was possible to expand the universe of electoral districts (seats) to 780 (see Table 7.2). The decision to select electoral districts at this level as the units of analysis also was influenced by the significant political role played by the republics and provinces in Yugoslav politics during the period being analyzed (a stage that might be termed the confederal phase of political development), as well as the opportunity accorded by this approach to explore cross-regional comparisons within one country.

As Table 7.2 indicates, data were obtained for 506 electoral districts in four of the six republics (Slovenia, Croatia, Bosnia, and Macedonia), and one of the two provinces (Vojvodina, an autonomous province of Serbia).* Each electoral district was a single-member constituency, electing one individual to the republican or provincial chamber in the particular assembly.

One problem in using electoral districts as the units for analysis is that the district (constituency) boundaries are drawn on the basis of population size and are rarely coterminous with administrative district boundaries, which are used for the collection and reporting of census data. It therefore becomes difficult to relate political data (such as voter turnout), which are reported for each electoral district, to socioeconomic data (such as level of industrialization), which are reported on the basis of administrative districts (in Yugoslavia the basic administrative unit is the commune, of which there were 501 in 1969). The problem, by no means unique to Yugoslavia, had a major influence on the selection of variables for analysis.

---

*We do not have access to the official register for Montenegro.

The officially published results of the 1969 election to the Republican Chamber of Serbia offered only data on the number of votes received by the winning candidate. One might speculate that the absence of more complete returns is the result of local political sensitivity due to the large number of upsets against regime- (league) sponsored candidates (the so-called "cases") and negative manifestations of electoral behavior, which occurred in this republic in both 1967 and 1969. It also may reveal a more cautious stance toward political data and "scientific" inquiry by administrators of the Serbian documentation services. Unfortunately, the election results reported in the press were too partial to compensate for the deficiency of the official sources. In the case of the province of Kosovo, the uniqueness of the electoral system employed prevented comparability with the other regions of the country.

TABLE 7.2

Electoral Contests for Republican and Provincial Assemblies, 1969

Republics and Provinces	Yugoslav Universe		Sample Structure							
	Total Districts (Seats)[a]	Total Candidates Slated[b]	Total Districts in the Sample[c]		Type of Election					
					Single-Candidate Contests		Multi-Candidate Contests		Total Electoral Contests	
			N	(%)	N	(%)	N	(%)	N	(%)
Slovenia	90	157	88	17.4	31	35.2	57	64.8	88	100.0
Croatia	120	260	113	22.3	39	34.5	74	65.5	113	100.0
Serbia	120	221	—	—	—	—	—	—	—	—
Bosnia	120	191	119	23.5	74	62.2	45	37.8	119	100.0
Macedonia	100	199	97	19.2	43	44.3	54	55.7	97	100.0
Montenegro	70	139	—	—	—	—	—	—	—	—
Vojvodina	90	172	89	17.6	28	31.5	61	68.5	89	100.0
Kosovo	70	80	—	—	—	—	—	—	—	—
Total	780	1,425	506	100.0	215	42.5	291	57.5	506	100.0

[a]Each district elected one member to the republican or provincial chamber. In Macedonia only 98 out of 100 districts actually held elections on the appropriate day, April 13, 1969.

[b]"Slated" refers to official confirmation by republican and provincial electoral commissions after a complex multistage nomination process. The actual number of candidates on the ballot for election day differed very slightly from the number slated because of withdrawals and so on.

[c]In republics and provinces for which data were available a small number of districts were not included because of incomplete information.

Source: Table shows contests for the popularly elected republican chamber and provincial chamber in the republics and provinces. The source for the Yugoslav universe is *Predstavnicka tela drustveno-polititckih zajednica: izbori i sastav* (Belgrade: Savezni Zavod za Statistiku, 1969), Statisticki bilten, 590, p. 8.

Summary of Variables and Questions for Analysis

In order to explore patterns of electoral behavior in Yugoslavia we have selected several variables for analysis. Four of the variables express various aspects of socioeconomic and political structure, and three others measure different dimensions of political behavior. The underlying assumption of the study is that there are some identifiable relationships between the structural (independent) variables and behavioral (dependent) variables, that may be qualitatively, as well as quantitatively, described and explained. In this preliminary report we will concentrate on the general recognition of the relationships among variables rather than assigning any precise tests of statistical significance or correlation. In summary form, the major independent and dependent variables are presented below.

Independent Variables

Political Competitiveness: This variable is defined by the number of candidates standing for election in a particular district. We shall refer to a district as politically competitive if the number of candidates is in excess of the number of places (seats) to be filled. As the districts being analyzed are all single-member constituencies, a politically noncompetitive district is one in which only a single candidate is on the ballot for a given legislative seat. For purposes of analysis this variable will be expressed as a dichotomy (noncompetitive races/competitive races) or as a trichotomy (noncompetitive races/two-candidate races/multi-candidate races).

In the context of this analysis we do not assume that plural-candidate legislative contexts indicate the existence of electoral opposition, that is, some form of "goal differentiation between available candidates in harmony with the constitutional requirements of a given system."[26] As Otto Kircheimer has aptly pointed out "any form of political opposition necessarily involves some kind of competition. The reverse does not hold true: political competition does not necessarily involve opposition."[27] The concept of political competitiveness used in this study is similar to the idea of contestation without opposition developed by Jerzy Wiatr and Adam Przeworski for their study of political pluralism in Eastern Europe.[28]

It should be noted that, although for purposes of summary presentation political competitiveness is treated as an independent structural variable likely to influence certain dimensions of political behavior (voter dissent, participation), competition in terms of the amount of choice given by the regime (the number of candidates available in a district) also may be viewed as dependent on other structural variables (ethnoterritorial region, economic region, urbanization). Viewed in terms of an overall framework for the analysis of voting behavior presented below, political competition therefore may be seen either as an independent variable having some equivalency to other independent structural variables or as a dependent variable (part of the structure of political choice) contingent on the social and economic structure.

Ethnoterritorial Regions: This variable is defined by the constituent units of the Yugoslav federation, the six republics and two provinces. Five of these regions are included in our sample (see Table 7.2). The existence of deep and persistent ethnic and regional cleavages is perhaps the most notable feature of Yugoslav society. Identification of the precise contours or boundaries of regional cleavages varies considerably in the voluminous literature on the subject and depends largely on the particular criteria employed by each study: nationality, geography, religious divisions, political culture, national character, "race," economic differences.[29] For analytical purposes this study will employ the regional boundaries drawn by Yugoslav constitutional architects in establishing the present federal structure of the country. Although none of the republics and provinces is ethnically homogenous (Slovenia, which is 94 percent ethnically Slovene, comes closest), they each display relatively distinctive clusters of dominant ethnic and cultural characteristics within one constitutionally defined territorial unit. Moreover, during the past decade official policy and political realities, particularly the diffusion of power within the League of Communists, have encouraged the continuation or formation of separate ethno-territorial identities in each of the republics and provinces.[30]

Of the several criteria employed when the present political-administrative divisions of Yugoslavia's federation were established in 1946, the primary consideration was that of nationality. Five of the six republics (Serbia, Croatia, Slovenia, Montenegro, and Macedonia) reflected the concentration of one numerically dominant nationality group. In the sixth republic, Bosnia-Hercegovina, where the intermixture of different nationalities was greatest, no single ethnic group had an absolute numerical majority. In recent years, however, the regime has encouraged the formation of a distinctive "Moslem" ethnic identity in Bosnia. (Moslems are now the largest portion of the population in Bosnia, 39.6 percent).[31] A similar trend has taken place in the province of Kosovo, which has become the special domain of its majority (73.7 percent) Albanian population. Vojvodina, composed mainly of Serbs (56 percent) and a large Hungarian minority (22 percent), remains a special case. The independent historical development of the Serbs in Vojvodina, however (compared with their ethnic brethren in "Serbia proper"), along with the "territorialization" of power throughout Yugoslavia, gives the province a separate regional identity. One of the major aims of this study is to examine to what extent the ethnoterritorial regions influence patterns of political behavior, as expressed through aggregate voting data. It also will be interesting to see if regional patterns of voting behavior correspond at all to other empirically delineated political configurations within Yugoslavia (such as distinctive political cultures as revealed through survey research on attitudes and values).

Economic Macro-Regions (Developed North/Less-developed South): This variable is based on the conventional Yugoslav and foreign breakdown of the republics and provinces into economically "developed" and "less-developed" areas. The division into economic macro-regions follows a rough north/south line across Yugoslavia and clusters the eight ethnoterritorial regions referred to above on the basis of per capita income. The income differentials between the two macro-regions in 1969, as well as the individual territorial units of which they are composed, is illustrated in Table 7.3.[32]

TABLE 7.3

Yugoslavia: National Income Per Capita (Social Product Per Head), by Economic Region

	Social Product Per Head, 1969 (current prices, new dinars)	Index, 1969 (Yugoslavia = 100)
Yugoslavia	6,525	100
Developed north	7,920	121
Slovenia	12,189	187
Croatia	8,000	123
Vojvodina	7,176	110
Serbia "proper"	6,724	103
Less-developed south	3,885	60
Montenegro	4,540	70
Macedonia	4,260	65
Bosnia-Hercegovia	4,223	65
Kosovo	2,046	31

Source: Adapted from Mary B. Gregory, "Regional Economic Development in Yugoslavia," *Soviet Studies* 26, no. 1 (January 1974): 214.

Of the 506 electoral districts included in our sample, 290 districts (57.3 percent) in Slovenia, Croatia, and Vojvodina fall into the "developed north" macro-region, and the remaining 216 districts (42.7 percent) in Macedonia and Bosnia fall into the "less-developed south."

Urbanization (Metropolitan/Rural): This variable was defined by the classification "urban territories" in official Yugoslav census reports. In 1969, some 70 places of an "urban character" were designated based on combined statistical criteria including the density of population and the structure of social and economic activities. As each of the 70 urban territories combined a central core city and various suburban localities "connected by common public utility funds and services," we refer to them as metropolitan areas (the Yugoslav term "urban agglomerations" being rather awkward), as distinguished from the remaining territory of the country, which we treat as rural areas.[33] Of the 506 electoral districts in our 1969 sample, 185 (36.6 percent) are in metropolitan areas and 321 (63.4 percent) are in rural areas.

Dependent Variables

Vote Fragmentation: This variable is defined by the division or split of the votes among alternative candidates in competitive races. Vote fragmentation is similar to the variable used in other studies to measure the degree of competitiveness, but should be clearly distinguished from our use of political competitiveness above to denote the structure of competition. These are two closely related but fundamentally distinct concepts. Quite simply, as used here, political competition is the choice given to the electorate, in terms of the number of alternative candidates available in an election; and vote fragmentation is choice taken by the electorate from among the alternatives. Although vote fragmentation is a central variable in our general inquiry on electoral behavior, various operational difficulties with the data analysis did not allow us to consider the variable in this report.[34]

Voter Turnout: This variable is the least complex in terms of conceptualization and measurement. The level of turnout is defined by the number of votes cast as a percentage of all registered voters. Voter turnout was converted into a dichotomy (above mean/below mean) by separating the individual electoral contexts in the sample into those above or below the mean percent of voter turnout for the entire sample of 506 electoral contests, that is, 86.089 percent.

Political Dissent: This variable is defined by the number of invalid votes as a percentage of the total votes cast. The level of invalidity is treated as a dichotomy by separating all the individual contests in the sample into those above or below the mean percent of invalid votes for the entire sample of 506 electoral districts, that is, 6.8 percent.

In recent years several pioneer studies of electoral behavior in Communist countries have pointed to both voter abstention (nonvoting) and invalid votes (void or spoiled ballots) as useful indicators of political dissent.[35] In the Soviet Union, where regime-induced voter mobilization is the most intensive and thorough, almost any type of voting behavior not officially condoned, such as abstaining or invalidating a ballot, assumes the character of a political act. Soviet electoral procedure does, however, allow for the possibility of registering dissent, and each year large numbers of Soviet voters cast "negative" votes and appear to escape any severe sanctions from the regime. As Jerome Gillison pointed out in a seminal article on Soviet elections, "it is virtually impossible to miss voting by accident, only design or sheer physical incapacitation can account for absenteeism. . . . Because of this rather awe inspiring organization, one can assume, that in the vast majority of cases, absenteeism is the result of purposeful abstention—one must be an artful dodger, and not merely absent-minded."[36]

Under the condition of highly organized voter mobilization that exists in the Soviet Union, as well as most other Communist party states, it seems reasonable to combine the number of absentee votes with the number of negative (invalid) votes as one measure of political dissent. As we pointed out above, such a combined measure of electoral dissent was also applicable to Yugoslavia during the period of "safe" elections. The marked decrease in the use of Soviet-type electoral mobilization techniques by the Yugoslav leaders, however, along with the other liberal measures adopted in the mid-1960s, had an important influence on the nature of voting, and thus on nonvoting. While the regime continued to encourage and characterize voter participation as a demonstration of support for the political system, voter abstention was no longer considered a litmus test of unpatriotic behavior. Voting was still officially regarded as a civic duty, but the normal absence of some voters on election day, due to lack of political commitment or apathy, was now expected and tolerated.

Empirical studies of the underlying motives for electoral turnout in this period revealed that the number of voters who participated simply due to a fear of sanctions or reprisals if they abstained was relatively low and mainly concentrated among citizens having little or no education.[37] The nonvoters interviewed were concentrated exclusively among the illiterate and those with less than a secondary school education (see Table 7.4). As pointed out above (see Table 7.2), the number of nonvoters rose steadily from 1963 to 1969 and was interpreted in Yugoslavia as a "rather positive development, if we bear in mind that our citizens were free in making their choice this time."[38] Obviously, the number of people who abstain includes many who are consciously protesting against the regime by failing to participate in the electoral process, and is an important measure of the political climate in a particular electoral district as well as the country at large.[39] The act of invalidating or spoiling a ballot, however, requires in most cases a more conscious and deliberate expression of political dissent.

Thus, although it is impossible to precisely determine what proportion of valid ballots, invalid ballots, and nonvoting citizens represent individuals who harbor antiregime beliefs, or to differentiate among such beliefs according to their specific character and intensity, we nevertheless feel that under the conditions in Yugoslavia during 1969, the number of citizens spoiling their ballots is the soundest measure of political dissent in the electoral process. In the following analysis, therefore, invalid votes will be treated separately from abstentions (a phenomenon already encompassed by our variable on voter turnout described above). Of course it should be noted that even invalid votes cannot be considered a pure measure of political dissent. According to the 1969 election law:

TABLE 7.4

Motivation to Vote by Level of Education: A Survey of Yugoslav Citizens, 1969

Motivation to Vote*	Illiterate	Four Years of School	Eight Years of School	Secondary School, Including School for Skilled Workers	Higher Institutions, University	Total
1. Civic consciousness and duty	69.3	59.1	58.3	52.4	40.6	55.7
2. A desire to influence political decision-making	5.1	10.2	10.5	14.6	23.0	12.5
3. Fear of encountering unpleasantness as a consequence of abstention	11.8	11.4	9.6	4.1	1.0	7.7
4. Consciousness of the importance of voting for the development of democracy	4.2	15.4	17.7	26.5	33.0	20.4
5. Did not vote	8.9	2.4	2.4	1.9	—	2.5
6. Other answers or unknown	.7	1.5	1.5	0.5	2.4	1.2
Total (N = 614)	100.0	100.0	100.0	100.0	100.0	100.0

Note: The table reflects a survey of 614 individuals conducted by the Institute of Social Science (Belgrade) in 23 Yugoslav communes. Unfortunately, as in many Yugoslav monographs, there is no breakdown of the absolute number of respondents falling into each category of the table.

Question: What is the basic reason you participated in the election and voting?

Source: Mijat Damjanovic, "Birac kao subjekt izbornog procesa" [The voter as the subject of the electoral process] in Milan Matic, et al., eds., *Skupstinski izbori 1969* [Assembly elections: 1969] (Belgrade: Centar za Istrazivanje Javnog Mnenja, 1970), pp. 112-14.

FIGURE 7.2

The Analytical Framework of Electoral Behavior

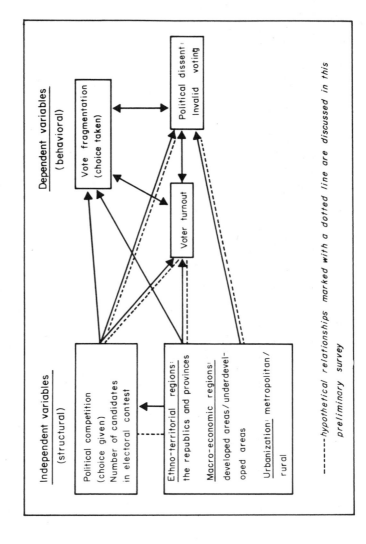

Source: Compiled by the author.

Electoral ballots are declared nonvalid on which the number beside the name of more than one candidate is circled, a ballot on which a new name is written and circled, a ballot which is not filled out, and also a ballot which is filled out so that it isn't possible with certainty to determine for which candidate the elector voted.[40]

Invalid votes defined and reported in this manner make it impossible to rigorously distinguish the highly politicized invalid votes from those due to apathy or misunderstanding about correct electoral procedure. It is unlikely, however, that the number of invalid votes deriving from indifference, ignorance, or negligence is very high. As one Yugoslav student of electoral behavior indicated, invalid ballots are

an indicator of the political mood because their number can be an expression of concealed protest at the ballot or at the political situation, and also the inability of voters to fill out the ballot. However, we can discount the second factor, because where real interest in the election exists, there is little probability that the voter will not seek help if he doesn't know how to complete the ballot, or that he will fill it out partially or incorrectly.[41]

In order to explore the relationship among the variables described above, the study is guided by the following general questions:

1. Are the dependent (behavioral) variables—voter turnout, political dissent, and vote fragmentation—related to the independent (structural) variables of political competition, ethnoterritorial regions, macroeconomic regions, and urbanization?
2. Is political competition (choice taken), which may be considered an independent "structural" variable influencing electoral behavior, related (dependently) to the other structural variables?
3. How are the three dependent variables interrelated?

Those questions, which have served to orient the preliminary data analysis, are schematically illustrated in Figure 7.2.

RESEARCH FINDINGS

Patterns of Electoral Behavior

A summary of the general findings on patterns of electoral behavior follows. Only a brief outline of preliminary results and tabular illustrations will be presented at this stage of the project. A more complete description and effort to explain the findings will be offered in the final report.

Voter Turnout

The mean percent of voter turnout for our entire sample of 506 electoral districts is 86.1 percent. The range of turnout across the sample varied from one district in Vojvodina where turnout was 97.5, to a low of 62.1 percent in a Macedonian district. In sharp contrast with Soviet-type elections, only 28.3 percent (143) of the districts had a turnout level of over 90 percent.

By ethnoterritorial region: Of the regions sampled, Vojvodina stands out with the highest mean turnout (90.7 percent) and the largest number of electoral

TABLE 7.5

Voter Turnout, by Territorial Unit, Economic Macro-Region, and Level of Urbanization

	Level of Voter Turnout*		
	Contests Above Mean (%)	Contests Below Mean (%)	Total (N)
Territorial unit (republic or province)			
Slovenia	80.7	19.3	88
Croatia	58.4	41.6	113
Vojvodina	87.6	12.4	89
Macedonia	27.8	72.2	97
Bosnia	29.4	70.6	119
Total	54.7	45.3	506
Economic macro-region			
Developed north	74.1	25.9	290
Less-developed south	28.7	71.3	216
Total	54.7	45.3	506
Level of urbanization			
Metropolitan	40.0	60.0	185
Rural	63.2	36.8	321
Total	54.7	45.3	506

*Voter turnout refers to number of votes cast as a percentage of all registered voters. The level of voter turnout was converted into a dichotomy by separating the individual electoral contests in the sample into those which were above or below the mean percent of voter turnout for the entire sample of 506 electoral contests, that is, 86.089 percent.

Source: Compiled by the author.

contests above the sample mean (see Table 7.5). While only 28.3 percent of all the districts sampled had a turnout level over 90 percent, the figure was 62.9 percent in Vojvodina. Slovenia and Croatia also had high levels of mean turnout (88.3 percent and 87.3 percent, respectively). Slovenia far exceeded Croatia, however, in the number of contests above the sample mean. The analysis revealed lower levels of mean turnout in Bosnia (82.7 percent) and Macedonia (82.4 percent). Macedonia had the largest number (72.2 percent) of electoral districts below the sample mean. Various explanations of this behavior can be sought in the rich body of literature on regional political behavior in Yugoslavia (an aspect of the study that will be given more detailed consideration in the final report).

By economic macro-region: The level of voter turnout appears very closely related to different levels of economic development: 74 percent of the electoral contests in the "developed north" were above mean, and only 28.7 in the "less-developed south" (again, see Table 7.5).

By urbanization: Voter turnout appears to be considerably higher in rural electoral districts than in metropolitan ones. This finding corresponds to a number of studies by Yugoslav social scientists, as well as several comparative studies, which have noted lower levels of voter participation in urban than in rural areas.[42]

A number of different explanations, usually linked to country-specific factors, have been advanced concerning the high level of rural participation. The following interpretation by a Yugoslav author, accounting for the high level of rural participation at voters' meetings, is representative of a recurring theme in the literature:

> In contrast to the city, greater significance is attached to familial relationships in the village, and as a result the role of tradition and custom is greater, social mobility is more restricted, creating a relative homogeneity among people. Gathering together at a voters' meeting is one of the rare opportunities for people to meet, to jointly discuss various matters and news, which traverses the confines of their limited environment, and often a definite isolation. The voters' meeting in the village is almost a basic framework which socially organizes and connects people. . . . In the city however, numerous institutions are developed to which citizens belong, and in which they participate. Voters in the city attend voters' meetings in smaller numbers, because they have other meeting places at their disposal, means and channels to influence communal politics that are not always accessible to the village voter.[43]

In addition to possibly explaining the high level of rural voter turnout, the above quotation also draws attention to the fact that the electoral process fulfills functions, for both the political elite and the individual citizen, beyond that of simply selecting candidates or mobilizing support. The election serves as a vehicle for the social and political integration of a large segment of the population—mostly rural, but also many urban voters—that is otherwise on the periphery of sociopolitical life. The integrating function of elections is particularly important in view of the relatively low level of party (league) membership among Yugoslavia's rural population. This finding also would support the argument made by one student of French political behavior, that politicization and partisanship are two related, but yet fundamentally distinct concepts.[44]

Political Dissent

The mean percent of invalid votes for our entire sample of 506 electoral districts is 6.9 percent. The range of invalidity varied from 0.01 percent in one district in Macedonia to 32.2 percent in a Croatian district. Some 79 (15.6 percent) districts in the sample had an invalidity level of over 10 percent of the votes cast. (A detailed analysis and explanation of electoral dissent in these districts will be the subject of a forthcoming report.)

By ethnoterritorial region: Vojvodina, with a mean invalidity rate of 9.0 percent, again stands out among the regions sampled (see Table 7.6). One-third (32.5 percent) of Vojvodina's districts have over 10 percent invalidity, or over twice as many as the whole sample. (Macedonia was next highest, with 19.6 percent of its districts reporting over 10 percent invalidity.) Of the contests in Vojvodina, 70.8 percent were above the sample mean on this measure. When this finding is combined with Vojvodina's very high rate of turnout, the level of politicization in this area emerges more sharply.[45] This takes on added importance when it is noted that Vojvodina had one of the highest rates of invalidity in Yugoslavia in both the 1945 and 1953 elections. (In the November 1945 election for the Assembly of Nationalities to the Constituent Assembly, Vojvodina had the highest level of antiregime votes, that is, those cast in the "box without a list," or 19.4 percent. Montenegro was lowest with 2.7 percent.) Explanations for the findings on Vojvodina may derive in part from the region's high level of ethnic heterogeneity (24 different nationalities of which 56 percent are Serb, 22 percent Hungarian, 7 percent Croat, 3 percent Romanian, and 4 percent Slovak), and the fact that a large portion of the province's present population includes partisan veterans and their families from various less-developed and war-ravaged areas of the country (about 250,000 people, mainly Serbs from Bosnia and Croatia) who, after the war, were rewarded by resettlement on expropriated German and Hungarian farmland.[46]

Other inter-regional differences on this variable do not appear very significant, although we suspect that a more detailed analysis of within-region (district-by-district) variation may reveal pockets or "subcultures" of electoral dissidence that relate to other variables. For example, of the seven electoral districts in the sample with over 25 percent invalidity, five are in Macedonia, although as a

TABLE 7.6

Invalid Votes by Territorial Unit, Economic Macro-Region, and Level of Urbanization

	Level of Invalidity*		
	Contests Above Mean	Contests Below Mean	Total (N)
Territorial unit (republic or province)			
Slovenia	39.8	60.2	88
Croatia	22.1	77.9	113
Vojvodina	70.8	29.2	89
Macedonia	39.2	60.8	97
Bosnia	21.8	78.2	119
Total	37.0	63.0	506
Economic macro-region			
Developed north	42.4	57.6	270
Less-developed south	29.6	70.4	216
Total	37.0	63.0	506
Level of urbanization			
Metropolitan	38.9	61.1	185
Rural	35.8	64.2	321
Total	37.0	63.0	506

*Invalid votes refers to void or spoiled votes as a percentage of votes cast. The level of invalidity was converted into a dichotomy by separating the individual electoral contests in the sample into those above or below the mean percent of invalid votes for the entire sample of 506 electoral contests, that is 6.877 percent.

Source: Compiled by the author.

single ethnoterritorial region, Macedonia doesn't exhibit an extremely high level of invalidity. This also suggests that local structure and situational factors may prove the underlying explanatory variables explaining extremes of political dissent.[47]

By economic macro-region: The level of dissent appears to be lower in the less-developed south than in the more economically advanced region of the country. Of the electoral districts in the south, 70.4 percent are below the mean for the entire sample. However, closer inspection reveals that this finding is due to the inclusion of Vojvodina in the "developed north economic macro-region," which, it should be remembered, is a composite of Vojvodina (an autonomous section of the Serbian republic) along with the republics of Slovenia and Croatia.

When Vojvodina is excluded, the developed north has 70.1 percent of its contests below mean and 29.9 percent above, or nearly the identical figure as the south. Considered in this way, the variable again underlines Vojvodina's unique electoral behavior.

By urbanization: Levels of invalidity do not appear to differ appreciably between metropolitan and rural regions.

Political Competition

By ethnoterritorial region and economic macro-region: As pointed out above, between 1967 and 1969 it was official regime policy to offer the voters as much choice as possible within the single-party framework, through the nomination of more than one candidate on the ballot. Survey interviews by Yugoslav institutes during this period revealed that the majority of the public also desired some choice among candidates in the electoral process.[48] Of the regions sampled, the data indicate that considerably more choice was given in the northern republics, with Vojvodina again standing out, this time as the most competitive region; see Table 7.7. (Data on plural candidacies in the 1974 election, although with a completely revised institutional framework, also reveal a larger number of competitive contests in the northern regions.)

This finding is probably influenced by a combination of factors, the most important being regional differences in political culture and political history. Historically, for example, the northern region of the country had more experience with "competitive" politics vis-a-vis the Austria-Hungarian monarchy. Recent attitudes toward political competition among regional Communist elites also have been shaped by current political disputes in the country, particularly regarding the distribution of economic resources. Thus, during the 1960s the controversy between the economically more advanced and the less developed republics over the source and allocation of funds for industrial development became closely connected with differences about how political power was to be divided and exercised in Yugoslavia. The proponents of more centralized political control and the use of more "administrative" measures were heavily concentrated in the less developed regions, while groups favoring decentralization of authority and a reliance on more "liberal" forms of state control, including direct and competitive elections, were more prevalent in the economically advanced regions.[49]

By urbanization: There are somewhat more competitive races in metropolitan than in rural areas. This variables does not, however, appear to account for much variation in the area of political competitiveness.

Political Competition and Voter Turnout

It has been frequently noted in the literature on multi-party states that the level of voter participation is higher in electoral districts where there are

TABLE 7.7

Competition by Territorial Unit, Economic Macro-Region, and Level of Urbanization

	Level of Competition		
	Noncompetitive (one candidate)	Competitive (two or more candidates)	Total (N)
Territorial unit (republic or province)			
Slovenia	35.2	64.8	88
Croatia	34.5	65.5	113
Vojvodina	31.5	68.5	89
Macedonia	44.3	55.7	97
Bosnia	62.2	37.8	119
Total	42.5	57.5	506
Economic macro-region			
Developed north	33.8	66.2	290
Less-developed south	54.2	45.8	216
Total	42.5	57.5	506
Level of urbanization			
Metropolitan	36.2	63.8	185
Rural	46.1	53.9	321
Total	42.5	57.5	506

Source: Compiled by the author.

competing parties than in "safe" districts where one party captures the majority of the vote. As a political system becomes more competitive, or "more inclusive," it is argued that politicians and parties reach out to mobilize adherents, thereby heightening the level of politicization and participation in elections.[50] Does an increase in political competition in terms of choice among alternative candidates belonging to the same party have the same effect on the electorate? The preliminary evidence from our study appears to confirm the hypothesis that competition is directly related to higher levels of voter turnout, but only when the comparison is between noncompetitive (single-candidate) and competitive two-candidate electoral contests (see Table 7.8). As the number of candidates increases beyond two, however, the level of voter participation often shows a marked decrease. Thus, when electoral races having more than two candidates are considered together, they reveal almost an identical number of cases above and below the sample mean as the noncompetitive contests.

TABLE 7.8

Competitiveness (Number of Candidates) and Voter Turnout in Yugoslav Electoral Races

Level of Voter Turnout	Competitiveness			
	Noncompetitive	Competitive		
	Single-Candidate	Two-Candidate	Multi-Candidate	Total
Contests above mean	49.3	63.2	48.9	54.7
Contests below mean	50.7	36.8	51.1	45.3
Total contests in sample	100.0	100.0	100.0	100.0
	(N = 215)	(N = 201)	(N = 90)	(N = 506)

Source: Compiled by the author.

This finding seems to correspond closely to comparative studies of countries having several party organizations, which reveal that electoral turnout tends to be higher with *bi*party competition than with *multi*party competition, and indeed that electoral mobilization tends to be even lower in multiparty contests than in districts where one party or candidate is uncontested. As one author noted, "the number of candidates bears, at most, a diminishing relation to the spectrum of electoral preferences; it can be argued that beyond some number, the multiplicity of candidates tends to confuse when it does not simply roll off the electorate, members of which in turn vote less surely than they otherwise might."[51] In short, increasing the range of choice beyond a small number is at least as likely to bewilder and immobilize those eligible to vote as it is to stimulate their interest and participation. The probability that the existence of several alternatives will cross-pressure citizens and cause them to abstain is undoubtedly even more important in a country such as Yugoslavia, which has only a very limited experience with the norms and habits of electoral choice.

Political Competition and Political Dissent

To what extent have invalid or negative votes in Communist elections reflected the existence of protest against the absence of choice in the political process? Or, put another way, does the opportunity to choose among alternative candidates, albeit only among "socialist alternatives," lessen the amount of political dissent? These questions are of central concern to our research on Yugoslav electoral behavior.

The preliminary findings indicate that the provision of competitive contests in 1969 was inversely related to the incidence of political dissent in the election. When an opportunity for voters to choose among candidates was offered by the political regime, it appeared to integrate or incorporate a segment of the population that otherwise might have actively dissented by spoiling ballots (see Table 7.9).[52] In fact, unlike the impact of political competition on the degree of voter turnout (where as we saw above an increase in the number of alternative candidates beyond two tended to dampen the participation of the electorate and lead to more nonvoting), the level of invalidity tended in almost all cases to steadily decrease with each additional candidate on the ballot.

It would seem, then, that at the minimum, the opportunity provided the electorate to exercise even a limited degree of choice among candidates, and the general liberalization of the electoral process in Yugoslavia served to reduce dissent against the regime, at least as expressed at the ballot box. Despite the success of plural candidacies as a mechanism for reducing dissent (a fact officially acknowledged in Yugoslavia at the time[53]) other so-called "negative"

TABLE 7.9

Competitiveness (Number of Candidates) and Dissent (Invalid Votes) in Yugoslav Electoral Races

| | Level of Invalidity | | |
	Contests Above Mean	Contests Below Mean	Total (N)
Competitiveness			
Single-candidate race	45.6	54.4	215
Two-candidate race	33.8	66.2	201
Multi-candidate race	23.3	76.7	90
Total	37.0	63.0	505
Noncompetitive race (single candidate)	45.6	54.4	215
Two-candidate race	33.8	66.2	201
Three-candidate race	25.8	74.2	62
Four-candidate race	22.2	77.8	18
Five-candidate race	12.5	87.5	8
Six-candidate race	—	100	2

Source: Compiled by the author.

byproducts of electoral democracy ("struggles for power," "private-candidates"), were apparently too potentially explosive in the regime's view to permit continuation of its short-lived experiment with political competition in direct popular elections for regional and federal legislative assemblies.

CONCLUSION

The foregoing analysis indicates that research on voting and the electoral process in a Communist state can provide important insights concerning patterns of political behavior and political development. Our study of the 1969 election points to significant differences among the various ethnocultural and economic regions of Yugoslavia that, although frequently noted, are rarely systematically examined. The findings also underline the hazards of making sweeping country-wide generalizations about political behavior in Yugoslavia, and demonstrate the need for more crossregional comparative inquiry on multinational states. The continued divergence in the political behavior of urban and rural areas, despite the rapid industrialization of the country (the proportion of the economically active population engaged in agriculture declined from 72.7 percent in 1948 to 47.3 percent in 1971), and the unique pattern of voting behavior exhibited in the province of Vojvodina might also help orient future research.

Although the present data analysis focuses on one election, it is hoped that the longitudinal analysis of voting behavior now in progress, including electoral returns from 1953 to 1974, will shed light on various continuities and changes in political behavior. The question of vote fragmentation, which was not treated in this study, may prove the most important factor when examined over several years and during different phases of political development. For example, although cleavage among voters in districts having plural-candidate contests may not have been very great when such competition was first introduced in the 1950s (for example, a 90/10 or 70/30 division between voters in most two-candidate contests), it would be intriguing to see if this changed over time to a more polarized (fragmented) pattern, and if such changes are related to specific demographic and political factors. Commentaries on political dissent often focus on individual personalities (Djilas and Mihajlov) or on specific events (the student uprising of 1968, the 1971-72 purge of nationalist leaders) but there is almost no research on patterns of mass political cleavage over time. On the republican-provincial level, data are available for the analysis of voter fragmentation over six elections in a two-decade period.

With respect to macro political development, our findings regarding the inverse relationship between competition (choice offered) and dissent, although not entirely unexpected, are most suggestive. The analysis indicates that the proportion of the population least supportive of the regime (and likely to spoil their ballots) did in fact respond more positively when an opportunity to choose among the legislative candidates was offered, but that from the party leadership's perspective, the other "negative," consequences of the competitive process were too great a cost to bear. Briefly, in 1969, the regime seems willing to tolerate a 5 to 10 percent level of invalidity in electoral districts throughout the country (and roughly double that amount of abstentions in each consituency) rather than face the possibility of losing control over the electoral process and possibly, although this is less likely, control of the country.

The Yugoslav case demonstrates the obstacles facing all one-party states when they attempt to broaden the scope of their support and minimize the forces in society that may potentially challenge their rule, or detract from its effectiveness. The most important issue, which of course the data cannot help answer, is how long and at precisely what cost the party leaders in a "mixed" regime can continue to constrain the degree of choice in order to maintain their hegemony. For the moment at least the evidence from Yugoslavia (and here we refer not only to electoral practice but to the entire course of recent political development[54]) indicates that the party leadership is determined to closely manage and very narrowly delimit the scope of legitimate participation and political choice in order to achieve what it regards as more important objectives and to deal with more pressing problems. In doing so the leaders appear temporarily willing to ignore the observation made by one of their own poets. "Freedom" he remarks "is not one freedom":

> Freedom is not a huge, unified prescribed guaranteed freedom. Freedom is not a holy illusion. Freedom is a mixture of small and different freedoms. . . .
>
> Those who yielded to freedom's temptations are afraid. Such freedom surpasses their notion of freedom, it crops up in the most unexpected places. Freedom is hard to control, impossible to predict.[55]

NOTES

1. Robert A. Dahl, ed., *Regimes and Opposition* (New Haven: Yale University Press, 1973), pp. 13-15. Referring to the transformation of the "European Leninist regimes," Kenneth Jowitt has recently observed that we are "witnessing the appearance of amalgam-regimes based on selective, tentative and to varying degrees fragile combinations of inclusion and mobilization." Although Jowitt asserts a "continual conflict" between inclusion and mobilization, the "partially complementary relationship" of these two strategies in his "amalgam-regimes" contrasts with the much sharper "repression or explosion" dilemma of the "mixed regime" posited by Dahl. See "Inclusion and Mobilization in European Leninist Regimes" *World Politics* 27 (October 1975): 69-96. Some of the more important studies that treat the question of political change and modernization are: Robert A. Dahl, *Polyarchy: Participation and Opposition* (New Haven: Yale University Press, 1971); Chalmers Johnson, ed., *Change in Communist Systems* (Stanford: Stanford University Press, 1970); Samuel Huntington, *Political Order in Changing Societies* (New Haven: Yale University

Press, 1968); Huntington, ed., *Authoritarian Politics in Modern Society* (New York, 1970); Ghita Ionescu and Isabel de Madariaga, *Opposition* (Baltimore: Pelican, 1972); John H. Kautsky, *The Political Consequences of Modernization* (New York: John Wiley, 1972); David Apter, *The Politics of Modernization* (Chicago: University of Chicago Press, 1965), *Political Change* (London: Frank Cass, 1973), and *Choice and the Politics of Allocation* (New Haven: Yale University Press, 1971); Barbara N. McLennen, ed., *Political Opposition and Dissent* (New York: Dunellen, 1973); Leonard Schapiro, ed., *Political Opposition in One-Party States* (London: Macmillan, 1972).

On Eastern Europe and the Soviet Union specifically, see: Charles Gati, ed., *The Politics of Modernization in Eastern Europe: Testing the Soviet Model* (New York: Praeger Publishers, 1974); Zvi Gitelman, "Beyond Leninism: Political Development in Eastern Europe," *Newsletter on Comparative Studies of Communism* 5, no. 3 (1972): 18-43; William Taubman, "The Change to Change in Communist Systems: Modernization, Post Modernization, and Soviet Politics," in *Soviet Politics and Society in the 1970's,* eds. Henry W. Morton and Rudolf L. Tokes (New York: Free Press, 1974); Paul H. B. Godwin, "Communist Systems and Modernization: Sources of Political Crisis," *Studies in Comparative Communism* 6, nos. 1-2 (Spring/Summer 1973): 107-34; Andrej Korbonski, "Comparing Liberalization Processes in Eastern Europe: A Preliminary Analysis," *Comparative Politics* 4, no. 2 (January 1972): 231-50, and "The Prospect for Change in Eastern Europe," *Slavic Review* 33, no. 2 (June 1974): 219-39.

2. Some of the most notable studies of the Yugoslav electoral system for foreign scholars are: Thomas T. Hammond, "Jugoslav Elections: Democracy in Small Doses," *Political Science Quarterly* 70, no. 1 (March 1955): 57-74; Dennison L. Rusinow, *Yugoslav Elections, 1969,* a three-part report of the American Universities Field Staff, Southeast Europe Series, vol. 16, nos. 4-6 (1969); R. V. Burks and S. A. Stankovic, "Jugoslawien auf dem Wag zu Halbfreien Wahlen," *Osteuropa* no. 3 (1967): 131-46.

3. There is a small but growing body of studies on the political importance of elections in Communist regimes, See, for example, Jerzy J. Waitr, "Elections and Voting Behavior in Poland, in *Essay on the Behavioural Study of Politics,* ed. Austin Ranney (Urbana: University of Illinois Press, 1962), pp. 225-31; Frank Dinka and Max J. Skidmore, "The Functions of Communist One-Party Elections: The Case of Czechoslovakia, 1971," *Political Science Quarterly* 88, no. 3 (September 1973): 395-422; Max Mote, *Soviet Local and Republic Elections* (Stanford: Hoover Institution, 1965); Jerome Gillison, "Soviet Elections as a Measure of Dissent," *American Political Science Review* 62, no. 3 (September 1960): 814-26; Everett W. Jacobs, "Soviet Elections: What They Are, and What They Are Not," *Soviet Studies* 22, no. 1 (July 1970): 61-76; Ronald J. Hill, "Continuity and Change in USSR Supreme Soviet Elections," *British Journal of Political Science* 2, part 1 (January 1972): 47-68.

See also the interesting discussion of elections in Jaroslaw Pielkaliewicz, *Communist Local Government: A Study of Poland* (Athens: Ohio University Press, 1975) pp. 90-106.

4. Branko Petranovic, *Politicke i pravne prilike za vreme privremene vlade DFJ* (Belgrade: Institut drustvenih nauka, 1964), p. 203. For the immediate postwar elections, see also Michael B. Petrovich, "The Central Government of Yugoslavia," *Political Science Quarterly* 62, no. 4 (December 1947): 504-30. Two good English-language works on the political background during the periods 1945-53 and 1953-63 are: Woodford D. McClellan, "Postwar Political Evolution," in *Contemporary Yugoslavia* (Berkeley: University of California Press, 1969), and A. Rose Johnson, *The Transformation of Communist Ideology: The Yugoslav Case, 1945-1953* (Cambridge, Mass.: Mill Press, 1972).

5. Hammond, "Jugoslav Elections," p. 58.

6. Jovan Djordjevic, "The Electoral System and the Results of the Elections for the Federal People's Assembly," *New Yugoslav Law* 5, nos. 1-2 (January-June 1954): 3-18:

"a citizen is not bound by law to vote, i.e., non-participation in the elections is not subject to sanctions at all . . . . However, this does not imply that citizens are not conceiving suffrage as their civic duty" (p. 17).

7. Wiatr, "Elections," p. 239. Wiatr distinguishes both safe and consent elections from "competitive elections." Elections have been classified in a variety of ways. W. J. M. MacKenzie distinguishes between "muddled elections," "stolen elections," "made elections," "elections by acclamation," and "free elections." In MacKenzie's view, there are four conditions "ideally necessary" for the introduction of "free elections": (1) an independent judiciary to interpret electoral law; (2) an honest, competent, nonpartisan administration to run elections; (3) a developed system of political parties offering alternative candidates to the electorate; and (4) a general acceptance throughout the political community of "certain rather vague rules of the game which limit the struggle for power." *Free Elections* (London: Allen and Unwin, 1958), p. 14. On the functions and types of electoral systems, see also: Richard Rose and Harve Mossawir, "Voting and Election: A Functional Analysis," *Political Studies* 15, no. 2 (1967): 173-201; A. J. Milnor, *Elections and Political Stability* (Boston: Little, Brown, 1969).

8. Hammond, "Jugoslav Elections," pp. 69-70.

9. See Lenard J. Cohen, "Conflict-Management and Political Institutionalization in Yugoslavia: A Case Study of the Parliamentary System," in *Legislatures in Plural Societies: The Search for Cohesion in National Development*, ed. Albert F. Eldridge (Durham, N.C.: Duke University Press, forthcoming).

10. Winston M. Fisk, "A Communist Rechtstaat?–The Case of Yugoslav Constitutionalism," *Government and Opposition* 5, no. 1 (Winter 1969-70).

Ghita Ionescu, "Notes Toward a Study of Political Institutionalization," paper presented at the Seventh World Congress of the International Political Science Association, September 1967; Jovan Djordjevic, "Political Power in Yugoslavia," *Government and Opposition* 2, no. 2 (January-April 1967): 205-18. A useful analysis of the changes in the period from 1963-70, is Winston Fisk, "The Constitutionalism Movement in Yugoslavia: A Preliminary Survey," *Slavic Review* 30, no. 2 (June 1971): 272-97.

11. See for example: Najdan Pasic, "Interesne grupe i njihovo mesto u nasem politickom sistemu," *Gledista*, no. 10 (October 1964): 1297-1305; Svetozar Stojanovic, "Socijalisticka demokratija i SKJ" in *Marks i savremenost* (Belgrade: Institut za izucavanje radnickog pokreta i Institut drustvenih nauka, 1964), pp. 26-37, 156-200; Janez Jerovsek, "Konflikti u nasem drustvu," *Sociologija*, no. 4 (1968): 160-67; Inge Perko-Separovic, "Konflktni interesi u socijalisticka drustvu," *Gledista*, no. 1 (January 1969): 63-68. For a more recent discussion of conflicts see *Drustveni konflikti i socijalisticki razvoj, Jugoslavije*, (Portoroz: Jugoslovensko udruzenje za sociologiju, 1972), three parts; and Joseph Fisera, "Recherches recentes sur les causes des conflits dans la societe Yougoslave," *Revue de l'Est* 3, no. 2 (April 1972): 203-14.

12. Jovan Djordjevic, *Demokratija i izbori* (Zagreb: Informator, 1967), esp. "Political Pluralism and Elections," pp. 74-87.

13. See for example, Stevan Vracar, "Pluralizam u socijalistickoj demokratiji," *Pregled* 17, nos. 1, 3 (1966): 211-34.

14. Djordjevic, *Demokratija i izbori*, p. 80.

15. See, for example, Leon Gerskovic, "Problemi i perspektive razvoja skupstinskog sistema Jugoslavije," *Rad Jugoslavenska Akademija znanosti i um jetnosti* (Zagreb, 1967), pp. 37-38; Jovan Djordjevic, *O samoupravnim i odgovornom drustvu* (Belgrade: 1971), p. 409; Pavle Nikolic, *Savezna skupstina u ustavnom i politickom sistemu Jugoslavije* (Belgrade: Saveza Udruzenja Pravnika Jugoslavije, 1969), p. 129. During recent years Yugoslav theorists have condemned any separation of power among political institutions. See, for example, Cazim Sadikovic, "Koncept' Jedinstva Vlasti' u novom ustavnom sistemu," *Arhiv za pravne i drustvene nauke* 59, nos. 2-3, (April-September 1973): 377-84.

16. *Aktuelna pitanja kadrovske politike i pripreme za skupstinske izbore, Teze usvojene VI za skupstinske izbore, Teze usvojen na VI Plenumu Saveznog odbora SSRNJ od 28, septembra, 1964, godine* (Belgrade: Komunist, 1964), p. 29.

17. *Izborni sistem u uslovima samoupravljanja,* (Belgrade: Institut Drustvenih Nauka, 1967), p. 329. Also in the same volume Slavko Milosavlevski, "Broj kandidata u izborima za predstavnicka tela u Jugoslovenskom izbornom sistemu," pp. 174-77. Mileslavevski makes a strong argument for multi-candidate elections in Yugoslavia as a means for the electorate to gain control over legislative representatives, by turning the candidates attention away from political cliques and toward the voters.

18. *Socijalisticki savez: zbornik dokumenata: 1945-1969,* (Belgrade: Export Press, 1969), p. 219.

19. For a description of the changes in the nomination of legislative candidates during the period, see Susan Bridge McCarthy, "Gate Keeping in the Nominations Process in Yugoslavia," paper delivered at the 1974 annual meeting of the American Political Science Association, August 29-September 2, 1974.

20. See Rusinow, *Yugoslav Elections, 1969,* part 3, which includes a review of the 1967 results. The official analysis of the 1967 electoral "problems," is in Dragoslav Zoric and Vladen Cetkovic, *Izbori u celini politickog sistema Jugoslavije* (Belgrade: Export Press, 1968).

21. Najdan Pasic, "Otkud izborni konflikti," *Borba* (November 24, 1969), p. 9. See also Mico Carevic, "Funkcionsanje izbornog sistema u opstini," *Socijalizam,* no. 5 (May 1970): 618-38; Mijat Damjanovic, "Izborni konflikt-politicki konflikt," *Drustveni konflikti i socijalisticki razvoj Jugoslavije,* part 1, pp. 245-54; V. Pupic, "An Assessment of the Elections," *Socialist Thought and Practice,* no. 34 (April-June 1969): 58-64. For the institutional structure and operation of elections in this period, see "Assembly Elections in 1967," *Yugoslav Survey* 8, no. 4 (November 1967): 9-18, and "Assembly Elections in 1969," *Yugoslav Survey* 10, no. 4 (November 1969): 13-28. The elections of 1965, 1967, and 1969 were studied by a team of researchers working for the Institute of Social Sciences in Belgrade; see *Skupstinski izbori, 1965; Skupstinski izbori, 1967, Skupstinski izbori, 1969* (Belgrad: Institut Drustvenih, 1966, 1968, 1970).

22. Rusinow, *Yugoslav Elections, 1969* part 3, p. 12.

23. See Hrvoje Bacic and Milan Matic, "The System of Elections for the Delegations of Basic Self-Managing Organizations and Communities and of Delegates of the Assemblies of the Socio-Political Communities," *Yugoslav Survey* 16, no. 1 (February 1975): 21-53. See also Pavle Nikolic, "Basic Characteristics of the System of Delegates: Abolition of the Classic Parliamentary and Electoral System," *Review of International Affairs* (Belgrade) 25, no. 576 (April 5, 1974): 1-3; and "Yugoslavia's New Electoral System," *Radio Free Europe Research: Communist Area,* two parts (April 17 and May 13, 1974).

24. The official analysis of the 1974 election is Trajo Trajkovski, "Prvi izbori na delegatskom principu i sastavu delegacija i skupstina," *Socijalizam* 17, nos. 7-8 (1974): 781-95.

25. Data for this study are drawn from the official registers of the Yugoslav republics and provinces: *Narodne Novine, Sluzbeni List Socijalisticke Republike Havatske,* 25, no. 21 (May 3, 1969): 334-41; *Sluzbeni List SR Bosne i Hercegovine* 13 (April 25, 1969): 223-24; *Sluzben Vesnik na Socijalisticka Republika Makedonija* 17 (May 5, 1969): 371-76; *Uradni List SR Slovenije* 15 (5.V. 1969): 340-42; and *Sluzbeni list Socijalisticke Autonomne Pokrajini Vojvodine* (April 23, 1969): 234-40.

26. Frederic S. Burin and Kurt L. Shell, *Politics, Law, and Social Change: Selected Essays of Otto Kirchheimer* (New York: Columbia University Press, 1969), p. 237. Yugoslav

candidates seeking legislature seats in multi candidate races were not allowed to exhibit the "goal differentiation" that Kirchheimer identifies with "loyal opposition" in constitutional regimes, but were all obliged to accept the "electoral program" of the socialist Alliance. The vagueness of the program (general support for self-management, direct democracy, the equality of nationalities, solving the problem of unemployment) and the fact that some candidates took very personal positions on how to approach the country's problems did not change the fact that any real competition of principles or programs was constricted.

27. Ibid., p. 237.

28. Jerzy J. Wiatr and Adam Przeworki, "Control Without Opposition," in *Government and Opposition* 1, no. 2 (February 1966): 227-39. For an interesting study of electoral competition in two African one-party states, see Goran Hyden and Colin Leys, "Elections and Politics in Single-Party Systems: The Case of Kenya and Tanzania," *British Journal of Political Science* 2, part 4 (October 1972): 389-420.

29. Representative studies illustrating different approaches and conclusions include: Jovan Ovijic, "Studies in Jugoslav Psychology," *The Slavonic Review* 9, no. 26 (1930-31): 375-90, and no. 27 (1930-31): 662-81; Vladimir Dvornikov, *Karakterologija Jugoslovena* (Belgrade, 1939); Dinko Tomasic, *Personality and Culture in East European Politics* (New York: George Stewart, 1948), Bogdan Denitch, "Political Cultures and Social Mobility in Yugoslavia," (paper presented at the Seventh World Congress of the International Sociological Association, September 1970); Gary K. Bertsch and M. George Zaninovich, "A Factor-Analytical Method of Identifying Different Political Cultures: The Multi-National Yugoslav Case," *Comparative Politics* 6, no. 2 (January 1974): 219-44; Ivan Lucev, "Socijalni karakter i politicka kultura," *Sociologija* 16, no. 1 (1974): 23-44. For the most recent historical interpretation of regional differences by Yugoslav writers to appear in English, see Vladimir Dedijer et al., *History of Yugoslavia* (New York: McGraw-Hill, 1974).

30. Frits W. Hondius, *The Yugoslav Community of Nations* (The Hague: Mouton, 1968) pp. 137-45. Hondius observes that the 1946 "Yugoslav Constitution and constitutional theory accepted the five component peoples and their six countries as given data. There was a conspicuous absence of any theory as to exactly why these nationalities found their political expression in various units of the Yugoslav state" (p. 139).

31. On the relationship of religion to ethnicity in Bosnia-Hercegovina, see David A. Dyker, "The Ethnic Muslims of Bosnia—Some Basic Socio-Economic Data," *The Slavonic and East European Review* 50, no. 119 (April 1972): 238-56.

32. A very useful study of economic regionalism including methodological issues is Deborah Milenkovitch, "Yugoslav Economic Development and Regional Disparities: 1947-1974," mimeo, notes for a lecture delivered to the Graduate Seminar on Comparative Economic Systems and on Labor-Managed Economies, Cornell University, May 1974. See also Nicholas R. Lang, "The Dialectics of Decentralization: Economic Reforms and Regional Inequality in Yugoslavia, *World Politics* 27, no. 3 (April 1975): 309-38.

33. Statisticki Godisnjak, *SFRJ: 1969* (Belgrade: Savezni Zavod za Statistiku, 1969) pp. 60-63, 619. The special classification of 70 "urban territories" in 1969 should not be confused with the more general breakdown of locations as "urban" or "rural" in Yugoslav statistics, which relates total population density to the percentage of nonagricultural population. According to the more conventional classification, there were 330 communities as urban in 1971. Most of these so-called "urban" settlements are really small towns. Thus, 191 of all 330 "urban" communities in 1971 had under 10,000 inhabitants, while only 21 had populations of 50,000 or more. In view of this, we found the special classification of 70 urban centers a more useful basis to define urbanization. See Ivanka Ginic, "Dinamika Gradskog Stanovnistva Jugoslavije prema prvim rezultatima popisa od 1971.godine," *Stano-*

vnistno 9, nos. 1-2 (January-June 1971): 25-41; Dennison I. Rusinow, "Some Aspects of Migration and Urbanization in Yugoslavia," *American Universities Fieldstaff Reports: Southeast Europe Series* 19, no. 2 (1972).

34. The definition and measurement of "voter fragmentation" is the subject of a special report by Professor James Hardy of Queens College, City University of New York, "A·Draft Note: On the Measurement of Electoral Competition, Fragmentation, and Fractionalization in the 1969 Yugoslav Republican Elections," mimeo, 1974.

35. Gillison, "Soviet Elections as a Measure of Dissent"; Wiatr, "Elections and Voting Behavior in Poland"; Jacobs, "Soviet Local Elections."

36. Gillison, "Soviet Elections as a Measure of Dissent;" pp. 819-20.

37. Mijat Damjanovic, "Birac kao subjekt izbornog procesa," in *Skupstinski izbori 1969* ed. Milan Matic, et al. (Belgrade: Centar za Istrazivavje Javnog Mnenja, IDN, 1970), pp. 112-14.

38. V. Pupic, "An Assessment of the Elections," *Socialist Thought and Practice,* no. 34 (April-June 1969): 61.

39. A pioneer survey of electoral behavior in the United States undertaken half a century ago concluded that political protest was not a major factor in voter abstention. Charles Edward Merriam and Harold Foote Gasnell, *Non-voting: Causes and Methods of Control* (Chicago: University of Chicago Press, 1924), p. 123. See also Kurt Lang and Gladys Engel Lang, *Voting and Non-Voting* (Walthan, Mass.: Blaisdall), pp. 66-86.

A study of the Netherlands demonstrated that when compulsory voting legislation was removed in the election of 1970, nonvoting increased among those politically alienated. Galen Irwin, "Compulsory Voting Legislation: Impact on Voter Turnout in the Netherlands" *Comparative Political Studies* 7, no. 3 (October 1974): 300-01. The presence of tacit political alienation or dissent among citizens who vote for established parties appears to be considerable in both Communist and non-Communist countries that employ sanctions against nonvoters.

40. *Zakon o izboru poslanika skupstine Socijalisticke Republike Srbije* (Belgrade: Republicki zavod za javnu upravu, 1969), p. 110 (article 107). The definition of invalid votes for 1969 was the same in each republic and province and corresponded to the federal law on elections.

41. Milan Benc, *Demokratizacija izbornog postupka i izborna apstinencija* (Zagreb: Institut za drustvena istrazivanja, 1969), p. 7

42. See, for example, Sidney Tarrow, "The Urban-Rural Cleavage in Political Involvement," *The American Political Science Review* 65 (June 1971): 341-57, esp. 344-46; Junicki Kyogoku and Nobutaka Ike, "Urban-Rural Differences in Voting Behavior in Postwar Japan," *Economic Development and Cultural Change* 9 (October 1960), part 2, pp. 167-85, esp. 170-72; Jae-on Kim and B. C. Koh, "Electoral Behavior and Social Development in South Korea: An Aggregate Data Analysis on Presidential Elections," *Journal of Politics* 34, no. 3 (August 1972): 826-59, esp. 841-42. See also the studies of India and Japan in Roger W. Benjamin, et al., *Pattern of Political Development* (New York: David McKay, 1972), pp. 70-127, 140-48; David R. Cameron, et al., "Urbanization, Social Structure, and Mass Politics: A Comparison Within Five Nations," *Comparative Political Studies* 5, no. 3 (October 1972): 273. For two studies of Yugoslavia using survey data that show higher levels of politicization in rural areas, see Dean E. Frease, "A Politicization Paradigm: The Case of Yugoslavia," *The Sociological Quarterly* 16 (Winter 1975): 33-47; G. Wayne Bradley, "Political Alienation in Yugoslavia," paper delivered at the sixty-seventh annual meeting of the American Political Science Association, September 1971.

43. Dusko Milidragovic, "Zborovi biraca kao oblik ucesca gradana u samoupravljanju opstinom," *Arhiv za pravne i drustvene nauka* 57, nos. 2-3 (April-September 1971): 236. See also Stojan Tomic, "The Relationship Between Urbanization and Citizen Participation,"

in *Participation and Self-Management*, vol. 6 (Zagreb: Institute for Social Research, University of Zagreb), pp. 143-50, and Benc, *Demokratizacija*, pp. 31-32. For similar findings and interpretation on citizen participation in Communist government in Yugoslavia, see Eugen Pusic, "Intentions and Realities: Local Government in Yugoslavia," *Public Administration* 53 (Summer 1975): 133-53.

44. Tarrow, "The Urban-Rural Cleavage in Political Involvement," p. 346.

45. The significance of this finding is underscored by the fact that Yugoslav surveys reveal Vojvodina to be in the regime with the highest level of interest in politics and the highest level of general satisfaction with the standard of living in the country. See T. Djordjevic, "Opste interesovanje za politicka pitanja," in *Jugoslovenski javno mnenje o aktuelnim politickim i drustvenim pitanjima 1965*, ed. Firdus Dzinic (Belgrade: Institut Drustvenih Nauka, 1965), pp. 12-13; Dragomin Pantic, *'Barometar'—zadovoljstva i nezadovoljstva gradjana* (Belgrade: Institut Drustvenih Nauka, 1967), pp. 73-74.

46. An analysis based on the 1961 census revealed that of 1,854,965 people living in Vojvodina, 373,236 or about 20 percent migrated to the region from other areas of Yugoslavia, the highest percentage for any section of the country. *Migracije Stanovnistva Jugoslavije* (Belgrade: Institut Drustvenih Nauka, 1971), pp. 114-15, 222. Although the particular ethnic composition of Vojvodina may have some relationship to its unique pattern of participation, according to one Yugoslav study the citizens of the province exhibit the least "ethnic distance" from one another of any region in the country. Dragomic Pantic, *Etnicka Distanca u SFRJ* (Belgrade: Institut Drustvenih Nauka, 1967), pp. 16-17.

47. The significance of local "political climate" as the key factor explaining the level of invalid voting was reported in a study of Croatian electoral behavior on the communal level in 1969. See Benc, *Demokratizacija*, pp. 41-47. In a more recent study of the 1969 communal elections in Croatia, Benc reports a slight inverse correlation between the level of economic development in a district and the number of invalid votes: the higher the level of development, the fewer invalid votes. His claim, however, that a survey of Yugoslavia by republics for individual electoral periods from 1946 to 1969 reveals the same tendency, is not supported by the evidence. See Milan Benc, *Izborno Ponasanje Gradjana* (Zagreb: Centar za sociologiju sela, grada i prostora Instituta za drustvena istrazivanja sveucilista Zagreb, 1974), pp. 68-69. It should be noted that, despite certain flaws, the 1974 study by Benc (in English, "The electoral behavior of citizens") represents a pioneer contribution to Yugoslav empirical political socilogy.

48. See Mijat Damjanovic, "Opravdanost usmeravanja izbornog procesa u uslovina drustvenog samoupravljanja," in *Izborni sistem a uslovima samoupravljana*, pp. 146-49; Slavko Milosavlevski and Milan Nedkov, *Izborniot sistem i izbornata demokratija vo praktika* (Skopie: Institut za socioloski i politicko-pravni istrazuvanja, 1968), pp. 130-33.

49. Dennison Rusinow, "Yugoslavia: 1969," *American Universities Fieldstaff Reports, Southeast Europe Series* 16, no. 8 (August 1969).

50. See Dahl, *Polyarchy*, pp. 23-25.

51. Peter McDonough, "Electoral Competition and Participation in India: A Test of Huntington's Hypothesis," *Comparative Politics* 4, no. 1 (October 1971): 77-88. Our preliminary research on voting in *interwar* Yugoslavia supports the same view; see *Statistika izbora narodnih poslanika kraljevine Srba, Hrvata, i Slovenaca* (Belgrade, 1924), p. XXI.

52. "Free elections are useful means of reducing the level of dissent, and of increasing the level of accord between governed and government. This would be a statement of the minimum function [of elections] so far as consent is concerned." P. H. Partridge, *Consent and Consensus* (New York: Praeger Publishers, 1971), pp. 143-44. A direct relationship between constricted competition and invalid voting is noted in Rodney P. Stiefbold, "The Significance of Void Ballots in West Germany Elections," *American Political Science Review* 59, no. 2 (June 1965): 406-7.

53. See "Assembly Election 1969," *Yugoslav Survey*, p. 25.

54. For a description of these developments, see Alex N. Dragnich, "Yugoslavia: Titoism without Tito?" *Current History* 67 (March 1976): 111-13, 133; Slobodan Stankovic, "Yugoslavia: Workers' Self-Management vs. One-Party Rule" Radio Free Europe, *Background Report* no. 147 (October 1975): 1-12; Melanie Anderson, "The Trial of Mihajlo Mihajlov," *Index* 5, no. 1 (Spring 1976): 3-12.

55. Matija Beckovic, "On Freedom," in Mitija Beckovic and Dusan Radovic, *Che: A Permanent Tragedy, Random Targets* (New York: Harcourt Brace Jovanovich, 1970), pp. 78-80.

8

PARTICIPATORY REFORMS AND POLITICAL DEVELOPMENT IN ROMANIA
Mary Ellen Fischer

Until 1975 elections to state organs in Romania—the Grand National Assembly (GNA) and local people's councils—followed a procedure typical in the Soviet Union and Eastern Europe since World War II: One candidate for each office was nominated by the Socialist Unity Front and then elected by an over-whelming majority of the voters. In 1971 Ceausescu indicated that the electoral procedures should be improved to ensure "heightened responsibility" of candidates toward the masses.[1] The first national elections after he made this suggestion were held in March 1975 and indeed almost 40 percent of the candidates for the GNA and 76 percent of all candidates were opposed in these elections.[2]

The purpose of this essay is twofold: First, to describe briefly the political reforms in Romania since 1965, and second, in the context of these reforms, to examine in as much detail as possible the first multi-candidate elections—which candidates were faced by opponents, the occupations of these candidates, the nomination and election procedures, and the results of the voting. Unfortunately, the number of votes received by each candidate remains confidential; only the total votes cast and the names of the winners have been published (see Tables 8.1 and 8.2). Nevertheless, the available information reveals a great deal about the concept of multi-candidate elections as perceived in Romania. The published data have been supplemented by interviews with election officials and informal discussions with Romanian citizens, both before and after the elections.

CEAUSESCU'S REFORMS

The introduction of multi-candidate elections in Romania must be analyzed in the context of other political reforms in the last decade under

TABLE 8.1

Results of Romanian General Election of March 2, 1969

County	Registered Voters	Votes Cast Number	Votes Cast %	Votes for Socialist Front Candidates Number	Votes for Socialist Front Candidates %	Votes Against Number	Votes Against %	Null Votes Number	Null Votes %
Alba	259,040	258,963	99.97	257,447	99.41	1,515	0.59	1	—
Arad	376,095	376,021	99.98	375,204	99.78	803	0.22	14	—
Arges	372,523	372,432	99.98	371,665	99.79	733	0.20	34	0.01
Bacau	370,524	370,445	99.98	370,073	99.90	370	0.10	2	—
Bihor	428,859	423,673	99.96	427,767	99.79	865	0.20	41	0.01
Bistrita-Nasaud	175,565	175,510	99.97	174,340	99.33	1,113	0.64	57	0.03
Botosani	288,014	287,928	99.97	287,796	99.96	127	0.04	5	—
Brasov	338,800	338,362	99.87	335,769	99.23	2,426	0.72	167	0.01
Braila	237,426	237,356	99.97	237,205	99.94	151	0.06	—	—
Buzau	333,251	333,067	99.94	332,693	99.89	348	0.10	26	0.01
Caras-Severin	268,855	268,771	99.97	268,442	99.88	316	0.12	13	—
Cluj	455,953	455,527	99.91	452,705	99.38	2,597	0.57	225	0.05
Constanta	352,227	352,089	99.96	351,357	99.79	628	0.18	104	0.03
Covasna	125,772	125,729	99.97	125,297	99.66	422	0.33	10	0.01
Dimbovita	297,899	297,809	99.97	297,408	98.86	385	0.13	16	0.01
Dolj	500,696	500,551	99.97	500,109	99.91	399	0.08	43	0.01
Galati	334,219	334,134	99.97	333,881	99.92	253	0.08	—	—
Gorj	216,420	216,356	99.97	216,029	99.85	327	0.15	—	—
Harghita	197,459	197,423	99.98	197,130	99.85	292	0.15	1	—
Hunedoara	340,566	340,491	99.98	339,025	99.57	1,415	0.41	51	0.02
Ialomita	237,821	237,812	99.99	237,722	99.96	67	0.03	23	0.01
Iasi	405,844	405,767	99.98	495,181	99.86	491	0.12	95	0.02
Ilfov	539,340	539,233	99.98	539,657	99.97	152	0.03	24	—
Maramures	288,492	288,322	99.94	287,469	99.71	697	0.24	156	0.05
Mehedinti	224,635	224,615	99.99	224,416	99.91	160	0.07	39	0.02
Mures	382,450	382,336	99.97	381,024	99.66	1,312	0.34	—	—
Neamt	307,007	306,940	99.98	306,720	99.93	220	0.07	—	—
Olt	334,357	334,226	99.96	334,058	99.95	122	0.04	—	—
Prahova	511,354	510,744	99.88	508,039	99.47	1,571	0.50	46	0.01
Satu-Mare	239,952	239,882	99.97	239,504	99.84	144	0.06	134	0.03
Salaj	177,207	177,160	99.97	176,937	99.88	215	0.12	234	0.10
Sibiu	294,489	294,330	99.95	292,520	99.39	1,705	0.58	8	—
Suceava	376,705	376,578	99.97	376,175	99.89	367	0.10	105	0.05
Teleorman	377,390	377,279	99.97	377,232	99.99	43	0.10	36	0.01
Timis	488,348	488,260	99.98	487,392	99.82	811	0.17	4	—
Tulcea	152,859	152,750	99.93	152,595	99.90	118	0.08	57	0.01
Vaslui	264,074	263,998	99.97	263,888	99.96	89	0.03	37	0.02
Vilcea	266,859	266,779	99.97	266,385	99.85	362	0.14	21	0.01
Vrancea	231,226	231,172	99.98	230,932	99.90	230	0.10	32	0.01
Municipiul Bucuresti	1,211,677	1,211,325	99.97	1,204,911	99.47	5,387	0.45	1,025	0.08
Total	13,582,249	13,577,143	99.96	13,543,499	99.75	30,748	0.23	2,896	0.02

Source: *Scinteia*, March 4, 1969, p. 1.

TABLE 8.2

Results of Romanian General Election of March 9, 1975

County	Electoral Districts	Candidates	Registered Voters	Votes Cast Number	Votes Cast %	Votes for Socialist Front Candidates Number	Votes for Socialist Front Candidates %	Votes Against Number	Votes Against %	Null Votes Number	Null Votes %
Municipiul Bucuresti	28	45	1,453,707	1,453,516	99.99	1,441,991	99.19	11,461	0.80	64	0.01
Alba	7	11	280,165	279,971	99.93	276,794	98.87	3,177	1.13	1	—
Arad	8	11	392,801	392,742	99.98	388,239	98.85	4,502	1.15	—	—
Arges	10	13	417,765	417,676	99.98	411,285	98.47	6,391	1.53	—	—
Bacau	11	14	414,387	413,941	99.89	408,292	98.63	5,649	1.37	—	—
Bihor	10	14	448,797	448,797	100.00	443,787	98.88	4,997	1.12	13	—
Bistrita-Nasaud	5	6	188,687	188,414	99.86	186,231	98.84	2,183	1.16	—	—
Botosani	8	11	286,721	286,677	99.98	283,980	99.06	2,692	0.94	5	—
Brasov	8	10	398,059	397,886	99.96	389,922	98.00	7,854	1.97	110	0.03
Braila	6	9	261,586	261,539	99.98	258,638	98.89	2,901	1.11	—	—
Buzau	9	13	356,407	356,370	99.99	352,544	98.93	3,826	1.07	—	—
Caras-Severin	6	8	284,434	284,382	99.98	281,582	99.02	2,800	0.98	—	—
Cluj	11	14	504,521	504,442	99.98	493,847	97.89	10,569	2.10	26	0.01
Constanta	9	13	427,034	426,730	99.93	422,560	99.02	4,154	0.98	16	—
Covasna	3	4	136,530	136,477	99.96	134,675	98.68	1,802	1.32	—	—
Dimbovita	8	11	332,923	332,912	99.99	330,736	99.35	2,164	0.65	12	—
Dolj	12	17	534,103	533,817	99.95	530,138	99.31	3,674	0.69	5	—
Galati	9	12	380,114	379,968	99.96	374,549	98.58	5,408	1.42	11	—
Gorj	6	9	240,141	240,141	100.00	238,757	99.42	1,384	0.58	—	—
Harghita	5	6	220,328	220,286	99.98	217,658	98.81	2,628	1.19	—	—
Hunedoara	9	11	368,589	368,559	99.99	363,612	98.66	4,938	1.34	1	—
Ialomita	7	10	254,499	254,465	99.99	252,543	99.24	1,921	0.76	1	—
Iasi	12	16	458,412	458,349	99.99	450,795	98.35	7,549	1.65	5	—
Ilfov	13	18	568,397	568,014	99.93	564,110	99.31	3,891	0.69	13	—
Maramures	8	11	314,504	314,402	99.97	310,914	98.89	3,474	1.10	14	0.01
Mehedinti	5	7	228,850	228,850	100.00	226,934	99.16	1,916	0.84	—	—
Mures	10	13	413,189	413,043	99.96	405,465	98.17	7,578	1.83	—	—
Neamt	9	12	337,027	337,008	99.99	334,464	99.25	2,544	0.75	—	—
Olt	9	13	362,339	362,279	99.98	359,659	99.27	2,595	0.72	25	0.01
Prahova	13	17	567,915	566,628	99.77	554,343	97.83	12,171	2.15	114	0.02
Satu-Mare	6	8	258,463	258,403	99.98	254,907	98.65	3,496	1.35	—	—
Salaj	5	7	185,066	185,605	99.97	181,893	98.32	3,088	1.67	24	0.01
Sibiu	8	10	324,423	324,284	99.96	316,122	97.48	8,162	2.52	—	—
Seceava	11	16	398,965	398,965	100.00	394,909	98.98	4,056	1.02	—	—
Teleorman	9	14	391,705	391,491	99.95	388,820	99.32	2,587	0.66	84	0.02
Timis	11	17	528,500	528,340	99.97	522,391	98.87	5,903	1.12	46	0.01
Tulcea	4	6	170,573	170,454	99.93	169,218	99.27	1,234	0.73	—	—
Vaslui	8	11	274,424	274,392	99.99	270,614	98.62	3,776	1.38	2	—
Vilcea	7	11	288,987	288,656	99.89	283,987	98.38	4,669	1.62	2	—
Vrancea	6	9	245,995	245,923	99.96	243,634	99.07	2,289	0.93	—	—
Total	349	488	14,900,032	14,894,185	99.96	14,715,539	98.80	178,053	1.20	593	0.003

Source: Scinteia, March 11, 1975, p. 1.

Nicolae Ceausescu. Communist leaders in power have made use of various strategies to maintain themselves at the apex of their respective political systems. Three of the most important of these strategies have been use of the individual's prestige as revolutionary leader, violence (or terror), and foreign support. The names Lenin, Mao, Tito, Castro (as well as Ho Chi Minh and Kim Il-sung) immediately come to mind as men who have been able to use their revolutionary prestige in the postrevolutionary struggles for power. Violence, or terror, has been even more widespread; the key name that comes to mind here is, of course, Stalin, but so far no Communist leader has been able to keep himself and his party in power totally without the use of this technique. The third source of power, foreign support, has been crucial in Eastern Europe, where in most cases the role of the Soviet army was the major factor allowing the local Communist party to seize and retain political control.

All three of these strategies were used extensively by the leader of the Romanian Communist Party (RCP) from 1944 to 1965, Gheorghe Gheorghiu-Dej. In the early days of party rule in Romania, foreign support—occupation by the Soviet army—undoubtedly was the crucial factor. This foreign support was accompanied by the extensive use of terror, and Gheorghiu-Dej until his death maintained his personal control over the Romanian police through his subordinate and close friend, Alexandru Draghici. Finally, although the Romanian Communist Party had not actually had an independent "revolution," Dej had been one of the major party leaders in the prewar period, and was one of the few ethnic Romanians who played an important role in the indigenous Communist movement.

None of these strategies has been available to Nicolae Ceausescu, head of the Romanian Communist Party since 1965. Although Ceausescu was involved in underground party activities before World War II, and spent many years in prison as a result of his revolutionary zeal, he was by no means an important Communist leader who could claim personal responsibility for the success of the Romanian revolution. Nor could he make extensive use of terror in 1965 to establish himself firmly in power, since at that time not he, but one of his major rivals (Draghici), controlled the Romanian secret police. Even more remarkable, Ceausescu has kept his position despite the opposition of the Soviet leadership to many of his policies. In fact, much of his success has been due to the hostility of the Soviets, rather than to their support. Yet after eleven years in office, he seems to be completely in control of his party and state, and is surrounded by a personality cult unsurpassed by any postrevolutionary leader except Stalin.

How did he do it? What strategies did Ceausescu find that enabled him to consolidate his power over the RCP so thoroughly that the March 1974 Central Committee Plenum created the office "president of the republic" especially for him? Since revolutionary prestige, terror, and foreign support were not available to him in 1965, he resorted to an intensive and tactically brilliant use of the following three strategies: (1) personnel manipulation, (2) policy consensus within the collective leadership, and (3) creation of a popular sense of regime legitimacy through political reforms including such mobilization techniques as nationalism and "participatory" democracy. These three strategies have been employed to varying degrees by other Communist leaders, but usually in combination with one or more of the other sources of power described above. The absence of these other possibilities forced Ceausescu to rely upon personnel change, policy consensus, and "legitimacy" in establishing his personal leadership of the Romanian political system.

The nature and relative importance of each of these strategies has varied during the years that Ceausescu has been party leader. Personnel manipulation and policy consensus within the top leadership will always remain important in the perpetuation of Ceausescu's personal rule inside the party. However, as the Romanian economy and society become more modern and complex, the need for popular support of the RCP itself becomes more acute. Ceausescu is attempting to establish as many sources of "legitimacy"[3] for party rule as possible. For example, he stresses traditional Romanian heroes in his speeches, and the national roots and positive role of the RCP in Romanian history. He encourages nationalism in his anti-Soviet speeches. He would like to become a charismatic leader in the eyes of the Romanian population, hence the extreme personality cult. (Sophisticated Romanian officials explain the cult in terms of the "backwardness" of the society and the need for a charismatic leader.) He also would like to develop a rational-legal basis of legitimacy for the regime by demonstrating its legality, efficiency, and representative nature.

Multi-candidate elections and certain other political reforms are part of this attempt to increase the rational-legal basis of RCP rule in Romania. Of course, other goals are apparent in some of the reforms (for example, centralization and personalization of power), but the major themes of the domestic reform movement have been legality, equity, efficiency, and mass "participation." The success of this domestic strategy is doubtful. Ceausescu has certainly created at least a partial legitimacy for his regime based upon foreign policy— especially his ability to keep Soviet troops out of Romania. Even the most disaffected Romanian, who complains about domestic political and economic conditions, usually praises Ceausescu for his foreign policy and accepts his leadership on this basis.* However, with recent economic problems even this support has become questionable. Whether Ceausescu has been able to mobilize support for his domestic policies is still more uncertain, and remains the key issue that the regime must face in the coming years.

---

*Likewise, most Romanians were unable to understand the Watergate crisis; Nixon's foreign policy successes should have justified any domestic irregularities.

Ceausescu's political reforms could be generally characterized as codification, equalization, centralization, and participation. For example, in recent years a new labor code and new collective farm statutes have been introduced, with the announced intention of codifying procedures and equalizing economic remuneration for all citizens.[4] An educational reform is still being debated; it would equalize access to education, increase the work requirements for students and the practical economic application of education and research, and reduce "inefficiencies" and "overlapping responsibilities."[5] For example, the maintenance of two chemistry faculties in Bucharest—at both the University and the Polytechnic Institute—had to be eliminated. All these reforms emphasized the need for legality, equality, and efficiency.

PARTY/STATE UNIFICATION

One of the most far-reaching reforms in the political arena aiming at increased efficiency is at the same time unique within the socialist commonwealth.* This is the unification of party and state offices in one individual at many levels within the political structure. Ceausescu has not always favored such a policy. In fact, at the Ninth Party Congress in 1965, just four months after he assumed the top party post, he strongly supported the new Article 13(b) of the party statutes, which would prevent one person from holding a full-time office in both party and state. In 1965 he defended this separation of offices as a guarantee of party control, assuring the independence of both party and state officials in fulfilling their duties.[6] Of course, the new rule forced one of Ceausescu's major rivals, Alexandru Draghici, to relinquish his position as minister of the interior. Less than three years later, at the December 1967 party conference, Draghici was removed from the Central Committee Secretariat, and in April 1968 he was severely criticized and ejected from political office.

At the same December 1967 conference that removed Draghici from the Secretariat, Ceausescu reversed his stand on the separation of party and state offices, and Article 13(b) was eliminated from the statutes. He had hinted in May 1967 that "parallel forces are wasted on carrying out the selfsame tasks,"[7] and at the December conference declared it necessary that "both along the party channel and state channel, one single comrade . . . deal with one and the same

---

*At least it was unique when introduced in Romania in 1968. The Polish reforms of 1974-75 were in several ways similar to the earlier Romanian reorganization. A dual-level administrative system was established in both countries, and the first party secretary at the intermediate level (voivodship in Poland, county in Romania) simultaneously became head of the people's council.

field of activity."[8] The immediate result of this change was Ceausescu's election as chairman of the Council of State:

> it becomes obvious that the parallelism between the activity of the State Council and that of the higher Party organs must be eliminated. Hence I proposed that the function of Chairman of the State Council be carried out in future by the Secretary General of the Party Central Committee.[9]

But not only was Ceausescu to hold both offices. The first secretary of each county was to be chairman of the county people's council, and each city, town, or commune was to have its own *primarul*, the prewar term for mayor, who would combine party and state leadership in one person. Thus the parallel hierarchies of party and state were to be tied together at key points from top to bottom.

These ties were extended at the November 1972 Central Committee Plenum, which announced that the economic party secretaries were to be elected vice chairmen of their parallel people's council, and placed in charge of socioeconomic activity, including economic planning. Propaganda secretaries also were to be made vice chairmen of the people's councils, to administer directly culture and education. Even the secretaries for labor problems were to be placed on the councils of the socialist unity front for their area of jurisdiction.[10] The major goals of the unification were given as simplification of procedures, improved coordination, and more operative leadership.[11] It was, however, emphasized that "control of internal party activity," including the selection of new members, verification of cadres, and the "custody and release of party documents" were to "remain the exclusive prerogatives of the party organs and apparatus."[12]

This desire for "improved coordination" and "elimination of parallelism" has resulted in the creation of a large number of new party/state organs in recent years. Among these are the Supreme Council of Economic and Social Development, the Defense Council, the Council on Socialist Culture and Education, and the National Council for Science and Technology.[13] Perhaps the most important new party/state organ was instituted at the March 1974 Central Committee Plenum: the Bureau. The exact function of this new organ remains uncertain (in June 1975 the chairman of the Romanian Legislative Council asserted that it would take several more years to clarify the role of the Bureau[14]), but its small size and position at the apex of both party and state hierarchies immediately under Ceausescu himself indicate its potential importance.

When it was created in March 1974, the Bureau was considered a party organ replacing the Presidium and responsible to the party Executive Committee. (The nine-member Politburo had been replaced in 1965 by a seven-member Presidium and an Executive Committee of 15 members and 10 candidate members; both of these organs had been somewhat enlarged by 1974.) The Bureau was to consist of about fifteen ex officio members, plus others chosen by the Executive Committee.[15] However, this new organ contained among its ex officio members not only the top party administrators (the Central Committee secretaries) but also the highest officials of the Council of State and the Council of Ministers. By its ex officio members, therefore, the Bureau was in fact a party/state body; it has since been officially recognized as such, although its membership has been significantly altered.

At the March 1974 Plenum the Bureau had been charged with the "operational coordination" of party and state activity, but it was obviously too large for such a task. Ceausescu himself had complained in 1965 that the Politburo of nine members had proven unwieldy for daily decision making, that because of its size daily decisions under Gheorghiu-Dej had usually been resolved not collectively, by "a statutory party organ," but by "a single person" (*unul singur*) "through consultations with a number of comrades."[16] The new party leader had denounced this tendency at the Ninth Party Congress in favor of collective leadership. The size of the Bureau was, in fact, drastically reduced immediately following the Eleventh Party Congress in November 1974. It now contains only five members, charged with the "operational coordination of party and state activity." This change was made not by the congress itself, as might have been expected, but by the new Central Committee elected by the congress. The party statute that described the composition of the Bureau was read to the congress by Gheorghe Pana for ratification exactly as it had been passed by the Central Committee the preceding March, that is, with over 15 members. However, due to certain proposals about other changes (a dramatic intervention by Petre Blajovici), the congress decided to empower the new Central Committee to rework the statutes. The amended version, which appeared after the congress, left the composition of the Bureau up to the Executive Committee, stipulating only that those elected be members of that body, and include the secretary general. The Bureau as elected contained only five members: Ceausescu, M. Manescu (president of the Council of Ministers), Gheorghe Oprea (vice president of the Council of Ministers), Ion Patan (another vice president and minister of foreign trade), and Stefan Andrei (Central Committee secretary for foreign relations). Congress proceedings are from this author's notes taken at the Congress; members of the new Bureau were announced in *Scinteia* two days later, November 30, 1974.[17]

Although it is elected by, and responsible to, the party Executive Committee, the Bureau is classified by Romanian officials as a party/state organ (described as such to this author by the president of the Legislative Council). Its new composition indicates that it will concentrate on economic and foreign policy problems that need immediate attention. Whether it will actually function as a collective organ, and whether it will replace the Executive Committee as an officially acknowledged major policy-making body, still remain to be seen. (It is now officially regarded as merely an administrative body, subordinate to the Executive Committee. The latter is the policy-making organ. In addition, membership in the Bureau is not generally mentioned in listing an official's major offices, and one member of the Bureau (Andrei) is not even a full member of the Executive Committee.)

PARTICIPATORY REFORMS

The unification of party and state from top to bottom has certainly been one of the most important political reforms to emerge in Romania during the past decade. However, additional reforms have been introduced within the state hierarchy. Unlike the unification, which aims mainly at improved efficiency and coordination, other changes have been introduced with the stated goal of increased mass participation in the political process. Both types of reforms should contribute to the legal-rational legitimacy of the regime if they indeed improve performance and stimulate significant mass input into the decision-making process. But the success of the changes in achieving these goals remains highly questionable.

The participatory reforms can be divided into three general categories: increased "consultation with interested groups and individuals at all levels, but mostly in local decision making; a more important role for the Grand National Assembly and its committees in the formulation of legislation; and the recent multi-candidate elections. One form of "consultation" has been the holding of regular national conferences for workers in various sectors (such as agriculture and construction), preceded by extensive local discussions at meetings and in the press preparing for the larger "exchanges of opinions." At one of the first of these national conferences, Ceausescu declared that "the broad discussions . . . are part of our party's current practice of conferring with the broad masses. . . . The participation of the masses in the solution of public matters . . . is the guarantee for the strength of our system."[18]

Other types of "consultation" have been introduced. For example, Ceausescu himself has made a series of whistle-stop tours throughout the country during which he often has made a point of talking with ordinary citizens on the street as well as with local political figures.[19] Romanian television has instituted a program in which citizens' complaints are investigated and the official who has failed to pave a street or make repairs on a building is brought before the camera to explain his negligence; followups several months later report on what has been accomplished, and officials have been replaced as a result of these inquiries. Citizens' complaints and suggestions are frequently published in the press, and there is now a strict statutory limit on the length of time that any public organ can take to respond to citizens' communications. (Such

limits are not always observed, as Ceausescu has frequently complained.) At the
local level, the people's councils make extensive use of the committee system to
increase citizen input into political decisions; these committees may be standing
committees on perennial problems such as housing construction, road maintenance, or beautification, or they may be ad hoc committees set up to deal with a
specific new project: a city hall, stadium, or whatever.

The goal of this "consultation" has clearly been an increased sense of
participation on the part of the masses in the political process. This would contribute to the rational-legal legitimacy of the regime, to the extent that the citizens believed they were effectively participating in problem solving. Unfortunately, many of these innovations have themselves become ritualized into mere
formalities.

THE GRAND NATIONAL ASSEMBLY

The second category of participatory reforms involves the GNA and its
committees. The constitution adopted in August 1965 implied increased
responsibility for the GNA. Important state organs—the Council of State, the
Council of Ministers, the Supreme Court, and the prosecutor general—were
thereafter required to submit to it reports on their activity.[20] A new Constitutional Commission was to be elected to "control the constitutionality of laws,"
presenting reports to the Assembly "at its own initiative" or at the request of
other GNA bodies.[21] Other standing commissions or "temporary commissions
for any problem" were to be elected to report on bills or other matters,[22] and
reports on the work of these groups began to appear frequently in the press.
Thus this representative body was to be more important within the government
hierarchy, and individual deputies were to have a sense of participation in the
drafting and preparation of legislation.

At the December 1967 Party Conference, Ceausescu called for still further
improvement in the activity of the GNA. He indirectly criticized the Council of
State by insisting that its practice of passing decrees as laws, and subsequently
submitting them to the Assembly for discussion, must stop. "As a rule," he went
on, "important normative acts [should be] passed as laws and discussed as such
by the GNA." This would involve examination and discussion of proposed laws
by the standing commissions of the Assembly. These commissions should not
only play a larger role in drafting laws, but also "hear reports presented by
ministers . . . on the way laws are put into operation."[23] To accomplish this, the
Assembly would have to hold "open sessions of longer duration." Again the
stress was on discussion and legality in the legislative process, that is, participation and codification.

As early as 1965 Ceausescu had described the GNA as a major forum for
"discussion and participation."[24] His choice of words is significant: policy

formulation—the setting of political priorities—was to remain a party function, highly centralized within a highly centralized hierarchy. The role of the GNA was limited to discussing the form of new legislation. Nevertheless, such legislation was henceforth to be enacted into law according to a constitutional, codified procedure, rather than the previous informal and arbitrary process, which had operated without regard to the constitution.

This emphasis on legality and the GNA has been a constant feature of the past decade. But what have been the concrete results? The president of the GNA Legislative Council singled out two changes since 1965.[25] First was an increase in direct (as opposed to representative) democracy; as he explained it, the direct participation of the citizen in the political process, and not the mere expression of satisfaction or dissatisfaction through a vote. He then mentioned some of the "consultative" measures outlined above. The second change was a reversal in the relationship between the executive and legislative branches of government: In his opinion, the previous supremacy of the executive over the legislative has been reversed, and the GNA has become the superior organ. This is, of course, the official viewpoint; whether it is accurate remains a matter of opinion. But at least it is recognized that in the past the GNA functioned largely as a rubber stamp, and officially the goal has been to change that situation.

What evidence is given to support the contention that the Grand National Assembly has indeed become the superior organ? First of all, there is the existence of the Legislative Council itself, a body of the GNA that was created in November 1971 and started work in March 1972. Its role is mainly to advise on drafts of all normative laws (GNA) or decrees of the Council of State (which must be ratified by the GNA) to be sure there are no ambiguities or conflicts with existing law. In addition, the Legislative Council conducts studies of its own in order to modernize or eliminate contradictions in existing legislation, and to point out the need for new laws.

Also cited as evidence of the Assembly's increased role are the various GNA commissions, whose meetings are frequently reported in *Scinteia*. The most important such commission is the Juridical-Constitutional Commission, formed in March 1975 out of two previous bodies. This group analyzes all proposed legislation, while the other commissions deal only with legislation within their particular sectors. It is impossible for this author to analyze the work of these commissions, since I was never able to attend any of their sessions. They do meet but, except for the Juridical-Constitutional Commission, they meet only for several hours in conjunction with a GNA session, so it is difficult to conclude that they spend a great deal of time working out legislation.

What about the meetings of the Grand National Assembly itself? Has it really become a forum for open discussion of legislation? Its sessions have not been substantially lengthened, despite Ceausescu's 1967 suggestion. The size of the body has been reduced from 465 to 349 members (see Tables 8.1 and 8.2), with the stated goal of increased discussion. (When this announcement was made in the summer of 1974, some Romanians skeptically concluded that the real motive was not increased discussion but financial savings.) The one meeting of the GNA that I did attend was in July 1975, just after its membership had been reduced, and the proceedings were even more of a formality than the Eleventh Romanian Party Congress. Motions were put and carried in rapid succession, with no time allowed for voices to be raised in opposition or abstention (although the questions were formally put to the floor). It is true that this was a time of extreme emergency in Romania, just after the 1975 floods, but a Central Committee meeting several days before had dealt at length with the recent catastrophe. The floods were not discussed by the Grand National Assembly. The explanation was given at the time that the Central Committee proposals had not long been available for analysis by the GNA, and indeed those questions were discussed by the Assembly in the fall. But this indicates the absence of spontaneous discussion in the Romanian parliament. Even more important, it demonstrates that the first large body called together to deal with the emergency was not the Grand National Assembly, but the Party Central Committee, thus reaffirming the continued superiority of the latter. This superiority is also reflected in terms of personal prestige: membership in the Central Committee carries much greater honor and many more privileges than election to the GNA.*

If, as seems to be the case, full meetings of the GNA are still completely formal with no spontaneous discussion, then the crucial decisions are made in advance. So how are laws proposed for GNA approval? Evidently the process differs formally according to the initiator. The right to initiate legislation belongs to the following groups: the Party Central Committee; the Socialist Unity Front; the Bureau of the GNA; any group of 35 delegates (usually a commission); the Council of State; and the Council of Ministers. According to the president of the Legislative Council, legislation is most often initiated by the Council of Ministers. This process has reportedly been much simplified in recent years. Previously, a law was first worked out by a group in a particular ministry. Once signed by the minister, it would be circulated to all other ministries for their approval or suggestions; this could take two to three months. Then it would be rewritten and recirculated until all disagreements had been worked out. It would then be presented by the originating minister to the Council of Ministers, and any remaining disputes would be resolved at that level. Now,

---

*Romanians themselves are unofficially still very skeptical about the role of their parliament; most people were simply unable to understand why I even wanted to attend the session. One concrete indicator of the low status of GNA delegates is their high turnover rate. Only 129 of the 349 delegates were reelected (37 percent), and 105 of these 129 individuals were important national figures whose prestige in no way depended upon membership in the GNA. In contrast, 133 out of 184 full members of the Central Committee elected in 1969 were reelected in 1974, and an additional 18 were given positions of comparable prestige (a total of 83 percent).

however, the original draft is worked out by a group in which all ministries and the Legislative Council are represented, and the approval of those representatives is taken to signify approval of the ministry. Then it is presented to the Council of Ministers. All ministries still collaborate on the draft, but the cooperation is immediate and direct rather than written. Once the Council of Ministers approves the draft, it is submitted to the Grand National Assembly, or to the Council of State if immediate action is necessary. If a body other than the Council of Ministers initiates a piece of legislation, the law is prepared by a group of "specialists," passed by the initiating body, and then submitted to the GNA or the Council of State.

Two other apsects of the legislative process must be mentioned here. First of all, according to Romanian legislators, the party is kept informed throughout the process, and it is "possible" that the party organ at the relevant level will change, approve, or disapprove specific legislation to ensure that it is "in the party spirit." No outsider is privy to information on unpublished party decisions, and the relationship between the party and the state is one aspect of the political process on which no Romanian will comment officially. Secrecy remains a major factor in the Romanian political process, especially when the party is concerned. An observer can infer that the party, and frequently Ceausescu himself, remains the most important initiator of legislation, but this cannot be proven.

At least two factors do support such an inference. First, departures from previous policies are usually initiated publicly by Ceausescu himself in a major speech. Second, legislation is often enacted without a thorough study of its implications. The laws affecting foreigners passed in 1974 are obvious examples. One such law required all foreigners to exchange the equivalent of ten dollars per day: this went into effect before exceptions (diplomats, exchange students, and their relatives) had been decided upon. The same was true of the law forbidding foreigners to rent living quarters from Romanians, even through the official tourist agency, ONT. This resulted in such confusion that a three-month period of grace was eventually granted.

The second aspect of the legislative process that should be mentioned is that many important laws and decrees are indeed put to public debate before they are enacted in final form. Such debate takes place in the press (articles, editorials, letters), on radio and television, and at public meetings, and suggested changes are frequently incorporated into the final legislation. Again, it is difficult to judge how much of this discussion is orchestrated and how much is spontaneous. What is important for an evaluation of the GNA is that effective discussion still takes place outside, not within, that body, and that most (but by no means all) Romanians remain quite skeptical about the influence of the GNA in the decision-making process. This would indicate that the Grand National Assembly still has a long way to go before it becomes an effective organ in the political system, and that attempts to increase the rational-legal legitimacy of the regime by emphasizing the legality and participatory nature of the parliamentary process have not yet met with the desired level of success.

MULTI-CANDIDATE ELECTIONS

The first multi-candidate elections organized by the Romanian Communist Party were held in March 1975. We know the names and occupations of all candidates; we have the formal press accounts of their nominations and of the electoral meetings held prior to the elections. Unfortunately, our knowledge of the results is limited. We know the winner, the total number of votes cast in each country for candidates of the Socialist Unity Front, the total votes against the candidates, and the number of null votes. However, we do not have the totals for each candidate, nor do we have any way of determining how geographical or social groups cast their ballots (see Tables 8.1 and 8.2).

There were 488 candidates for 349 seats in the GNA; that is, 139 or almost 40 percent of the candidates were opposed. None of the highest party leaders, members of the RCP Political Executive Committee, were opposed, and all were nominated and elected.* Of the 361 full and candidate members of the Central Committee, 173 were electoral candidates, 16 or about 9 percent were opposed, and 6 of the 16 were defeated.† From this we can see that comparatively few top political officials had to compete for reelection.

The Candidates

Nominations took place during a ten-day period beginning February 3, just a month before the March 9 elections.[26] Individuals were nominated by the Socialist Unity Front at public meetings held in each electoral district. The candidates themselves can be divided into three general groups. First, there were the officials holding important posts in the central party and state organs (about 30 percent of those elected); at least one such candidate was nominated in each

---

*The only exception was Chivu Stoica, a candidate member of the Political Executive Committee, who did not run for reelection. He had been an important member of Gheorghiu-Dej's inner circle, and Ceausescu's predecessor as chairman of the Council of State. He is now 67, and gradually retiring (or being retired) from top office.

†The defeat of 6 out of 16, or over 37 percent of the Central Committee members opposed, cannot be construed as a major embarrassment for the regime since one of the two full members who lost was beaten by a candidate member; and of the four candidate members who lost, two were defeated by full members and one by another candidate member. So actually only one full and one candidate member, 2 out of 16, lost to nonmembers.

county, frequently with little or no formal connection to that county. (Indeed, many of the Central Committee officials were elected to the Central Committee from one area of the country, and to the GNA from a totally different place.) These officials were almost always unopposed, and usually nominated first, along with the first party secretary of that county. The latter official belongs to the second major group of candidates (about 20 percent of the GNA): those holding an important post in the county political structure. These individuals had important ties to their constituents (although some were in addition members of central organs such as the Central Committee or the Political Executive Committee), were usually among the first nominated, and were usually unopposed.

It is within the third group of candidates, just over 40 percent of the delegates, that the term "multi-candidate" election is actually applicable; these were local residents working in industry, agriculture, education, and so on. This group tended to be nominated later than the others, and frequently two candidates ran for the same seat. In almost every case, however, when two candidates opposed each other, they came from the same occupational category—both were presidents of agricultural collectives, both were teachers, both were researchers, both were local party or trade union secretaries, or both were directors or deputy directors in a particular sector of the economy, such as machine building, petroleum products, or wood processing. In other words, a "balanced" composition was insured for the GNA by opposing candidates with similar responsibilities. (In fact, 96 of the 139 races—almost 70 percent—included candidates with exactly the same "objective" qualifications: economic sector, professional expertise, and level of promotion.) Even sexual balance was guaranteed; there were only about three races in which a man and a woman were opposed. About 55 women were elected, and about 38 (almost 70 percent) ran against other candidates. Most were concentrated in the fields of education, light industry, or agriculture, in contrast to the overall GNA where managers in heavy industry were second only to full-time party workers.

The Elections

During the month between nomination and election, public meetings were held in the electoral districts. Usually both candidates appeared at the same meeting and spoke to their constituents to solicit votes. Since all the candidates had been nominated by the Socialist Unity Front, both were considered "objectively" fit to hold office: They had in some way made a major contribution to society and so were worthy of election. Consequently, the voters' decision could not be based on issues—both candidates supported the same platform—but on personalities. As Romanian officials explained, "subjective" factors were decisive: which candidate had the personal qualities to become a public figure. In electoral meetings, each candidate tried to impress the voters with his sincerity, and his ability to represent them effectively. Since the "same program and means" were available to both candidates, the voters had to "sense tiny differences in nuance, in decisiveness, for example."[27] Too often, victory went "to him who is known," which in some cases was "regrettable, but inevitable." The most publicized example was the defeat of a Central Committee member and director of the national theater, classical actor Radu Beligan. Although well known himself, Beligan was opposed by Octavian Cotescu, a professor at the Institute of Theater and Cinematography, who had been involved in many movie and television comedies and therefore was more widely recognized and more popular. (This was the one case in which a Central Committee member was defeated by a nonmember. The interpretation given here of his defeat was that current in Bucharest in the summer of 1975.)

Skeptical Romanians had recognized this "regrettable" possibility when the announcement was made in the summer of 1974 that, in order to improve the activity of the GNA, "more candidates will run for a seat, the citizens thus being afforded the possibility to elect those who prove more competency, resourcefulness, energy, ardor and managerial skills, more firmness and responsibility in the implementation of party policy."[28] Some citizens asserted then that the quality of government would not be improved by multi-candidate elections since most voters would know neither of the individuals nominated, and, if they did, would favor one for the wrong reasons. The Beligan case seemed to support these contentions, but another result of the voting is even more significant in this respect: Many voters did not exercise their right to choose between the candidates, but merely turned in a ballot favoring both.

We do not know exactly how many voters did this. We know only that Ceausescu himself, soon after the elections, announced that "in *most* cases, the citizens preferred to vote for *both* candidates."[29] His own interpretation of such an action was that the voters "considered both candidates to have the necessary qualifications."[30] Romanian officials indicated (without prior questioning) that of course other interpretations can be given to this failure on the part of the voters to exercise their choice. The alternate possibility they saw was "disinterest": that the failure to choose could result from either satisfaction or indifference, and it is impossible to distinguish between the two. Ceausescu himself, I was told, complained about "indecisiveness" after the election. This "indecisiveness," the failure to choose one candidate over another, could indeed have resulted from the ignorance predicted before the elections. It could in some cases have been a form of protest against the absence of a choice based on concrete issues. It also could have resulted in part from the electoral procedure itself.

When a Romanian citizen appeared to vote, his name was checked off on the registration list and he was given a ballot. He could then, as in the past, merely register a favorable vote by dropping the ballot into the ballot box. This constituted a vote for both candidates, and according to Ceausescu, this is what most voters chose to do. If he wished to vote against a candidate (that is, for one or the other), he had to go into the voting booth, pull the curtain, and then cross out one name. Habit dies hard, and previously such an action indicated that the voter was voting against the party's candidate. In fact, in this election, when entering the booth to vote privately had no official stigma attached to it, the number of votes against the regime jumped from 0.23 percent of the voters (30,748) in the last elections of March 2, 1969, to 1.2 percent (178,053) (see Tables 8.1 and 8.2). This also was mentioned by Romanian officials as a serious problem resulting from multi-candidate elections. Either discontent has risen sharply since 1969 (a conclusion that I would not dispute), or more voters felt free to vote against the regime under the new procedures. Nevertheless, "most" voters still chose to follow the previous routine of dropping their ballot openly into the box. They thus guarded against the charge of voting down the official candidates, but also failed to exercise their right to choose.

CONCLUSIONS

What can we conclude about these multi-candidate elections in Romania? First of all, they were not, and were not intended to be, multi-candidate elections in the Western sense. There was no difference between the candidates on substantive issues. (Of course, it can be argued that this is frequently true of elections in the United States, but that is not the intent of elections there.) Both candidates were nominated by the Socialist Unity Front with the approval of the party, and so their platforms assumed support for official policies. In most cases, major political officials ran unopposed,* and so there was no way to register discontent with the top leadership except by voting against all candidates. Often there was no real connection between the candidate and his constituents, although even major candidates were required to at least put in an appearance in their electoral district between nomination and election. Finally, the composition of the GNA itself was predetermined by the selection of candidates and their opponents within certain occupational categories. The overall outcome of the elections was assured by the carefully organized nomination process.

What, then, was the purpose of holding multi-candidate elections? Within the context of the other recent political reforms described above, it is clear that

---

*When questioned on this point, Romanian officials mentioned the "disequilibrium" that would result from nominating a candidate to oppose a major official. Of course, all candidates were proposed locally (the explanation went on), and usually the local officials decided that the candidate was so outstanding that no opponent was necessary.

a major purpose involved in the elections was an increased sense of participation on the part of the voters and the candidates. If the citizens could be convinced that they had been allowed real input into the political system, then a sense of legality, of representational legitimacy, would have been created. And if the citizens felt that the quality of politicians was improved by multi-candidate elections, and if the delegates felt a heightened sense of responsibility to their constituents, then the instrumental legitimacy of the regime would have been increased. Unfortunately, the high number of ambiguous ballots illustrates the difficulty faced by the RCP in trying to create such legitimacy. The population did turn out in overwhelming numbers to vote; however, popular indifference still remained high and the voters for the most part did not bother to choose between candidates.

Romanian political scientists frequently complain about the low level of "political culture" and "political responsibility" in their country, explaining that Romanian citizens still have to be educated into democracy. This certainly is one aspect of the failure of multi-candidate elections in Romania in 1975. There is no strong tradition of active political participation in Romania; on the contrary, fear of participating probably played some role in the recent outcome. But another reason for the widespread apathy shown at the polls is the general sense of disappointment and disillusionment prevalent in Romania at the time of the elections.

The summer of 1974 was a time of relatively high optimism, perhaps the highest since before the Soviet invasion of Czechoslovakia in 1968. Romanians were hoping for a major reorientation in political and economic priorities to be initiated by the Eleventh Party Congress in November. Not only were the multi-candidate elections to the GNA announced, but stress was placed upon the increased incomes and shorter working hours to be introduced. The proposed recycling of Central Committee members (under which at least one-third of the members would be elected anew at each Party Congress) excited even some of the usual skeptics. Then the Eleventh Party Congress never voted on this last proposal and it was eliminated from the changes in the party statutes; the long-range economic directives passed by the congress made it clear that investment in heavy industry would take an even higher proportion of the budget.

Disillusionment set in. A number of other reforms negatively affected the status of particular groups within the society: writers, for example, can no longer live on their royalties; work norms have evidently been raised in some industries to impossible levels, in effect reducing the minimum wage although it has officially been raised. In addition, there is increased pressure to report contacts with foreigners, and foreigners can no longer stay in Romanian homes. This not only makes it harder for foreigners to meet Romanians and more expensive for them to travel in Romania, but it makes it impossible for Romanians to exchange hospitality at home for an invitation to visit abroad. A large number of factors, then, combined to disillusion Romanian voters just before these first multi-candidate elections and lessened any positive impact they might have had. (These reforms were introduced and discussed while I was in the country.)

The general sense of disillusionment that has recently characterized Romanian politics indicates the continued failure of the RCP to establish a rational-legal basis of legitimacy for its rule. Even so, a prerequisite for disillusionment is hope. It would be easy to dismiss the multi-candidate elections of March 1975 and the other attempts at political reforms as failures: No choice was offered to the voters on issues, important leaders were not opposed, and most important, the voters usually did not exercise their right to choose. Many forms of "consultation" with the masses have become routinized and formalized, destroying their original purpose. Finally, the Grand National Assembly has not yet become a forum for spontaneous debate, nor is it even a major policy-making organ. Yet small steps have been taken toward codification, equalization, centralization, and participation. The last is the most difficult: It will take a great deal of time to convince ordinary citizens that their participation is actually desired by the leaders, especially since the regime remains totally unresponsive to certain popular demands.

Perhaps the major problem faced by the RCP has not really been touched by these tentative steps toward reform. The reforms have concentrated mostly upon procedures, rather than policy content. The indisputable fact remains that, while Ceausescu has been able to mobilize a consensus on policy within the party leadership, the population as a whole does not support his high investment priorities. Hopes were raised and dashed in 1974; the population then responded in 1975 with indifference. Only when Ceausescu can convince most Romanians that their priorities and those of the party are the same—as in foreign policy— does he have any hope of establishing a rational-legal basis of legitimacy for his regime. A dramatic increase in the living standard would seem to be the prerequisite for such legitimacy, since that is the overwhelming priority for the majority of Romanian citizens. But as long as the current economic directives remain in effect (the long-range plan runs until 1990), there seems little chance for such improvement.

The RCP has been the leader in the drive for rapid modernization in Romania. Since 1971 it has also led the attack on certain unacceptable side effects of the modernization process: social stratification, overspecialization, weakening of ideological drive. Such attacks have reduced the security of various elites within the society without significantly improving the lives of lower-income groups. Ceausescu constantly stresses the need for self-sacrifice and social responsibility in the hope of changing human nature. But it is impossible to live in Romanian society without breaking rules, given the generally low standard of living. Ceausescu is caught in a bind: He cannot change ethical standards without improving the economic situation, yet his high investment and egalitarian biases make any improvement very slow. Without such progress, he cannot create a general sense of regime legitimacy, and without such legitimacy, there is no chance for a significant change in the nature of the political process in Romania.

There have, however, been incremental improvements in the form of politics during the past decade. If this continues, and is accompanied by incremental economic progress, the negative short-term conclusions of this study may prove too pessimistic. But the many intervening variables—leadership changes, natural calamities, the international situation, and increasing the consciousness of relative economic deprivation—preclude any positive long-term prediction.

NOTES

1. In his speech to the Central Committee Plenum of February 10-11, 1971; see Nicolae Ceausescu, *Romania on the Way of Building Up the Multilaterally Developed Socialist Society* (Bucharest: Meridiane, 1971), p. 468. These are Ceausescu's collected works, hereafter cited as Ceausescu, plus volume number.

2. According to the president of the Romanian Legislative Council in an interview, July 1975; figures on the GNA agree with published sources.

3. This term is used here in its broadest sense: A ruler is "legitimate" if he is "believed by those subject to his rule to have a right to it." See Carl J. Friedrich, *Man and His Government* (New York: McGraw-Hill, 1963), p. 233. For simplicity, the Weberian classification is retained below: Legitimacy may be based upon tradition, charisma, or rational-legal factors (procedural or instrumental). In a sense, we are seeing in Romania an attempt at what Dallin and Breslauer have termed the postmobilization "shift from coercive to normative power"; see Alexander Dallin and George Breslauer, "Political Terror in the Post-Mobilization Stage," in *Change in Communist Systems*, ed. Chalmers Johnson (Stanford, Cal.: Stanford University Press, 1970), pp. 191-214, esp. p. 210.

4. The new goal is a ratio of one to six between lowest and highest incomes; see *Programme of the RCP* (Bucharest: Meridiane, 1975), p. 93.

5. See, for example, Ceausescu's speeches to the Central Committee Plenum, June 18-19, 1973, and to a conference of cadres in higher education, September 13, 1974, in Ceausescu VIII, 586-600; X, 699-726.

6. *Congresul al IX-lea al PCR* (Bucharest: Editura Politica, 1966), esp. pp. 79, 803.

7. In an article on the 45th anniversary of the RCP; see Ceausescu, II, p. 274.

8. Ceausescu, II, p. 554.

9. The nomination was made by the chairman of the Council of State, Chivu Stoica; *Scinteia*, December 8, 1967, p. 7.

10. This decision was printed in *Scinteia*, November 23, 1972, p. 2. The Plenum itself was reported in *Scinteia* on November 21, and Ceausescu's explanation on pp. 1-4. Extensive personnel changes had taken place at an Executive Committee meeting the preceding month as a preliminary to the Plenum; see *Scinteia*, October 12, 1972, p. 1.

11. *Scinteia*, October 12, 1972, p. 1.

12. *Scinteia*, November 23, 1972, p. 2.

13. Other examples are the Council on Economic-Social Organization, the Central Council of Workers' Control of Economic and Social Activity, and the Committee for the Problems of People's Councils. See Academia de Stiinte sociale si politice a RSR, *Organizatiile obstesti in sistemul organizarii politice din RSR* (Bucharest: Editura Academiei RSR, 1973), p. 24.

14. In an interview with this author.

15. According to *Scinteia*, March 27, 1974, p. 1, the Bureau would consist of the general secretary and Central Committee secretaries of the RCP; the president of the republic and president of the Council of State; those vice chairman of the Council of State who "assure the permanent activity" of this body, the president of the Council of Ministers; the president of the Central Council of Workers' Control of Economic and Social Activity; the president of the State Planning Committee; the head of the trade unions; and others chosen by the Executive Committee. Ex officio members would thus be Ceausescu; Andrei, Burtica, Constantinescu, Gere, Pana, Popescu, Verdet; Bodnaras, presumably, from the Council of State; M. Manescu; Draganescu; Dalea.

16. *Congresul al IX-lea*, p. 732.

17. The new party statutes can be found in *Congresul al XI-lea al PCR* (Bucharest: Editura Politica, 1975); Article 24, p. 595, describes the Bureau.

18. At a conference of construction workers, *Scinteia*, February 27, 1966, p. 1.

19. Between July 1965 and January 1973 he made 147 such tours, usually of more than one day each. For details, see *Omagiu* (Bucharest: Editura Politica, 1973), p. 20.

20. Articles 69, 75, 99, and 108.

21. Article 53.

22. Article 52.

23. Ceausescu, II, pp. 557-58.

24. *Congresul al IX-lea*, p. 70.

25. In an interview with this author. He chose to mention this date, so the trends are associated in his mind with the Ceausescu period. Much of the material here comes from a series of interviews with this official, or from other interviews arranged by him.

26. The material here is based upon a careful reading of the national and local press for the month preceding the election.

27. These explanations are from interviews with Romanian election officials in July 1975.

28. See the draft *Programme of the RCP* (Bucharest: Agerpres, 1974), p. 109. The final form of the *Programme*, published by Meridiane in 1975, omitted all the above qualifications except "managerial skills," and "firmness and responsibility." See pp. 137-38.

29. Italics added; see his speech to the joint plenum of the Central Committee and the Socialist Unity Front, *Scinteia*, March 18, 1975, p. 2.

30. Ibid.

9

COALITION POLITICS AND
SOVIET INFLUENCE IN
EASTERN EUROPE
Kent N. Brown

This essay seeks a new perspective on the nature of Soviet-East European relations. While the paradigm suggested here does not necessarily exclude or supersede existing theories on Soviet bloc interaction, it does provide a larger framework for analysis than either the totalitarian or unitary-actor models of Communist systems. Before presenting the major hypothesis of this study, it will first be necessary to review the general literature on Soviet-East European relations.

There are, generally speaking, three approaches to the study of Soviet-East European relations. The first, which I term the historical orientation, attempts to periodize the Soviet-East European relationship. The second, the systematic approach, seeks to explain the relationship through an analysis of specified variables. Finally, the dependency approach looks primarily at the economic linkages between large and small states. These are neither mutually exclusive nor do they encompass the entire range of possible perspectives. However, this categorization does provide us with more or less manageable parts.

The historical approach is best exemplified by Zbigniew Brzezinski's *The Soviet Bloc*. Because this remains the most comprehensive study of its type, it merits a thorough review. Brzezinski traces the interplay of ideology, power, and dependence through five historical phases. He begins by noting that the ideology and outlook of Soviet leaders inevitably led them to attempt to impose their own domestic institutional processes on the interstate system. During the early 1950s East European leaders' personal loyalties toward and interaction

The views expressed herein are solely those of the author and do not necessarily reflect the views of the U.S. government.

with Soviet leaders engendered self-imposed (based on "local anticipation of Soviet desiderata"[1]) as well as Moscow-imposed restrictions on their behavior, ideology, and policy making. Gradually the Soviet monopoly over ideology and power diminished, resulting in limited diversity in views and policies. Stalin's death induced a preoccupation with domestic affairs. Soviet leadership ambivalence on many issues and institutional decentralization both enhanced the freedom of movement of East European leaders, despite their uncertainty as to which direction to pursue.

The dilemma for these leaders, according to Brzezinski, was to balance conflicting ideological commitments with self-interest. Stalinist precepts were not only difficult to abandon but, for many within the East European elite, also provided a rationalization of positions, prerogatives, and policies. This difficulty was intensified when Malenkov and Khrushchev initiated domestic and foreign policies that deviated from those pursued by Stalin. Many East European leaders stalled on reforms, thus creating a "domesticism," that is, a domestic policy diverging from the Soviet example, a phenomenon previously limited to Yugoslav revisionism. Soviet primacy was still a function of the potentials of "military strength and industrial development," but actual power and influence in East Europe "depended now to an unprecedented degree on the support of centralists in the leadership of other states."[2] The dependency was mutual; the leaders still depended on Soviet support but, as Brzezinski implies, the Soviet leadership also depended on them to maintain influence in those countries.

De-Stalinization and desatellitization were viewed by the East European leaders as completely separate processes. Greater independence from Soviet hegemony was desirable, but domestic experimentation that could weaken their own power bases was not. Both processes proceeded (or failed to proceed) at varying paces in the different states, depending on homogeneity of leadership, attitude toward Germany, assessments of the possibility of China as an alternative source of political support and the West as an alternative source of economic support, and the ability of the Soviets to "intrigue within a ruling elite, taking advantage of factions."[3] Brzezinski, however, failed to link these explicitly with de-Stalinization and desatellitization.

In his final section Brzezinski examines the interplay of domestic and external forces. He notes that the 1960s were characterized by an increasing tendency for "a ruling Communist Party to view the communist camp from the standpoint of domestic interests and to evaluate it in terms of the camp's capacity to satisfy these interests."[4] This was simultaneously a cause for and consequence of the erosion of ideology resulting from increasing diversity. Brzezinski maintains that the degree to which one party can involve itself in the affairs of others has demonstrated observable changes. However, he contends that the "totalitarian" nature of these Communist systems is constant and asserts that factional conflict is the sole linkage between Soviet power and internal developments.

Let us now examine what I term the systematic approach to the study of East Europe and its relationship with the USSR. One approach is the checklist, which designates certain factors as responsible for the restricted nature of the domestic policy options on East European regimes,[5] such as geographic proximity, Soviet troop presence, fear of Germany, and ideological similarities. An analysis of the relative importance of these factors, how they change over time, and how they are actually perceived by the Soviets and East Europeans is almost totally neglected. More sophisticated works utilize social science methodology to examine more objectively internal and external forces operative in Eastern Europe.

In this regard important contributions have been made by such political theorists as Linden, Triska and Johnson, and Jamgotch.[6] Triska and Johnson discuss the utility of two different types of analysis for the study of political change in Eastern Europe. Their evidence suggests that, inter alia, the USSR is the major "impact-source" of domestic change in Eastern Europe, that the Soviets are increasingly cognizant of the necessity of differentiating between their bloc partners, and that pressures and demands for change are much stronger in East Europe than in the USSR. Incapable of understanding these leadership responses to civil demands in East Europe, the Kremlin leaders react by inducing their own political changes in East European regimes.

Of greater relevance to this essay is the Triska-Johnson analysis of the relationship between national and subsystem autonomy. Particularly significant is their contention that leaders are becoming increasingly dependent on domestic actors to perform their functions, and relatively less dependent on Soviet leadership support for securing their offices. The leader's position "becomes precarious. The sustained balancing of the two constituents of [his] own power grows heavy."[7] In the Triska-Johnson scheme, this balance will be crucial to the future of Eastern Europe. This situation necessitates prudence among East European leaders and Soviet recognition of this balance as a prerequisite to system maintenance.

Linden is primarily interested in measuring the degree of "normative" integration in Eastern Europe. By statistical analysis he concludes that, the more economically developed an East European state, the less "deviant" from the norm acceptable to the USSR it tends to be (Triska and Johnson's study corroborates this conclusion). Linden further suggests that the degree of trade dependence manifests no significant relationship to deviance from behavior acceptable to the Soviets, and that a secure military position vis-a-vis the Soviets is correlated with deviance. "Positive deviance," that is, favoring the Soviet perspective more than the Kremlin itself, can be as much an obstacle to normative integration as "negative" deviance.[8] For this reason, it should be a prime consideration of Western scholars. Linden relies heavily on data biased toward leadership interaction. One of his coding devices accords a high priority to visits of top-level leaders to each other's capitals, whereas he accords little value to visits by low-level, expert, and working delegations.

Jamgotch concentrates on the ideological underpinnings of the intrabloc relationship. In his argument, the East European alliance is essential to the Soviets for goal attainment and domestic legitimacy. The Kremlin has realistically and purposefully appraised the relationship and has developed strategies and tactics, including accommodation to pluralism within the East European subsystem, designed to regularize its hegemony and assure the security of bloc regimes. According to Jamgotch, the Soviets are concerned with systems maintenance, not expansion, and recognize that a certain degree of dissidence within the system is tolerable.

Tangential to his main theme is Jamgotch's contention that Western scholars must understand the process of communicating political change in Eastern Europe to Soviet decision makers. This includes East European sources of information, the attitudes of the Soviet officials who collect the data, and how the data are processed in Moscow. He suggests that such a study would facilitate a comprehension of different levels of Soviet tolerance to diversity in different countries.

Dependency theorists, who still attempt to develop a meaningful paradigm for exploring transnational linkages, utilize the Soviet-East Europe relationship to test some of their hypotheses. Some scholars have defined dependent countries as those "unable to exert substantial influence over the basic decisions affecting their national economies," whose policies are determined "directly or indirectly by international structures and processes."[9]

As Marer notes, the usual characteristic of imperialism, historically the central concept of dependency theory, is political domination for the purpose of economic extraction; in the case of Eastern Europe, however, evidence suggests that the Soviets have been paying economically for the political benefits of their relationship. Through a variety of measures, including artificial supplementation of economic institutions and trade policy, the USSR has made Eastern Europe economically dependent in order to cement bloc unity.[10]

Several studies of Soviet influence in Eastern Europe have referred to some form of dependency in the Soviet-East European relationship. This subject requires additional research on the different types of dependency—political, bureaucratic-technological, or economic, and on their roles historically in various international subsystems.

Despite the diversity of these approaches to the study of Soviet-East European relations, there are some general observations we can make. First, these works do not tell us how abstract concepts such as power, ideology, or dependence are actually perceived, measured, and implemented by Soviet and East European decision makers. How, for example, does the Polish leadership translate Soviet "power" into "pro-Soviet" policies? How does this leadership measure external power against domestic considerations? How indeed does the policy-making process operate in Eastern Europe? Perhaps we should view power and obligation as only two inputs into the decision maker's thinking. Power and obligation are materialized only when they are represented by individuals and groups considered relevant to a particular immediate issue by the decision maker. He must weigh them against other, often conflicting inputs. Moreover, individuals who are not directly involved in some aspect of policy making must share some of the leader's perceptions, or recognize the legitimacy of his decisions, if the system is to function at all.

Second, the concept of domestic pluralism requires expansion and must be related to the international system. Western scholars seem to believe that East European leaders treat domestic forces in isolation from external forces. The view that the East European leader must balance Soviet influence with domestic interest neglects the fact that neither the Soviet leadership nor the domestic public is unified in purpose, degree of influence, or kinds of demands on decision makers.

Instead of examining a dominant actor system or subsystem, we need a perspective that focuses on several overlapping internal systems or on an individual domestic system in which external actors are influential.

We should look at the interaction of various domestic and external factions, tendencies, and groups and how this interaction generates policy formulation. Unfortunately in recent years, there have been intensive studies of the influence of the political processes of bargaining and conflict on domestic policy making in Communist systems, while the study of their influence on interstate relations has been neglected.[11]

GENERAL STATEMENT OF HYPOTHESIS

We hypothesize that most policy making in Eastern Europe is the result of a process of coalition formation and interaction within a particular country's political system. Factions within the Soviet leadership, and additional Soviet groups and individuals, must be viewed as participating in the East European domestic coalition process. Soviet influence on East European policy making is a function of the dependence of domestic individuals and groups on their Soviet "partners" within coalitions.

DEFINITIONS AND CONCEPTS: COALITIONS, GROUPS, AND DECISION MAKING

The idea that groups exist and play a role in Soviet and East European political systems has been suggested by H. Gordon Skilling and others.[12] There is considerable controversy, however, regarding the definition and extent of influence on policy making of a particular group. In my scheme, coalitions, similar to what have been termed informal groups,[13] make a substantial contribution to decision making in terms of "suggestions" based on expertise. Institutional structures and formal groups in Communist countries are characterized by compartmentalization, fragmentation, and resistance to change. Despite the strong efforts of Communist parties, lack of coordination and poor vertical and horizontal communication inhibits closely planned, centralized "system dominant" decision making. Under these conditions the party is forced to accept political bargaining at the intermediate level, as well as within the party and leadership itself, as a method of policy-alternative formulation and input into the policy process.

Moreover, the leaders of formal groups also are forced to participate in the bargaining process. These group leaders depend for their survival on their ability to impress the national and party leaders that they are able to some extent to satisfy the needs of the group rank and file. If a group's leadership has completely alienated its members, it undermines the legitimacy of the system, of which the formal group is recognized as an integral part, and seriously weakens its own ability to transmit downward instruction and "education" from above. Communist leaders will therefore insist that the group leadership act as much as possible in accord with the desires of its rank and file. However, because the leader of a group realizes that official channels are often adverse to meaningful communication, he is forced to seek allies outside the system for the process of bargaining over the division of the resources.

Recognition of a shared interest in a policy outcome on an issue or cluster of issues and a consequent unified effort to influence the policy-making process results in the formation of a coalition. By virtue of the organizational and ideological obstructions to individual initiative and interaction in Communist systems, coalitions will usually result from the interaction of the leaderships of formal groups, such as the writers' unions, youth groups, trade unions, party commissions, and governmental structures and substructures.

Subunits or factions from these groups and from the leadership may, however, comprise a coalition. Some members of the writers' union, for example, may form an alliance with certain members of the party ideological commission with a similar perspective or interest on an issue. This alliance would perform two functions: It would strengthen the power of those who seek to directly influence the leadership, and it would provide support to those who are trying to influence the eventual position adopted by the group. In the latter case, the writers who wish to encourage their union to adopt a particular stance on the issue of publication royalties, for example, may seek to persuade the union as a whole by pointing to the support of the proposal by certain members of the party commission.

SOVIET GROUPS AND EAST EUROPEAN COALITIONS:
THE DYNAMICS OF INFLUENCING POLICY

This process of coalition formation and performance provides the means by which Soviet influence permeates East European political systems at several levels and on a large diversity of issues. My hypothesis is that East European groups often depend on the support of actors and groups within the Soviet system to influence policy making within their own systems. Their dependence on this political support is manifested in their willingness to express support for their domestic leaders' "pro-Soviet" domestic and foreign policies.

Admittedly, we lack sufficient data on decision making in the Soviet and East European political systems to confirm the accuracy of my hypothesis. Nevertheless, specific case studies of East European policy decisions suggest, if not demonstrate, how this political process might function.

My first example concerns the decision by the post-1968 Czechoslovak leadership regarding political trials. In the summer of 1969 hardline members of the Czechoslovak leadership began a campaign for political trials of the leading 1968 reformers. Dubcek and Smrkovsky in particular were mentioned in the provincial press and indicted as "traitors" to socialism. Husak, however, vowed in several major speeches that there would be no political trials. Despite the Soviet ambivalence with respect to the issue of political trials, in 1972 there were trials for "subversion" of several middle- and low-level 1968 reformers.

Despite the dearth of information on the positions of Husak, the Soviets, and the hardliners, my hypothesis can serve to explain these events. The Czechoslovak leadership was divided among those who favored proceeding with the political trials of former reformist leaders for "subversive" activities and those who did not. Let us assume that both the proponents and opponents sought to secure support for their respective positions. For example, those opposing the trial may have adopted a strategy of seeking out internal groups who willingly expressed their opposition to political trials. Moreover, each member of both leadership groups tended to depend on "clients" for occasional support. Thus coalitions of purely domestic forces evolved because of the issue. Of course, the power of the coalition members varied according to their particular relation to the issue.

If a faction sensed itself incapable of dominating the policy outcome, it would seek out Soviet contacts for support. The Czechoslovak hardliners in the leadership probably sought direct support for their positions from their hardline counterparts in the Kremlin. They could have justified their argument by assigning the case to the larger and more dominant issue of general stability within Czechoslovakia, mutual interests (such as establishing a precedent for future "rightists, opportunists, and counterrevolutionaries"), or by appealing to favors owed to them for having formerly supported unpopular Soviet-dictated decisions. This resulted in the increased dependence of the Czech hardliners on the Soviets.

In general, one possible result of introducing the Soviet element would be to ensure the resolution of the issue by Soviet leaders. It is unlikely that either the moderate Czechoslovaks or the hardliners would really favor this—for it prolongs their dependence on the Soviets and consequent Soviet-oriented policy. For the Soviets, moreover, this would be an additional issue to overburden decision makers. Such factors as the number of members in the CPSU Politburo at a given time, the nature of existing Politburo factions, dominance of the party leader, would be instrumental in determining whether the Soviets will consider the issue.

Obvious Soviet pressure on the crucial issue of political trials would not be manifest—because of the reluctance of the Kremlin to appear to directly interfere in the affairs of another state. Moreover, the pressure of the Soviet presence (however invisible and deliberately unobtrusive) is mitigated by the divisive tendencies among Soviets. True, the participating Czechoslovak factions never made crucial decisions without the scrutiny and approval of Soviet counterparts. The Czechoslovak leadership made the decision based on the relative importance of the dominant Soviet position vis-a-vis the positions of the internal coalitions, or other impressive Soviet interests, and the implications of certain actions of Czechoslovak leaders. Most likely moderate or compromising elements within the leadership (I would argue that this has become a major role of a Party leader) will attempt a compromise—in the Czechoslovak case, instead of reducing the charges and penalties, they arrested and tried individuals who were relatively unknown domestically and internationally.*

My second example involves the issue of managerial reform and technology importation in Hungary. In 1968 the Hungarian regime initiated the process of economic reform. Some reforms were in effect moderations of the Czechoslovak system of economic management and planning reforms under Novotny. Moderates and liberal elements in Hungary realized that some changes were necessary to improve the performance of the economy. Because the reforms deviated from narrowly defined socialist principles, the conservative politicians and economists

---

*The appearance of an overwhelming role for the Soviets in East European decision making seems to contradict this example. I believe two factors help explain why the Soviets are not as involved in East Europe as we sometimes think they are. First, conservative forces have tended to dominate party, institution, and group leaderships and pursue what we identify as pro-Soviet policies out of self-interest. Second, as discussed below, groups and their leaders have become dependent on Soviet support for getting their share of the resource pie and for maintaining their positions. They reciprocate by communicating upward domestic demands for pro-Soviet policies.

tried to moderate the reforms. This resulted in increased factionalism and the initial dominance of the moderate-liberal faction. The Czech example exacerbated Soviet suspicions regarding the potential result of factionalism. Hungarian opponents of reform attempted to influence antireformist Soviet politicians and economists who condoned strong central planning.

Within this setting, we can envisage a group of managers in an industrial enterprise in Hungary, who seek to import a new Western technology despite the competition with other groups for resources. They proceed to develop alliances around the issue or, perhaps, will join or attempt to create a coalition around the broader issue of importing technology from the West in order to further economic reform. These managers realize that because the technology, vital to further production and general economic improvement, cannot be obtained in the East, it must be imported and assigned priority over expenditures of hard currency for other products.

The extent to which the "pro-technology" group of managers will be required to enlist the aid of Soviet pro-technology groups depends on the existence and composition of the opposing or competing coalitions, on internal bureaucratic obstacles to influencing the policy process, and on their assessment of the strengths of the corresponding issue in the Soviet Union. If the Hungarian managers perceive that their Soviet counterparts have had some success in influencing technological importation in the USSR, they will be more likely to attempt to obtain their support. This support could come in the form of, for example, a private statement of support for the importation of the technology at a meeting of Hungarian and Soviet managerial delegations, the context of which would reach Hungarian decision makers at a higher level. Crossnational collaboration among Soviet and East European specialists in the formulation of a strategy for influencing national and multinational decision processes on given issues[14] is a possibility.

The phenomenon of crossnational coalitions enhances Soviet influence in East European countries at levels in addition to the leadership and party levels. In our example, the Hungarian managers, by seeking Soviet assistance, were obligated to their Soviet colleagues, to the extent that the Soviet "vote" tipped the balance toward their goal. This dependence on Soviet counterparts promotes a tendency within East European formal groups and coalitions to support what is perceived to be the Soviet perspective on a variety of issues. Soviet leaders could, for example, request the leaders of Soviet groups or delegations to East Europe to encourage their counterparts to adopt a pro-Arab stand on the Arab-Israeli conflict. Thus, if the Hungarian leadership decides to adopt a more "independent" outlook on the Middle East, it will have to contend not only with the Soviet Union and the CPSU but also with internal factions committed to Soviet policy.*

---

*This will create problems for the Soviets when they are trying to encourage shifts in policy. Perhaps one of the reasons some East European countries dragged their feet on

While this is ostensibly a somewhat tenuous basis of support for Soviet policies, I would argue that, in addition to individual issues, the process of dependency on Soviet groups has become institutionalized to such an extent in some East European countries that independent policy definition and coalition formulation would be almost revolutionary. Most major groups in the East European countries have found the system, as described above, to function in their favor at least some of the time. Furthermore, the Soviets favor a resource distribution in East European countries, which ensures that at least the most influential domestic leaders are moderately satisfied with the system.

SUBHYPOTHESES

A series of subhypotheses on the parameters and dynamics of the interaction of coalitions and political dependency can further explicate the general hypothesis of this essay.

First, the degree to which crossnational coalitions play a role in East European politics on an issue or issue cluster is inversely proportional to the degree of unity within the East European leadership.

If a politburo is united on an issue or policy, it will be extremely difficult for a coalition of forces, even with Soviet support, to oppose or modify it. Coalitions in East European politics, moreover, are often initiated not only by leadership factions but also by the publicity the alleged issue receives. A united leadership can control communication, debate, and the implementation of "bargaining" on any issue that reaches its attention. Further research into the Romanian case may reveal that Soviet influence has been reduced in Romanian policy making because of the relative unity of Romanian leaders. On the other hand, that the Czechoslovak leadership appears to be fairly evenly divided on almost the entire spectrum of issues forces the competing groups to seek Soviet supporters, and induces a consequent dependency on the Soviets.

Second, the more relevant the issue to Soviet sensitivities, the less necessary the coalition process.

Several factors will determine the nature of Soviet involvement with an East European leadership over an issue. In crisis situations (domestic, bitlateral, or international), interaction among leaders is not subject to the limitations of the political process described previously. Nevertheless, the nature of the coalition process, and the degree of influence of the Soviets in that process, have established certain restrictions for East European leaders in times of crisis. The degree to which the leadership, its factions, or other political groups have

---

detente was due to prior "socialization" of group leaders into an anti-West mindset. Many leaders may have had difficulties in turning the antidetente conservatives, who were in positions of power in their formal groups, around on the issue.

depended on Soviet support in the past will define the choices available to the East European leadership in confronting direct Soviet pressure.

As a corollary, we can hypothesize that the sensitivity of an issue is defined by the sensitivity of the group concerned with the issue. For example, an issue affecting journalists is less likely to be hashed out by coalitions of forces. Moreover, the Soviets have established closer intergroup "dependency" bonds with leaders of journalists' unions. The latter phenomenon would seem to preclude the total creation of "issues" in this sphere, since Soviet interest and willingness to exert influence (1) relieves the journalists of the need to procure domestic allies and (2) encourages such sensitive groups to refrain from making "demands" upon the system.

Third, the high degree of Communist leadership control of sensitive groups is in part designed to prevent sensitive issues from being subject to the consideration of groups and coalitions not directly affected by those issues.

This is a lesson the Soviets learned during the Prague Spring, when many formerly closed issues were disputed publicly. The Czechoslovak leadership lost a certain amount of control over the extent to which issues were subject to bargaining, and thus was unable to control the democratic or "liberal" forces that coalesced to influence decision makers on formerly closely held matters. The Soviets learned that the East European party leaders could not always be trusted to control issues and groups. The dependence of sensitive groups on Soviet support provides a measure of insurance against a repeat of the events of 1968.

Fourth, group leaders depend on Soviet support to maintain their positions within their respective organizations. In addition, the consequent dependence of the entire group or coalition on the leaders is responsible for the pro-Soviet group perspective.

As suggested earlier, group leaders must balance the often contradictory interests of their rank and file with those of the national leaders, and thus are particularly vulnerable to dependency on the support of their Soviet counterparts and/or the Soviet leadership to maintain their positions. In addition to the precariousness of their position, group leaders often lack the competence to manage their areas of specialization. The Soviet connection thus helps to raise the standards of performance. The head of an East European party commission, for example, may be considered incompetent by his national party leadership and may be almost entirely dependent upon expressions of support from the Soviet Union to keep his job. In return, he adopts a pro-Soviet stance on every issue within his scope and will argue the Soviet case with his subordinates on the commission as well as with the party leadership. He also will tend to coalesce with groups and individuals favoring the perceived Soviet line.

East European party leaders who have appointed as group leaders independent men highly respected by their rank and file have thus removed a potential source of Soviet influence. Most party leaders, however, fear the challenge that independent and capable group leaders represent to their own authority and control. Thus, they continue to appoint less capable individuals, which in the long run undermines the national leaders' independence from the USSR.

Fifth, the unity of the group or coalition on issues is necessary to goal achievement up to a certain level, beyond which it threatens opposing groups, the party, or most important, the Soviets.

Groups and coalitions are frequently defined by the immediate issue because long-term alliances based on a variety of issues threaten the role of the party, both politically and ideologically. Furthermore, the continued existence of a coalition of domestic forces could eventually undermine the role of Soviet actors, their influence on these coalitions, and the process in general, since an institutionalized domestic coalition could lose its dependence on the Soviets. On the other hand, if a powerful and cohesive domestic coalition were to arise, it could force a closer dependency link between the national leaders and the Soviets. A strong domestic challenge would thus generate increased party leadership dependence on Soviet support.

Finally, sudden sweeping changes in group leaderships in an East European country may sever the dependency link with the Soviets at the subleadership level. Under such circumstances, Soviet influence may be expected to decrease in the short run, regardless of whether the party leadership remains the same.

If an East European leadership undertakes a purge of the leaderships of other institutions, new appointees will not be sufficiently socialized to comprehend the intricacies of their interaction within the coalition system and assume their roles. Crossnational dependency will be disrupted and the pro-Soviet views of those who have been displaced will no longer be communicated upward, downward, and laterally. Such a purge would render difficult the formation of coalitions, thus providing the leadership with more power, but less expertise, for making decisions.

The same result would ensue if the Soviet leadership were to engage in a similar domestic purge—links with East European groups would be at least temporarily disrupted. One could predict (on the basis of this hypothesis) that significant changes of this nature will result in a period of instability in a country's bilateral relations with the Soviet Union. Because of a perceived Eastern European tendency for greater independence, the Soviets could be expected to attempt to prevent such cadre changes.

Several additional hypotheses could be extrapolated from this theory; hopefully this brief review has suggested some insights into the difficult field of Soviet-East European relations. Unfortunately, at this stage it is difficult to accumulate the necessary data to determine if and how the coalition process operates. One question I have largely neglected is the linkage between official Soviet policy toward Eastern Europe and the crossnational coalition process. If we assume that Soviet domestic and foreign policies result, at least to some extent, from the interaction of groups, coalitions, or tendencies, then we must consider the influence of the crossnational contacts of these actors into general Soviet attitudes, behavior, and policy on relations among Communist states.

For example, do Soviet individuals, as a result of their interaction with East European counterparts, feel that Eastern Europe deserves more sympathy and consequent autonomy or more comradely guidance and control? According to Jamgotch, the issue of who is providing feedback to the Soviet leadership may well be critical to understanding Soviet policy toward East European states. For example, the Soviet official who thinks the Czechs need more self-discipline may recommend a policy radically different from one suggested by the official who admires the Romanians for their treatment of dissidents.

More relevant is the question as to whether there is "interdependence" crossnationally. Do Soviet coalitions, for example, rely on the support of East Europeans in their attempts to influence Soviet policy making? If so, do the Soviet coalitions lobby for the increased autonomy of the East Europeans? The latter seems unlikely, for if Soviet actors regard their relationship with bloc colleagues as profitable, they will avoid encouraging policies disruptive of that relationship.

CONCLUSION

Internal differentiation and pluralism in East European countries will not necessarily lead to greater independence from Soviet influence. There is no guarantee that increased specialization and the parties' increasing reliance on specialists and inputs from outside groups will generate a decrease in the Soviet role in Eastern Europe. Indeed, the reverse might hold true—increasing fragmentation of interests in these countries may force those who hold such interests to become more and more dependent on Soviet actors to achieve the kind of influence they seek on policy making.

The decisive factor is the future political environment in the Soviet Union. If the CPSU loses its leading role or becomes so dependent on outside expertise that groups attain high levels of autonomy, then the kind of crossnational dependency link I have suggested here may cease to function or, perhaps more ominously for party dominance in Eastern Europe, may provide a justification for Soviet and East European coalitions and groups to collaborate to attack and subvert the position of the parties. Presumably, however, the parties are fully cognizant of the ideological and political dangers of according too much freedom to coalition actors. Efforts to recentralize and improve the planning function are at least in part inspired by a concern that party policy makers must dominate the decision-making process.

One note of caution: The process I have outlined here is juxtaposed against a complex background of historical, ideological, and power relationships that affect all individuals in the groups, factions, and coalitions. Their group identities alone will not determine their reactions in a given situation—additional inputs into their individual decision-making processes also will affect how they perceive and exploit their roles within the political system.

NOTES

1. Z. Brzezinski, *The Soviet Bloc* (Cambridge: Harvard University Press, 1967), p. 137.

2. Ibid., p. 329.

3. Ibid., pp. 454-55.

4. Ibid., p. 500.

5. See A. Gyorgy, "External Forces in Eastern Europe," in *The Communist States in Disarray, 1965-71,* eds. A. Bromke and T. Rakowska-Harmstone (Minneapolis: University of Minnesota Press, 1972).

6. R. Linden, "Normative Integration in Eastern Europe," unpublished; J. Triska and P. Johnson, "Political Development and Political Change in Eastern Europe," unpublished; N. Jamgotch, "Alliance Management in Eastern Europe," *World Politics* (April 1975).

7. Triska and Johnson, "Political Development," p. 43.

8. Linden, "Normative Integration," p. 37.

9. R. Kaufman, H. Chernotsky, and D. Geller, "A Preliminary Test of the Theory of Dependency," *Comparative Politics* (April 1975): 304.

10. P. Marer, "The Political Economy of Soviet Relations with Eastern Europe," in S. Rosen et al., *Testing Theories of Economic Imperialism* (Lexington, Mass.: Lexington Books, 1974).

11. At least two sources have suggested the possibility of an international linkage of domestic groups. Bromke, in his "Polycentrism in Eastern Europe" (in *The Communist States in Disarray,* eds. Bromke and Rakowska-Harmstone), notes that "there have been numerous examples of group interactions cutting across national boundaries, such as those of economic reformers . . . because of the influence that these groups exert on their own societies, the interdependence of their actions has often been crucial in the process of leveling of reforms in the area as a whole" (p. 5). Skilling, in *Change in Communist Systems,* ed. Chalmers Johnson (Stanford, Cal.: Stanford University Press, 1970), states that "there is a significant interaction of political groups across the frontiers of every Communist system . . . in recent years political groups . . . have had an even more direct impact on each other, owing in no small part to the greater ease and frequency of communication" (pp. 232-33).

12. Especially H. Gordon Skilling and F. Griffiths, eds., *Interest Groups in Soviet Politics* (Princeton, N.J.: Princeton University Press, 1971).

13. Griffiths, in ibid., distinguishes informal and formal groups by describing the latter as "goal seeking aggregates of men taken by profession or formal organization" (p. 341), and refers the reader to Skilling's definition of "opinion" groups for a possible definition of informal groups; Skilling says, "In opinion groups, members may move from one group to another at different times and on different issues, so that the boundaries of groups may be constantly shifting." It should be noted that Griffiths takes issue with the group approach in general for various reasons, and substitutes his "tendency analysis" for the approach.

14. For some indication of the extent of crossnational group communication, see K. Hager, "In Close Order: On Ideological Cooperation Between Fraternal Parties," *Pravda,* May 14, 1974 (translation in *Daily Review,* May 23, 1974, p. 4). According to Hager, "In

the field of the social sciences alone the GDR Academy of Sciences has bilateral agreements with Academies in other fraternal countries on 40 complex topics and more than 60 special research subjects. Bilateral commissions on problems of the historical sciences have been set up . . . . Our universities and colleges have concluded 178 friendship treaties and working agreements with their partners . . . . It has become a good tradition to prepare and hold joint meetings between scientists, commissions and scholars specializing in individual branches of science."

CHAPTER

10

PROSPECTS FOR INTEGRATION IN EASTERN EUROPE: THE COUNCIL FOR MUTUAL ECONOMIC ASSISTANCE
Paul Marer

Is the following statement, summing up conventional wisdom, true or false?

> Economic developments in the last few years on the world market—the energy crisis, accelerating inflation, the enlargement of the European Common Market, and the world-wide recession—have seriously impaired the ability of the East European (EE) countries to continue in the future their rapid expansion of trade with the West. EE is becoming more economically dependent on the Soviet Union, which in turn is giving a new impetus to integration in the Council for Mutual Economic Assistance (CMEA), a tendency that obviously benefits the USSR.*

If the statement is intended only to paint a broad-brushed picture of recent developments affecting the CMEA, it is essentially correct. But beyond that, it is an oversimplification for several reasons. First, at any one time there are numerous centrifugal and centripetal forces pushing member states against or toward

From Paul Marer, "Prospects for Integration in Eastern Europe: The Council for Mutual Economic Assistance," *International Organization* 30, no. 4 (© 1976 by the Regents of the University of Wisconsin).

*The CMEA here refers only to the USSR and the six EE countries of Bulgaria, Czechoslovakia, the German Democratic Republic, Hungary, Poland, and Romania, even though Cuba and Mongolia also have full membership in the organization.

regional economic integration. Therefore, it would be more accurate to say that recent developments on the world market strengthened latent centripetal forces for CMEA integration, but it is by no means certain that these forces will over-come the strong obstacles to integration in the CMEA region.

Second, the statement implies a strong interest and commitment on the part of the Soviet Union to CMEA integration. Clearly, Soviet commitment is a critical factor. But, as will be documented, it is not a foregone conclusion that the Soviets will want to push economic integration much further than it now stands. The catalyst providing CMEA its integration momentum in recent years has been Soviet willingness to supply a growing volume of energy and raw mate-rials to EE. It is at least conceivable that the Soviets will find it necessary in the future to ease up on this commitment.

There is still another way in which the opening statement is simplistic. It implies that increased East-West commerce and deepening CMEA integration are mutually exclusive trends. In some respects, that is of course true: A conven-tional measure of integration is the share of total trade members of a bloc con-duct with each other. Thus, if East-West trade grows less rapidly than intrabloc trade, there is basis to conclude that CMEA integration is becoming stronger. But it is also possible that even a relatively slowly expanding East-West com-merce may help these countries to transform the "exchange of inefficiencies" that has characterized much of intra-CMEA trade in machinery and equipment up to now into a more genuine intrabranch specialization.

An analytically useful way of looking at the future is to assess both the so-called centrifugal forces against and the centripetal forces for CMEA inte-gration. Which forces have the upper hand at any particular moment, and why? Which internal developments within CMEA and external influences from with-out are changing the strength of these forces, and how?

The CMEA countries have recently gone through a period in which devel-opments largely external to the region strengthened centripetal integration forces within the bloc. After a brief summary of the institutional evolution of the CMEA, this essay will describe some of the readily identifiable economic and political forces that affect the speed and direction of the economic inte-gration process in the region.

EVOLUTION OF THE CMEA INSTITUTIONS
AND PROGRAMS

At the risk of oversimplification, the evolution of CMEA since it was formed in 1949 may be sketched by identifying three historical stages, as follows:

Stage 1 was characterized by inactivity throughout the 1950s, with CMEA affairs consisting almost entirely of bilateral relations between the Soviet Union and individual EE countries. A phrase coined by Fred Pryor describes the period well: "Soviet Embassy system of coordination."[1]

Stage 2 encompassed the period of the 1960s, which began with Khrushchev's hasty attempt to transform CMEA into a supranational organization. After the attempt was abandoned in the face of strong resistance from several countries, the substance of integration during the mid-1960s became identified with plan coordination. Since this "coordination" consisted largely of an exchange of information on domestic plans already approved by the national authorities, the changes recommended by CMEA organs encountered benign neglect or express resistance. The principal interest of members in "coordination" was to ensure from each other the supplies needed to fulfill domestic plans.

The main achievement of CMEA during this period was the free exchange of technical information (which, however, soon became a brake rather than a force for further integration); the creation of two banking institutions with considerable (but unused) integrative potential; the construction of a coordinated transport network; and the building of a multinational oil pipeline and an electricity grid. It should be noted that the last two joint CMEA projects, although multinationally planned, did not involve capital transfers across borders because each country was responsible only for constructing the sections located on its own territory.

The second half of the 1960s also was a period of debate and experimentation. Limited changes in central planning were introduced in some countries, comprehensive reforms in the economic mechanisms of other countries. Proposed approaches to CMEA integration reflected these differences among member states. Some countries favored greater reliance on a regionwide socialist market mechanism, visualizing better prospects for both the realization of gains from regional specialization and greater national autonomy.[2] Other countries, the Soviet Union foremost among them, again proposed (but much more cautiously than earlier) supranational planning, to be implemented by a network of bilateral agreements among members.

The 1960s also was a period of finding out what integration schemes would not work; learning that the more far-reaching a scheme, the more coordination problems and resistance from particular countries will be encountered.

Stage 3 is the period of the 1970s, beginning formally with the 1971 unveiling of a new comprehensive program for integration. The program decided in favor of a planned rather than a market approach, with emphasis on sectoral joint planning. Much of the work is to be carried out by regional industrial associations, which are analogous to the middle-level industrial associations in the individual CMEA countries because both have a degree of decision authority in the area of foreign trade and CMEA cooperation. The program recognizes that effective coordination of investment plans is crucial to integration efforts. Therefore, member states are urged to undertake joint planning in selected areas.[3]

The program reflects the spirit of the limited reforms in central planning introduced in the 1960s by the Soviet Union and Romania rather than the spirit of the comprehensive reforms introduced in Hungary and, earlier, in Czechoslovakia. The aspects of the program that appear more in keeping with a market-type approach to integration, such as a timetable for moving toward the convertibility of member currencies, are inconsistent with the program's major thrust and their implementation is lagging.[4]

The CMEA's institutional framework is neither supranational nor one in which every decision requires unanimity. Any member of CMEA declaring a lack of interest in an activity can opt not to participate. In practical terms, the present arrangements ensure that issues of major national interest to all members on which a unanimous agreement cannot be reached will not come up for joint decision.

The existing institutional framework also means that each member has some freedom to decide in which joint projects it wishes to participate, and what degree of commitment it is willing to give to each. A country's decisions in this regard will be influenced by a host of ideological, political, and economic factors, which must be continually weighed. Hence, an understanding of the centrifugal and centripetal integration forces affecting CMEA members is important. To a discussion of these we turn next.

CENTRIFUGAL FORCES HINDERING CMEA INTEGRATION

Few subjects of interest to economists are as mushy as the economics of CMEA integration. As J. M. Montias stated a few years ago, "There is no recognized methodology for analyzing problems in this field; the problems themselves have not been rigorously formulated or put down in precise language."[5] This is still true today.

According to the comprehensive program mentioned earlier, integration is defined as progress toward production and trade specialization and a growing number of joint investment projects, designed and implemented through coordinated or joint planning among CMEA members.

One should note that specialization is not simply a question of rapid increase in intrabloc trade or having a large share of a member country's total trade with bloc partners, which could obtain even if trade included many "exchanges of inefficiencies." Real specialization, based on natural or manmade differences in resource endowments among countries, should mean that different states specialize in the production of relatively labor-intensive, or capital-intensive, or resource-intensive products, with specialization carried out through an exchange of goods, or of factors of production, or both. One problem faced by the CMEA is that a certain portion of trade is not based on real specialization but on an exchange of products, such as garden-variety machinery and other manufactures, that buyers don't really want but must import, either because they are tied to other goods the purchaser really needs, or because this enables the buyer to find a market for the goods it produces but cannot readily export. This is what is meant by an "exchange of inefficiencies," and it lowers the gains from trade for both partners. Exchange of inefficiencies is caused by some of the institutional and systemic obstacles to trade and integration, which include the following:

1. The existing structure of production in EE: By following a Soviet-type strategy of industrialization in the immediate postwar period, all EE countries created or expanded parallel productive capacities, much of this in machine building, which hinders specialization. The production of consumer goods, a branch where gains from specialization are particularly large, had been given low priority. Postwar Soviet import demands, serviced either under war-related indemnities or on a commercial basis, created special industries in the EE countries, geared toward bilateral trade with the USSR rather than multilateral trade involving all CMEA members.

2. Problems of coordination: Just as vertical channels of coordination and control weaken links between producing and trading enterprises in a given country, so do coordination problems among countries inhibit specialization. For example, trade delegations that are supposed to make specialization decisions are several removes from the enterprises that are to produce the exports or use the imports. These problems make it especially risky for planners and enterprises to depend on foreign suppliers.

3. Inefficient domestic and CMEA price systems: Domestic prices are set on the basis of arbitrarily defined costs and remain unchanged for long periods. For these reasons, the prices at which the CMEA countries trade with each other are not based on the domestic prices or costs of the members; instead, world market prices, lagged and averaged over several years, are employed. But the prices that would balance supply and demand on the rather insulated CMEA market are quite different from the lagged world prices at which CMEA countries value their intrabloc trade. Parallel development strategies created surpluses in machinery, much of it not modern, which is not reflected in the prices of engineering products traded. At the same time, concentration of production by each country in heavy industry, which gobbles up material inputs, combined with wasteful use of these inputs, has led to a rapid growth in demand for energy and raw materials.

Since each CMEA country wants to be self-sufficient as a nation, or at least the bloc as a whole, each extracts, produces, and cultivates some scarce materials far beyond what would be considered the margin of minimum return in the West. This makes the marginal cost of energy and raw materials high. The combination of high demand and high costs of production has created a shortage of primary products in CMEA that, during the 1960s and early 1970s, was not reflected in the trading bloc's relative prices.

The dilemma of intrabloc price information is that, if relative prices in the CMEA deviate substantially from world prices, this will induce buyers of relatively high-priced goods to import them from the West, and sellers of relatively low-priced goods to find buyers elsewhere, creating dangerous centrifugal pressures. Such pressures have in fact been felt for some time, especially in Soviet trade with the countries of EE (see below).[6]

4. Bilateralism: These price distortions and the lack within CMEA of a convertible currency (whose introduction in turn is hindered by the price distortions) contribute decisively to the bilateral character of trade, under which not only total imports and exports but trade within each commodity group must be bilaterally balanced. Bilateralism, in turn, is a serious obstacle to regional specialization and trade.

5. Noncompatible economic guidance mechanisms: The introduction of comprehensive economic reforms in some CMEA countries devolved some production and trade decisions to enterprises. Specialization agreements are difficult to plan and implement when some parties to the agreement have undertaken such reforms and others have not.

6. Inability to compare investment costs and contributions: The economic rationality of investment decisions, especially those involving joint investment projects, is difficult to establish to everyone's satisfaction. Joint financing of new industries and joint investment projects in the extractive industries require calculations of comparative costs, hindered greatly by lack of uniformity among countries in their methods of administratively determining prices and costs. Where the availability of raw materials is the decisive factor in undertaking a joint investment, the decision presumably can be made largely on geological grounds. But even such projects require bringing to a common denominator the value of each member's contribution to the project, setting interest rates on loans, and arriving at profit distribution methods acceptable to all participants—which are not easy to accomplish.

The obstacles to integration can be presented not only in the abstract but also by reference to concrete problems in Soviet trade relations with the countries of EE. These relations are the single most important factors in setting the direction and speed of CMEA integration.

Close regional cooperation is clearly in the political interest of the USSR. But, from the Soviet standpoint, economic considerations may push the Soviets in the other direction. Why EE may be viewed by the Soviets as an economic liability is an important issue whose assessment requires some historical background and a brief discussion of the difficulties of quantifying and interpreting the evidence on which the conclusions must be based.

TABLE 10.1

USSR Trade with East Europe by Major Commodity Categories
(millions of devisa-rubles)

Year	Total	Fuel and Raw Materials	Agricultural Products and Food	Machinery	Industrial Consumer Goods	Unspecified
USSR exports						
1955	1,777	845	270	296	26	340
1960	3,074	1,730	498	390	74	383
1965	4,553	2,661	364	787	74	666
1970	6,083	3,365	409	1,267	124	918
1971	6,517	3,510	501	1,483	129	894
1972	6,727	3,715	87	1,689	137	1,100
1973	7,381	3,924	282	1,987	157	1,030
1974	8,705	4,304	371	2,378	232	1,420
USSR imports						
1955	1,657	601	113	734	76	134
1960	2,795	651	182	1,209	511	243
1965	4,673	817	383	2,114	882	478
1970	5,970	728	556	2,657	1,365	664
1971	6,533	786	621	2,800	1,608	718
1972	7,687	897	663	3,400	1,718	1,009
1973	8,093	903	679	3,810	1,720	981
1974	8,600	949	736	4,004	1,767	1,144
Surplus (deficit)						
1955	120	244	157	(438)	(50)	206
1960	279	1,079	316	(819)	(437)	140
1965	(120)	1,844	(19)	(1,327)	(808)	188
1970	113	2,637	(147)	(1,390)	(1,241)	254
1971	(16)	2,724	(120)	(1,317)	(1,479)	176
1972	(960)	2,818	(576)	(1,711)	(1,581)	91
1973	(712)	3,021	(397)	(1,823)	(1,563)	49
1974	105	3,355	(365)	(1,626)	(1,535)	276

Note: To convert to 1971 $U.S. (= SDRs), 1 devisa ruble = $.90.
Source: International Trade Information Management System (ITIMS) of Indiana University (based on official Soviet sources).

As a consequence of EE's development strategy, poor endowment in natural resources, and wasteful use of materials, the consumption of energy, raw materials, and foodstuffs grew rapidly during the postwar period. The four less developed countries—Bulgaria, Romania, Poland, and Hungary—absorbed an increasing share of their total output of primary products domestically and redirected some raw material exports to the West. Czechoslovakia and East Germany had been net importers of primary products even before the war. During the postwar period, the USSR became a large, and by the mid-1960s the only net supplier within CMEA of energy and raw materials, to the extent of nearly $3 billion worth by 1970 and $3.7 billion (1971 dollars or SDR units) by 1974. During the 1960s EE paid for this net import of fuel and industrial raw materials primarily with machinery, but by the 1970s these purchases came to be balanced with a net surplus of machinery and industrial consumer goods in about equal proportions (see Table 10.1).

One interesting fact that can be noted in Table 10.1 is that, although the USSR's surplus (EE's deficit) of fuel and raw material exports has been rising for two decades, the rate of increase in this surplus has been steadily declining. From 1955 to 1960 the surplus more than quadrupled; from 1960 to 1965 it rose by 71 percent; from 1965 to 1970 it climbed 43 percent; but during the four years 1970-74 it increased by only 27 percent. Soviet writers have been noting for more than ten years that it is increasingly unprofitable for the USSR to provide fuel and mineral resources to meet rapidly growing EE demand. Soviet spokesmen make two points: First, since most of the new fields are in Siberia, costs have risen rapidly; second, EE countries pay for energy and raw materials, which can readily be sold on the world market for hard currency, with manufactures that are low in quality and cannot readily be sold for hard currency.

Is EE an economic liability to the Soviet Union? The available information is neither comprehensive nor detailed enough to permit a definitive answer. But the available information suggests that this is a strong possibility.

The actual distribution of gains and losses in Soviet-CMEA trade in 1960 and 1970 was estimated by two Western scholars. Under ordinary circumstances, when two nations engage in trade both partners are expected to benefit, even though the distribution of gains from trade may not be equal. Defining gains from trade as the ratio of the estimated resource cost of exports to the potential resource cost of full import substitution, Edward A. Hewett found that trading with CMEA actually results in a loss for the Soviet Union.[7] That is, by these calculations, in 1960 it cost the USSR 38 percent more resources to export to CMEA than it would have cost to substitute domestic production for imports from CMEA. In contrast, all CMEA countries except Romania were able to save anywhere from 3 to about 30 percent of the resources they would have had to expend had they been forced to produce domestically the commodities imported from the Soviet Union (although Romania "lost" 19 percent).

By 1970 both CMEA foreign trade prices and the commodity structure of Soviet-CMEA trade had changed. Assuming that only prices changed (that is, that the commodity composition in 1970 would have remained the same as it was in 1960), Hewett calculates that the Soviet loss on trade with CMEA would have increased to 67 percent. This is largely because fuels and ores have had to be extracted in increasingly remote Asian regions, where production and transport to the borders of East Europe cost more. The actual loss was only 28 percent because of changes in the structure of trade: By 1970 a larger proportion of Soviet exports to CMEA was comprised of machinery than a decade earlier (see Table 10.1). In spite of changes in the commodity composition, CMEA countries had increased their gains from trading with the Soviet Union by 1970 as compared with 1960 (gains for Poland remained about the same).

Somewhat similar results were obtained, via a different methodology, by Carl H. McMillan.[8] Using the so-called Leontief method, he calculated the capital, labor, and natural resource requirements of a typical basket of Soviet exports as well as import replacements. He found that in 1959 (the only year for which he was able to perform these calculations) Soviet exports contained absolutely greater amounts of labor, capital, and natural resources than those of import substitutes of equivalent value. McMillan found that the overall losses had originated in trade with the more developed CMEA partners: East Germany, Czechoslovakia, Hungary, and Poland. That is, Soviet exports to these countries used up more labor, capital, and natural resources than it would have required to produce the manufactured goods that made up the bulk of Soviet imports from them.

Because of data problems and the simplifying assumptions, the results should not be interpreted as precise measurements and neither of the two experts cited claim more. For example, the finding that exports of the raw material exporter contain absolutely greater amounts of labor and natural resources than those of its import substitutes is not that surprising, considering that exports are exchanged for relatively sophisticated machines, ships, and other manufactures that embody substantial skilled labor inputs. Also, there is no information on the volume and price of military equipment shipped from the Soviet Union to EE (scattered evidence suggests that the prices charged are high), which could influence not only the magnitude but also the direction of the results. Many other relevant items also had to be omitted, such as the grant equivalents of EE's interest-free or subsidized capital transfers to the USSR.[9]

Be that as it may, the question of cost can be approached from still another perspective, which is perhaps more relevant, given the way in which the Soviets are likely to think about the problem.

The Soviet Union continues to face a declining rate of growth of national product, attributable to a substantial slowdown in the rate of growth of labor force (due to demographic factors), of capital stock (as an increased proportion of new capital must replace rather than add to the existing stock), and of productivity (due to the chronic deficiencies of Soviet planning and faltering technological progress). The relevant trends can be discerned in the slowdown in the rate of increase in output:[10]

Period	Real National Income (Soviet official data)		Real GNP (Western data)
	"Produced"	"Utilized"	
1950-55	11.4		6.3
1955-60	9.1		6.2
1960-65	6.5		5.5
1965-70	7.7	7.1	5.5
1970-75		5.1	4.2
1975-80 (plan)		4.4-5.1	

To halt the decline in economic growth, a more rapid improvement in productivity is needed. In the view of the current leadership, this requires increased Western capital plus technological and management knowhow. These imports must be purchased, currently or as credits are repaid, largely with Soviet energy and raw material products. The more pressing the Soviet need for Western imports and the larger the share of Soviet convertible-currency exports to CMEA partners, the more EE is viewed as an economic liability by the Soviets. The poor harvests of 1972 and 1975, as well as the likelihood of future poor harvests, also must enter the equation.

In late 1973 and in 1974, as world prices of energy and raw materials increased rapidly, with the price of such commodities as oil soaring spectacularly, the Soviet Union found itself in a dilemma. On the one hand, it became more and more costly to continue with the 1970 bilateral agreements under which increased quantities of energy and raw materials were to be supplied to EE during 1971-75 at fixed (average 1966-70) world prices.* On the other hand, to abruptly raise export prices before the agreements expired, or to ship less than the promised quantities, would seriously damage Soviet prestige. More important, such actions would cause serious economic difficulties and reduce

---

*More than any other commodity, oil illustrates the problem. In 1974 the Soviet Union shipped about 60 million tons of crude oil and petroleum products to the five European members of CMEA (Romania did not purchase oil from the USSR), at $16 to $20 per ton (depending upon the mix of crude and oil products), for a total revenue of $1.0 to $1.2 billion. During the same year the Soviets sold approximately 40 million tons of oil in the West at the then current average world market price of about $70 per ton, for a total revenue of about $2.8 billion. If we make the admittedly unrealistic assumption that the USSR could have sold the 60 million tons of oil to the West rather than to CMEA, we find that it could have earned $3 billion additional hard currency revenue, increasing the $7.5 billion actual earnings by 40 percent.

living standards in EE, possibly triggering dangerous political instability in the region.

The Soviet Union chose what may be considered a middle course to resolve the dilemma. It used world price developments to enforce its demand for a higher price on its exports to CMEA, but it raised prices in steps rather than demanding current world prices at once. It renegotiated intra-CMEA foreign trade prices, which were supposed to remain fixed from January 1971 until December 1975, substantially to its advantage, effective January 1, 1975. The justification for discarding the old agreement earlier was that the dramatic changes in world price and supply conditions could not have been foreseen in 1970, when the five-year price and quantity agreements were signed. Most important, the price of oil sold to EE was doubled from 18 to 37 rubles, but the price was still less than two-thirds the world market price.* Other selected price increases also were negotiated, involving both Soviet exports to and imports from EE. The price revisions substantially improved Soviet terms of trade with EE, thereby reducing but not eliminating (what the Soviets claim to be) unfavorable trading arrangements with CMEA. To be sure, even before the prices were changed, the Soviets had taken "compensatory" actions for what they view as the economic liability of supplying EE with cheap energy and raw materials. Most important among these was obtaining large, low-interest credits from EE to develop energy and raw material resources in the USSR.

In a move of major significance, the method of determining intra-CMEA prices after 1975 also was changed. Beginning with 1976 the old system of maintaining fixed prices for five years was replaced by a moving average price base. Prices are now based on average world market prices in the five years immediately preceding the year for which the newly calculated prices are applicable. Thus, prices in 1976 were established across the board on the basis of average world prices of 1971-75, in 1977 on the basis of average prices in 1972-76, and so on.

What is the portent of these developments for EE? Focusing on that most important and visible commodity, oil, the 1975 doubling of price meant that, in 1975 alone, EE had to find ways to pay at least an additional $1 billion. On the assumption that until 1980 the price of oil on the world market will remain at the level of $84/ton (or $12/barrel), the new CMEA pricing mechanism means that by 1978 EE would almost pay the current world market price. On the 1974 quantity of about 60 million tons this would mean an oil bill approximately double again, from its 1975 level of $2 billion to about $4 billion. Each $1 billion

---

*It is important to note that the nominal revaluation of the ruble vis-a-vis the dollar increases the nominal dollar but not the actual ruble value of intra-CMEA trade. Thus, when calculating the real burden of intra-CMEA price changes in dollars, an unchanged ruble/dollar exchange rate must be used.

(of unchanged 1971 purchasing power) additional cost means that EE's exports to the Soviet Union must rise by about 10 percent in real terms.

As far as the USSR is concerned, recently published incomplete plan figures suggest that a conditional commitment was made to continue to supply energy and raw materials to EE. This was announced after considerable bargaining, which included the Soviets obtaining commitments from the countries of EE to participate on a very large scale in the CMEA joint investment projects, which are located mostly in the USSR. But the Soviet supply commitment, especially for the period beyond the current five year plan, is far from unequivocal. A Soviet spokesman stated:

> The major part of the CMEA nations' fuel and energy requirements is provided by the Soviet supply which will continue to grow after 1980 as well. But this depends largely on the condition that the interested countries take part in building up the additional oil and gas extracting capacities and recognize the expenses needed to maintain the production of these important crude products at an adequate level . . . to meet the requirements of other socialist countries for crude products.[11]

CENTRIPETAL FORCES FOR INTEGRATION

Recent developments on the world market have given a renewed impetus to CMEA integration, largely through their impact on East-West trade.

Trade with the West averages about one-third of the value of EE's total trade turnover (ranging from a low of about one-fifth for Bulgaria to about one-half for Romania and Poland). This trade plays a crucial role in the economies of EE: Raw materials and foodstuff imports provide their industries essential products unavailable or in scarce supply in CMEA;[12] machinery imports make an essential contribution to the modernization of industries; and Western consumer goods improve the quality and assortment of retail items. Since consumerism is one of the most potent political forces in the CMEA, particularly in EE, this dependence on Western consumer goods, even if marginal in terms of total consumer spending, is critically important. The EE countries pay for their purchases with a net export surplus in food, raw materials, and semimanufactures to the industrial West.

Among considerations that push the EE countries (not the USSR) toward greater reliance on the CMEA market and on CMEA suppliers is the increasing hard-currency indebtedness of these countries. These are the most important determining factors:

1. The energy crisis: In 1973 the world economy was shaken by a threefold increase in the price of oil. The immediate impact on EE was not

unmanageable since about 80 percent of the region's oil and petroleum product imports came from the USSR which, according to long-term agreements signed in 1970, continued to supply the scheduled quantities at fixed, pre-1970 world prices. In 1973 the six EE countries combined imported about 11 million tons of crude oil from sources other than the USSR.[13] Assuming that the price of a ton of crude oil increased from approximately $20 to $60, the initial hard-currency expenditure for EE was $400 to $500 million annually, somewhat less than 10 percent of EE's total 1973 exports to the West of over $6 billion.

2. Western inflation: The second adverse development for EE was double-digit inflation in key Western countries, triggered or fueled by the oil price rise. Since the prices of EE consumer-good and agricultural exports did not increase as much as the prices of their imports, EE's terms of trade with the West deteriorated. The extent to which this contributed to these countries' balance of payments problems varied, depending upon their structure of exchanges with the industrial West.

3. Western recession: The third adverse development now facing EE is reduced Western demand for EE exports, triggered by world recession and the balance of payments problems of several West European countries, which has forced cuts in their imports. Especially hurt were EE agricultural exports, which formerly encountered the least resistance in penetrating Western markets. Hungary and Romania were dealt a severe blow, for example, when in 1974 the Common Market placed an embargo on beef exports to members of the community.

4. Enlargement of the Common Market: Another, and in the long run perhaps even more adverse development for several EE countries was the 1972 enlargement of the Common Market, under which intra-Common Market tariffs are being reduced to zero by July 1977 in five stages. Since several of the countries that joined the Common Market, (such as the United Kingdom) or became associated (such as Austria) are key markets for EE goods, this reduction of intra-West European tariffs, while maintaining pre-1972 tariff levels on imports from nonmembers, is hurting EE countries especially. Hardest hit are foodstuffs and basic materials which, for example, represent more than half of Hungary's exports to Austria. Further problems are created by European Community rules of origin, increasing the difficulty of exporting goods manufactured under industrial cooperation, because the share of a product manufactured in nonmember third countries may not surpass the percent fixed by the European Community if it is to be eligible for preferential intra-market tariffs.

To be sure, we must not lose sight of the fact that the fundamental difficulty facing all the EE countries in East-West trade is their inability to produce and market in adequate quantities modern, good-quality manufactures that can be readily sold in the West for hard currency. The recent developments only exacerbate this problem.

5. Impaired credit standing: While recent developments adversely affected EE exports to the West, the EE appetite for Western goods and technology has not abated. During 1974 imports from hard-currency countries rose by nearly 50 percent (a good portion of which was due to price inflation, but imports also rose significantly in real terms), and purchases continued to increase rapidly during 1975. The combination of a sluggish rise in EE exports and rapid growth in EE imports resulted in several EE countries running record trade deficits with developed Western countries during 1974 and 1975, so that at the end of 1975, EE's combined hard-currency indebtedness, excluding the USSR, approached $18 billion.[14]

Large deficits can be bridged temporarily with credits, which have become easier to obtain as relations between East and West improved and as Western countries, anxious to increase their own exports for balance of payments and employment reasons, compete with each other in providing large official credits to promote sales to the USSR and EE. But growing indebtedness causes serious concern to Western creditors as well as to the EE planners. First, if indebtedness goes beyond a certain point (which is admittedly not clearly defined), it damages the credit-worthiness of a country, with obvious consequences for both the availability and cost of credit. But perhaps of more immediate concern to EE is that a rising debt-service burden impairs ability to secure a growing volume of imports, which are needed (and cannot be obtained from CMEA), if an increasing share of export earnings is required to service debts rather than to pay for current imports.

6. More attractive intra-CMEA trade: As imports from the West are more difficult to secure, obtaining an increased flow of scarce goods from CMEA becomes more important. As certain CMEA members become more critical suppliers of essential imports, more attention inevitably will be paid to facilitate obtaining these imports. CMEA suppliers can become more critical either because what in the past were assured deliveries become uncertain supplies, contingent upon, say, the importing country's policies with regard to CMEA integration. These developments strengthen the hands of those in EE—ideological purists and enterprise managers foremost among them—who argue that it makes more sense in any event to specialize production for the more stable and less demanding Soviet and CMEA than for the more capricious Western markets.

A related, less tangible phenomenon is the effect on the Weltanschauung of EE leaders of Western recession, inflation, monetary crisis, and the continued discrimination against EE exports in the West, such as the Common Market preference and lack of most-favored nation status or official credit support in the United States. As EE decision makers weigh their commercial policy options, the difficulties of closer cooperation with CMEA in general and the USSR in particular probably appear more attractive today, by comparison, then when the waters of the Western economies were calmer.

7. Gain in trade bloc importance: Still another intangible factor pushing EE in the direction of closer cooperation within CMEA is the growing importance of trade blocs, as shown by the experience of the Common Market, the highly successful OPEC (Organization of Petroleum Exporting Countries) oil cartel, and prospects that similar groups might emerge elsewhere. To be sure, EE countries are not likely to be in a position to form OPEC-like cartels. But they might improve their economic position against outsiders, such as the Common Market, by negotiating not individually but as a bloc. For example, the CMEA countries are increasingly forced to come to terms with the process of West European economic integration, which they initially rejected as "imperialistic." The rapid expansion of economic relations between individual EE countries and European Community members during the 1960s and early 1970s prompted the USSR to try to channel these relations formally through the CMEA. Although the individual EE states as well as the European Community members are more interested in bilateral relations than multilateral relations, the Soviet Union prefers direct agreements between the two blocs because this would strengthen the dependence of EE countries on the CMEA, which the Soviet Union, by its economic and political weight alone, necessarily dominates. The Common Market Commission also seems to be edging toward advocating agreements between the two blocs, although its interest in negotiating with individual CMEA members in its capacity as a supranational organization is more pronounced.[15] Decision makers in EE must consider how much they could improve their negotiating clout if they face Brussels jointly rather than singly, even though the economic and trade interests of individual CMEA countries vis-a-vis the Common Market differ. To be sure, letting the Russians serve as chief spokesmen for all CMEA countries might be an unwelcome tradeoff.

8. Halt to further experimentation with economic reforms: Economic instability in the West discourages or halts comprehensive economic reforms of the type that devolves more autonomy to producing and trading enterprises. More central controls may in fact be reimposed as a defense against imported inflation and worsening balance of payments problems. While this may not be conducive to regional integration, such actions, as McMillan points out, are at least consistent with the spirit of CMEA integration, which stresses traditional-type joint planning.[16]

9. Abatement of pressures for supranationalism: A subtle and interesting observation was made by Andrzej Korbonski in relation to the previous point.[17] Soviet pressure on CMEA members to conform closely on all matters, but especially on making CMEA a supranational body, has apparently been muted for some time. This must have gone some way toward allaying the fears of the EE countries that closer economic integration would be a first step toward loss of sovereignty, and ultimately perhaps national identity.

10. World market price changes on energy and raw materials: One consequence of higher world energy prices is that Soviet oil and gas fields and mineral

deposits, which a few years ago seemed economically marginal and thus uninviting for investment, have suddenly become feasible investment propositions. Another consequence of higher world energy and raw material prices is that the increase justifies raising the CMEA prices of these goods. This brings relative prices in the bloc more in line with relative scarcities in the region, without releasing dangerous centrifugal forces. This contributes to an improved climate for making investment and specialization decisions, supporting integration efforts.

Along the same lines, accelerating world inflation triggered, paradoxically, a CMEA decision to get rid of the inflexible system of intrabloc foreign trade pricing. Since large discrepancies between relative prices on the CMEA and on the world markets induce centrifugal forces, bringing CMEA prices relatively closer to world prices annually rather than once every five years should be more supportive of CMEA integration than was the previous, inflexible system.

11. Fewer obstacles to ruble convertibility: Many obstacles stand in the way of achieving even partial (intrabloc) convertibility of the ruble. One is the Soviet disinclination to pool monetary reserves with the scarce reserves of its EE partners. Another has been Soviet concern that the USSR would remain a large and perennial debtor vis-a-vis EE, requiring it to make settlements in hard currency or gold. With its substantially improved terms of trade, the Soviet Union now has less reason to fear this eventuality.

12. EE borrowing of hard currency through CMEA banks: As EE countries accumulate larger and larger hard currency debts, they will find it advantageous to borrow hard currency through the two CMEA banks. Not only can these banks borrow on better terms than the individual EE countries can, but, given implicit Soviet backing of these loans, Western credit also becomes more readily available through this channel. For example, to finance part of the largest joint CMEA project under way to date—construction of the Orenburg pipeline, which will deliver large quantities of Soviet gas to all EE countries and will cost an estimated $1.5 billion—the CMEA International Investment Bank borrowed $300 million Eurodollars from a consortium led by the Deutsche Bank of West Germany. Some of the funds are being loaned to Poland to enable it to purchase pipes and equipment in the West to construct its segment of the pipeline in the USSR; the other EE countries will probably receive similar credits.

13. East-West industrial cooperation as a spur to CMEA integration: Current research on the U.S. perspective on East-West industrial cooperation reveals that many U.S. companies are large multinational firms and that many have signed or are negotiating industrial cooperation agreements in more than one EE country. The worldwide expansion of multinational firms and the EE countries' desire to obtain Western technology and management knowhow have given rise to a gradual shift in East-West commerce from international trade to licensing and management contracts, coproduction arrangements, and in some EE countries, contractual or equity joint ventures. But since the economic feasibility of

many industrial cooperation agreements depends on having a market of more than national size or being able to combine resources from several CMEA countries, Western firms are carefully assessing bloc-wide production and marketing opportunities. By contrast, socialist enterprises in CMEA countries have neither the motivation nor the opportunity today to venture into each other's territory (there are a few exceptions to this generalization), so they leave the field, by default, to Western multinationals, whose activities may, in certain respects, be integrative. In fact, there may be a possible analogy between the role U.S. subsidiaries played in helping to integrate Western Europe during the late 1950s and 1960s and the role U.S. multinationals and other Western firms may be playing in helping to integrate Eastern Europe during the 1970s and 1980s.*

CONCLUSIONS

One conclusion of this essay is that the Soviet attitude and commitment to CMEA integration is a critical factor that will decide how the centrifugal and centripetal forces now battling in the CMEA will be resolved. It is by no means a foregone conclusion that the Soviets will push integration much farther. They may decide in a few years that it is too costly for them to continue to provide a growing volume of energy and raw materials to EE, goods that the Soviets may themselves need to pay for much-needed Western imports.

However, it should be noted that recent developments in the CMEA on the price and investment fronts have gone a long way toward reducing EE as a Soviet liability, if such liability ever existed. Moreover, even if the Soviet Union would find it profitable to diminish its economic links with its CMEA partners, it surely views EE's increased economic dependence as a political asset, as its EE partners must continuously weigh the economic cost of noncompliance with Soviet political demands.

---

*An example of how the expansion of East-West commerce can contribute to CMEA integration: Shortly after EE countries began to purchase Western licenses on a regular basis, CMEA decided to introduce (in 1967) a system of payments for the transfer of licensing and knowhow among CMEA countries—an indispensable first step toward improving the effectiveness of intra-CMEA technology transfer. Another example is the establishment of a central CMEA office for purchasing Western licenses proposed by the USSR to avoid duplication. This would be linked to CMEA funding of joint specialization projects. McMillan further points out that when an EE country is committed under an East-West cooperation agreement to payment in convertible currency for royalties or parts and service, it will undoubtedly press for hard currency payment when the resulting products are exported to CMEA partners. In fact, the joint venture agreements of Romania explicitly provide for this possibility.

Another conclusion is that recent economic developments in the West have slowed, at least for the time being, the rapid expansion of East-West commerce, and this is forcing the EE countries to rely more on their CMEA trade partners. One consequence of EE's increasing hard currency balance of payments problem is that these countries might find it necessary to continue to open up to direct Western participation in their economies, through East-West industrial cooperation projects. Paradoxically, such projects might in the future play a significant role in improving the regional specialization, trade, and investment decisions of the CMEA countries.

NOTES

1. Frederic L. Pryor, *The Communist Foreign Trade System* (Cambridge, Mass.: MIT Press, 1963).

2. Carl H. McMillan, "Some Remarks on Socialist Integration and East-West Relations," remarks prepared for the Airlie House Conference on Eastern Europe—Stability or Recurrent Crises? November 13-15, 1975.

3. A recent comprehensive review of institutional developments in the CMEA can be found in Zbigniew M. Fallenbuchl, "East European Integration: COMECON," in U.S. Congress, Joint Economic Committee, *Reorientation and Commercial Relations of the Economies of Eastern Europe* (Washington, D.C.: U.S. Government Printing Office, August 1974).

4. McMillan, "Some Remarks."

5. J. M. Montias, "Obstacles to Economic Integration of Eastern Europe," *Studies in Comparative Communism* 2, nos. 3-4 (July/October 1969).

6. Paul Marer, *Postwar Pricing and Price Patterns in Socialist Foreign Trade (1946-1971)* (Bloomington: Indiana University International Development Research Center Report no. 1, 1972).

7. Edward A. Hewett, "Prices and Resource Allocation in Intra-CMEA Trade," paper prepared for Conference on the Consistency and Efficiency of the Socialist Price System, University of Toronto, March 8-9, 1974.

8. Carl H. McMillan, "Factor Proportions and the Structure of Soviet Trade," *ACES Bulletin* 15, no. 1 (Spring 1973). Critical comments on this article and further original findings are presented in Steven Rosefielde, "The Embodied Factor Content of Soviet International Trade: Problems of Theory, Measurement and Interpretation," *ACES Bulletin* 15, nos. 2-3 (Summer-Fall 1973).

9. For a listing of additional considerations and further discussion, see Paul Marer, "Has Eastern Europe Become a Liability to the Soviet Union—the Economic Aspects," in *The International Politics of Eastern Europe,* ed. Charles Gati (New York: Praeger Publishers, 1976). See also an earlier study by the same author which discusses the early postwar period as well as more recent developments: "Soviet Economic Policy in Eastern Europe," in *Reorientation and Commercial Relations of the Economies of Eastern Europe.*

10. Abram Bergson, "Russia's Economic Planning Shift," *Wall Street Journal*, May 17, 1976.

11. N. Ptichkin, "The 29th Session of the Council for Mutual Economic Assistance," *Foreign Trade* (Moscow), October 1975.

12. For example, Czechoslovakia buys approximately one-third of industrial raw material and semimanufactures imports from the industrial West. *Svet, Prace,* November 12, 1974, p. 4.

13. Robert W. Campbell, "East European Trade in Crude Oil and Petroleum Products, 1965-1974," unpublished paper, 1975.

14. Author's estimate, based on Lawrence J. Brainard, "Financing Eastern Europe's Trade Gap: The Euromarket Connection," *Euromoney,* January 1976, pp. 16-18. The indebtedness figure is a gross estimate, that is, without subtracting EE's relatively small hard-currency assets, held mainly in the form of Eurocurrency deposits.

15. Max Baumer and Hans-Dieter Jacobsen, "Integration of COMECON Into the World Economy?" *Aussenpolitik* [German foreign affairs review] (Hamburg) 27, no. 1 (1976).

16. McMillan, "Some Remarks."

17. Andrzej Korbonski, "Detente, East-West Trade, and the Future of Economic Integration in Eastern Europe," paper presented at the annual meeting of the American Association for the Advancement of Slavic Studies, Atlanta, Georgia, October 1975.

11

EXTERNAL INFLUENCES ON POLITICAL CHANGE IN EASTERN EUROPE: A FRAMEWORK FOR ANALYSIS

Sarah Meiklejohn Terry

It has been observed elsewhere that Eastern Europe, if only by virtue of its hapless geography, "has traditionally been on the receiving end of foreign influences . . . [as] an object rather than a subject in international politics."[1] This fact notwithstanding, those foolhardy enough to attempt to evaluate the role of such influences in the politics of the region should at least have the prerogative of prefacing their remarks with a caveat or two about the pitfalls of that task.

As James Rosenau, a pioneer in the development of cross-system analysis, has admitted: "Recent years have witnessed substantial clarification of the dynamics that underlie political behavior at the individual, local, national, and international levels, but the capacity to move predictively back and forth among two or more of these levels is presently lacking."[2] Yet, where Rosenau could attribute this problem as a general phenomenon to the near infinite "variability in politics,"[3] our task is further complicated by the fact that in Eastern Europe we have not as yet witnessed that "substantial clarification" of the dynamics of domestic political behavior—in other words, by our inadequate understanding of the very political processes whose susceptibility to external influences we are trying to evaluate. Most serious is the lack of empirical data concerning the input side of decision-making processes. To be sure, the gaps in our knowledge are not

This essay originated in an effort to expand upon themes relevant to this volume which were introduced by Andrzej Korbonski in his "External Influences on Eastern Europe," in *The International Politics of Eastern Europe,* ed. Charles Gati (New York: Praeger Publishers, 1976). The author wishes to acknowledge her debt to Professor Korbonski and thank him for his generous counsel. She is also grateful to Robert Legvold of Tufts University for his helpful comments.

nearly so disabling as in the worst days of Stalinism; nonetheless, one is still forced to rely primarily on policy outputs as the best indicators of system performance, and of the impact thereon of foreign influences. Moreover, in part as a result of this scarcity of data, Eastern Europe has figured infrequently in the literature experimenting with such theoretical approaches to cross-system analysis as the transnational, transgovernmental, or linkage concepts.[4]

A second caveat concerns the particular perspective from which this essay seeks to evaluate external influences. Generally speaking, influence is narrowly defined as a deliberate effort on the part of one party to alter the behavior of a second "so that it redounds to the policy advantage" of the first.[5] The focus is primarily on the motives of, the means employed by, and the policy benefits to the source of the influence. Without challenging the usefulness of this approach, I propose to use a concept of influence that is both broader and differently focused. Specifically, my central concern is with the target or receiver of the influence and with the primary product of the influence process—that is, the change (or lack of change) in the behavior or institutions of the target system. Moreover, viewed from this perspective, external influences need not be limited to deliberate attempts by outside parties to elicit particular responses. The influence process may be inadvertent, or may even be initiated by the target; likewise, the source may be a passive party, or may not even be a specific actor. This is not to say that I am disinterested in the nature of the source or its relationship to the target, any more than those using the more traditional approach are disinterested in aspects of the target system that affect its response. Rather, it is a question of emphasis; I am primarily concerned here with political processes in the East European systems and with the impact on those processes of all manner of external phenomena—be they events in other systems, changes in the international climate, or deliberate policy actions.

With these considerations in mind, the purpose of this essay must perforce be limited. It is not intended as a substantive contribution to our knowledge of East European politics. Rather, it is an attempt to think systematically about such evidence ("hard" or "soft") as we now possess regarding external influences, and to identify promising directions for future research. Toward those ends, I propose:

1. To establish a tentative framework, in the form of a checklist or series of questions, for analyzing both sides of the influence equation—that is, both the external factors and relevant aspects of the target system.

2. To apply this framework to selected examples drawn from the several external environments that have exerted some influence on Eastern Europe in the past two decades.

3. To identify those external environments and factors that appear most likely to influence the future course of East European political development.

For purposes of this essay, Eastern Europe will be defined as comprising those seven countries that do now or did in the past belong to what is loosely called the Soviet bloc (Albania, Bulgaria, Czechoslovakia, East Germany, Hungary, Poland, and Romania), but excluding Yugoslavia and the Soviet Union, both of which are viewed as part of the external environment. With respect to sources of influence, the emphasis will be on non-Soviet and non-Western factors, although both of these sources will be treated tangentially: Soviet influence as a factor conditioning the penetrability of Eastern Europe by other external influences; Western influences not as specifically "Western" but as a component of other differentiated environments (global, regional, identity references) to which the East Europeans relate. With respect to the targets or receivers of influence, where possible the emphasis will be on the impact on domestic as opposed to foreign policy behavior, although it is understood that the two are never wholly separable.

CONDITIONS OF INFLUENCE PENETRATION

A Checklist for Analysis

In light of the perilous state of the art of cross-system analysis in the study of Eastern Europe—in light also of the dearth of data on the input side of political processes—how, then, should one go about evaluating external influences on the politics of that region? One way, and the one that will be attempted here, is to break down the concept of "external influences" into its component factors, which in varying combinations determine the effectiveness of influence penetration. These relate to: (1) the origin or source of the influence; (2) the content of the influence being transmitted or the nature of the potential change it would induce; (3) the agents or channels by which it is transmitted; and finally, (4) those aspects of the target system that determine its receptiveness to a given influence.

Sources of Influence

When analyzing the source of an external influence, one should always define it in relation to the prospective target of penetration. For example, does the influence originate in an environment in which the latter is not directly involved and over which it has no control? Or is the source one with which the target system interacts directly? The answer to these questions is not always clearcut. The target system may interact directly with the source at one level but not with respect to the influence in question, as when the former is affected indirectly by relations between the latter and a third party. This may apply particularly to smaller states, such as those of Eastern Europe, which at best play a secondary role in global politics. The relationship between source and target may also change with time. What was originally an independent variable in the external environment may, after the initial impact has been absorbed (or deflected), become a dependent or semidependent variable in that the system being influenced may gain some control over its further effect; in other words, the original target begins to manipulate that influence toward its own ends. Conversely, it can happen that an influence initially admitted by conscious decision of the target system may acquire a degree of independence by virtue of the fact that its removal would entail undesirable or destabilizing consequences for the receiver; this would be the case where a target system initiating the influence penetration then becomes dependent on that external input for the pursuit of its own goals.

A second set of questions concerns the proximity of the external source to the target. Proximity is used here not only in the geographical sense but also in terms of such indicators as historical experience, cultural affinity, political systems and values, economic interests, or levels of socioeconomic development. In some cases, proximity in one sense will reinforce proximity in another; in other cases, the pressures will be countervailing. On the one hand, geographical proximity may breed historical animosities or economic inequities that can never fully be overcome by the centripetal pull of a shared ideology. On the other hand, geographical proximity may coincide with shared historical experiences or economic interests, which together may be enough to break down barriers of political and ideological hostility. Or, shared political values may compensate for great distance and the lack of common historical, cultural, or economic interests. The possible combinations are almost infinite, and the relationships are apt to be complex.

One final variable pertaining to the source of an external influence is its magnitude in relation to the receiving system. Other things being equal, the larger the former in relation to the latter, the greater on balance will be the prospects for influence penetration—while a very large country, especially one with strong holds over its population, stands a far better chance of rendering even major foreign inputs insignificant.[6] But this is not a question of size alone; magnitude will vary with such factors as distance, the type and importance of the input to the target system, and changes in the international climate. The sole source of a product critical to the receiver will gain influence regardless of relative size. On the other hand, a large but distant power may exert a dominant political and economic influence over a smaller state in times of relative instability, but will quickly lose that influence if it cannot deliver military protection in a time of crisis.

Varieties of Influence

Turning to the question of the nature of the influence being transmitted, we must first ask whether the input, if absorbed, would itself directly cause a change in the receiving system, or whether it would be more of a conditioning factor—that is, one that would affect that system only indirectly by enhancing or diminishing the prospects for some change generated either by indigenous forces, or by some other external influence. An example of the former might be as dramatic and unequivocal as a change of leadership or the imposition of a new political system as the result of direct military intervention. The latter might be as diffuse as a shift in the general international climate, or in some aspect of a state's relations with the outside world, which alters the balance among competing groups on the domestic level, or which allows a system to ward off other pressures from outside. Here again, the dividing line is not always easy to draw.[7]

Next we must inquire into the nature of the potential change that would be induced, whether directly or indirectly, by the external input. Would it involve basic alterations in the macropolitical structure of the society, or would it be of an incremental nature, in the subordinate economic or social systems? Would it challenge the sacred cows of the political order, or would it leave ideological values and the distribution of decision-making authority more or less untouched? Finally, would the induced change be perceived within the system, or by important sectors thereof, as a positive or negative contribution to the achievement of its overall goals—which, in addition to system maintenance, may include legitimation, economic growth and efficiency, and social justice, among others?

If we now combine these variables with those relating to the sources of external influences, we can begin to see the subtleties and complexities that condition influence penetration. At one end of the spectrum, a broad systemic change emanating from an ideologically alien system and challenging the authority of established elites clearly could not be absorbed short of war or revolution. Conversely, influences that impinge only indirectly on the political sector—for example, via the economic and/or social systems—and that originate in ideologically compatible systems, at more or less the same level of socioeconomic development, could be easily digested. But the possible gradations between these extremes are many. It does not follow, for instance, that, because broad systemic change from an alien system is unacceptable, no inputs from that system can contribute positively to the achievement of the target system's nonpolitical goals or be so perceived by the latter's elites. Nor does it necessarily follow that all inputs from a compatible system will be positively construed, even though they promise to preserve or reinforce the existing political structure, if they would have negative consequences for the economic development and political stability of the target system, or if they would be in conflict with other values (as of a cultural or historical nature).

Agents and Channels of Influence Transmission

In assessing the effectiveness of agents and channels of influence transmission—be they international organizations, representatives of foreign governments, cultural and educational institutions, or private individuals—the key questions appear to be the following: What is the frequency and intensity of contact? Does the bearer of potential influence enjoy credibility with his contacts? Also, at what level does the agent interact with the target system? The fact that the interaction occurs at the highest political level (rather than lower in the bureaucratic structure, with nongovernmental elites, or with the society at large) by no means guarantees that it will be more effective. That will depend, as we have already seen, on many other factors. But it will determine how the external influence is absorbed (assuming it is absorbed in some form) into the system—for example, as a direct input into the decision-making process, rather than as a possible instrument (or victim) of bureaucratic tugs-of-war, or even as a source of social malaise.

A particularly important factor on the receiving end is the degree to which the linkage group is either integrated into or alienated from the target system. Karl Deutsch has observed: "A linkage group becomes much more susceptible to the inputs from abroad if its ties to the domestic system are weakened—if it is, for instance, a segregated or a discriminated minority or if it is an economic class or social class which is disadvantaged or alienated."[8] On the other hand, for this very reason the most susceptible groups may be the least effective channels for penetration of the system itself.

Finally, we should ask whether there are multiple channels through which an influence can reach its target. A message transmitted without response through one channel may strike home when transmitted, possibly in somewhat altered form, through another channel and to a different audience.

Conditioning Factors in a Target System

Apart from such variables as historical experience and political culture touched upon earlier, the time element—in the sense both of the stage of development of a political system and of its "generational age"—appears to be one of the most critical determinants of its vulnerability or receptivity to influence penetration from outside. Samuel Huntington has suggested that, while a system is most vulnerable to outside influences during the early stages of its development when it is experiencing political instability and governmental weakness, its barriers to such influences also tend to be high. Later the barriers are lower but, because the system is more mature and integrated, it is less vulnerable to disruption and presumably more capable of tolerating selective influence penetration.[9] Closely related to the question of stages of development is that of leadership generations. As Huntington has written elsewhere, "generational age" is a "measure of adaptability":

> So long as an organization still has its first set of leaders, so long as a procedure is still performed by those who first performed it, its adaptability is still in doubt. The more often the organization has surmounted the problem of peaceful succession and replaced one set of leaders with another, the more highly institutionalized it is . . . . An organization may also change leadership without changing generations of leadership. One generation differs from another in terms of its formative experiences. Simple replacement of one set of leaders by another . . . is not as significant as a shift in leadership generations. . . .The shift from Lenin to Stalin was an intra-generation succession; the shift from Stalin to Khrushchev was an inter-generation succession.[10]

Moreover, by the time this generational shift occurs, a system has presumably undergone a degree of functional differentiation that in itself facilitates influence penetration at multiple levels.

Pushing the Deutsch and Huntington observations one step further, one might ask whether, as a general rule, a system in crisis regardless of its stage of development is more vulnerable to outside influences at the societal and intellectual levels (that is, among the groups most likely to be alienated) but more resistant to the same influences at the higher political echelons—and, conversely, whether in more stable times these positions are at least partially reversed, because the society is better integrated while the leadership is more capable of taking risks.

This, then is the tentative checklist that I will use to explore selected aspects of international-national interactions in Eastern Europe. It is, admittedly, a complex and possibly confusing framework, subject no doubt to a multitude of qualifications and refinements. But I believe it will help illuminate the various factors—some of which are now hotly debated on more impressionistic grounds—that determine the extent to which external forces influence the politics of the region. Before turning to that task, however, we must consider one additional factor that conditions and limits the impact of all other external influences on Eastern Europe: the influence of the Soviet Union.

The Soviet Factor

One factor this essay is specifically not intended to discuss is the impact of the Soviet Union on its client states in Eastern Europe.[11] It is essential for the broader purposes of the discussion, however, to examine briefly Moscow's changing desire and capacity either to isolate those states entirely from all other sources of external influence, or to mediate such influence.

Clearly, the origin of the East European Communist states at the end of World War II profoundly altered the normal pattern of external influences during their early stages of development (thus providing a partial exception to Huntington's observations just cited). Having come into being as a direct result of Soviet military and political intervention, they were "highly penetrated and the national-international linkage [was] the key to explaining internal political development." On the other hand, the fact that they were saturated by inputs from one quarter, and a vastly more powerful one at that, did serve to reinforce their isolation from "other sources of influence, even those emanating from other satellites."[12] Thus "absolute conformity to the Stalinist model ... [could be] quickly imposed in the name of 'one road to socialism,'"[13] with little regard to differences of history, culture, or economic development and rationality.

It hardly seems necessary to detail here the changes in center-satellite relations that have attended de-Stalinization and the gradual replacement of a bipolar international system with a multipolar one. The salient facts are that the Soviet Union, on the one hand, no longer automatically demands total conformity from its erstwhile puppets, but has been willing (or forced) to tolerate both a degree of diversity within Eastern Europe as well as increased contacts between that region and the outside world; yet, on the other, it continues to exercise the dominant influence over the region, not only as a source of inputs but as a monitor of inputs from other external sources. As Vernon Aspaturian recently wrote:

> The decisive character of the Soviet Union's role as boundary policeman [boundary here in both its figurative and literal meanings] is verified by the fact that whenever ... the Soviet leaders are perceived as either unable or unwilling to exercise the monitor function, individual countries of Eastern Europe have attempted to free themselves from the system fetters imposed upon them .... This was the case with Hungary and Poland in 1956 and Czechoslovakia in 1968.[14]

From the standpoint of the task at hand—that of evaluating the susceptibility of the East European states to non-Soviet external influences—the problem here is to establish, at least in rough fashion, first, the degree of diversity that Moscow is willing to tolerate in the region and, second, what factors might cause this level of tolerance to change. Both are formidable tasks in themselves, and I can only summarize here some of the conclusions that others have come to.

Since it is often difficult to know in advance precisely what the Soviets will tolerate (which accounts for some of the peculiarities of East European behavior that make it so difficult to trace external influences on these countries), one way of approaching the problem is to determine on the basis of historical experience what they will not tolerate. This is the approach taken by Zvi Gitelman in his essay on "the diffusion of political innovation" within the Soviet bloc. Here Gitelman has identified some "rules of the game" that determine the acceptability of innovations within member states, as well as innovation transfers among them. Thus, changes that would tamper with the leading role of the party, party control of the mass media, or a state's membership in Comecon or the Warsaw Pact are viewed as out of the question. Likewise, criticism of the Soviet Union and claims on the part of the innovating state "to be elaborating an alternative, competitive 'model' of socialism" are both unacceptable.[15] Yet, as Gitelman himself suggests, these "rules" may not all be as inflexible as they would appear at first blush. While some have been rigorously enforced, the record on others is ambiguous. For instance, despite the formal taboo against elaborating a competititve model of socialism, systemic differentiation in Eastern Europe is a growing reality, and evidence suggests that innovations in one country are carefully watched for their possible utility in others. Similarly, while the prohibition against withdrawing "directly or indirectly" from Comecon or the Warsaw Pact remains valid in theory, Romania has for some time been a member of both organizations "mostly on paper without incurring Soviet sanctions."[16]

What this suggests is that the system boundaries set down by the Soviet Union are subject to continual redefinition and, therefore, that the latitude for interaction with and influence penetration from non-Soviet environments is also subject to pressures for change. We will speak here only of the pressures that may affect Moscow's behavior. One such pressure stems from the conflict of interest inherent in the Soviet Union's dual role as both superpower and regional leader; where in the latter role it strives to perpetuate its dominant position, its promotion on the international level of such principles as peaceful coexistence, equality, and noninterference in internal affairs offers its East European client states opportunities to expand their scope for independent action.[17]

A second set of pressures derives from the fact that the Soviet Union and Eastern Europe currently suffer from the same problem—to wit, the inadequacy of the Soviet model of development beyond the industrialization phase—and, therefore, that the Soviet Union as well as the East European countries is faced with the necessity either of generating modernizing innovations from within or of adapting them from abroad.[18] This, together with the additional fact that continued imposition of the Soviet model on its clients has transformed them into economic liabilities, suggests several reasons why Moscow, despite its obvious preference for cohesion and standardization within the region, may feel compelled to bend the rules of the game as well as to allow greater influence penetration from outside.

First, the Soviet leadership may be presumed to have an interest in limited experimentation in Eastern Europe—even experimentation that threatens to encroach on the political boundaries of the system—to the extent that it promises to make these countries more stable politically and economically. Second, Moscow (or more likely particular groups within the leadership) may view the smaller systems of Eastern Europe as laboratories of sorts in which to experiment (or permit experimentation) with institutional or socioeconomic innovations on a limited scale before considering them for adoption at home.[19] In this way, they can assess the efficacy of a given reform, as well as its potential for spillover into the political and ideological realms, without incurring the destabilizing effects themselves and, equally important, without legitimizing it for use elsewhere in the bloc. Finally, in its search for solutions to its own economic problems, the Soviet Union has turned to the noncommunist industrialized world for massive infusions of capital and technology. Since "that which is politically legitimate in the USSR will be politically available to Eastern Europe,"[20] this has opened the way for greatly expanded interaction between that region and the outside world. Yet this is another instance in which Moscow's economic self-interest may be in conflict with its interest in political stability within and control of the East European countries, in that influences that may not produce destabilizing consequences in one system may do so in others where the conditioning factors are different. This is a complicated and much debated question, and I shall have more to say about it later.

With these considerations in mind, let us turn to the question of the impact on East European politics of the several external environments in which these countries operate. I shall look first at the international communist environment and then, more briefly, at several aspects of Eastern Europe's interaction with the noncommunist world. The treatment will be analytical rather than historical, and in some cases distinctly episodic.

EASTERN EUROPE AND ITS FOREIGN ENVIRONMENTS: THE COMMUNIST WORLD

There are a number of ways one could cut the international communist pie in order to examine the influence of some pieces on others. For the purposes of this essay, I have chosen to examine the Chinese and Yugoslav influences on Eastern Europe, as well as intra-East European interaction. But I do so in full recognition of the fact that I could just as easily have chosen other perspectives— as, for example, international Communist organizations as instruments of influence penetration or the impact of the more important nonruling Communist parties.[21]

The Chinese Factor

There are no natural bonds—whether of the geographical, historical, cultural, or economic variety—between China and the countries of Eastern Europe.

They form part of the same community only by self-definition as Communist states. Even here, Peking's relationship with any particular East European capital is a function of their respective attitudes toward Moscow and the on-going Sino-Soviet split. "In short, the links that tie China to Eastern Europe do not form a line but a triangle."[22]

Still, the Chinese factor in East European politics is a particularly useful one for purposes of evaluation, in part because of this triangular relationship, in part also because the historical evidence on which we can draw now spans a period of 20 years, but even more because it affords examples of so many variables and contrasts. I shall focus primarily on China's impacts on Albania, Romania, and Poland—each of which represents a different pattern of influence penetration—and touch only briefly on the other countries.

The defection of Albania in 1961 is, of course, the most dramatic example of Chinese penetration of Eastern Europe, and the only example to date of full desatellization. What makes it such an interesting case is not so much that China and Albania, as the Mutt and Jeff of the Communist world, are such an unlikely match, but rather: (1) that there were so many ways in which the interests of these two seemingly disparate countries meshed; and (2) that from the perspective of more recent events it helps to demonstrate some of the limits of influence penetration from afar.

With respect to the first, one can safely say that Albania was (and to a somewhat lesser extent remains) the only East European country with which China shared (and shares) a significant number of interests, not so much in the sense of common traits as of traits or interests of a complementary nature. Most prominent in the rhetoric of the alliance has, of course, been their shared perceptions of the world—on such matters as the impossibility of peaceful coexistence or a peaceful transition to communism, and the beneficial consequences of nuclear war for the cause of world socialism—views that have set them apart from the rest of the bloc and were most likely a function of their extreme isolation and weakness.

However, questions of vital national interest vis-a-vis Moscow unquestionably were most important in cementing the relationship. From the Albanian side, the critical points were Tirana's fear of the probable consequences for its independence of a second Soviet-Yugoslav rapprochement, together with the Hoxha regime's understandable distaste for de-Stalinization and for the deemphasis on industrialization, which they rightly feared would leave Albania in the permanent status of poor cousin in the socialist bloc. Although for somewhat different reasons, China could share these objections to the post-1956 direction of Soviet policies. Hence the common emphasis on the principles of national sovereignty, equality, and noninterference in the internal affairs of others.[23]

It is interesting to note that the great differences of distance and size actually favored the alliance in its early years. From Tirana's viewpoint, China fit nicely into the dominant pattern of Albanian strategy over the centuries—that is, reliance on a distant mentor for protection from more predatory neighbors.[24]

Indeed, this was the role that the Soviet Union had played in protecting Albania from Yugoslavia between 1948 and 1955. Also, the distance between Tirana and Moscow made Peking's patronage more credible than if the two had shared a boundary. Similarly, Albania's minute size in relation to China meant that the latter could provide economic subsidies without undue hardship. In sum, then, it would appear that the physical relationships were as important as the political ones and that Chinese support, while not the root cause of Albania's defection, was a necessary condition.

The evidence of Chinese influence on the internal politics of Albania is more ambiguous. Despite their common aversion to de-Stalinization, despite even Albania's emulation of China's Cultural Revolution, the Chinese model of development seems unlikely to have any lasting effect on Albanian political behavior. In fact, the most important domestic consequence of Peking's tutelage seems to have been to save Albania from—or at least to delay the onset of—the cycles of partial reform and retrenchment that have followed de-Stalinization in the rest of Eastern Europe, and to permit its leaders to proceed with their policy of modernization in the harsh, sometimes violent, and clannish style that has long been the hallmark of Albanian politics.

Because of the coincidence and similarities of the two Cultural Revolutions, perhaps a few more words on this point are in order. There can be little doubt that the Albanian version, which lasted from 1966 through 1969, was organized in direct response to the Chinese, or that many of the targets were the same (bureaucratism, revisionism, petty-bourgeois remnants). As with the search for distant protectors, however, the adoption of external forms to please the patron of the historical moment has become something of a national way of life in Albania, and has served both as a means of deflecting the full impact of foreign influences (as under the Ottoman Empire) and as a kind of smokescreen behind which to pursue the country's own ends. Thus beneath the superficial and admittedly real similarities, one can detect important differences of style and content. In its implementation, Tirana's version was more carefully orchestrated and controlled from the top. As one observer has written:

> The Albanian Ideological and Cultural Revolution was not marked by an intense intraparty power struggle, or by the virtual deification of the party leader . . . . It did not result in the enhancement of the political power of the military, nor did it lead to the establishment of distinct revolutionary political institutions or the weakening of existing mass organizations. It did not entail violence, the public humiliation and degradation of leading cadres, or temporary economic disruption. It did not bring a radical restructuring of the educational system. Nor did it involve a repudiation of the Western cultural heritage or a sudden accentuation of Albania's isolation from the outside world.[25]

In addition, some of the prime targets were specific to the Albanian situation, including the three religions of the country and the traditional status of women, both of which the regime viewed as obstacles to modernization.[26] Moreover, domestic developments since 1969 tend to confirm that the Albanian experience will be shaped largely by the regime's efforts at modernization and socialization and, to the extent that foreign influences are important, it will be Albania's traditional European rather than Chinese ties that impinge.[27]

In the international realm as well, recent years have seen a subtle change in the Sino-Albanian alliance. First, the Soviet invasion of Czechoslovakia in 1968, followed by the Sino-Soviet border clashes in 1969, demonstrated to both sides that the relative weight of the physical variables could be drastically altered by shifts in the international climate. For Tirana, the value of China's political and economic support paled in direct proportion to the possibility of a Soviet attack, while the Chinese suddenly came to see the virtue of good relations in quarters of greater strategic import than a Balkan mountain range.[28]

The Peking-Tirana axis is far from dead; China remains Albania's most important trading partner, and a new economic assistance agreement was signed in July 1975. Nonetheless, in the wake of Sino-American detente, Albania has begun a cautious search for alternative sources of support, involving even fitful attempts to mend its fences with Yugoslavia (although, it should be noted, not with the Soviet Union).[29] This raises a major question for the political future of Albania, namely, whether a regime that has staked so much on a single relationship can survive a significant weakening of that relationship without itself coming under challenge from within. The recent shakeups in Tirana's military and economic establishments, accompanied by the unveiling of a "pro-Soviet plot," provide hints that the Hohxa regime may indeed be facing such a challenge.[30]

At least on the surface, there are several similarities between the 1961 Albanian defection from the Soviet camp and Romania's partial withdrawal, which began two years later. The disenchantment of both countries had its origin in part in a desire not to sacrifice their industrialization plans to the interests of the more developed countries in the bloc. Therefore, Romania, like Albania, has insisted on the application to relations among Communist states of the principles of sovereignty, equality, and noninterference. Likewise, Romania has taken advantage of the escalating Sino-Soviet rift to increase its independence from Moscow and, as in Albania, this policy shift was facilitated by the existence of a tightly knit regime under a strong leader capable of resisting pressures from either Moscow or domestic pro-Soviet elements. But here the parallels end, with respect not only to the policies of the two countries but also to the relative impact thereon of Chinese influences. The reasons are many, and all have dictated a less important role for Peking in Bucharest's script.

First, the issue of national sovereignty and (Soviet) noninterference was from the outset their only common ground. On all other questions of doctrine and in their perceptions of the world, the Romanians have been much closer to the Soviet than to the Chinese position. Second, factors of distance, and the relative magnitude of the potential Chinese input, have played a very different role here than in Albania. Not only does Romania share a border with the Soviet Union, it is also dependent on the latter for numerous goods and materials; moreover, its economy is many times larger than Albania's, too large for Peking to subsidize to any meaningful extent. Still a third and very important consideration is the fact that, where Chinese support was a sine qua non of Albania's defection, it was only one of several external factors favoring Romania's deviation. Unlike Albania, Romania was far from isolated; Yugoslavia and, in the Western world, both France and West Germany offered alternative sources of support—sources that were more relevant to Bucharest's substantive goals and needs. The real function of China in this context was to provide additional leverage and legitimation within the Communist world for Romania's independent course.

Thus, Bucharest's position has been both more precarious and more flexible than Tirana's. More precarious because a Gheorghiu-Dej or Ceausescu could scarcely afford a Hoxha's brazen defiance of Moscow. For this reason, as well as for more basic ideological ones, the Romanians have had to remain steadfastly neutral in the Sino-Soviet split. On the other hand, their position has been more flexible in that, since they have not been wholly dependent on Peking's support, they have been better situated to manipulate the Chinese influence for their own purposes and to resist pressures to take sides in the dispute—even to tell Chou En-lai, as they did in 1966, that he could not use Romania as a platform for his attacks on the Soviet Union.[31]

Bucharest's first realization of the limitations of the Chinese connection began with the Cultural Revolution which, from the Romanian point of view, reduced Peking's usefulness as leverage against Moscow. But, as with Albania, the full weight of these limitations became clear only after the Czechoslovak invasion and Moscow's vehement anti-Yugoslav and anti-Romanian campaign of 1971. (To wit, Chou's remark in the midst of that campaign: "Distant waters cannot quench fire.") Likewise, Sino-American detente has meant that Romania, like Albania, is less important to Peking. At the same time, its alternative sources of support in the West have become less credible due to rising trade deficits and Western reluctance to subsidize the Romanian economy further—the latter in large part a function of broader East-West detente, which has noticeably diminished the West's desire to nettle Moscow.[32]

Although it is difficult to isolate and assign a relative weight to the Chinese factor here, it is clear that the essence of these developments has been a substantial loss of flexibility for Romania. Moreover, economic and geographic proximity to the Soviet Union has dictated that Bucharest's response to changing circumstances be rather different from Tirana's. Thus, the last few years have seen a partial normalization of relations with Moscow, including agreement by the Romanians to participate in several joint ventures within the bloc (although, it should be noted, without conceding their basic position on integration). Again, it is unlikely that we have seen the last of the special Sino-Romanian relationship; the Ceausescu regime shows no lessening of resistance to Moscow's attempts to further isolate the Chinese or expel them from the fold. But neither is it likely to be again as close or as useful to either side. At the moment, Bucharest is seeking to regain flexibility, not by reviving the Chinese tie but by cultivating relations with the nonaligned third world countries[33] and with the more independent-minded nonruling Communist parties.[34]

With respect to domestic policy, one could say that Peking's influence has been negligible in the sense that the Chinese model has even less relevance to the Romanian than to the Albanian scene. Undoubtedly it was important internally, as in the triangular Bucharest-Peking-Moscow relationship, that the Chinese input was orchestrated at the very highest level of the Romanian leadership. Whatever attraction Chinese policies might have had at lower levels, the internal disorder and economic disruption that accompanied the Cultural Revolution could hardly have appealed to Ceausescu and his colleagues. Thus here, as in Albania, the domestic impact of Chinese influence has, at least until recently, been as a stabilizing factor reinforcing the regime's ability to pursue its chosen nationalistic course.

But it would be a mistake to conclude that because Peking's domestic impact has been indirect, or has recently been weakened by changing circumstances, the Chinese link was unimportant to Romania's political development. On the contrary, emerging as it did at a critical juncture both in Romanian-Soviet relations and in domestic Romanian politics (the death of Gheorghiu-Dej), China's stabilizing influence was undoubtedly a contributing factor in the success of Ceausescu's strategy of national integration and legitimation. One might speculate here as to why the Romanians have apparently been more aggressive (and successful) than the Albanians in translating temporary external support into more lasting domestic strength. One likely reason is the very precariousness of the formers' position, especially the immediacy of their exposure to Soviet pressures, compared to the relative isolation of the latter. A second possibility is that the emergence of the Sino-Romanian relationship coincided with a generational change in the Romanian leadership; by contrast, Albania seems destined to experience the shift from revolutionary to postrevolutionary leaders at a time when its main source of support is on the wane. For this reason alone, the diminution of the Chinese presence in the Balkans is far less likely to entail destabilizing consequences in Bucharest than in Tirana.

In this connection, I should mention the evidence that Kenneth Jowitt brings to our attention concerning Bucharest's growing interest in North Korea as a country "whose scale, ethos and organization" more closely approximate those of Romania than "the populist, guerrilla, or 'wall-poster' strains found in China." As signs of similarity between the two, Jowitt points to North Korea's emphasis on economic self-reliance and national independence as well as the one-man focus of the regime.[35] Certainly it is tempting to infer here a new "external influence" on Romanian politics. In light of the Chinese experience, however, it is worth asking to what extent Ceausescu is actually seeking a model to emulate, or to what extent he is attracted to North Korea as a model with which he can identify and which will provide both leverage and a degree of legitimacy within the Communist world for policies he is (and has been) intent on pursuing—policies that are a reflection more of domestic values, traditions, and goals than of foreign influences.

The impact of Chinese influence on the course of Polish politics over the past 20 years provides some striking contrasts to the Albanian and Romanian cases. Rather than broaden the scope of Poland's autonomy, Peking's policies have on balance pushed that country closer to Moscow. Likewise, Chinese intrusions at the domestic level, while sporadic and somewhat unpredictable, have most certainly not been conducive to internal cohesion and stability.

On the surface it would be easy simply to point to Poland's geopolitical misfortune, particularly the then unsettled boundary with Germany, as evidence that the Chinese stance was at best irrelevant and at worst inimical to Warsaw's most vital interests. In fact, the reasons for the contrasts appear to have been more subtle and were related in the first phase (1956-58) to shifts in China's position vis-a-vis Warsaw, compounded initially by illusions on the latter's part. Later, changes in Poland's domestic and international situations made the leadership less receptive to, or capable of exploiting, Peking's overtures. Finally, the Chinese input has not in this instance been channeled through a unified leadership but has intersected at lower levels in the political structure.

The irony of the relationship is not that the Poles and Chinese had nothing in common—like the Albanians and Romanians, the Poles were eager at times to increase their autonomy from Moscow—but that, from the Polish point of view, the Sino-Soviet split came too late. In retrospect, we can see that the period in which Gomulka was most capable of loosening ties with Moscow, both in terms of domestic strength and a relatively propitious international environment, coincided with Mao's efforts to "reconstruct a center."[36] It is true, of course, that Peking's early role in persuading Moscow not to intervene and the subsequent endorsement of the October gains, as well as China's own "hundred-flowers" campaign, had encouraged the Poles to believe that China would be a source of support for Poland's right to pursue its own course. As we now know, this hope proved illusory. By the end of 1956 Peking had become alarmed at disintegrative tendencies in the bloc, and a year later, at the November 1957 Conference of Communist Parties in Moscow, it was Chinese pressure more than anything else that forced a reluctant Gomulka to acknowledge Soviet leadership.

Chinese influence also contributed, although in a less direct way, to the retreat from October on the domestic level. Gomulka was not the only one who understood that the vehemence with which Peking joined in the "antirevisionist" campaign against Yugoslavia in the spring of 1958 was also a sign of Chinese displeasure with Poland's unorthodox course. Taking their cues from China's "Great Leap Forward," some of his opponents began intimating that Poland needed its own economic and ideological "great leap."[3][7] It is a safe assumption that the use of Chinese imagery here did not signify (as it did in Bulgaria, for instance) a genuine interest on the part of Polish Stalinists in the Chinese model, but was instead an indication of their distaste for Khrushchev's reformism as well as Gomulka's. Nonetheless, its introduction into intraparty dialogue most likely enhanced the impact of China's antirevisionist stance and, to this extent, contributed to the growing conservatism of the Gomulka regime.

To the extent that Peking contributed to retrenchment in Poland at the end of the 1950s, it also contributed to one of the factors that later made it impossible for Warsaw to exploit the opportunities offered by the Sino-Soviet split, and which once again allowed pro-Peking sentiments to become a disruptive factor in intraparty politics. By the early and especially mid-1960s the Polish regime was, if not a regime in crisis, at least a regime in disarray and creeping paralysis. Gradual retrenchment had whittled away at the broad basis of support that Gomulka had enjoyed among liberals and moderates both in and outside the party on his return to power. Yet his "neither fish nor fowl" policies had also failed to mollify his opponents at the other end of the political spectrum. Thus, while the Albanian and Romanian regimes were challenging Moscow against a backdrop of internal cohesion, the Polish leader was facing a two-pronged challenge at home.

One of these was the challenge mounted by Kazimierz Mijal, the Stalinist-turned-anti-Soviet who, after a two-year clandestine campaign against the Gomulka regime, fled in February 1966 to Albania, where he announced the formation of a "true" Communist Party of Poland and began broadcasting vitriolic tirades back to Poland over Radio Tirana.[3][8] One is tempted to dismiss the Mijal affair as little more than comic relief in an otherwise dreary scene. After all, whatever appeal his anti-Soviet message could be expected to have among the Poles (according to rumor, either Mijal or the Chinese embassy distributed maps showing Poland enlarged at Soviet expense) would have been cancelled out by the prospect of a return to Stalinism. Still, to the extent that his pro-Peking antics demonstrated the inability of the Polish party to maintain order in its own house, and to the extent that he contributed to the progressive leftward drift of Gomulka's policies (for example, the failure to implement the 1964-65 economic reform, the mid-1960s crackdown on dissident intellectuals, and the stepped-up campaign against the Catholic Church), Mijal merits some credit for helping to undercut the stability and legitimacy of the Gomulka regime.

A second and even more important factor conditioning Warsaw's response to the widening gap between Moscow and Peking was the deterioration of Poland's international position, which reached alarming proportions with

Khrushchev's overtures to Bonn in 1964 and the prospect that the West Germans might acquire nuclear arms through a multilateral nuclear force. At this point, the critical element in the Polish-Soviet relationship was less the often cited fact that Poland was wholly dependent on the Soviet Union for the security of the Oder-Neisse boundary, although this was true enough, than it was the equally valid fear that Moscow was in a position to compromise that boundary. This fear receded with Khrushchev's removal, but it was shortly replaced by a second in the form of West Germany's Ostpolitik, which the Poles rightly or wrongly viewed as an attempt to isolate them in their own camp. These were dilemmas of which the Chinese were well aware—and which, in fact, they obliquely tried to exploit on at least one occasion. But from the Polish vantage point, they were dilemmas in which Peking's influence could count for little.[39]

One consequence of these domestic and external weaknesses was that Warsaw became highly vulnerable to Soviet pressures to conform and, therefore, that it was far easier for Moscow to limit the manner in which the Poles tried to profit from the split with Peking than was the case with either the Romanians or the Albanians. For instance, the Poles could, and for long periods did, remain silent on the issue; they could on occasion quietly oppose attempts to isolate or expel the Chinese from the international communist family; or they could use explicit support for the Soviet position on China to move Moscow closer to Warsaw on some matter of more immediate import to them.[40] What they could not do was exploit the conflict to increase the distance between Warsaw and Moscow. In other words, Poland's primary interest in the 1960s came increasingly to be not autonomy but regional unity—or, to borrow from William Zimmerman's discussion of "hierarchical regional systems," increasing the "salience" or "rigidity" of regional boundaries.[41]

Although the particulars vary from country to country, the other East European states all adhere more closely to the Polish than to the Romanian (not to mention Albanian) pattern, in that they have been unable to any significant degree to broaden their sphere of independent action by manipulating the Sino-Soviet conflict. Again, the ideological predilections of a given leadership appear not to have been the prime determinant of its fidelity in toeing the Soviet line on China. (Bulgaria, for instance, was the only country apart from Albania for which the Chinese model could have had genuine relevance and the only one actually to experiment with the "great leap" at the end of the 1950s; yet, since then, Bulgaria has been among the most loyal to Moscow.[42]) Rather, as in the three cases just examined, the critical factors seem to have been those such as a regime's internal cohesion, its legitimacy in the eyes of the population, as well as the extent of its international exposure, all of which have in turn conditioned its vulnerability to counterpressures from Moscow.[43]

Thus, for the most part the Chinese factor has remained an independent variable in East European politics: an elusive influence that they might occasionally use to express displeasure at some aspect of Soviet policy,[44] and from which they might benefit indirectly to the extent that the Romanians were successful in preventing Moscow from tightening its grip on the region as a whole, but an influence that nonetheless remained beyond their power to control and might from time to time intrude in their domestic politics in unpredictable ways.[45] Only for the two recalcitrant Balkan regimes has it been a semi-dependent variable—that is, one they could manipulate within limits for their own ends. Yet they, too, have been unable to control the decline of that influence, the consequences of which we are only beginning to discern.

What would have happened had it not been for the Cultural Revolution is hard to say. As other of the East European regimes gained greater legitimacy at home, it is possible that they would have attempted to follow Romania's example as one way of reducing the rigidity of the system's boundaries. At just that point, however, China ceased for the most part to be credible as an alternative source of support—not merely because of the harsh rhetoric and violence of the Cultural Revolution, but more likely because the isolation and weakness it engendered made China an unreliable alternative. Since then, its potential usefulness to the region as a whole has been diminished by the same factors that have led to declining Chinese influence in Romanian and, to a lesser extent, Albanian policy—that is, by the invasion of Czechoslovakia, which demonstrated all too clearly the limits that distance placed on Peking's support, and by the escalation of the Sino-Soviet conflict to the stage of armed border confrontation, which probably made it too risky a lever for most of these regimes to attempt to exploit. For its part, China's increasing international acceptance has decreased the need for East European proteges, while the latters' all too apparent ineffectiveness as counterweights to Soviet power has made them distinctly less useful to the Chinese. Hence Peking's growing interest, at least for the moment, in strengthening ties with Western Europe, especially with West Germany, and in expounding the virtues of a strong NATO. One piquant detail of this new venture is that the Chinese are once again displaying their bent for redrawing the map of Europe, this time by supporting the idea of German reunification—a cause hardly destined to enhance their stock among the East Europeans.[46]

The Yugoslav Factor and Intra-East European Influences

In lumping Yugoslav influences on Eastern Europe together with the influences exercised by the East European countries upon each other, I recognize that there are essential differences between the two categories. First, Yugoslavia, like China, is a source of inputs from outside the Soviet-dominated bloc. Second, not having undergone full Stalinization and not having been subject to the same restraints on political development as its neighbors within the bloc, Yugoslavia represents an older and more fully developed alternative to the Soviet model. On the other hand, like their later East European counterparts, the original Yugoslav reforms were a reaction to the inadequacies of that model; nor have they been the most radical reaction in all respects. Moreover, by virtue of geography, history, language, culture, and level of economic development, Yugoslavia has as much in common with some of its neighbors within the bloc as they have with each other. Thus, the dynamics of influence penetration have been more or less analogous, as are the problems of evaluation.

The mere fact that organizational, institutional, or theoretical innovations in one East European country have tended to surface in others is, I would suggest, neither surprising nor in itself particularly interesting. To a certain extent, similarities in reform efforts are inevitable if only because all members of the region are proximate to each other in various respects, and because all have in one way or another come face to face with the same problem—the limitations of the Soviet model for their further development. Therefore, it is almost axiomatic that, with the post-Stalin renewal of direct contacts among them, innovations devised in one country would have at least a superficial relevance for and potential appeal in another.

What seems more significant than the abundant evidence of interest (largely of the journalistic variety) in what goes on elsewhere in the bloc is the fact that, despite the similarities in the problems they face, there is relatively little direct evidence of intraregional influence penetration—and that, where evidence does exist, the impact of such influences on the various countries has been so uneven. This is due in part to the fact, mentioned earlier, that we simply do not possess sufficient information on decision-making processes. As Roger Kanet noted in a recent article on "modernizing interaction" in Eastern Europe: "The best that can be hoped for at present is to indicate that (1) innovation occurred in one country, (2) decision makers in a second country were aware of that innovation, and (3) innovations occurred in the second country that were similar to the original ones."[47]

It is also due in part to one aspect of Moscow's role in the influence transmission process that tends to cause the East European regimes to play down the importance of inputs from elsewhere in the bloc (a point to which I shall return momentarily). Still a third reason, and one that seems to be overlooked in the general enthusiasm to find evidence of comparability and emulation among these countries, is the fact that beyond the initial catalytic stage, where events elsewhere in the region often do play an important role, there seem to be definite limits to the applicability in countries "y" or "z" of innovations taking place in country "x." Thus, rather than simply trace the impact of, say, Yugoslav workers' councils or the post-1956 Polish economic model (to mention only two of the best-known examples), I shall try to sort out the ways in which the several factors in my original checklist either facilitate or impede influence flows within Eastern Europe. (Although, clearly, I can hardly do more than scratch the surface of such a complex topic in the space of a few short pages.)

Perhaps the best place to start is with the factor responsible not only for the ultimate decision as to which influences are admissible, but also for some rituals of intrabloc interaction that tend to complicate the task of evaluation. I am speaking again, of course, of the Soviet factor, which in this case plays a somewhat ambivalent role. The most obvious aspect of Moscow's role is that of bloc monitor, in which capacity it has generally determined the timing as well as the substance of permissible intraregional influences. That is, Titoism burst on the East European scene in June 1955 rather than in 1950 or 1951, not because the East Europeans were previously ignorant of what was taking place in Yugoslavia, but because it was Khrushchev's reconciliation with Tito and his acknowledgment of "many roads to socialism" that legitimized (seemingly, at least) the Yugoslav road for consumption elsewhere. Similarly, the initial impact of Polish economic ideas was effectively cut off by the "antirevisionist" campaign of 1958, and only later revived following publication of Liberman's views in the Soviet Union.[48]

However, this legitimizing function, while serving as a reasonably effective (if sometimes crude) form of control, produces some side effects that are probably inadvertent and undesirable from the Soviet point of view, and also tend to distort patterns of influence penetration within the bloc. On the one hand, the very fact that Moscow has put its imprimatur on an idea originating in one country—even if by miscalculation, as with Yugoslavia in 1955-56, or by inattention, as with Czechoslovakia before 1968—tends to magnify the impact of that idea on the others. Because they generally will have at least marginal relevance, and because inputs from outside the bloc are inadmissable, innovative ideas from within the region tend to have a catalytic effect on would-be reformers who are looking for guidelines and for "safe" bargaining positions from which to push for change at home.[49] On the other hand, to the extent that Moscow's response is uncertain or negative, the effect will be to understate influence; and where emulation does occur, it will be disguised or covert.

It would be easy, however, to exaggerate the Soviets' role in either initiating or restricting influence flows among their East European clients. On more than one occasion, individual regimes have taken the initiative either in resisting influences they viewed as undesirable (for example, East Germany and Czechoslovakia in 1956) or in soliciting Moscow's aid in so doing (Poland and East Germany with respect to the 1968 Czech reforms). Moreover, unlike the early post-Stalin era, when it was in fact Soviet policy that provided the impetus for change (for example, the "New Course" and de-Stalinization), the weight of evidence since then suggests that the timing and substance of more recent reform efforts have been determined by the internal dynamics of a given system. (As one Czech economist aptly put it, the main stimulus for change in Czechoslovakia was "failure."[50]) Finally, the Soviet role is of little use in explaining the unevenness of influence flows within the region. For clarifications of these disparities, we must look to a variety of other factors concerning both relations among the countries in question and aspects of their respective domestic situations.

Looking first at the way in which a particular East European country is perceived as a potential source of inputs by its neighbors, we may speculate that its credibility and appeal will be determined by a combination of its relative status within the bloc, its success as an innovator, as well as past relations with the prospective target of influence. Thus, in very general terms it was Poland that initially exerted the greatest influence, both as the strongest member of the European Communist alliance apart from the Soviet Union, and because the changes occurring there in 1956-57 were revolutionary by comparison with the rest of the bloc.[51] After 1957 Poland's influence dwindled because of its failure to implement the proposed economic reforms; but the relative freedom of expression allowed in that country remained an attraction to other populations and caused the Poles to be regarded by other regimes as a source of contamination. By contrast, the repercussions of the Hungarian revolution, while potentially more destabilizing for the bloc as a whole, were short-lived—although the Hungarian experience remained a potent object lesson to others in how not to conduct a reform. In fact, the aura of illegitimacy probably continued to exert a negative influence long after the Kadar regime had become one of the most innovative in Eastern Europe.

Czechoslovakia provides perhaps the most dramatic example. Not only had it enjoyed considerable prestige as the most developed and democratic of the East European states prior to the communist takeover; for years thereafter, the country had remained (at least in relative terms) something of an economic showcase and, in 1960, had been the first to be allowed to call itself a "socialist republic." All of these facts contributed to the explosive and irresistable impact that the reforms of the Prague Spring would unquestionably have had throughout the region had they been allowed to continue, although since the invasion Czechoslovakia's influence, like Hungary's after 1956, has been virtually nil.

At the other end of the spectrum, Albania, as non-Slavic and largely non-Christian as well as the least developed state in the region, has always been the "odd man out." Bulgaria, too, has traditionally carried little weight; whether Moscow's concerted efforts to transform it into a model of the "developed socialist society" succeed in altering this perception remains to be seen.[52] Romania probably stands somewhere in-between. By virtue of its relative backwardness and its own sense of ethnic and cultural separateness, Romania, too, has traditionally carried little weight. On the other hand, the fact that its semi-independent course since 1963 has not been emulated by others is, as we saw earlier, due at least in part to other constraints; and there is some evidence, admittedly circumstantial, that other area leaders discreetly admire Ceausescu's domestic success.[53]

Finally, Yugoslavia as a source of influence represents a special case in that, as the only ready-made alternative to Stalinism, its initial impact on the other East European countries was bound to be enormous—both as an attraction to their populations and as a threat to the stability of their regimes.[54] Since the late 1950s, however, both the appeal and the threat have been tempered: First, by some fine tuning in Moscow of Yugoslavia's relationship to the bloc, which has by and large kept the most radical aspects of Titoism outside the bounds of tolerance; second, because in the end the practice of Titoism has turned out to be neither as radical nor as attractive as the theory. In particular, the recentralization of Yugoslav political life has reduced the distance from neighbors within the bloc, while persistent economic woes and nationalist hostilities stand as reminders of the possible risks of following a Titoist course.

Obviously these generalizations do not hold true in all cases and may be altered by such additional factors as past patterns of friendship or hostility between particular countries. Thus it is a matter of historical record that sympathy for Poland was an important element in triggering the Hungarian revolt in 1956. Conversely, it seems likely that the lack of mutual sympathy between the Czechs, on the one hand, and the Poles and Hungarians, on the other, played some role in the Prague's indifferent response to the 1956 events. Elsewhere, the unsettled Macedonian question has probably provided an effective (and, from Sofia's viewpoint, useful) barrier to Yugoslav influence in Bulgaria. Similarly, traditional hostility toward the Germans among several of the East European peoples, combined with a lingering reputation for domestic weakness, has likely prevented the GDR from exercising the influence that its economic success might otherwise afford.

Turning next to the relationship between the effectiveness of influence transmission and the nature of the influence being transmitted, and particularly the degree of change that it would induce, several observations are useful, mostly in demonstrating the limits of intraregional interaction. First, while it is scarcely surprising, it should nonetheless be noted that, even among Communist states, inputs that directly affect the political system are far less likely to be absorbed (or will be absorbed much more slowly) than those affecting it only indirectly. The former category includes not only explicit changes in political institutions or practices but, equally important, any changes in the economic structure that would significantly alter the distribution of decision-making power, since in a Communist system this is as much a political as an economic function. Thus economic reforms of the radical decentralizing variety have proven almost as resistant to diffusion as changes affecting the leading role of the party—and precisely because reforms of this type do potentially undercut the party's role. On the other hand, reforms that tinker with the economic mechanism in order to make it less cumbersome and more efficient, but without shifting the locus of major economic decision making, are more easily digested and have been tried out in in one or another form in all of the countries in question.[55] The reaction can be swifter still when the inputs involve merely policy shifts rather than structural changes, even of a modest nature; witness, for example, the immediate reaction to the 1970 Polish worker riots that precipitated Gomulka's demise—several other East bloc regimes were spurred to take measures aimed at improving the living standard of their populations.[56]

Second, while it is generally true that, the more comprehensive the reform movement, the more likely one is to find evidence of political inputs from neighboring Communist states, there seems to be no particular correlation between these inputs and the end product. Rather, they seem to be more an indicator of the greater breadth of political and intellectual inquiry in these countries than of the ultimate scope and direction of the indigenous reform. It is true, of course, that workers' councils on the Yugoslav model sprang up spontaneously in both Poland and Hungary in 1956, but in neither case were they central to the changes taking place. Moreover, while Yugoslavia's nonalignment policy was undoubtedly an important element in Nagy's decision to leave the Warsaw Pact, the domestic political reforms proposed by the Hungarians—particularly the reintroduction of a Western-style multiparty system—went far beyond anything ever contemplated by Tito. Later, during the 1965-68 period, there is no question that the Czech reformers were thoroughly familiar with the Yugoslav model; they went so far as to send delegations to study the self-management system, and they were the only ones in Eastern Europe to show active interest in Yugoslavia's innovative multichamber legislature. Still, in the final analysis, the planned Czechoslovak enterprise councils resembled less the Yugoslav variety than a combination of the Czech factory councils from the 1945-48 period and Western-style boards of directors. And while it seems likely that a Yugoslav-style legislature would have been proposed at Extraordinary Fourteenth Party Congress scheduled for September 1968, it is clear that this was only one aspect of a more comprehensive program that would have ended the Communist Party's monopoly within the National Front and reinstituted traditional parliamentary controls on the exercise of power—both features that were missing from the Yugoslav system.[57]

Third, when one moves away from inputs of the broad systemic variety, even though there is evidence of freer exchange,[58] there are still issues that remain so locked in the canons of Marxism-Leninism that open, objective discussion is impossible. One striking example is the question of alcoholism, which is a serious, even growing, social problem everywhere in the region, but is still officially regarded as a "vestige of the past." Thus, even though there exists in each country a group of specialists who do not share the official view, the channels of communication are so blocked by the ideological hang-up over the question of alienation under socialism as to preclude cooperation among them, not to mention influencing one another's policies. This is, in fact, one instance in which specialists in the individual East European countries seem more interested in communicating with their Western counterparts than with each other.[59]

Turning finally to conditioning factors in the domestic environment, I shall look briefly at five variables that seem to have played an important role over the last two decades in determining receptivity to intraregional influences: leadership characteristics, stage of political development, level of socioeconomic development, agents and channels of influence transmission, and domestic political culture and experiences. (By and large, these observations also apply to inputs from nonbloc sources as well.)

With respect to leadership characteristics, there are obviously many intangible and unpredictable variables—education, life experiences, personal qualities—that make a leader rigid or flexible, narrow- or broad-minded. One factor that may be more predictable than others, however, and should be taken into consideration is what Huntington calls "generational age."[60] The differences between a Gomulka and a Gierek, an Ulbricht and a Honecker, a Novotny and a Dubcek, or a Rakosi and a Kadar are probably not entirely accidental. Likewise, it is probably not accidental that the two countries most resistant to change either from within or under the impact of external influences—Albania and Bulgaria—have been those whose leaderships are still dominated by the revolutionary generation. A change in generations among middle-level elites will also hasten the process of influence absorption, especially when it coincides (as it did in Czechoslovakia) with a new and sudden exposure to foreign environments.[61]

Closely related to generational age is the stage of political development of a given regime. In line with Huntington's observations noted earlier, it is probably a valid assumption that all the East European regimes have made sufficient strides toward establishing their legitimacy and stability that they would not be as vulnerable today to the kind of convulsive upheavals they feared in 1956 under the combined impact of de-Stalinization and Titoism, or even in 1968 from the Prague Spring. Indeed, the two regimes least perturbed by the Czech reforms at the time, the Hungarian and Romanian, were the two that already enjoyed substantial domestic viability.[62] By the same token, if Huntington is correct, they should now be more capable of withstanding selected external inputs without destabilizing consequences (a matter to which I shall return in the following section on influences from outside the bloc).

The third variable, the relative level of socioeconomic development, so far appears to be only marginally useful as an indicator of receptivity to outside influences. For instance, if this were a reliable indicator, one would expect to find the highly developed countries as those most receptive to radical economic reform, in that they would be the first to feel the dysfunctional effects of the command-type economy and extensive growth; conversely, the less developed could be expected to be least receptive. While this pattern holds true for the latter—in Albania, Bulgaria, and Romania—it cannot explain why it was Poland that led the way in the 1950s (or Yugoslavia, if we include it in the region for this purpose), or why Czechoslovakia and East Germany were initially so resistant. On the other hand, with much of Eastern Europe moving into a new stage of economic technological growth, this variable will remain an important one to watch.

In assessing the role of agents and channels of influence transmission, the critical issue at the receiving end is that of access to decision-making processes. Access itself is an elusive factor in that it depends not only on the level at which an outside influence is introduced, or whether the bearer or receiver of the influence is regarded as reliable or unreliable, but also on a variety of situational factors: the openness of a leadership to change at a given moment, whether it is in command of a situation or in a state of disarray, the presence or absence of cooperation among key groups in the society, and so on. Judging by events in Hungary and Poland in 1956, external inputs can gain easy, if temporary, access even through "unreliable" groups (students, workers, dissident intellectuals) if a regime's control mechanisms and authority have broken down; whereas the same influences were quickly isolated by the more coherent East German, Czechoslovak, and Bulgarian regimes. Clearly, access in itself is not a sufficient condition for effective influence penetration, but it is a necessary condition. Moreover, the higher the political level at which an input is allowed to be introduced, the smoother the process of absorption or adaptation when it does take place. For example, both the careful consideration given to Yugoslav institutions by the Czech reformers, and the frequent contacts between Czech and Hungarian planners during the preparation of their respective economic reforms,[63] were possible only because a decision to undertake these reforms had been made at the highest level in each country.

While all the above variables play some role in conditioning the impact of external influences, probably the single most important determinant—and the one that more than any other sets the limits to intraregional interaction—is the disparity among the East European peoples with respect to their political cultures and experiences. As one looks back at the various reform efforts that have taken place, one is struck less by their similarities than by their differences and, even more, by the continuities in the behavior of a given country. Nor should this be surprising. To the extent that reforms have been prompted by the need to correct economic distortions left over from the Stalinist era, from which all of the countries have suffered, some similarities were to be expected. To the extent, however, that a regime desired or was forced to try to instill a sense of its political legitimacy, it has had to respond (although only within the limits tolerated by Moscow) to the particular traditions of the nation, with the result that innovations or policy changes in one country may not be transferable simply because they aren't as relevant in another. Thus, Poland's policies toward the Church or in agriculture have never elicited the same response as its economic ideas; similarly, Ceausescu's blend of communism and nationalism has probably attracted little overt interest elsewhere in part because it is so specifically Romanian. By the same token, a regime that can tap a strong domestic tradition has less need to look to others for inputs; thus the Czechoslovak reform movement, although it examined the experiences of others, was primarily an indigenous affair.[64]

On the other hand—the apparent contradiction notwithstanding—the fact that at the macropolitical level none of these countries has been able to move beyond a Leninist-type system means that, just as the Soviet Union no longer provides an adequate model for East European development, they are unable to provide one for each other.[65] We may merely be witnessing the low point in a cycle; but it seems clear that the crushing of the Prague Spring and, more recently, the gradual constriction of the New Economic Mechanism (NEM) in Hungary have brought an end to the heady days when reform-minded East Europeans could look hopefully to other systems in the region for solutions to their fundamental problems of development. This applies as well to Yugoslavia as a source of inputs, particularly in light of the recent recentralization of political life in that country.

This is not to suggest that the East Europeans have nothing to gain from observing and occasionally emulating each other. Because they all operate under the same major constraint, changes in one system are still relevant in others as a rough guide to what is permissible[66] and as leverage for aspiring reformers.[67] Likewise, as the reaction to the 1970 Polish riots showed, they can look to each other for strategies in maintaining or restoring stability. But, at least in the present context, the fact that they continue to influence each other at all is primarily a function of "the politics of system boundaries."

EASTERN EUOPE AND ITS FOREIGN ENVIRONMENTS: THE NONCOMMUNIST WORLD

In light of the fact that Western influences on Eastern Europe are the focus of a separate chapter, this chapter will not deal with such influences as specifically "Western." However, it is impossible to ignore the West completely in that it figures centrally in other variously defined noncommunist environments in which the East European countries operate. Although often less direct, the impact of these environments may be as profound as that of influences from within the Communist world, and is of particular interest from the standpoint of emerging trends. I shall therefore look briefly at three aspects of these environments: (1) the impact on Eastern Europe of changes in the general international climate, particularly in East-West relations; (2) the potential consequences of increased East European participation in specialized international organizations, as well as more informal regional relationships that cross bloc boundaries; and (3) the implications of the tendency on the part of at least some of the East European regimes to establish "identity references" with groups of states beyond the Communist world.[68]

With respect to changes in the international climate, I shall focus primarily on the impact of reduced East-West tensions. Here, rather than a simple one-dimensional relationship, it would appear that detente in its various manifestations over the last 20 years has had at least three discernible (and sometimes contradictory) effects on Eastern Europe. The most obvious one, and the one on which those who today take an optimistic view of detente pin their hopes, involves the increased opportunities that international relaxation brings for lessening the economic and military dependence of the region on the Soviet Union. Thus, the halting steps toward detente in the mid-1950s, in the form of the "Spirit of Geneva," contributed to the development of Nagy's neutralist views by tempering the perception of a world sharply divided into two hostile camps. Elsewhere the repercussions were less dramatic but nonetheless marked: the Rapacki Plan in Poland, and a more general trend toward an expansion of economic and cultural relations and personal contacts. Later, Romania took advantage of the first signs of West German Ostpolitik and French initiatives to increase its economic independence.

On the other hand, as the Hungarian case shows only too well, to the extent that the Western powers are interested in cultivating relations directly with the Soviet Union, they will be less likely to support efforts on the part of the East Europeans to assert their independence. Thus, the 1956 Hungarian experiment in neutralism lasted a matter of hours; likewise, in 1968 the West chose not to risk Moscow's ire by openly encouraging the Dubcek regime. And, as we saw earlier, the flexibility that the Romanians derive from Western trade and credits has decreased in direct proportion to the rise in Western interest in promoting economic relations directly with the Soviet Union. While it is hardly my intention to make light of the difficulties inherent in fostering Eastern Europe's autonomy (expressed most recently in the so-called Sonnenfeldt doctrine[69]), the fact remains that an overriding concern for improved relations with Moscow strengthens the latter's hand in its dealings with the region.

Third, whether reduced international tensions will tend to reinforce or undermine a particular East European regime depends very mucy on the domestic circumstances in that country. To the extent that a regime has come to rely on international pressures of one sort or another as a substitute for establishing its legitimacy at home, the removal of those pressures will weaken that regime by leaving it more vulnerable to pressures from below. Poland provides an excellent case in point. The reasons why popular demands in Poland proved more containable than in Hungary in October 1956 were, first, precisely because the external pressures (specifically Western nonrecognition of Poland's western boundary) were not removed to the same extent and, second, because in the preceding months the Polish regime had moved more deliberately to respond to those demands.

By 1970, however, the situation was entirely different. The Gomulka regime had long since lost its popular base and had, for some years, freely exploited the threat of a "revanchist" Germany as one of its main pillars of domestic stability. In December of that year, when Gomulka apparently hoped that the negative popular reaction to drastic price reform would be offset by the positive effect of the signing of the Polish-West German treaty, the response proved just the opposite. Having been told for years that their deprivations were due to the need to maintain defenses against German revisionism, the Polish workers were justifiably enraged at being told they would have to pay more for their bread and meat only days after Bonn's final recognition of the Oder-Neisse boundary. Thus, what should have been the crowning achievement of Gomulka's career contributed instead to his demise.[70]

At this point we should ask what lessons we can learn from these earlier experiences that might help us evaluate the possible effects of the current phase of detente on political change in Eastern Europe. Unfortunately, we are faced here with several difficulties: First, earlier periods of relaxation have been quite short, a fact that makes it risky to try to forecast long-term consequences; and, second, history never repeats itself exactly, and different combinations of circumstances may significantly alter the outcomes. With these disclaimers in mind, the following observations seem to be in order.

With respect to the argument over the relationship between increased trade and technology transfer on the one hand and domestic reform on the other, it can be cogently argued that, in the short run at least, there is no relationship or even that it is inverse—that is, that the import of capital and technology may be a substitute for internal reform or may even go hand in hand with stepped-up domestic repression.[71] Certainly East Germany, Romania, and the Soviet Union provide exhibits one, two, and three of countries that, despite considerable exposure to outside economic influences, have retained relatively centralized economies and have undergone little if any political liberalization. In Poland, too, the rise in economic cooperation with the West over the last few years has had a stabilizing effect by supplying both consumer goods and the technology essential for continued rapid growth. On the other hand, the long-term impact may be quite different and may vary substantially from country to country. One might speculate a la Deutsch, for instance, that a given level of economic and technological exposure, which has no political spillover effects in a country as large and as relatively isolated as the Soviet Union, may by virtue of size, geography, as well as a variety of cultural and historical factors, have just such effects in some of the more vulnerable East European countries.[72] Even in the absence of overtly political repercussions, the flexibility necessary for competing successfully in world markets over the long term can be expected to increase pressures for economic reform.[73]

Moreover, two special circumstances in the current regional and global economic environments may well combine to produce their own disruptive effects in the very near term. First, while it is true that the relative share of nonbloc countries in East European trade is not much higher today than it was ten or twelve years ago (Poland being the lone exception[74]), that trade is now concentrated in two areas that form the basis of the popular legitimacy recently achieved by several of these regimes: Western technology and consumer goods. Thus, while economic cooperation may not in itself foster economic or political liberalization, the termination or reduction of such cooperation could well have destabilizing consequences—the seriousness of which would depend on the degree of interdependence—because it must result either in unsatisfied consumer expectations or in the failure of ambitious modernization plans on which these regimes have staked their futures. (This is, incidentally, a good example of an external influence that, although initially admitted by conscious decision of a regime, becomes a semi-independent variable to the extent that that regime is dependent on the continuation of the inputs for the success of its policies.[75])

The second special circumstance is, of course, the energy-raw material price spiral of the last few years, which has put the relatively resource-poor East European countries in an especially painful balance of payments squeeze. Not only were they ill-prepared to cope with the ensuing inflation in capitalist markets, but they have found that trade within the bloc is no longer insulated from global economic trends—and that they even may have to compete with hard currency countries for their traditional markets and sources of supply within Comecon, particularly in the Soviet Union. It is by no means clear whether the ultimate consequence of these developments will be to draw these countries into a relationship of greater interdependence with the outside world or to force them back into their former isolation and one-sided dependence. On the one hand, Moscow's increasing reluctance to subsidize its East European clients, and especially to satisfy their future energy needs, will tend to propel them toward more intensive participation in world markets, with all the economic and political consequences that such openness may bring. On the other hand, the sharply higher prices that they must now pay for Soviet-supplied raw materials (especially oil), together with the enormous investments that they are being required to make in the development of additional Soviet resources, would seem to portend a massive reorientation of trade and investment capital away from domestic development and other external markets.[76] Perhaps the only certainty at the moment is that the necessary near-term adjustments will place serious strains on the economic, and therefore also the political stability of the region.[77]

In a more positive vein, one of the more significant changes in the international relations of Eastern Europe has been the expansion in the participation by these countries in a variety of international and regional organizations. In addition to the network of specialized agencies under the umbrella of the United Nations (to which all of them now belong since East Germany's admission in 1974), three (Hungary, Poland, and Romania) have recently become full members of the General Agreement on Tariffs and Trade (GATT); and one (Romania) is a member of the International Monetary Fund (IMF), with others likely to follow suit. Several also belong to the Danube Commission, a particularly interesting case of a one-time Soviet-bloc organization becoming a vehicle for reducing Eastern Europe's isolation through the inclusion of nonbloc states (Yugoslavia, Austria, and West Germany).[78] Equally significant has been the recent tendency on the part of several of the countries to gravitate toward more loosely defined regional associations that, at least by implication, would exclude the larger powers: for example, Romania and Bulgaria toward the Balkans;[79] Hungary toward the smaller Danubian states, and especially Austria;[80] Poland and East Germany toward the Baltic area, and in the Polish case especially toward Sweden.[81]

As Korbonski has observed, it is a safe assumption "that most if not all of these organizations [do] not see themselves as active agents of influence diffusion" that could seriously affect the political systems of member countries. "Indeed, most of them would strenuously deny harboring such intentions," and it is largely for this reason that the East European countries have been able to participate.[82] Nonetheless, to the extent that this proliferation of overlapping memberships signifies a desire for serious cooperation with nonbloc states—very likely involving policy coordination in various fields such as health, pollution abatement, energy, transportation, and flood control—it will mean long-term exposure to policy making and administrative practices in other systems. And, while it would be unwarranted to look for major changes in the political practices of the East European regimes as a result, we certainly can expect this type of interaction to reinforce any existing tendencies toward a progressive depoliticization of issues and greater specialist input into decision-making processes.

Looking finally at the tendency toward establishing "identity references" across system boundaries, this would seem to be a particularly fascinating phenomenon in that, unlike the proliferation of organizational memberships which may be undertaken for strictly utilitarian reasons, this would appear to involve a deliberate attempt on the part of some East European countries (or specific groups within them) to lower the barriers to influences that might otherwise be deemed unacceptable. I have already mentioned Romania's self-proclaimed identification with third world nations (although they would appear to have little in common). It has yet to be seen what influence, if any, this will have on the future political development of Romania; at the very least it provides a rationalization for remaining longer in the mobilization phase, as well as for seeking preferential trade and credit terms.[83]

Rather more promising from the standpoint of potential substantive inputs into East European politics is the growing awareness, on the part of the more advanced members of the region, of their community of interests and problems with modern industrialized states, irrespective of social or political systems. The implications of this common identity are intriguing, if not immediately dramatic, in that it tends to legitimize the admission of selected influences from what would otherwise be regarded as alien sources. Two recent examples from the Polish experience may illustrate the point—one dealing with an issue of social policy, the other with political processes. The first instance concerns a parliamentary review begun in 1974 of Poland's family code, in the process of which various committees of the Sejm examined the experiences of a large number of industrialized societies, both socialist and nonsocialist. Although the review is still in progress, the first concrete result was the establishment of a state alimony fund, a rather innovative solution that seems to have emerged from a process of selective adaptation rather than direct emulation.[84]

The second example involves the legislative function itself. In this case it would appear that, among Polish legal scholars and parliamentary deputies, there is growing interest in revitalizing both the legislative and oversight functions of the Sejm. In the process, they are showing an intent curiosity about the ways in which other modern societies handle such matters as information retrieval systems for their legislatures, committee staffing, legislative oversight of the executive, and so forth.[85] One hesitates even to whisper "separation of powers" or "checks and balances"—the Poles themselves would strenuously deny it—yet the incipient signs are there.

It is probably worth emphasizing again that neither of these emerging trends—that is, neither the expansion of East European participation in international and regional associations nor the establishment of identity references beyond the Soviet bloc—is likely to induce major systemic changes in the foreseeable future. Both will, however, facilitate the gradual depoliticization of social and economic life in these societies. Moreover, what these trends suggest for the directions of future research on external influences in Eastern Europe is that we should look less at the macropolitical level, where both indigenous and Soviet constraints are apt to be greatest, and more at the aspects of the system that are susceptible to ideological neutralization.

It is also worth emphasizing that there is nothing inevitable about the direction of political development in Eastern Europe. If nothing else, the experiences of the last decade should convince us that, in the short run at least, there are no irreversible trends. In this respect, the rather hopeful trends just referred to must be viewed as essentially marginal phenomena—that is, they have been possible because of the small margin of confidence and legitimacy afforded by steady improvements in the quality of life enjoyed by the populations of these countries. Should that margin disappear, these trends as well could prove all too reversible.

Finally, and by way of conclusion, the following anecdote emerged from a meeting of Western diplomats and journalists with several politically prominent Poles in Warsaw in the summer of 1975, at which discussion focused on the degree of autonomy available to the several East European regimes in their domestic and foreign policies.

"Let us suppose," said one of the Poles by way of illustration, "that a meeting of all the fraternal socialist states is being held in Moscow. In the conference room, there is the usual circular table, the name plates, the comfortable armchairs. The only difference is that on each chair there is a tack. The delegates gather and begin to take their places. The first to find his seat is the East German: He spies the tack but, with scarcely a moment's hesitation, he turns around, sits down—and smiles. Next the Czechoslovak delegate: He, too, sees the tack, whereupon he takes two more from his pocket, places them on his chair; then he sits down, and he smiles. Then the Hungarian finds his place: When he sees the tack, he pauses ever so briefly, sits down with a barely audible sign, and he doesn't smile. Next the Romanian: He looks at the tack, picks it up and reads on the bottom 'made in the USSR,' whereupon he puts it in one pocket; from his other pocket he takes a second tack, on the bottom of which is stamped 'made in the People's Republic of China,' places it on his chair, sits down, and he smiles. Finally the Polish delegate enters, finds his chair, observes the tack, which he discreetly brushes aside as he gingerly sits down—and grimaces."[86] This by way of a pointed reminder that, in the final analysis, it is still Moscow that determines the admissibility of external influences into the region.

NOTES

1. Andrzej Korbonski, "External Influences on Eastern Europe," in *The International Politics of Eastern Europe*, ed. Charles Gati (New York: Praeger Publishers, 1976), p. 253.

2. James N. Rosenau, "Theorizing Across Systems: Linkage Politics Revisited," in *Conflict Behavior and Linkage Politics*, ed. Jonathan Wilkenfeld (New York: David McKay, 1973), p. 25.

3. Ibid., p. 30.

4. For a brief survey of the treatment of the East European case (or, more accurately, the lack thereof) in this literature, see Korbonski, "External Influences," pp. 254-55.

5. Alvin Z. Rubinstein, "Assessing Influence as a Problem in Foreign Policy Analysis," in *Soviet and Chinese Influence in the Third World*, ed. Alvin Z. Rubinstein (New York: Praeger Publishers, 1975), p. 10. See also J. David Singer, "Inter-Nation Influence: A Formal Model," *American Political Science Review* 57 no. 2 (June 1963): 420-30. Singer writes (p. 421) that "the tendency . . . in both political science and social psychology is to define an influence attempt as one in which A seeks to modify the behavior of B, or to identify A's influence over B in terms of 'the extent to which he can get B to do something that B would not otherwise do.'" Singer himself objects to this definition, and the article is an attempt to go beyond it; nonetheless, he retains the source perspective.

6. Karl W. Deutsch, "External Influences on the Internal Behavior of States," in *Approaches to Comparative and International Politics*, ed. R. Barry Farrell (Evanston, Ill.: Northwestern University Press, 1966), p. 11.

7. There are certain parallels here to Rosenau's categories of "penetrative" and "reactive" linkage (linkage being defined as "any recurrent sequence of behavior that originates in one system and is reacted to in another"). But where he is talking about types of behavior by the source or target at either end of a linkage, I am speaking here of the content of the link itself. See James N. Rosenau, "Toward the Study of National-International Linkages," in *Linkage Politics*, ed. James N. Rosenau (New York: Free Press, 1969), pp. 44-63.

8. Deutsch, "External Influences," p. 12.

9. Samuel P. Huntington, "Political Development and Political Decay," *World Politics* 17, no. 3 (April 1965): 405-6; see also his "Transnational Organizations in World Politics," *World Politics* 25, no. 3 (April 1973): 366-67.

10. Huntington, "Political Development and Political Decay," p. 396.

11. For a recent analysis, see Vernon V. Aspaturian, "The Soviet Impact on Development and Modernization in Eastern Europe," in *The Politics of Modernization in Eastern Europe: Testing the Soviet Model*, ed. Charles Gati (New York: Praeger Publishers, 1974), pp. 205-53.

12. William Zimmerman, "National-International Linkages in Yugoslavia: The Political Consequences of Openness," paper presented at the annual meeting of the American Political Science Association, September 1973, New Orleans, mimeo., pp. 1-3.

13. Korbonski, "External Influences," p. 257; see also Zbigniew K. Brzezinski, *The Soviet Bloc: Unity and Conflict*, rev. ed. (Cambridge, Mass.: Harvard University Press, 1967), Chapters 5-7.

14. Aspaturian, "The Soviet Impact," p. 220.

15. Zvi Gitelman, "The Diffusion of Political Innovation: From Eastern Europe to the Soviet Union," *Sage Professional Papers in Comparative Politics* 3, no. 27 (1972): 29-33.

16. Korbonski, "External Influences," p. 261.

17. See William Zimmerman, "Hierarchical Regional Systems and the Politics of System Boundaries," *International Organization* 26, no. 1 (Winter 1972): 18-36; Zimmerman uses the notion of system boundaries here in the figurative as well as literal sense.

18. Aspaturian, "The Soviet Impact," p. 252.

19. See, for example, Gitelman's discussion of Soviet reactions to Hungarian reforms; "The Diffusion of Political Innovation," pp. 49-53.

20. Ibid., p. 6.

21. Undoubtedly one of the more promising topics for future study will be the influence of the Italian Communist Party, whose political fortunes and ideas are followed with great interest in Eastern Europe. See, for example, Hansjakob Stehle, "Polish Communism," in *Communism in Europe: Continuity, Change, and the Sino-Soviet Dispute*, ed. William E. Griffith (Cambridge, Mass.: MIT Press, 1964), vol. 1, pp. 145-47; A. H. Brown, "Pluralistic Trends in Czechoslovakia," *Soviet Studies* 17, no. 4 (April 1966): 457, 464.

22. Robin Remington, "China's Emerging Role in Eastern Europe," in Gati, ed., *The International Politics of Eastern Europe*, p. 82.

23. On the origins and course of the Sino-Soviet dispute, see Brzezinski, *The Soviet Bloc*, especially Chapters 15 and 16. For various treatments of Albania's role, see: William E. Griffith, *Albania and the Sino-Soviet Rift* (Cambridge, Mass.: MIT Press, 1963); Peter R. Prifti, "Albania and the Sino-Soviet Conflict," *Studies in Comparative Communism* 6, no. 3 (Autumn 1973): 241-79; Nicholas C. Pano, "The Albanian Cultural Revolution," *Problems of Communism* 23, no. 4 (July-August 1974): 44-57.

24. See, for example, Norman J. G. Pounds, *Eastern Europe* (Chicago: Aldine, 1969), pp. 814-23; also Griffith, *Albania*, pp. 3-9, 168-75.

25. Pano, "The Albanian Cultural Revolution," p. 54.

26. Ibid., p. 52; Prifti, "Albania and the Sino-Soviet Conflict," p. 248.

27. Pano, "The Albanian Cultural Revolution," pp. 54-57; Prifti, "Albania and the Sino-Soviet Conflict," pp. 261-66.

28. For details of the growing divergence in the strategic outlooks of the Chinese and Albanian regimes, see Dorothy Grouse Fontana, "Recent Sino-Albanian Relations," *Survey* 21, no 4 (Autumn 1975): 121-44; also Peter R. Prifti, "Albania's Expanding Horizons," *Problems of Communism* 21, no. 1 (January-February 1972): 30-39.

29. Prifti, "Albania and the Sino-Soviet Conflict," pp. 249-61. Concerning more recent inconsistencies in Albanian-Yugoslav relations, see Radio Free Europe Research, *RAD Background Reports* 91 and 166, June 2 and December 2, 1975.

30. See, for example, Radio Free Europe Research, *RAD Background Report* 161, November 24, 1975: "Changes in Albanian Leadership Signify Struggle for Succession to Power"; also reports in New York *Times*, May 1 and 4, 1976.

31. For several treatments of these events, see Robert R. King, "Rumania and the Sino-Soviet Conflict," *Studies in Comparative Communism* 5, no. 4 (Winter 1972): 372-412; Robert R. King, "The Problems of Rumanian Foreign Policy," *Survey* 20, nos. 2-3 (Spring-Summer 1974): 105-20; Kenneth Jowitt, "Political Innovation in Rumania," *Survey* 20, no. 4 (Autumn 1974): 132-51.

32. King, "Problems of Rumanian Foreign Policy," pp. 107-13.

33. Ibid., pp. 115-17.

34. For evidence of Romania's growing identification with the "independent" Communist parties of Western Europe (plus Yugoslavia), see Kevin Devlin, "The Interparty Drama," *Problems of Communism* 24, no. 4 (July-August 1975): 18-34; also his "Historic Triumph for Independent Communist Parties," Radio Free Europe Research, *RAD Background Report* 142, October 15, 1975.

35. Jowitt, "Political Innovation in Rumania," pp. 133-35, 148-51.

36. For a detailed account of this period, see Brzezinski, *The Soviet Bloc*, Chapter 12, also p. 260.

37. Stehle, "Polish Communism," pp. 106-16.

38. Concerning the Mijal affair, see: Radio Free Europe Research, *Polish Situation Reports*, May 22, 1964, February 24, March 31, and September 12, 1966; *Foreign Report* (biweekly of the London *Economist*), November 17, 1966; and Jan Nowak, "The Stalinist Underground in Poland," *East Europe*, 14, no. 3 (March 1965): 2-15.

39. Stehle, "Polish Communism," pp. 148-56.

40. See especially the Polish statements of April 1964 and September 1966, in ibid., pp. 155-56; and Radio Free Europe Research, *Polish Situation Report*, October 3, 1966.

41. Zimmerman, "Hierarchical Regional Systems," esp. p. 26.

42. J. F. Brown, *Bulgaria Under Communist Rule* (New York: Praeger Publishers, 1970), pp. 83-90, 116-19; see especially his comments concerning lingering pro-Chinese sentiments in the Bulgarian party and the unusual lengths to which the regime felt compelled to go to demonstrate the unsuitability of the cultural revolution for Bulgarian conditions.

43. For a brief country-by-country rundown, see J. F. Brown, *The New Eastern Europe: The Khrushchev Era and After* (New York: Praeger Publishers, 1966), pp. 164-78.

44. Thus, in the late 1950s the East Germans and Czechs apparently used praise of radical Chinese policies as an oblique means of criticizing Khrushchev's reformist tendencies; see Brzezinski, *The Soviet Bloc*, pp. 384-86.

45. The most dramatic such intrusion was, of course, the crushing of the Hungarian revolt in 1956, in which Chinese approval was apparently an important factor in the Soviet decision; see ibid., p. 278; and *Khrushchev Remembers*, ed. and trans. Strobe Talbott (Boston: Little, Brown, 1970), pp. 417-19. But this is not the only example of the unpredictable effects of Chinese influence; despite earlier pro-Chinese sentiments (read anti-revisionist—see previous note), one observer maintains that the emergence of the Sino-Soviet conflict was one of several factors at work in stimulating the Czech reform movement, in that "it led to a questioning of apparently eternal verities" and "tended to weaken the position of the die-hards and Marxist-Leninist fundamentalists." A. H. Brown, "Pluralistic Trends in Czechoslovakia," *Soviet Studies* 17, no. 4 (April 1966): 456-57. (Although Brown does not mention it, the conflict also aggravated the economic crisis by closing off a sizable market for Czech industrial exports.)

46. See, for example, Craig R. Whitney, "Peking Wooing Bonn to Offset Moscow," New York *Times*, March 7, 1976.

47. Roger E. Kanet, "Modernizing Interaction within Eastern Europe," in Gati, ed., *The Politics of Modernization in Eastern Europe*, p. 286.

48. According to A. H. Brown ("Pluralistic Trends," p. 457), "until 1964 . . . no major Polish economic work had been published in Czechoslovakia" (although the timing here may have been determined as much by domestic considerations as Soviet policy).

49. With respect to the Czech reform, Brown commented (ibid.): "For anyone but a member of the Politburo, it is of importance to be able to quote a top communist in support of his own criticisms, and the views of Tito (still slightly suspect), and more especially those of Kadar, Gomulka and Togliatti have served this technical purpose. The fact that changes were already under way in other communist countries was both a stimulus to change in Czechoslovakia and a useful tactical device in the hands of those who wished to hasten the process."

50. Quoted in ibid., p. 456. Much the same could, of course, be said about Poland in 1970, East Germany in 1963, and to a lesser extent, Hungary in inaugurating the NEM—although in that case, it was more the fear of economic stagnation than the reality that prompted change.

51. Korbonski, "External Influences," p. 259. See also Andrzej Brzeski, "Poland as a Catalyst of Change in the Communist Economic System," *The Polish Review* 16, no. 2 (Spring 1970): 3-24; and Adam Bromke, "Poland's Role in the Loosening of the Communist Bloc," in *Eastern Europe in Transition*. ed. Kurt London (Baltimore: Johns Hopkins Press, 1966), pp. 67-92.

52. See, for example, F. Stephen Larrabee, "Bulgaria's Politics of Conformity," *Problems of Communism* 21, no. 4 (July-August 1972): 42-52.

53. Note, for example, Gierek's merger of party and state functions at the local level; even Tito may have profited from Ceausescu's style in his recent retreat toward recentralization and discipline.

54. See Brzezinski, *The Soviet Bloc*, Chapter 9.

55. For a recent survey, see Michael Gamarnikow, "Balance Sheet on Economic Reforms," in *Reorientation and Commercial Relations of the Economies of Eastern Europe*, ed. John P. Hardt (Washington, D.C.: Joint Economic Committee, U.S. Congress, 1974), pp. 164-213.

56. Korbonski, "External Influences," p. 271; and Kanet, "Modernizing Interaction," p. 292.

57. Galia Golan, *Reform Rule in Czechoslovakia: The Dubcek Era 1968-1969* (Cambridge: Cambridge University Press, 1973), pp. 42-46, 149-54; Vladimir V. Kusin, *The Intellectual Origins of the Prague Spring* (Cambridge: Cambridge University Press, 1971), Chapter 11; Kanet, "Modernizing Interaction," p. 289.

58. See, for example, the series of articles by Andrzej Wasilkowski under the general title, "In the Countries of the Socialist Commonwealth," which appeared more or less weekly during June and July 1975 in *Trybuna Ludu* (Warsaw); also Z. Szeliga, "The Hungarian Elections," *Polityka* (Warsaw), May 8, 1971, translated in Radio Free Europe Research, *Polish Press Survey*, no. 2303 (May 21, 1971).

59. From information provided by Professor David E. Powell, of the University of Virginia and the Harvard Russian Research Center, who is studying the problem of alcoholism in Eastern Europe and the Soviet Union.

60. See note 10 above.

61. A. H. Brown, "Pluralistic Trends," p. 457; and Korbonski, "External Influences," p. 270.

62. For instance, Kenneth Jowitt suggests that, despite the substantial differences in their internal development, the Romanian regime favored continuation of the Czechoslovak experiment because it offered them "the latitude necessary to work for change within the existing system and helped to maintain the belief that revision of existing relations was possible within the current boundaries of the bloc"; *Revolutionary Breakthroughs and National Development: The Case of Romania, 1944-1965* (Berekely and Los Angeles: University of California Press, 1971), pp. 270-71.

63. Korbonski, "External Influences," p. 269.

64. Concerning the indigenous roots of the Czech reforms, see: A. H. Brown, "Pluralistic Trends," pp. 453-54; Kusin, *Intellectual Origins*, passim.; Ota Sik, "Czechoslovakia," in *Reforms in the Soviet and Eastern European Economies*, ed. L. A. D. Dellin and Herman Gross (Lexington, Mass.: Lexington Books, 1972), pp. 59-62.

65. For an interesting discussion of the limitations of the Leninist model, see Zvi Gitelman, "Beyond Leninism: Political Development in Eastern Europe," *Newsletter on Comparative Studies of Communism* 5, no. 3 (May 1972): 18-43.

66. For instance, A. H. Brown ("Pluralistic Trends," p. 464) questions whether the intense interest that the Czechs showed in the Yugoslav model was not merely "a rationalization based on knowledge of the range of possibilities for Czechoslovakia in the immediate future." Much the same could be said with respect to Polish interest in the new election procedures in Hungary in 1971; see Szeliga, "The Hungarian Elections."

67. To wit, the comment made several years ago in a Polish article on Hungarian reform, implying that the latter had been more clever in escaping the constraints of the system: "It would appear that we have much to learn from our partners to the south. . . . It is no accident that there is a common saying in Europe that, if someone enters a revolving door behind you and exits in front of you, he is certain to be a Hungarian." *Polityka*, November 11, 1972.

68. For a discussion of "identity references" in the East European context, see comments by Kenneth Jowitt in *Eastern Europe in the 1970s*, ed. Sylvia Sinanian, Istvan Deak, and Peter C. Ludz (New York: Praeger Publishers, 1970), pp. 180-84.

69. For the official summary of remarks made by State Department Counselor Helmut Sonnenfeldt to a meeting of American ambassadors in Europe in December 1975, see New York *Times*, April 6, 1976; see also Barnard Gwertzman, "Eastern Europe a Delicate Issue," New York *Times*, April 7, 1976.

70. Based in part on information supplied by a Polish sociologist and party member, March 1973.

71. See, for example, *East-West Trade and Technology Transfer: An Agenda of Research Needs*, ed. Robert W. Campbell and Paul Marer (Bloomington: International Development Research Center, Indiana University, 1974), pp. 71-74 (especially remarks by Grossman and Schapiro); also Franklyn D. Holzman and Robert Legvold, "The Economics and Politics of East-West Relations," *International Organization* 29, no. 1 (Winter 1975): 306-7.

72. See note 6 above.

73. See, for example, Jerzy Kleer, "Koniunktura a handel," *Polityka*, April 3, 1976; also comments by Fallenbuchl and Berliner in Campbell and Marer, eds., *East-West Trade*, pp. 72-73.

74. For areawide comparisons, 1964-72, see the chapter by Charles Gati elsewhere in this volume; data for later years may be found in the foreign trade section of the Comecon statistical yearbooks (*Statisticheskii yezhegodnik stranchlonev Soveta Ekonomicheskoi Vzaimopomoshchi*) published by the Comecon secretariat in Moscow, although there are frequent discrepancies with data published elsewhere. Poland's trade with capitalist countries rose dramatically in the first half of the 1970s, and by 1974 reached 55.6 percent of its total imports and 44.3 percent of exports. See, for example: "Nasz handel zagraniczny w liczbach GUS," *Zycie Gospodarcze*, no. 24 (June 15, 1975); Pawel Bozyk, "Handel zagraniczny 1971-1974: korzystne przyspieszenie," *Zycie Gospodarcze*, no. 20 (May 18, 1975).

75. In this connection, the Poles have recently made unprecedented concessions in exchange for two large loans, setting an example that the Soviets may well not appreciate. In one instance, they allowed full disclosure of information on their copper industry in order to obtain a $240 million loan; in the second, they have agreed to permit the emigration of 120,000 ethnic Germans as part of an agreement including a credit of DM 1 billion

from the West German government. Thomas E. Heneghan, "Polish Trade and Polish Trends: Economic and Political Considerations," Radio Free Europe Research, *RAD Background Report*, no. 158 (November 13, 1975), pp. 11, 13, 20.

76. Concerning the potential magnitude and consequences of this reorientation, see ibid., pp. 21-29; Harry Trend, "Major Economic Changes Flow from Comecon Trade Development," Radio Free Europe Research, *RAD Background Report*, no. 44 (February 16, 1976); Wieslaw Szyndler-Glowacki, "Operacja Orenburg," *Zycie Gospodarcze*, no. 16 (April 20, 1975); "XXIX sesja RWPG," *Zycie Gospodarcze*, no. 26 (June 29, 1975). Although as of this writing only fragementary figures for 1975 Comecon trade were available, they indicate a jump of nearly 40 percent over 1974 in Polish-Soviet trade; see "Handel zagraniczny ZSRR w 1975 roku," *Zycie Gospodarcze*, no. 20 (May 16, 1976).

77. Indeed, warning signs were already in evidence by early 1976, in the form of the diversion of already scarce goods from domestic markets to help cover trade deficits, postponement or cancellation of industrial cooperation projects, reduction of imports from the West, and so on. See, for example, Heneghan, "Polish Trade," pp. 9, 24; Radio Free Europe Research, *Hungarian Situation Report*, no. 2 (January 21, 1976): 10-11; *Business Week*, May 3, 1976, pp. 118-19.

78. Zimmerman, "Hierarchical Regional Systems," pp. 30-36; Holzman and Legvold, "The Economics and Politics of East-West Relations," pp. 315-20.

79. See especially Robert R. King, "The Athens Conference and the Balkans: Old Variations on an Old Theme," Radio Free Europe Research, *RAD Background Report*, no. 55 (March 1, 1976); also nos. 40 and 41 (February 12, 1976).

80. Zimmerman, "Hierarchical Regional Systems," pp. 30-36.

81. Concerning the Polish-Swedish connection, see especially Wieslaw Szyndler-Glowacki, "Konstruktywne wspoldzialanie: po wizycie Edwarda Gierka w Szwecji," *Zycie Gospodarcze* 30, no. 24 (June 15, 1975); Heneghan, "Polish Trade," pp. 15-18; Radio Free Europe Research, *Polish Situation Reports*, nos. 23 and 31 (June 22 and September 14, 1973).

82. Korbonski, "External Influences," p. 262.

83. For a detailed interpretation of Romania's notives in this regard, see Jowitt, "Political Innovation in Rumania," passim.

84. Personal interview with a member of the Polish Sejm, September 1975; see also Wanda Falkowska, "Rodzina i prawo: zmiany w kodeksie," *Polityka*, December 13, 1975.

85. Ibid.; also: Wojciech Sokolewicz, "Changes in the Polish Sejm," *East Central Europe* 2, no. 1 (1975): 78-91; Sylwester Zawadzki, "The Future of Parliament in the Political Structure of Socialist Society in Poland," paper presented to the Second International Conference on Legislative Development, January 1975, in Albany, N.Y., mimeo.; Andrzej Gwizdz, "O zmianach w regulaminie Sejmu," *Panstwo i Prawo* 27, no. 10 (October 1972): 4-18.

86. As related to me by Bernard Margueritte, Warsaw correspondent of *Le Figaro* (Paris).

12

THROUGH DIPLOMACY OR "WESTERNIZATION": A CRITIQUE OF AMERICAN APPROACHES TO EASTERN EUROPE

Charles Gati

Broad explanations of the sources of continuity and change in Eastern Europe in the postwar world normally focus on three major factors or variables. The first is the Soviet impact on Eastern Europe, conceptualized either in terms of the strict "satellite" relationship of the Stalinist era or in terms of a somewhat looser "tutelary" relationship since the mid-1950s. The second factor is identified as various features in the domestic environment: historical background, tradition, political culture, national resources, and characteristics. The third broad explanatory variable has been Western influence: the impact of American and West European policies, attitudes, and trends on the politics of Eastern Europe.

This chapter—more a critical essay than a balanced research paper— explores this third source of East European politics, dealing with the impact of what the West has done vis-a-vis Eastern Europe and with the impact of what the West is as perceived in Eastern Europe. The very selection of the topic assumes Western presence as well as an element of choice for the states of Eastern Europe, for however pervasive Moscow's influence remains and however important national considerations have become, Eastern Europe is certainly challenged by, and responds to, the West in the realm of ideas, culture, technology, and way of life.

UNDERESTIMATED U.S. OPPORTUNITIES

In one form or another, revisionism has been the professed objective of Western, especially American, policies toward Eastern Europe since World War II.[1] The more radical version of revisionism, which was particularly current

315

during the first decade of the cold war, was said to have aimed at the prompt political transformation of the region: its liberation from Soviet control and the concurrent adoption of Western-style political pluralism. In an oft-quoted declaration, John Foster Dulles stated the expectation underlying this form of revisionism when he urged the United States to let it be known that "it wants and expects liberation to occur." He added, "The mere statement of that wish and expectation . . . would put heavy new burdens on the jailers and create new opportunities for liberation."[2] While emphasizing peaceful methods to obtain liberation, Dulles still expected radical and short-term political transformation that would lead to the introduction or reintroduction of competitive political systems.

In fact, however, and despite very genuine sympathies and hollow rhetoric about "liberation," the United States did not actively seek to change the pro-Soviet orientation of Eastern Europe. Contrary to scholarly consensus, and especially public perception, the United States consistently shied away from trying to negotiate a peaceful resolution of the future of Eastern Europe. In my view, moreover, during certain crisis situations in particular, the United States had several opportunities to reduce Soviet control through negotiations.

The first and probably most promising opportunity presented itself in the early days of World War II, in November 1941, when the Soviet Union made known its claim to the Baltic region. Even though the Soviet government was on the verge of military defeat then—having been evacuated from Moscow to Kuibyshev—Stalin was still able to convince a somewhat reluctant Britain and subsequently the United States that his postwar aims were modest and reasonable; after all, some members of the British foreign service felt, he could have asked for Poland and the Balkans as well. Negotiating from a position of extreme weakness, then, the Soviet Union successfully relied on its feeble condition to obtain a sympathetic hearing from its Western allies. Given Stalin's professed suspicions and what were seen as understandable Soviet security concerns, as well as the compelling needs of the wartime alliance, even Churchill felt he should advise President Roosevelt to comply. "The increase in gravity of the war has led me to feel," he wrote, "that the principles of the Atlantic Charter ought not to be construed so as to deny Russia the frontiers she occupied when Germany attacked her. . . . I hope therefore that you will be able to give us a free hand to sign the treaty that Stalin desires as soon as possible."[3]

Second, between late 1944 and the February 1948 coup in Czechoslovakia, the West still had certain opportunities to challenge the emerging Soviet design for Eastern Europe. As yet, most countries in the region only tilted toward the Soviet Union, political competition continued to exist, non-Communist governments were in fact in power. Contemporary documents from the archives of the State Department convincingly demonstrate that while the United States, primarily through the Allied Control Commissions, frequently objected to the exclusion of non-Communist elements from the political process,

U.S. representatives were instructed to avoid any confrontation with the Soviet Union. The department's confidential briefing paper on Hungary, for example, advised U.S. diplomats in 1945 that the United States "would not, of course, take the position of supporting Hungary against the Soviet Union. . . . The United States government recognizes that the Soviet Union's interest in Hungary is more direct than ours."[4] Essentially similar instructions were sent to other East European capitals. On the scene, most high-ranking diplomats pressed for a more assertive Western posture, but Washington prevailed and some representatives were reassigned or resigned in protest.[5]

Third, since the beginning of the cold war U.S. opportunities have gradually declined; as time went on, U.S. diplomatic leverage has admittedly eroded. The response was paradoxical. On the one hand, the American approach to Eastern Europe was now characterized by increasingly immodest, indeed vehement, verbal assurances and propaganda activities. "Liberation," for example, was essentially an exercise in anti-Communist sloganeering and posturing, not foreign policy; it was a largely political act aimed at intimidating both the Russians and the Democrats. On the other hand, however, the U.S. approach to Eastern Europe—a peculiar form of self-deception—served to conceal a disinclination to take advantage of legitimate diplomatic opportunities inherent in Soviet-East European relations. Significantly, the United States did not seek to exploit policy differences within the Soviet leadership on behalf of Eastern Europe. During the three major crises of post-1948 Eastern Europe—the 1953 East Berlin riots, the 1956 Hungarian revolution, and the 1968 Czechoslovak reform movement—the apparently divided Soviet leadership might well have entertained Western proposals aimed at finding an Austrian, Finnish, or Yugoslav solution for one or some of the countries involved. We will not know one way or the other, of course, because the West never sought to find out the degree to which Soviet leaders were in fact divided over the proper response to these crises. No diplomatic deal was offered; no official proposals are known.

It is instructive to recall, therefore, that in 1953, according to Khrushchev at least, Beria and Malenkov were prepared to liquidate East Germany as a socialist state, meaning they were not opposed to negotiations on the question of German reunification.[6] In 1956 the Soviet leadership in fact rejected the idea of military intervention at first, hoping that the ever-present threat of intervention would be sufficient to produce a pro-Soviet, although pluralistic, political order, somewhat on the Finnish pattern.[7] In 1968 the Soviet Union for several months sought to stem the tide of reform by subtle and then explicit signals, such as expressions of unity at multilateral (Warsaw Pact) meetings, an unparalleled politburo-to-politburo confrontation, and conspicuous military maneuvers. Only when these measures failed to slow the pace of reform and the West indicated it would not get involved did the Soviet Union and its Warsaw Pact allies send the troops in.

The U.S. lack of diplomatic response to any of these crises points to one of the seldom noted successes of Soviet propaganda, to wit, that over the years the West has come to accept the Soviet definition of what is and what is not negotiable, and what is and what is not realistic. The West has come to agree to the Soviet view that it would be "unrealistic" to raise the "non-negotiable" issue of Eastern Europe in a diplomatic setting, and took refuge in public-political polemics instead.

This apparent reluctance to test the limits of Soviet tolerance at the negotiating table—to see what tradeoffs if any might appeal to the Soviet leadership—has been influenced by two mistaken assumptions. One is that the Soviet system is so vulnerable that almost any political change in Eastern Europe would in fact constitute a grave threat. Surely this is not a proposition without merit, for the Soviet Union in its capacity as the professed leader of the Communist world needs Eastern Europe to demonstrate that the Soviet model of socialism contains potentially universal qualities.[8] It should be pointed out, however, that the Soviet Union has learned to live with the defection of Yugoslavia and Albania as well as China, and that it has come to tolerate, however grudgingly, Romania's foreign policy course. What has taken place, to borrow a phrase from John C. Campbell, is as much the Balkanization of socialism as it is the socialization of the Balkans.[9]

A second assumption that has informed U.S. fatalism is that the only basis for promising negotiations with the Soviet Union is military strength and that the West lacks such strength in Eastern Europe. Without suggesting the contrary, of course, it should still be recalled that Stalin, for one, negotiated from a position of considerable weakness when he obtained Western acquiescence in the sovietization of the Baltic states in 1941. Conversely, the Austrian Peace Treaty of 1955 demonstrates that the Soviet Union could, as it did, negotiate the withdrawal of its troops from a position of considerable strength. Under present conditions, it would be far more accurate to suggest that—given the deeply pro-Western orientation of the people of Eastern Europe, their governments' growing desire to fulfill certain national aspirations and economic needs, and the demonstrated Soviet aversion to military intervention—what the West lacks is not military strength but a proper appreciation of its opportunities for peaceful political engagement in Eastern Europe.

Thus, the underlying theme of the U.S. diplomatic approach to, and perception of, Eastern Europe has been one of underestimated American opportunities and overestimated Soviet determination.

DIPLOMACY OR FUNCTIONALISM

In the aftermath of the Soviet suppression of the 1956 Hungarian revolt, the professed American strategy toward Eastern Europe gradually changed.

Given Western inaction at the time, "liberation" showed itself to be an empty slogan. It was subsequently replaced by a more covert form of revisionism, called bridge building or peaceful engagement, that deemphasized short-term expectations, political incitement, psychological warfare, and generally open confrontation with the Soviet Union and the regimes of Eastern Europe. The new Western strategy sought to influence the political orientation of the region primarily by trade and cultural interaction, expecting long-term benefits both for the West and the peoples of Eastern Europe. West Germany's Ostpolitik, de Gaulle's grand design for a Europe from the Atlantic to the Urals, and the American policy of peaceful engagement and bridge building all followed more or less the same pattern of revisionism as they aimed at bringing Eastern Europe into closer economic and cultural contact with the West primarily in the non-political or apolitical realms. It was assumed that eventually (later rather than sooner) such economic and cultural bonds with the West would democratize or at least liberalize Eastern Europe, reduce Soviet influence, introduce pluralistic tendencies, and generally develop or reinforce a disposition toward Western political values.

This important assumption was, and to a lesser degree remains, rather deeply ingrained in Western political tradition as the interdependence of economics and politics, indeed an economic interpretation of history, has come to be widely shared by Marxists and non-Marxists alike. In the realm of foreign policy, the establishment of the postwar European recovery program, and somewhat later the extensive program of foreign aid to the developing countries, were meant to demonstrate that the improvement of economic conditions would lead to the introduction of a Western-style political superstructure. In the realm of political theory, functionalism provided the rationale, or justification, for such programs, by suggesting that where international political cooperation was not yet possible economic (or generally apolitical) cooperation was advisable as a first step or functional prelude to political harmony among nation-states. Moreover, functionalism also provided a political strategy that conveniently fit the apparent Western psychological need for optimism concerning the universal appeal of democratic values.

In Western Europe the record by and large seems to confirm the validity of the functional approach to democracy, although the causal link between economic cooperation and political harmony is neither clear nor proven. In the developing world, the dismal record of Western democratic experiments suggests that political pluralism (if that is the main feature of Western democracies) cannot be transferred or even adapted to the traditions of essentially autocratic polities, or at least that the transfer of economic goods does not guarantee the transfer of political values. (Indeed, the validity of the modernization theories that posit universal phases of development—claiming identical political and social reactions to "the pressures and demands of the modern, industrialized, and urban-centered world"[10]—should be seriously doubted.)

Significantly, Western assumptions and experiences are hardly unique in this respect. Eastern Europe provides several examples that demonstrate that economic dependence on the USSR, even when reinforced by ideological affinity and the presence of the Red Army, does not guarantee political imitation. Yugoslavia in 1948 turned against Moscow despite its overwhelming dependence on Soviet (and other East European) trade, and Romania defied the Soviet Union in the 1960s despite its lack of an immediate economic alternative. Albania is still another example, of course. Indeed, at no time in the postwar world could it be said that the more an East European country depended on the USSR economically, the more faithfully it served Soviet political interests or emulated Soviet political values. The political and social consequences of even extensive economic dependence are therefore unpredictable; surely, at least the same can be said of the political and social consequences of somewhat expanded Western trade.

Nonetheless, the United States and the West in general have come to rely on the economic and cultural instruments of foreign policy during the last 15 or 20 years in their effort to influence the politics of Eastern Europe. In part, this more "evolutionary" form of revisionism—called "peaceful engagement" by Zbigniew Brzezinski and William E. Griffith[11]—was a reaction to the glaring failure of the "liberation" approach. In part, it was an expression of the growing recognition of the limits of American power. In part, it evolved in the face of the Sino-Soviet rift and the opportunities that rift was presumed to offer to the various states of the region.

Peaceful engagement, as much as Ostpolitik later on, was covert revisionism. "It is no longer beyond the realm of possibility," Brzezinski wrote in 1965, "that in the course of the next decade or so the Soviet leaders will reluctantly conclude that their position in East Europe would be stronger if the East European states ceased to be unpopular and unstable dictatorships, and instead came to resemble Finland."[12] The Finlandization of Eastern Europe was thus seen as a possibility, at least partly because of the "nonideological character of industrial development."[13] True, "the prospects for the democratization of East Europe" in the shorter run were correctly judged to be "somewhat dim," yet in "the long run the attraction of a united Europe, the effects of closer contacts, and the opportunity to observe Western European welfare democracy will cumulatively tend to strengthen the process of social regeneration in East Europe and provide for wider public influence on decision making."[14] Hence the expectation of not only penetrating but "dismantling the Iron Curtain."

Brzezinski, Griffith, and others based their expectations on an active, though peaceful, policy of Western involvement that would have entailed diplomatic as well as economic and cultural engagement. Partly because of the Vietnam war, however, the official American approach—called bridge building by President Johnson and Secretary of State Dean Rusk—deemphasized diplomacy and relied instead almost exclusively on the more indirect instruments of foreign policy. What began, then, as a well-defined and multifaceted political approach to Eastern Europe gave way to an essentially non-political overture, based on the East European need for technological innovation, the appeal of Western managerial techniques, the magnetism of the Common Market experience, and the widespread East European longing for and affiliation with "Europe" and European culture. The ultimate convergence of divergent European political and social systems was widely predicted,[15] partly because of the prevailing aura of "developmental determinism," partly because of the post-Khrushchev uncertainty in the USSR, and partly because of the appeal of the West. The gradual political democratization of Eastern Europe was seen as likely if not quite inevitable.

Indeed, by the middle of the 1960s, some scholars no longer spoke of their expectations; by then, they spoke of the actual realization of these expectations. Ghita Ionescu, for example, in *The Politics of the European Communist States*, published in 1967, went so far as to maintain that the East European party Apparat was "dissolving under pressure from outside and from within"[16] and that "in the communist political societies of today the point has been reached where the Apparat's power is held in check by the newly separated constitutional powers."[17] Indeed, Ionescu concluded his study by drawing attention to "two irreversible trends": "The first is that the pluralization and the reinstitutionalization which follows from it will continue to lead to the dissolution of the Apparat. The second . . . is that the European communist states will in the future become more European than communist."[18] External (presumably Western and especially West European) as well as certain internal influences were thus said to have already led to the realization of the primary objectives of covert revisionism: the introduction of "plural checks," limited constitutionalism, political competition, the toleration of dissent, and perhaps most important, the Europeanization of Eastern Europe.

Reading such descriptions, Western policy makers could, and apparently did, congratulate themselves, for their revised strategy that involved only minimally increased trade and cultural contacts was thus said to have paid off handsomely, and probably far sooner than expected. In fact, however, if one were to speak of the Europeanization or Westernization of Eastern Europe, one must be far more discriminating, critical, and ultimately rather pessimistic.

WESTERN PRESENCE AND THE MYTH OF "DEVELOPMENTAL DETERMINISM"

Strictly speaking, any assessment of the "Westernization" of Eastern Europe is somewhat misleading. At least part of the region we now call Eastern Europe is in fact Central Europe, and much of the cultural and intellectual tradition there is Western. In almost every realm of human endeavor, but especially in culture, Western influences as much or more than Eastern influences have long been and are present: in architecture, music, literature, and so on. Historically and politically, the region always aspired to be at least "between" East and West, and preferably closer to West than East.

Moreover, Westernization is a notion that denotes a rather specific political tendency and aspiration. It is a relative notion, in the sense that when East Europeans speak of the West, of Westernization, or of Western influences, they invariably mean the reduction of Eastern, that is, Soviet influence. "Westernization," therefore, is part of competitive coexistence in Europe: competition between economic models and management techniques, between intellectual tendencies, between two ways of life, and between political models. Thus the question we are concerned with here is whether the West has or has not altered the balance of Eastern and Western influences in Eastern Europe, and if it has, what aspects of East European life have been affected.

First, in the economic realm, much, perhaps too much, has been made of the expansion of East European trade with the West. Any assessment here should take into account two criteria. The first is the element of time, for if one compares the present level of East European trade with the West with that of, say, 1950, the change is impressive; if, on the other hand, comparison focuses on the early 1960s vis-a-vis the early or mid-1970s, change is marginal. The other criterion is of a somewhat more technical nature: Should we consider the volume of trade or the relative share of Western trade (in contrast to the relative share of COMECON trade)?

As to the element of time, comparison between 1950 and 1972 or 1975 is not very instructive, for in comparison with the years of Stalinist autarky and isolation, Western economic presence in Eastern Europe has, of course, substantially and obviously increased. Nor is it very helpful to make much of trade volume if one is interested in the relative economic presence of East and the West.

Accordingly, Table 12.1 provides a picture quite different from what is commonly assumed. While the volume of East European foreign trade has grown, the Western share of East European trade has not. In sharp contrast to the popular image of expanding East-West trade, the data actually suggest only marginal changes: The Western share in the region's foreign trade has, if anything, declined in Czechoslovakia, remained about the same in Bulgaria, Hungary, Poland, and Yugoslavia, and increased somewhat in East Germany and Romania. Trade with the Soviet Union and within the region itself remains the important fact of economic life in Eastern Europe. Parenthetically, for rather complex economic reasons and for rather simple political reasons, the pattern of the last decade is not likely to change; if anything, East European dependence on Soviet raw materials will continue to assure extensive Soviet-East European trade relationships.

TABLE 12.1

Western Share of East European Trade, 1964-72
(Average of imports and exports in percentages)

Year	Bulgaria	Czechoslovakia	East Germany	Hungary	Poland	Romania	Yugoslavia
1964	22.3	26.8	23.6	31.1	36.3	31.6	68.5
1965	23.2	26.8	26.1	31.5	35.3	35.1	64.3
1966	27.0	29.7	26.9	33.4	37.0	40.4	65.2
1967	24.0	28.2	25.9	32.4	35.3	47.6	68.4
1968	22.3	28.5	23.9	29.8	34.9	44.8	68.4
1969	20.5	29.4	27.2	32.1	34.2	44.8	72.5
1970	22.2	22.4	28.4	29.2	33.8	36.5	62.3
1971	21.5	22.5	28.3	32.7	34.7	36.7	71.1
1972	13.9	21.4	25.9	26.6	32.2	37.2	60.6
1973	14.5	23.6	27.8	28.7	39.3	39.8	58.7
1974	n.a.	25.8	n.a.	n.a.	n.a.	n.a.	52.9

Sources: Alan A. Brown and Paul Marer, *Foreign Trade in the East European Reforms* (Bloomington: International Development Research Center, Indiana University, 1972), p. 80; Radio Free Europe (RFE), *East-West/4* (March 12, 1973); RFE, *Czechoslovakia/4* (April 1, 1974);RFE, *Romania/5* (April 3, 1974); U.S. Department of Commerce, Overseas Business Reports (June 1973), p. 20; *Facts on Czechoslovak Foreign Trade* (Prague: Chamber of Commerce of Czechoslovakia, 1973), p. 47; *Statistical Yearbook of Bulgaria, 1972: Hungary, Statistical Yearbook* (Budapest: Hungarian Statistical Office, 1974), p. 273; *Statistical Yearbook of Poland* (Warsaw: Central Statistical Office, 1973).

Aside from Western trade, much, perhaps too much, has been made of technology transfer.[19] Here we have little data to work with, and opinions do differ. But at a recent Indiana University conference on East-West trade and technology transfer, most specialists agreed with Gregory Grossman, who noted that the import of Western technology is "not incompatible with a conservative policy domestically." He added, "It does not, at least in the foreseeable future, require a drastic restructuring of domestic economic institutions, though it may require some adjustments, and it does not harbor the uncertainties and risks associated with a far-reaching economic reform." Grossman further noted that the political risk, normally assumed as a result of increased contact with Westerners, is minimal, for "the usual police methods can be used to insulate the bulk of the population from contact with the West."[20]

Thus, while the transfer of Western technology to Eastern Europe is taking place and advanced western products, machinery, and computers are generally admired, it does not necessarily follow that this process presents an insurmountable political problem in Eastern Europe. East Europeans have long been impressed by Western technology but, as we shall argue later, that attitude has little, if anything, to do with the question of political power in Eastern Europe or with Western influence over political decision making. One finds no evidence for the proposition that Western trade and technology transfer require economic decentralization, reforms of the pricing mechanism and of the monetary system, and that such economic reforms in turn require political decentralization (with some attention to group interests).

In this respect the Hungarian case is instructive. In that country, the New Economic Mechanism, introduced in 1968, grew out of domestic economic needs and considerations rather than as a consequence of Western trade; the expected political decentralization did not really take place; and in the end (by 1974) NEM itself was shelved. If there is a lesson in the Hungarian experience, it is that East European politics has its ups and downs, that it tends to move in a cyclical pattern, and that political considerations usually dominate economic considerations rather than the other way around.

In addition to trade and technology transfer, there is one other area of Western economic activity that is said to influence Eastern Europe: the experience and appeal of the Common Market. Officially, concern about the Common Market's discriminatory policies has been voiced time and again in Eastern Europe; officially and especially unofficially, East Europeans have expressed admiration for the ability of their West European neighbors to rise above petty rivalries and build an economically viable community. But, as Werner Feld pointed out as early as 1970 in the *Journal of Common Market Studies*, the utility of the Common Market "experience" and its institutional framework for COMECON cannot and should not be exaggerated.[21] Aside from economic considerations, the political weight of the Soviet Union makes COMECON a different sort of economic grouping, one that cannot easily learn from the structure and operational techniques of the Common Market. Thus, we are once again faced with a phenomenon that attracts East European attention and admiration, without the necessity of institutional adoption or even adaptation.

Second, in the realm of intellectual tendencies—that is, cultural influences and the competition of ideas—whatever hard data are available as well as observation on the scene unmistakably point to a cultural environment that is closely attuned to and even reflects Western tendencies. Whether the comparison is with the era of Stalinist isolation, when only Russian culture was considered worthy for import, or with the more relaxed era of the 1960s, the evidence is clear that Western books, movies, plays, music, and scholarship enjoy considerable freedom of access and enormous appeal in Eastern Europe. In some instances at least, it is also possible to demonstrate that it is not only the volume of Western culture that has increased but its relative share of the East European cultural scene (vis-a-vis Russian culture) as well.

Publishing trends in the region, and by implication the reading habits of East Europeans, are documented in Table 12.2. The conclusion is that, in all five countries for which data were collected, the relative share of Russian books translated into East European languages has been allowed to decrease, while translations from the major Western languages have considerably increased (especially in Romania). The contrast with the 1950s would be even more vivid.

THE POLITICAL DIMENSION OF WESTERNIZATION

Unfortunately, we do not have such comparative and comprehensive data about Western films, plays, and music. To give an example, however, Table 12.3 presents the number of feature films imported from abroad to Hungary, showing that the relative share of Soviet and East European films in Hungarian moviehouses also has declined, while the relative share of Western films has somewhat increased. Far more revealing would be some data showing the extent of popular interest in Western versus Eastern films; alas, such information is not available. Nor can we provide any hard data about plays at the present time, although it does seem safe to assume that trends similar to those observed in book publishing prevail throughout the region. While classic works by a Moliere or Shakespeare never disappeared from the repertoire of East European companies and selected works by such (formerly?) "progressive" playwrights as Arthur Miller were always shown, the present tendency is to perform even such politically controversial plays or musicals as *Fiddler on the Roof*—the talk of several East European capitals in the early 1970s. Finally, Western music, including rock and jazz, is probably as appealing to East European youth as it is to young people in the West. More important, such music can now be heard on local and especially Western radio stations, including Radio Free Europe. Indeed, most self-respecting teenagers in Eastern Europe know that Frank Sinatra is getting old,

TABLE 12.2

Book Translations from Major Languages, 1964-70
(in percent; N in parentheses)

Year	Russian	English/French/German*
Bulgaria		
1964	77.2 (292)	22.8 (86)
1965	72.9 (250)	27.1 (93)
1966	69.5 (210)	30.5 (92)
1967	63.0 (194)	37.0 (114)
1968	63.5 (193)	36.5 (111)
1969	66.4 (221)	33.6 (112)
1970	61.8 (162)	38.2 (100)
Hungary		
1964	36.9 (154)	63.1 (263)
1965	35.4 (146)	64.6 (266)
1966	32.0 (126)	68.0 (268)
1967	36.5 (112)	63.5 (195)
1968	32.9 (132)	67.1 (269)
1969	25.4 (92)	74.6 (270)
1970	28.0 (99)	72.0 (254)
Czechoslovakia		
1964	39.3 (285)	60.7 (440)
1965	38.5 (289)	61.5 (461)
1966	28.1 (198)	71.9 (506)
1967	31.1 (220)	68.9 (488)
1968	25.3 (201)	74.7 (595)
1969	17.4 (119)	82.6 (563)
1970	17.2 (120)	82.8 (576)
Poland		
1964	35.4 (172)	64.6 (314)
1965	35.7 (170)	64.3 (306)
1966	36.7 (202)	63.3 (349)
1967	32.7 (200)	67.3 (411)
1968	29.2 (182)	70.8 (442)
1969	30.4 (156)	69.6 (358)
1970	31.5 (152)	68.5 (331)
Romania		
1964	58.1 (182)	41.9 (131)
1965	38.0 (101)	62.0 (165)
1966	27.6 (72)	72.4 (189)
1967	24.2 (73)	75.8 (229)
1968	20.5 (66)	79.5 (256)
1969	12.9 (40)	87.1 (270)
1970	19.9 (69)	80.1 (278)

Note: The percentages given above are those of translations from the four major languages; the numbers in parentheses indicate the actual number of books translated.

*German translations include those from both West and East Germany.

Sources: UN Statistical Yearbook, 1966-72.

TABLE 12.3

Feature Films Exported to Hungary
(as percent of total)

From	1960	1965	1970	1971
USSR	37	20	20	25
Czechoslovakia	13	10	7	8
East Germany	7	8	6	6
Poland	1	6	7	6
England	7	5	5	10
United States	7	8	16	12
France	6	12	10	9
Italy	7	9	7	9

Note: The total percent does not add up to 100 because the countries exporting relatively few films to Hungary were left out of this compilation.

Source: Adapted from *Statistical Pocket Book of Hungary, 1972* (Budapest: Statistical Publishing House, 1972), p. 303.

that the Beatles no longer sing together, and that Elton John is a current king. In addition, there are now competent groups in such places as Poland and Hungary in particular who explicitly imitate Western rock and whose enormous popularity is officially tolerated.

In the natural and social sciences as well as the humanities, Eastern Europe has come a long way from the time when Russian textbooks provided all necessary information and insight, including references to Academician "Popov" and his comrades who were said to have made all the major discoveries of this, or for that matter the nineteenth, century. In comparison with the more recent past, cultural exchange—the exchange of scholars, books, periodicals, and information—continues to be complicated, cumbersome, and controversial, but Western presence is undoubtedly felt in every discipline, even the social sciences that are subjected to strict party control. Polish sociologists seem thoroughly familiar with Western methodology, and Hungarian historians can now contemplate the utilization of advanced quantitative techniques in the study of interwar Hungary. Generally speaking, serious scholars usually do have access to Western books and scholarly periodicals.

Still, it is premature to speak of the free flow of Western ideas. Nearly all cultural and other intellectual contacts have to be officially organized and sanctioned. The scholar who can read Western publications in his discipline is not necessarily free to read other Western publications. While the West has certainly begun to reassert its traditional place in East European intellectual life during the last 15 years or so, it has done so in the face of official protests against contamination and ideological subversion. The question this important development poses has been curiously neglected: Is there any linkage between improved cultural contacts and political relations?[22] Should one assume that Western cultural and ideological penetration, to the extent that it has occurred, is in fact a threat to the monopoly of party power as exercised in Eastern Europe?

This question, to which we shall return below, becomes more pertinent as we briefly consider the third cluster of influences: the challenge of the Western "way of life" to Eastern Europe. What we have in mind is not so much the impact of modernization;[23] rather we are concerned with the social aspect of that phenomenon: the emulation of Western trends, customs, habits, fads, and fashions—a phenomenon that is familiar enough to students of Eastern Europe. It consists of a changing transportation mode that idolizes The Car and de-emphasizes public transportation; it consists of miniskirts and wide lapels (when they are "in" in the West); it consists of the growing acceptance of (and improvements in the production of) readymade clothes for the well-to-do as well as the poor; it consists of long hair for guys and straight hair for gals; it consists of blue jeans and boots and a phlegmatic, unduly casual way of walking; it con-sists of teenage rebellion. The party ideologists criticize some or all of these trends and fads and the party and youth papers ridicule "self-styled Western imitators," but their harangues are of no avail. It seems that urban youth, in particular, have embraced Western patterns and lifestyles as the only alternative to that which is officially promulgated. In search of a complete belief system, they cannot easily turn to religion (although some do) and they do not know much about or find irrelevant pre-Communist national tradition or such nationalist ideologies as native populism. Accordingly, if they do not accept Communist ideology and norms of behavior, they have nowhere to turn but West, and thus they find the "fruits" of Western life, both the healthy and the rotten, quite delicious—perhaps because they remain partly forbidden.

Does the politics of Eastern Europe reflect the processes of Westerni-zation that have affected the region's way of life, its intellectual tendencies, and to a far lesser extent its economic subsystem? (It should be obvious that my dis-cussion of "system" and "subsystems" in Eastern Europe differs somewhat from the standard literature of systems analysis. I assume that in Eastern Europe it is the political system that is (1) the all-embracing general system and (2) the driving force and dominating element behind the various subsystems. In this sense, I would speak of a political system and such partly autonomous, partly subordinate subsystems as the social, economic, and cultural ones.[24])

Roughly speaking, there are three alternative answers or explanations in the scholarly literature. The first is that the Westernization of such subsystems has been and will continue to be thoroughly, if not fully, incorporated into and reflected by the political system. While specific institutional forms in Eastern

Europe may differ from those in the West, Western political values and structures are already expressed in Eastern Europe through greater political participation, group representation, certain constitutional limits on party power, and so on.[25] This perception of East European politics is, of course, influenced by Western "developmental determinism" (that is, "it has to happen"); it is also shared by Marxist ideologists, who assume that the political system is always a reflection of the social, cultural, and especially economic environments.

A second explanation posits a partial relationship and overlap between the essentially Soviet-style political institutions on the one hand and the partly Westernized economic, social, and cultural sectors on the other.[26] In this view, Western values reaching East Europeans during the last 15 years or so have reinforced the value orientation of the old and offered an alternative to the young, and this public immersion in Western ideas could not help but modify the political system. The conception here is of partial overlap: Some parts of the political system remain immune to Western influences (partly because of ideology, partly because of the lack of proper training for democracy[27]), while other parts of the political system are seen as responsive to Western influences (as expressed through wider political participation, decentralization, increased role of parliamentary bodies).

The third explanation is one that is most pessimistic concerning the prospects for political change in Eastern Europe through Western influences. It recognizes Western presence in and penetration of the various subsystems, but it assumes no significant infiltration of the political system. In other words, what the people think, what their lifestyles are, and to a lesser extent how the economy functions is one thing; how the party exercises political power is something else.[28] The party, despite its repeated denials to the contrary, can afford to tolerate the transplantation of Western values so long as its power remains firm in the political realm. This, then, is no longer totalitarianism in the sense used in the 1950s (or the way it was in Stalin's time); it is the monopolization of political power. As Adam B. Ulam observed:

> Perhaps a moment will come when some of the prophecies about the corrosive effect of "convergence," certain common traits of all "post-industrial" societies, "consumerism," etc., on Communist authoritarianism will be fulfilled. There are, to be sure, forces of economic and social change constantly pushing against the walls of the authoritarian state. Yet the controlling factor has always been the political one. . . . It is at least premature, then, to expect that the increased volume of economic and cultural contacts will produce a diminution of authoritarian controls in the East or crucially affect the pattern of relations between the Communist states in the area and the USSR. In fact, the local regimes—like the Soviet regime during the last few years—may well tighten their ideological and

political controls to protect themselves from any undesirable fruits
of more extensive contacts with the West, and they may also be less
willing to seek emancipation from their great friend and protector.[29]

Of these alternative explanations, the more optimistic ones were made in the
mid-1960s. At that time, in my judgment, there was ample evidence to support
the second, although perhaps not the first interpretation.[30] Between the fall of
Khrushchev in 1964 and the Soviet-led invasion of Czechoslovakia in 1968,
reformist tendencies in Czechoslovakia and Hungary, the promising areawide
public dialogue on "socialist pluralism," and the apparent Soviet tolerance
toward Romania's semi-independent foreign policy posture combined to give
credence to optimistic long-term evaluations. As a consequence of the preparation for the emerging Soviet-American detente, there was reason to be hopeful
about the East European states obtaining more elbow room that would lead to
political relaxation, liberalization, democratization, or simply more autonomy.

As demonstrated elsewhere, however, the promise of the mid-1960s—the
era that may come to be known in retrospect as a "golden age" in Eastern
Europe—is by and large gone.[31] The 1968 Czechoslovak events, for one, certainly contributed to Soviet-inspired efforts to reverse tendencies toward autonomy and experimentation. Detente, too, has had a harmful effect on Eastern
Europe so far, for it has resulted in stricter ideological measures curtailing
expressions of cultural pluralism. East-West trade and technology transfer continue, but energy shortages have made East European economies more
dependent on the Soviet economy than any other time since the mid-1950s. In
this respect, at least, chances for increased Western presence are practically
nonexistent.

It seems, then, that our apparent belief in and hopes for eventual political
Westernization in Eastern Europe through trade and cultural contacts—indeed,
our reliance on largely apolitical instruments of foreign policy to advance
reconciliation between the two halves of Europe—is an expression of Western
complacency. The present effort, devoid as it is of political and ideological
content, is similar to "liberation" in that both constitute self-deception, holding
out more hope for future transformation in Eastern Europe than we have reason
to expect; conversely, neither is likely to lead to political change of the type that
the West has professed to cultivate in Eastern Europe.

Diplomatically, Eastern Europe has become a "forgotten region"[32] and
is likely to stay that way, although Soviet ambitions in the Balkans, especially
after Tito's death, may still place Eastern Europe on the American agenda. In
the meantime, however, as Andrzej Korbonski convincingly argues, the prospects
for political change in the region depend primarily on domestic developments
and domestic influences—as well as on the Soviet Union.[33] Thus, the important
external variable as far as Eastern Europe is concerned could still be Soviet-
American relations, assuming the present U.S. approach to detente is modified

so as to emphasize negotiations aimed at achieving political deals. In other words, when the United States no longer considers the exchange of goods or scholars as a substitute for, or a first step toward, political adjustment and change and when summit meetings no longer seek pseudo-agreements that conceal failure and project a false sense of hopeful anticipation, then the West may expect to influence the direction of political change in Eastern Europe.

NOTES

1. President Woodrow Wilson's ideas about Eastern Europe at the end of World War I already constituted a form of revisionism. For an excellent analysis of U.S. policy toward the region, see Bennett Kovrig, *The Myth of Liberation: East-Central Europe in U.S. Diplomacy and Politics Since 1941* (Baltimore: Johns Hopkins University Press, 1973). For an up-to-date assessment, see Bennett Kovrig, "Peaceful Engagement Revisited," in *The International Politics of Eastern Europe*, ed. Charles Gati (New York: Praeger Publishers, 1976). Cf. Zbigniew Brzezinski, *Alternative to Partition: For a Broader Conception of America's Role in the World* (New York: McGraw-Hill, 1965); John C. Campbell, *American Policy Toward Communist Eastern Europe: The Choices Ahead* (Minneapolis: University of Minnesota Press, 1965).

2. As quoted in Kovrig, *The Myth of Liberation*, p. 110.

3. Winston S. Churchill, *The Hinge of Fate* (Boston: Houghton Mifflin, 1950), p. 327.

4. U.S. Department of State, *Foreign Relations of the United States: Diplomatic Papers, 1946*, vol. 6 (Washington, D.C., 1969), p. 275. For a detailed, country-by-country account of American policy at the time, see Geir Lundestad, *The American Non-Policy Towards Eastern Europe 1943-1974* (New York: Humanities, 1975).

5. This is not the place to enter into still another debate about cold war origins. For an excellent survey and analysis relevant to my argument here, see James L. Richardson, "Cold-War Revisionism: A Critique," *World Politics* (July 1972): 579-613.

6. Khrushchev's speech of March 6, 1963, as cited in Michel Tatu, *Power in the Kremlin: From Khrushchev to Kosygin* (New York: Viking, 1968), p. 314.

7. *Khrushchev Remembers*, vol. 1 (Boston: Little, Brown, 1970), pp. 415-29. Cf. Janos Radvanyi, *Hungary and the Superpowers: The 1956 Revolution and Realpolitik* (Stanford: Hoover Institution Press, 1972), pp. 12-17. Both Khrushchev and Radvanyi touch on the Chinese role in Soviet decision making, on which see also, "The Origin and Development of the Differences Between the Leadership of the C.P.S.U. and Ourselves," *Peking Review*, no. 37 (1963): 9-10.

8. Of course, the issue is far more complicated than I can indicate here. For a sophisticated, up-to-date analysis of the extent to which Eastern Europe is an asset or a liability to the Soviet Union, see the chapters by Vernon V. Aspaturian (political-ideological aspects), A. Ross Johnson (military-strategic aspects), and Paul Marer (economic aspects) in Gati, ed., *The International Politics of Eastern Europe*.

9. John Campbell, "Yugoslavia," in *The Communist States in Disarray*, ed. Adam Bromke and Teresa Rakowska-Harmstone (Minneapolis: University of Minnesota Press, 1972), p. 196.

10. Lucian Pye, cited in David Apter, *Political Change: Collected Essays* (London: Frank Cass, 1973), p. 153.

11. Zbigniew Brzezinski and William E. Griffith, "Peaceful Engagement in Eastern Europe," *Foreign Affairs*, July 1961, pp. 642-54.

12. Brzezinski, *Alternative to Partition*, p. 48.

13. Ibid., p. 74.

14. Ibid., p. 37.

15. Cf. Alfred G. Meyer, "Theories of Convergence," in *Change in Communist Systems*, ed. Chalmers Johnson (Stanford: Stanford University Press, 1970), pp. 313-41.

16. Ghita Ionescu, *The Politics of the European Communist States* (New York: Praeger Publishers, 1967), pp. 273-74.

17. Ibid., pp. 275-76.

18. Ibid., p. 271.

19. Cf. Robert W. Campbell and Paul Marer, eds., *East-West Trade and Technology Transfer* (Bloomington: Indiana University Developmental Research Center, 1974).

20. Ibid., p. 71.

21. Werner Feld, "The Utility of the EEC Experience for Eastern Europe," *Journal of Common Market Studies* 8, no. 3 (March 1970): 236-61.

22. The problem is briefly dealt with (emphasizing exchange with the Soviet Union) in George Urban, "A Conversation with Robert F. Byrnes: Cultural Exchange and Its Prospects—II," *Survey* 20, no. 4 (Autumn 1974): 41-66.

23. For appropriate definitions and a substantive discussion, see Charles Gati, ed., *The Politics of Modernization in Eastern Europe: Testing the Soviet Model* (New York: Praeger Publishers, 1974). The distinction between the concepts of modernization and Westernization is explored in that volume by Vernon V. Aspaturian, pp. 3 ff.

24. Cf. Morton A. Kaplan, *System and Process in International Politics* (New York: Wiley, 1957).

25. This is the view that has informed some of the writings of Ghita Ionescu and others. See especially Ionescu, *The Politics of the European Communist States* and *The Break-up of the Soviet Empire in Eastern Europe* (Baltimore: Penguin Books, 1965).

26. This view characterizes the writings of (probably) most American students of Eastern Europe. See, for example, Zbigniew Brzezinski, *Between Two Ages: America's Role in the Technetronic Era* (New York: Viking, 1970).

27. The problem of lacking adequate background and proper training for democracy, and the implications of this problem for Eastern Europe, was indicated by an anonymous Hungarian intellectual in the following vivid statement: "It's true, we can't expect to have democracy until international alignments change. But meanwhile, how about changing what we have inside the country, and in people's minds? So we can have democracy when the chance arises. What we have at the moment is more or less a socialist reproduction of what there was before the war. Instead of feudal capitalism, we have feudal socialism. And inside people's heads too, a feudal mentality, of either ordering others about or waiting to be ordered about. If there's going to be change, that's where it'll have to start." Paul Neuburg, *The Hero's Children: The Post-War Generation in Eastern Europe* (London: Constable, 1972), p. 321.

28. For a sophisticated analysis, see Gregory Grossman, "Economic Reform: The Interplay of Economics and Politics," in *The Future of Communism in Europe*, ed. R. V. Burks (Detroit: Wayne State University Press, 1968), pp. 103-40.

29. Adam B. Ulam, "The Destiny of Eastern Europe," *Problems of Communism* 23, no. 1 (January-February 1974): 12.

30. For a somewhat optimistic assessment based on tendencies of the 1960s, see Charles Gati, "Hungary: The Politics of Reform," *Current History* (May 1971): 290-94, 308.

31. The contrast between the 1960s and the 1970s—the contrast between Eastern Europe in the pre-detente and detente periods—is analyzed at greater length in Charles Gati, "East Central Europe: Touchstone for Detente," *Journal of International Affairs* 28 (1972): 158-74.

32. Cf. Charles Gati, "The Forgotten Region," *Foreign Policy* 19 (Summer 1975): 135-45.

33. Andrzej Korbonski, "Evaluating External Influences on East European Politics," paper prepared for delivery at the 1975 APSA Convention. See also his "The Prospects for Change in Eastern Europe," *Slavic Review* 33, no. 2 (June 1974): 219-39.

CHAPTER
13

NATIONAL-INTERNATIONAL
LINKAGES IN YUGOSLAVIA:
THE POLITICAL CONSEQUENCES
OF OPENNESS
William Zimmerman

Considerations of space rule out the possibility here of an all-encompassing treatment of the impact of international-national linkages on Yugoslav internal political development. (Even within the more limited focus of this essay, there are important gaps in our knowledge that, when filled, might produce some alteration in the nature of our assessments.) Instead the focus is on the consequences of a phenomenon unique to Yugoslavia among Communist countries, namely, the enormous migration, as a result of conscious policy choices by the Yugoslav regime, of workers abroad.*

How unique that phenomenon is when contrasted with patterns typically associated with Communist systems, and how much it typifies—and reinforces—

This essay is part of a larger, ongoing project, the theme of which is the impact of the international environment on Yugoslav political development. Data employed in the paper were obtained while in Yugoslavia as Fulbright-Hays Fellow in 1970 and during a brief visit in June 1973 under auspices of a Ford grant to associates of the University of Michigan's Center for Russian and East European Studies for research pertaining to mass migration, mobility, and social change. The author benefited from many conversations with Yugoslav scholars and wishes in particular to thank Professors Ivo Vinski of the Economics Institute (Zagreb) and Ivo Baucic of the Geographic Institute (Zagreb), and the Institute for International Politics and Trade (Belgrade), which provided with an office and seven months without committee meetings during the 1970 stay.

*I stress the role of conscious policy choices because I believe that in our effort ultimately to construct typologies of systems with regard to their degree of linkages to the international system, we are apt to focus on more ecological factors. Size, degree of authoritarianism, and the existence or lack thereof of a potential counterelite in exile all matter. Nevertheless, it is to policy choices primarily that we must look to explain the nature and consequences of the penetration of a national system.

much of the general orientation of the Yugoslav political system, is illustrated by a brief recapitulation of the two basic images of Communist systems that traditionally have been central to Communist studies. The first is the Soviet model, the second the satellite model. In terms of the relationship of the state and society to the international environment, the two models diverge diametrically in one major respect. While the image of the Soviet-type system shares little in common with general comparative politics models, it does presume that sources external to the nation-state are not of major consequence in explaining the state's political development.[1] Indeed, in terms of its relationship to its international environment, the Soviet-type system was an essentially closed system. In that respect, the Soviet model, to the extent it was actualized, was similar to the billiard ball model of the traditional states-as-actors approach.[2] In such an imagery, the political system would react to the international environment—but only in a mechanical sense; such reactions did not entail goal adaptation or internal organizational adaptation. Nor were non-national actors a part of the internal policy process. Great attention was attached to ensuring the impermeability of the nation-state's boundaries, again as in the billiard ball model. In particular, ideas and influences originating from outside the system were systematically prevented from entering the country and the outflow of the state's citizenry was rigidly regulated. Consistent further with their closed system imagery, Soviet-type political systems were economically autarkic.

In the satellite imagery, by contrast, the nation-state is highly penetrated and the national-international linkage is the key to explaining internal political development. The penetration, however, originates from only a single source; other sources of influence, even those emanating from other satellites, are excluded. Each satellite was connected, in Karl Deutsch's terms, to a "decision center outside the state from which decisions inside the state . . . [can] be predicted."[3] In extremis, the satellite imagery is one in which the putative nation-state is merely yet another traditional political institution assumed to have autonomous capacity that has been transformed into a mechanism for the downward communication of commands. To the extent a Communist system is truly a Soviet-type political system, to that extent it is automatically not a satellite, inasmuch as a Soviet-type system excludes penetration even by the Soviet Union; a substantial part of the story of relations among Communist states has centered on Soviet efforts to induce behavior on the part of other Communist states typical of that associated with satellite status—only to be rebuffed successfully by such states, in large part because they had been created in the Soviet image.

In other respects the two images shared much in common and bespoke a time when Western analysts and Communist commentators alike knew what they had in mind when they referred to a Communist system. As evidenced, inter alia, by the salience that borders acquired in both images, both models depicted systems whose leadership evidenced low trust in the citizenry of the respective state and whose efforts to control the sorts of influences to which the citizenry was exposed involved the virtual monopolization of the socialization process. The pattern of political controls was such that there was high unity of command within the polity and extensive penetration of the society by the political system. Just as the Soviet-type system insulated itself from the external environment, in both images the regime was insulated from society; the behaviorally relevant inputs originated in the political system itself and not in society. In neither case was there substantial role for autonomous actors within the system. Finally, Communist systems evidenced numerous characteristic public polity features, a fact often forgotten by Western specialists in their attention to control mechanisms and social system penetration. Thus, planner sovereignty rather than consumer sovereignty prevailed. Nationalization was widespread. Capitalism, the capital market, and capitalists, foreign and domestic, were eliminated; comparatively egalitarian wage policies were introduced and full employment approximated through the guise, primarily, of "political" factories and massive underemployment.

It should be noted that these two images no longer provide a highly accurate fit with the reality of the overwhelming majority of the European Communist systems. At a minimum, "domesticism"[4]—with its implication that the locus of the decisional center is within the state—characterizes the erstwhile satellites: They have, in many instances, substantially increased their ties with external sources other than the USSR and reduced the extent to which they are penetrated by the Soviet Union. In several European Communist systems the societies have been depoliticized to an appreciable extent; the demand for affirmation has been replaced by regime tolerance of mere compliance on the part of the citizenry.

In the Soviet case, too, there is a considerable recognition on the part of specialists that the impact of international-national linkages is greater than we had customarily thought. In the study of Soviet foreign policy, the early tendency to underplay even the reactive quality of Soviet foreign policy has long since dissipated. No longer is it the case that models that see Soviet foreign policy goals as deriving entirely from the internal dynamics of the Soviet system are regarded as conceptually adequate for explaining foreign policy behavior of a Soviet-type system. Indeed, mechanically reactive models or approaches to Soviet foreign policy have to a certain degree been supplanted by approaches that emphasize learning, institutional adaptation, and goal adaptation.[5] The impact of changes in international context on Soviet elite perspectives has been stressed.[6] Furthermore, there is a fairly widespread appreciation now of the feedback on domestic political processes resulting from foreign policy behavior: that foreign policy decisions have an impact on the institutional relationship within the Soviet Union, for instance, between the Politburo qua oligarchy and the general or first secretary qua dictator; that individual careers are influenced by the success or failure of foreign policy moves; and that the political position of key subelites and groups is influenced by events in the international system and the foreign policy of the Soviet regime.[7] Finally, it is reasonably well settled that extranational actors can and actually have played a role in the Soviet political process.[8]

Nevertheless, it is Yugoslavia, especially during the late 1960s and early 1970s, that stands out in greatest contrast to the Soviet and satellite-type models, both in general terms and with specific reference to the nature and sources of international-national linkages. In that time span, the authoritarian quality of Yugoslav politics has paled in comparison with that typically associated with Soviet-type systems and the regime has been generally committed to a posture of high trust in its citizenry. The regime's involvement in society has been markedly less intrusive and the reciprocal impact of societal forces on the polity manifestly more in evidence. The political system itself has been distinctly more pluralist (although here, especially, events in the past two years have greatly qualified this generalization). In the years 1966-70, furthermore, there were impressive steps in the direction of investing formal state institutions with functions associated with such institutions in Western constitutional systems. Finally, throughout the period the policies of the regime were generally such as to encourage, in several respects dramatically, the permeability of the country's borders to both the outflow of Yugoslavs and the inflow of external ideas and influences.

The most important of these policy choices were those made in connection with the economic reforms of 1965. The economic intent of the reforms (it was evident that for many there were political values to be served as well[9]) was to decentralize economic decisions from the planners to the market; to eliminate the immensely inefficient political factories with their attendant underemployment; to encourage the international mobility of resources, both labor and capital, by devaluing the dinar (and ultimately making it convertible); and to allow the international market to serve as the efficient allocator of values.

The opportunity to make these decisions, however, would not have occurred had not Yugoslavia in the immediate postwar period closely approximated the Soviet model. Primarily because the Yugoslav regime did successfully imitate the Soviet experience—it had a largely monolithic party organization, it had come to power largely on its own, and at that time was far in advance of other European democracies in the radical transformation of society—it was able to resist Soviet pressures whose intent was the satellitization of Yugoslavia. It was only after the Soviet-Yugoslav split that the Yugoslav regime moved in a thoroughgoing way toward what came to be known as Titoism.[10] The decisions, furthermore, probably would not have been made had it not been that during the years after the Soviet Union broke with Yugoslavia, both the Yugoslav citizenry and the United States proved highly willing to lend their support to the regime's conciliationist policies at home and independent policies abroad. The implementation of the decisions would probably not have progressed as far as it did, moreover, had not Aleksandar Rankovic been removed in 1966.[11] Rankovic apparently concluded (correctly) that the economic reforms were fraught with important political consequences. Yugoslavia would be integrated into (Western) Europe and into the (capitalist) international market to an extent far greater than any other Communist system. The international dimensions of the reform further threatened to increase the problems of internal political control and to make it more likely that the Yugoslav citizenry would be exposed to external influences from the West, in the long run producing a more Western-oriented Yugoslav foreign policy.

In the event, with the fall of Rankovic, the international dimensions of the reforms rapidly took shape. The borders became highly permeable. It is, of course, the case that many of the keys to Yugoslavia's future political evolution are largely internal (the imminent succession problem, nationality relations, economic tensions). Nevertheless, Yugoslavia is now sufficiently coupled to its international environment and sufficient subject to external influences emanating from plural sources that it is impossible accurately to describe the political evolution of Yugoslavia in the late 1960s and early 1970s (or to make intelligent extrapolations further into the 1970s) without great attention to national-international linkages. Not only are these linkages important per se but they have a significant bearing on the changing configuration of nationality relations, interclass and inter-regional income distribution, and may even play a role in the ultimate resolution of the succession problem. Moreover, the policy of opening the borders has come to serve as one of the key symbols (along with market socialism and self-management) of the distinct and positive in the Yugoslav socialist variant—so much so that a major alteration in the policy would constitute a fundamental reorientation in the Yugoslav system. Thus, for the purposes of examining the impact of national and international linkages on the internal evolution of a Communist system, Yugoslavia is an especially interesting deviant case.

The impact of international-national linkages on internal Yugoslav development is also highly topical. In the years after the fall of Rankovic, the criticism of the open borders policy became muted (except for the calls for a radical solution to the unemployment policy voiced in the student strikes of 1968) and the Yugoslavs could congratulate themselves in 1969 that "The policy of good neighbour relations and 'open boundaries' being pursued by Yugoslavia has yielded valuable positive experience not only as regard the feasibility of fruitful cooperation and peaceful coexistence between states with different social systems, but also at the level of establishing and expanding channels of communication for direct contacts between individuals and nongovernmental groups in society."[12]

In the 1970s, however, the consequences, intended and unintended, had begun to call forth substantial criticism, from various quarters, of at least facets of the decision so as to raise seriously the issue of whether the basic elements of the open border policy would continue. Moreover, the various critiques of the consequences of an almost classically liberal attitude toward the allocative function of the market and permeability of a country's boundaries come at a time when other European Communist countries, including the Soviet Union, are likely to be increasing their ties to the international economic system and increasing somewhat the permeability of their borders.

THE YUGOSLAV MIGRATION: A PROFILE

Central to the policy of opening Yugoslavia's borders was the decision to allow and indeed encourage Yugoslav citizens to go abroad "temporarily" to work—thus joining their confreres from other southern European countries in the massive economic migration to northern and western Europe, especially West Germany. The decision was part and parcel of an attitude shift: "From the end of the Second World War to the end of the 1950s, going to work in a foreign country was treated as well nigh a betrayal" and hence "in practical language it meant also political emigration."[13] But by the late 1960s the mainstream Yugoslav view cast aspersions on "the contemporary mentality of camp socialism" which seems "shocked by the fact that our people are so easily permitted to leave their homeland to return without any prejudices after a few years."[14]

With the liberalization of the passport service, the political conditions for massive economic migration were created. As Zvonimir Komarica put it, the constitutional provision that each person may choose his own employment became "applicable in the region of foreign migration."[15] With the reforms of 1965, the economic incentives were provided. These incentives were manifest: an immediate consequence of economic decentalization was a decrease in total number employed and a corresponding increase in "the number of people looking for employment"—to use the circumlocution of the Yugoslav *Statistical Yearbook*. Where there were 3,662,000 employed in 1965, there were 4,000 fewer in 1966 and still fewer (3,561,000) in 1967. After 1967 the number employed increases again. but it is not until 1969 that the number is in excess of that in 1965 (see Table 13.1). The number of unemployed increased steadily between 1965 and 1969. In 1969, the number of unemployed reached its peak and then decreased somewhat, but it still remained well in excess of the 1965-67 figures (see Table 13.2). At the same time the devaluation of the dinar greatly increased the attractiveness of working abroad. In Ivo Vinski's words, the new dinar exchange rate, "along with stimulating the import of goods and services, stimulated perhaps even more greatly the export of living labor in the sense of the employment of our workers abroad."[16]

And go they did—not only the unemployed but, as it turned out, a sizable number of the employed (including those with skills much in demand in Yugoslavia who were attracted by the relatively higher wages abroad). Exactly how

TABLE 13.1

Employed in Yugoslavia, 1964-70
(thousands)

Year	Number Employed
1964	3,608
1965	3,662
1966	3,582
1967	3,561
1968	3,587
1969	3,706
1970	3,850

Source: *Statisticki godisnjak Jugoslavije 1972* (Belgrade: Savezni zavod za statistiku, 1972), p. 89.

many are abroad is difficult to report; estimates vary considerably depending whether the source is reporting Yugoslav data or the data of the recipient countries (and on how many axes the author has to grind). One can find estimates for specific years or specific countries that are half again as large as those of more conservative sources.

TABLE 13.2

Unemployed in Yugoslavia, 1964-71
(thousands)

Year	Number Unemployed	Unqualified or Semiqualified	Skilled
1964	212.5	180.5	32.0
1965	237.0	198.6	38.4
1966	257.6	182.2	51.8
1967	269.1	179.2	66.0
1968	311.0	192.9	92.1
1969	330.6	215.2	88.9
1970	319.6	212.0	83.0
1971	291.3	156.7	81.7

Source: *Statisticki godisnjak Jugoslavije 1972* (Belgrade: Savezni zavod za statistiku, 1972), p. 100.

TABLE 13.3

Yugoslav Workers Abroad, 1964-72
(thousands)

Year	Workers in Europe
1964	100
1965	140
1966	220
1967	320
1968	400
1969	520
1969-70	566
1970	700
1971	608
1972	760

Source: 1964-70: Vinski, "Zaposljavanje Jugoslavena u inozemstvu," *Ekonomski presled*, nos. 7-8, July-August 1971. 1969-70: Ivo Baucic, *Porijeklo i Struktura Radnika iz Jugoslavije u SR Njemackoj* (Zagreb: Institut za Geografiju, 1970), p. 12. 1971: *Statisticki Bilten*, no. 679 (1971), "Lica na privremenom radu u inostranstvu"–this summarizes data acquired as a result of the March 1971 census; Vladimir Grecic points out in this thesis *Savremene migracije radne snage u Evropi* (Belgrade: Institut za Medjunarodnu politiki privredu, 1972), p. 230, that there is a gap of 152,000 in the expected and actual totals of the census. If all of these Yugoslavs were abroad and 89 percent of them were in Western Europe (as the census figures suggest) there were approximately 742,000 Yugoslavs in Europe in 1971. 1972: Ivo Baucic interview.

Nevertheless, a sense of the magnitude of the phenomenon can be achieved and an impression conveyed of the rapidity with which what began as a trickle became transformed into a spate and by the early 1970s had become a flood. How this came to be is suggested by Table 13.3 and Figure 13.1. At the onset of the reforms there were approximately 100,000 Yugoslavs working in Europe. By 1967 that number had trebled. By 1970 the number had more than doubled over the 1967 estimates. Finally, by 1973, while the rate of increase of migration to Western Europe had tapered off, the absolute number continued to increase; moreover, all indications were that the migration to countries outside Europe, Australia in particular had scarcely abated.

The figures reported by *NIN* in spring 1972, "drawn from the most recent statistics of the European countries and the testimony of our Yugoslav diplomatic representatives abroad" indicate that at the end of 1971 there were a total of 985,500 workers abroad, of which 785,500 were in Western Europe (478,000 in the Federal Republic of Germany) and roughly 100,000 in Australia (120,000), Canada, the United States, and New Zealand.[17] Ivo Baucic, perhaps

FIGURE 13.1

Thousands of Yugoslav Workers in Europe, 1964-72

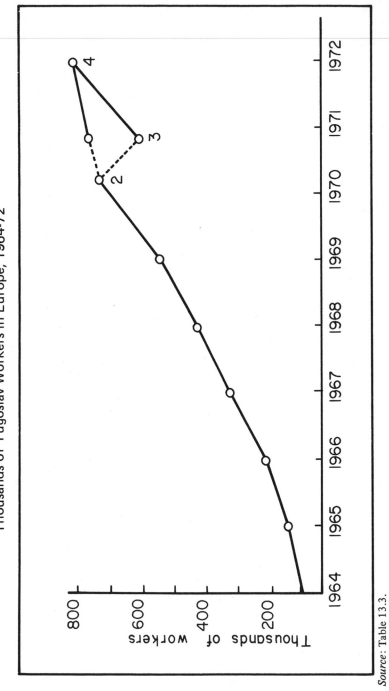

Source: Table 13.3.

the most careful student of Yugoslav migration, places the West European figure at the end of 1972 at 760,000 and that for Germany at 465,000. In 1973, what may have been the peak figure of 860,000 was reached. In 1974 and 1975 the recession in Europe produced a decrease in the number of Yugoslavs in Western Europe. In contrast to the 860,000 figure for 1973, by 1974 the number had decreased to 800,000 and then in 1975 to 770,000. (It remains to be seen whether the 1973 figure will be quickly re-attained.) In addition to those working in Europe, moreover, there were by the end of 1975 an additional 200,000 Yugoslavs working in Australia, Canada, the United States, and elsewhere outside of Europe, approximately 250,000 dependents of Yugoslav workers in Europe, and roughly 100,000 dependents among those Yugoslavs outside Europe. Thus it seems safe to assert that something on the order of a million Yugoslavs are working abroad, a number that plus dependents indicates that the total number of Yugoslav citizens abroad at the end of 1975 was approximately 1,340,000.[18] By way of comparison, the population in 1971 of Bosnia and Hercegovina was approximately 3,746,000; Montenegro, 530,000; Croatia, 4,227,000; Macedonia, 1,647,000; Slovenia, 1,725,000; and Serbia (including Vojvodina and Kosovo), 8,447,000. The Yugoslavs are only engaging in slight hyperbole when their workers abroad are termed "our seventh republic."

Were there a "seventh republic" composed of workers temporarily abroad, it would differ in many respects from an equivalent microcosm of Yugoslavia. A disproportionately large share of the workers abroad have emigrated from Croatia and/or are Croatian by nationality. The fraction of Yugoslavs abroad who are from Croatia was particularly high during the years 1965-68. In five studies treating that time span, estimates of the Croatian contribution to the European migration range between 40.5 and 59.4 percent of the Yugoslav total. (The latter estimate was obtained from a study conducted by the Sarajevo and Zagreb radio stations; presumably disproportionately large numbers of persons from Bosnia and Hercegovina and Croatia would be among those surveyed.[19]) Since 1968 the relative number of persons from Croatia as a percentage of the total Yugoslav population abroad has decreased; even so, about half again as many persons from Croatia (33.3 percent) are abroad as one would expect simply by extrapolating from the 1971 census. Among the other republics, only Bosnia and Hercegovina (20.4 percent) and Macedonia (8.3 percent) are represented abroad by a number larger than their percentages (18.3 and 8.0 percent, respectively) of the total Yugoslav population. The others either have a number abroad that approximates in percentage terms their fraction of the Yugoslav population, or is considerably lower, most notably in the case of Serbia proper (17.0 instead of 25.6 percent), Kosovo (3.6 rather than 6.1 percent), and Montenegro (1.2 percent of the total instead of 2.6 percent) (see Table 13.4).

TABLE 13.4

Yugoslavs Abroad, by Republic, 1971 Census

Republic	Percentage of Total Number Abroad	Percentage of Total Yugoslav Population
Bosnia and Hercegovina	20.2	18.3
Croatia	33.3	21.6
Macedonia	8.3	8.0
Montenegro	1.2	2.6
Slovenia	7.3	8.4
Serbia	29.6	41.2
Serbia proper	17.1	25.6
Vojvodina	9.0	9.5
Kosovo	3.4	6.1
Total	99.9	100.1

Source: Statisticki Bilten, no. 679, p. 9.

TABLE 13.5

Workers Abroad, by Nationality

Nationality	Percent Abroad	Percent Total Yugoslavia
Albanians	5.2	6.4
Croatians	38.9	22.1
Hungarians	2.9	2.3
Macedonians	5.7	5.8
Montenegrins	0.8	2.5
"Muslims"	6.4	8.4
Serbs	28.5	39.8
Slovenes	7.0	8.2
"Yugoslavs"	0.7	0.4
Others	3.9	4.2
Total	100.0	100.1

Source: Derived from *Statisticki Bilten*, no. 729 (1971); "Nacionalni sastav stanovnistva po opstiniama," p. 6; *Statisticki Bilten*, no. 671, p. 13; "Nacionalni mapa SFRJ," *NIN*, no. 1149 (January 14, 1973): 31-32.

Almost the same generalization obtains when the numbers abroad are computed in terms of nationality declared in the 1971 census. Slightly more than a fifth of Yugoslavs identified themselves as Croatian in the 1971 census (21.6 percent); slightly less than two-fifths (38.9 percent) of those abroad were Croatian. Of the larger nationalities, the Magyars (Hungarians) are the only other nationality with a larger percentage (2.9 percent) of the total abroad than of the total within Yugoslavia (see Table 13.5).

The age profile of the workers abroad also differs from that at home. Of the Yugoslav work force, 31 percent are women, and the same percentage abroad. Yugoslav women working abroad typically are much younger than the men. As a result, a composite age profile is somewhat misleading; needless to say, those who go abroad come largely from the ranks of those under 35. Nevertheless, the age of men working abroad appears to be on the average older than Yugoslavs widely believe. Table 13.6 enumerates: (1) age profiles of the men in Baucic's survey of Croatian workers abroad, (2) the age structure of those from Croatia working abroad, and (3) the age structure of all Yugoslavs working abroad. Briefly put, if Baucic's sample is representative, whereas 70 percent of the total Yugoslav population working abroad is under 35, almost half the men abroad are over 35.

Finally, the work skills of those who go abroad vary in significant ways from the profile of the Yugoslav domestic work force. There has been much confusion on this score in Yugoslav commentary, with great credence attached to the view that Yugoslav workers in Western Europe—in sharp contrast to the Italian, Spanish, Turnkish, Portuguese, and Greek workers—tend to be skilled

TABLE 13.6

Yugoslav Workers Abroad, by Age

Age	Baucic Study of Men Abroad[a]	Croatia[b]	Yugoslavia[b]
< 24	14.0	32.4	32.7
25-29	17.9	18.3	19.8
30-34	20.2	17.0	17.5
35-39	20.7	13.6	13.3
> 40	27.2	17.5	15.9
Unknown		1.2	0.8
Total	100.0	100.0	100.0

Sources:

[a] Ivo Baucic and Zivko Maravic, *Vracanje i zaposljavanje vanskih migranata iz SR Hrvatske* (Zagreb: Institut za geografiju, 1971), p. 29.

[b]*Statisticki Bilten*, no. 679, p. 10.

TABLE 13.7

Yugoslav Workers: A Skills Profile, December 1970
(in percent)

	Yugoslavia[a]	Croatia[a]	Croatian Workers Sample Abroad[b]	Men Among Croatian Sample Abroad[b]
Unskilled	24.5	14.3	48.6	43.1
Semiskilled	12.7	16.2	9.8	11.0
Skilled	25.2	28.9	29.9	35.7
Highly skilled	6.6	8.8	3.3	4.3
Elementary school	7.9	4.0	2.7	1.5
High school	14.2	15.5	4.4	3.2
University and advanced schooling	8.9	12.2	1.3	1.1
Total	100.0	99.9	100.0	99.9

Sources:
[a] Computed from *Statisticki godisnjak Jugoslavije 1972*, pp. 93, 357.
[b]*Statisticki Bilten*, no. 679, p. 10.

rather than unskilled. In part, this view stems from a German study of workers in Germany, which found that 55 percent of the Yugoslav workers in German factories were skilled and only 14 percent were unskilled.[20] In fact, however, all the evidence indicates that, overall, skilled workers go abroad in proportions comparable to their numbers in the Yugoslav work force, and that disproportionately it is the unskilled and semiskilled who go abroad (see Table 13.7). The first job that the Yugoslav peasant obtains after he leaves the land is in Munich.

What is also clear is that, of those who go abroad to work whom the Yugoslav Statistical Office classifies as workers—roughly two-fifths of the total—a rather large number (41.6 percent) are skilled workers; even among these workers (narrowly conceived), however, the fraction of nonskilled and semiskilled workers abroad is higher than the national average (see Table 13.8).

NATIONAL-INTERNATIONAL LINKAGES
AND THE YUGOSLAV MIGRATION

We have already suggested that the major variable explaining the phenomenon of the economic and presumably temporary emigration of Yugoslav workers abroad was a public policy choice that was one of the defining characteristics of the Yugoslav opening to the world. Given that decision, it is an intriguing illustration of the significance of national-international linkages to identify other elements that influence the magnitude or composition of the migration. As one enumerates a list of factors that are either direct or contingent causes of the migration, its volume, and its composition, it rapidly becomes apparent how inextricably linked even the most ostensibly "internal" variables are with events and actors in the environment external to Yugoslavia. Any such list, for instance, would include high politics narrowly conceived, level of development, informal communication networks, and individual preference patterns.

As we have seen, high politics mattered in 1965-66: Had not Rankovic been ousted, the implementation of the reforms—and with it the opening of the borders—would presumably have been modest in scope. The connections that Rankovic's police had with their Soviet counterparts were by all accounts a major element in his political demise; it is easily imaginable that some future major shift in the Yugoslav leadership might again occur, indirectly producing a significant change in migration behavior. One can say with near certainty that the extent and direction of Yugoslavia's general linkages with the international environment are still a matter of central import in the country's high politics.[21]

TABLE 13.8

A Skills Profile of Those Classified as Workers by the Yugoslav Statistical Office
(in percent)

	In Yugoslavia	Abroad
Unskilled	24.1	28.2
Semiskilled	10.4	10.6
Skilled	25.6	41.4
Highly skilled	6.6	4.0
Elementary school	7.2	3.7
High school	15.3	8.1
University and advanced schooling	10.3	3.7
Unknown	0.5	0.3
Total	100.0	100.0

Source: Drawn from *Statisticki Bilten*, no. 679, and computed by Ivo Vinski, "Privredni razvoj, zaposljavanje i nezaposlenost kadrova," in *Dadrovska funksija u udruzenom radu*, ed. J. Brekic (Zagreb, 1972), p. 66.

Furthermore, in the aftermath of Tito's well known "Letter," the purge of Marko Nikezic (the Serbian republic party leader), and the removal of Stane Kavcic (then Slovenian prime minister), all during fall 1972, there seemed for a while a genuine possibility that internal "consolidation" would imply the extensive use of administrative measures to restrict the outflow of Yugoslavs wishing to leave the country.[22]

Given political conditions allowing international migration, it turns out, not surprisingly, that knowing a country's level of development goes a long way toward explaining migration flows. Level of development is a relative measure. To explain Yugoslav migration in terms of level of development implies that Yugoslavia is highly integrated into the international economic system. Indeed, it is not inappropriate to regard much of Yugoslavia (as explained below I exclude the least developed regions from this statement) as constituting a part of (Western) Europe and to treat Yugoslav migration as simply one facet of an equilibrium mechanism of an economic market for labor labeled "Europe," where demands for services call forth a response in labor supply.[23] To do so, naturally, takes us well away from internal Yugoslav variables. Instead, Yugoslavia is approximated by one point on a straight-line regression equation for Europe as a whole. In that equation, gross national product per capita predicts whether a given country will be a net exporter or net importer of labor. An illustration of this approach is provided by Vladimir Grecic's thesis, *The Contemporary Migration of the Work Force in Europe*. Using figures largely drawn from 1968-70, he derives an equation that parsimoniously depicts ($r = 0.82$) European migration patterns; namely, where Y = gross national product per capita and X = migration, $Y = \$1,382.18 - 125.58x$ (see Figure 13.2).

A problem with Grecic's treatment is that in the Yugoslav case low GNP per capita is largely associated with low migration—although it is perhaps significant that the converse is not quite true. Croatia, as we saw, not Slovenia, heads the list. The reason, I suspect, is a simple one: Some parts of Yugoslavia—Kosovo and Montenegro in particular—are barely integrated into a Yugoslav market, much less a European market. Put somewhat differently, it is probably the case that there exists a certain threshold that is associated with "the passing of traditional society"[24]—to use Daniel Lerner's famous phrase—and that can be expressed in terms of dollar per capita. Below a certain level, say, $500 per person annually, an area (in this instance, a republic or an autonomous region) is largely self-sufficient economically and its citizens are generally not plugged into communication networks extending much beyond the village, nor have they sufficiently extricated themselves from a patriarchal and ordered society to be able to empathize in Lerner's sense—to imagine themselves in another role than the one in which they find themselves. To go from Kosovo to work in Slovenia is in this respect to go abroad.

The role of communications networks in affecting the decision to go abroad also significantly involves national-international linkages. Especially at

FIGURE 13.2

Migration and GNP Per Capita

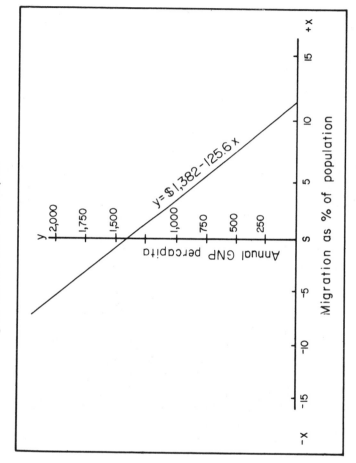

Source: Vladimir Grecic, *Savremene migracije radne snage u Europi* (Belgrade: Institut za medjunarodnu politiku privredu, 1975), p. 154.

the outset of the mass migration there was an important difference between areas where migration was well established before World War II or even World War I (such as the coastal and mountain regions of Croatia, Macedonia) and those where this was not the case; Grecic in his study reports estimates that "in 1931 the number of Yugoslav workers in Western Europe amounted to about 130,000 persons."[25] For persons from these areas there existed a relevant experience from a previous generation: "It is understandable that it will be easier to reach a decision to emigrate for a person whose father or grandfather has worked in some foreign country."[26] Moreover, there might well be a relative or close friend living abroad who could facilitate a move (providing temporary quarters, making inquiries about jobs).[27] Consequently, it is also not surprising that there are patterns with respect to where the workers migrate: the Croatians went initially primarily to Germany, while those from Serbia went primarily to France.[28] Once these linkages had been reestablished, persons continued to gravitate in directions where relatives, friends, and, as the process burgeoned, friends of friends resided—although presumably as the phenomenon became institutionalized (ads in the papers, announcements over radio and television, direct solicitation through federal or republic employment bureaus), the relative role of informal ties diminished.

Finally, in our list of factors ostensibly internal to Yugoslavia, there is the matter of individual preference patterns. We know something about the reasons Yugoslavs give for their departure abroad. The overwhelming number go abroad because they can earn more money than at home.[29] When asked why they went abroad, roughly two-thirds of a Bosnian sample responded "better wages" and a quarter indicated that they were unemployed.[30] In Baucic's study (based on interview data acquired from Croatians returning home during Christmas vacation 1970-71), the "possibility of employment" found a considerable response (36.3 percent), especially among women (61.2 percent). Nevertheless, for the total group the role of higher wages is as striking as in the Bosnian study: The Croatian workers who have jobs go abroad in order to earn more money (9 percent) and usually for a specific purpose: to build a house (19.1 percent), to buy an apartment (6.3 percent), farm equipment (6.5 percent), a private car (2.7 percent), or to open a business (6.2 percent).[31] Moreover, when asked what wages they would require to take a job in Yugoslavia, the respondents' average response was 50 percent greater than the earnings of the average worker in Yugoslavia—although much less than the average Yugoslav worker earns in Germany. To be exact, the average wage in Croatia in 1970 was 1,254 dinars monthly; the mean response of the Croatian workers sample was 1,820 dinars; their average salary in Germany, the equivalent of 3,300 dinars.[32]

If, in explaining the migration phenomenon it makes sense to couple "internal" factors with transnational phenomena and attitudes, there is all the more reason to accord attention to the conscious policies of major corporate actors external to the Yugoslav environment. These actors include not only states (the great powers, their interactions and their separate decisions; significant regional powers, most notably Germany; and contiguous states) but also international organizations and the permanent political emigration.

At first glance, the connection between the interaction of the superpowers and migration patterns may seem rather tenuous. Nevertheless, the improvement in U.S.-Soviet relations seems in 1972-73 to have furthered the general sense among the Yugoslav elite of the importance of going it alone—with the result that new legislation was specifically designed to prevent those who had not satisfied their military obligation from going abroad to work. Similarly, direct criticisms by Soviet commentators of the policy of allowing workers abroad, or even a more broad critique of the general Yugoslav orientation, may have a bearing on the policies adapted with a view to regulating the outflow of workers. At a time when Belgrade is clearly sensitive to Soviet remarks, observations in the Soviet press designed to undercut the arguments of "some persons in the West" (who accentuate the positive about the internal consequences of a mass migration policy) by stressing that West Germany "completely avoids any investment whatsoever in infrastructure (kindergartens, hospitals, schools)"; that "the facts reveal a slowing of economic growth in a number of countries exporting the main productive force—workers"; "that the emptying and degradation of entire geographic regions . . . [and] a worsening of the age structure of the population is taking place"; may find a distinct resonance in Yugoslavia.[33] That having been said, the Soviet willingness to in fact deliver a promised $1.3 billion in credits was much more likely to have an impact on the marginal propensity of Yugoslavs to migrate; for every Yugoslav impressed by arguments stemming from Soviet sources, there is another disposed to reject a proposal that smacks of the Soviet model.[34]

The same could also be said for the United States and the International Bank for Reconstruction and Development—the United States, by reducing the risks for private American investment in Yugoslavia, the IBRD, by its policy of encouraging infrastructural development in Yugoslavia and by its cultivation of Adriatic development schemes and, more recently, the development of the south.

It is probably the European Economic Community and Germany, however, that have the greatest capacity to influence Yugoslav migration patterns. There is little reason to quarrel with Svetislav Polovina's observation that "the signing of the Rome Agreement in 1957 and the founding of the European Economic Community represented the most significant step [in the liberalization of migration flows among countries]. And if the creation of the EEC included in the integration process only six West European countries, it constituted the beginning of an integrated European labor market inasmuch as the work force of countries which were not members of the Community (Spain, Portugal, Greece, Turkey, Yugoslavia) were included [in it]."[35]

Efforts to regulate the flow of workers entirely through employment bureaus will require extensive German cooperation. Germany would be most likely to counter the "lost human capital" argument and to provide transfers to cover the cost of schooling the Yugoslav children who remain at home while the parent or parents work abroad.[36] The mild 1967 recession sharply reduced the outflow of Yugoslav workers to Germany; any major alteration in the present number of Yugoslav workers in Germany (three-fifths of the total number in Europe) is likely to result either from a major German depression or, more probably, the bringing of the mountain to Mahomet—through German-financed factories in Yugoslavia.[37]

Finally, there is the political emigration; its existence surely had a deterrent effect on the critical decision to open the borders. Were it to have a substantial impact on the attitudes of Yugoslav workers abroad, this would almost surely have its impact on Yugoslav migration policies—not just in the already considerable efforts of the Yugoslav government to inform and shape the opinions of its workers abroad, but in the number and qualities of those allowed to go abroad.

THE OUT-MIGRATION OF WORKERS: POLITICAL CONSEQUENCES

We have written thus far of the linkages tying the Yugoslav national environment, directly or indirectly, to Yugoslav migration patterns. The other side of the coin is the impact of the workers abroad—a linkage group, in Deutsch's term—on Yugoslav political development.[38] What difference does the out-migration of workers make for internal Yugoslav political development? What are the political consequences of openness—and against whose criteria?

Measured against the criteria employed in deciding to allow the workers to go abroad, the policy must be judged successful. Although we do not know, as yet, much about attitude changes as a result of the workers' experience abroad, the absence of any drastic antiregime behavior involving those who have been abroad strongly suggests that in gross terms the confidence in the political trustworthiness of citizens has been justified.* The policy has paid off handsomely in terms of remissions; Yugoslav workers return more hard currency to the country than tourism earns. The export of labor is Yugoslavia's major

---

*Opinion surveys do exist that would allow us to ascertain whether those who have gone abroad, those who intend to go abroad, and those who have never gone abroad and have no intention of going abroad are different. It remains to be seen whether these materials (which are for internal use) will be made available to the foreign scholar.

industry. The hard currency earnings in turn contribute somewhat to other market socialist goals—the modernization of plant, gradual approximation of convertibility, and the linking of the Yugoslav economy to the international economy. The market for labor outside the country has absorbed enormous numbers of Yugoslavs who would otherwise have been unemployed.

It is largely the unintended consequences of the policy or the asymmetrical impact on various groups within Yugoslavia that have caused those who are not opposed in principle to the policy (at least as a temporary measure) to call for changes in aspects of the policy. In terms of the general Yugoslav orientation to the world, the mass migration of workers to Germany appears to have shown that Rankovic was right: Given spontaneity, Yugoslav citizenry will opt for a "one-sided link-up with Western Europe or Bavaria"[39] not to the liking of those in the ruling group who are concerned at a minimum to balance off Western connections with continued ties with East Europe and the Soviet Union. The departure of the workers in such numbers has fueled concern for the national security costs of their departure, leading Tito to claim that "three big armies" are missing and to wonder whether they would be able to get back to the country in a crisis.[40] (Ironically, this national security concern stems in part from improved U.S.-Soviet relations; it is even more a reflection of the scare prompted by the Croatian events of 1971 and Tito's age.)

There is scarcely any doubt that, through conspicuous consumption, the Yugoslav workers qua linkage group have exacerbated the already well developed consumer-oriented revolution of rising expectations. The fact that those with skills can readily double and in many instances quadruple their salaries abroad; that the skilled are to be found disproportionately in the north; that even the unskilled abroad earn far more than their counterparts at home; when taken together aggravate the stratification of Yugoslav society geographically, between the skilled and the unskilled, and between those who have been abroad and those who have not. "If low salries are paid to experts in an enterprise," Kardelj has recognized,

> Such persons will prefer to go to find work in Germany. . . . Are we going to curtail the freedom to travel abroad or are we going to take this fact into account, that is, take into account the circumstance that we live in a world that influences us. . . . Would it be possible. . to abolish at the present level of development of productive forces such production relationships as rest on income distribution according to labour performance without reverting to the system of . . . state ownership and the system of political absolutism, or even to the kind of forcible egalitarianism that would destimulate man in his work?[41]

It turns out additionally that "temporary," while difficult to specify precisely, is a rather long time—especially for Croatians who go abroad to work. What meager data there are indicate that the rate of return is low compared with other countries that export labor.* This is important not only in economic terms. Economically, part of the rationale for allowing workers with jobs to go abroad is that this amounts to a form of training (through the acquisition of better work discipline and a more responsible job abroad) to be used when they return. Moreover, it temporary means brief, then the "lost human capital" argument is far less compelling.

It is also important politically. Presently available evidence lends credence to the commonsense notion that duration abroad has a direct bearing on attitude change. Resocialization appears to accelerate progressively with number of years abroad. (Unfortunately the only data touching on this subject are not time series data but rather the responses of different people who have been abroad for different durations.) Edward Komarica, in his duscussion of the findings of an unpublished survey of Yugoslav workers, finds consolation in the fact that only 12.2 percent of the Yugoslav workers who were abroad responded that each would rather be a "small proprietor abroad than a well paid worker in Yugoslavia," while 84.8 percent indicated that they would prefer to be well paid workers in Yugoslavia rather than small proprietors abroad (3 percent did not answer).[42] For our purposes, however, what is interesting is that of those who answered, 5 percent who had been abroad for less than six months chose "small proprietor abroad," 16 percent of those abroad between a year and three years answered "small proprietor abroad," while 27 percent of those abroad more than three years expressed their preference for being small proprietor abroad rather than well paid worker at home. Other questions in the survey point to the same conclusion: Workers abroad for more than three years are more prone to advise children to go abroad to work, more likely to read the emigrant press, and less disposed to join a workers' organization abroad composed of Yugoslav workers (see Table 13.9).

Certain costs that have accrued from the workers' departure appear not to have been considered in 1965-66 and have proved troublesome in ensuing years. A number of small occupations have been decimated by departures abroad. Regions with a high percentage of women abroad (to wit, northern Croatia and norther Vojvodina) are troubled by juvenile delinquency.[43] Figures have been marshaled in the press to show that a sizeable percentage of marriages do not survive the experience of having one partner go abroad, and that children remaining in Yugoslavia while parents work abroad do relatively poorly in

---

*I was informed by one Yugoslav scholar that he had made inquiries of the police in order to obtain return figures. The data, he was told, simply did not exist. One official estimate by the Federal Employment Bureau put the return rate as of 1971 at 22 percent overall and 10 percent for Croatia.

TABLE 13.9

Time Abroad and Attitudinal Preferences
(in percent)

Time Abroad	Proprietor Abroad	Worker in Yugoslavia	Would You Advise Your Children to Go Abroad to Work?		Do You Read Emigrant Press?		Do You Participate in Yugoslav Workers Organization?	
			Yes	No	Yes	No	Yes	No
6 months or less	5	95	15	81	25	75	87	13
6 months to 1 year	7	93	13	82	27	73	88	12
1 year to 3 years	16	84	21	77	49	51	86	14
3 years or more	27	73	33	60	48	52	78	22

school.[44] Finally, it is pointed out that experience abroad entails enormous psychic strains on the individual isolated from a customary social milieu and that a disproportionately large number of persons abroad are likely to suffer from psychic disorders—most notably paranoia.[45]

Such concerns, however, are largely minimalist criticism. The policy prescriptions that flow from them imply an acceptance of the logic and desirability of a policy of open borders. The implicit or explicit prescriptions entail increasing the number of Yugoslav social workers and teachers in Germany and persuading Germany to provide transfer payments to cover the educational costs of Yugoslav children who do not accompany their parents to Germany. Even the concern for national security considerations need only imply—and seems ultimately only to have implied—regulations requiring fulfillment of military obligations prior to departure abroad for work. Nevertheless, the cumulative impact of all these objections suggests a broad consensus that the policy of allowing workers to go abroad, as it has worked out in practice and as its full ramifications became evident, is a matter for serious concern.

Other assessments have not accepted the premises on which the original policy was made, or at least view the redistributive consequences of the policy as of such salience as to call for major, rather than essentially incremental, changes in the migration policy—even if such changes require alteration in the fundamental orientation of the Yugoslav system as well.

One generalized critique was inspired by Croatian nationalist sentiments. In its most narrow construction it connected the number of Croatians working abroad and the heavy preponderance of tourism in Croatia—each of which is a major source of hard currency—with the currency issue, which was so central to Croatian claims, especially in 1971, that the Croatian republic was being exploited by the federation, by Belgrade, by the banks, and by the Serbs. For these Croats a reversal in migration trends was a condition for amicable republic-federation relations. Thus, in 1971 *Politika* cited the then president of the Croatian executive council, Dragutin Haramija, as saying, "I must frankly say: no federal government which in the period to come would consider the possibility of even more of our citizens departing for abroad and relying on their checks to solve Yugoslavia's balance of payments problem could expect support from Croatia."[46]

For other Croats, the tie was not between migration and currency questions but rather between migration and Croatia's population. Here the issue was not mere exploitation but rather a more sinister design to reduce the number of Croats and the influence of Croatia within Yugoslavia.[47] Within this group one element adopted the stance that the "autonomous position [samostalniji polozaj] of Croatia within the federation of the peoples of Yugoslavia"[48] would create conditions wherein Croatia could deal quickly and adequately with its overall population problems, including the regulation of its workers wishing to migrate abroad, and that, to quote the conclusions of a study of the Croatian

Pugwash Group (sic), measures in the regions of migration, employment, and population "are an inseparable part of the sovereignty of the Republic, the working class and the people of SR Croatia."[49]

Others among the more extreme Croatian nationalists, inside and outside the country, envisaged the workers' migration as a potential lever for enhancing Croatian nationalist, and conceivably separatist, aspirations. It has been suggested by Professor F. Singleton, plausibly in my view, that the Zagreb student strike that began November 25, 1971, started "prematurely, having originally been planned for January, when large numbers of Croatian 'Gastarbeiter' would have returned home from Germany for the winter holiday."[50] Tito himself gave credence to this idea in his December 1, 1971, speech in Karadjordjevo: "There was talk, and even reporting in the press, that a strike was forthcoming, that it would be large and would come in January. . . . It is not clear, however, why it was speeded up."[51] After the strike and after the purge of the Croatian leadership (Miko Tripalo, Savka Dabcevic-Kucar, Haramija, and colleagues), Josip Vrhovec charged that "It was only when the migration of our workers became more massive . . . that part of the political emigration" concluded that "the struggle can be won only in Croatia herself."[52] (Vrhovec had labeled the political emigrants' prior efforts, "apart from isolated subversive actions," as "insignificant and absurd.")

A second maximalist critique stems chiefly from strands in Yugoslav thinking that share much in common with old left—"Cominformist," in Yugoslav patois—and new left perspectives and are infused with strong overtones of Yugoslav nationalism. From such a stance, being linked to the international market is consider a dangerous and harmful policy—dangerous because of the likelihood of a European or German economic crisis; harmful because it places Yugoslavia in a neocolonialist position vis-a-vis (German) imperialism and strengthens the restoration of capitalism within Yugoslavia. The attendant acceleration of social stratification is not dismissed as "inevitable in the present historical period"; efficiency is to be traded off for a more egalitarian social structure. The individual who migrates, in this view, especially if he has specialized skills, is virtually disloyal and at a minimum should offset the cost of his training by depositing some kind of bond equivalent to the amount paid for his education prior to his departure abroad.[53] For the nation, migration constitutes a form of selling Yugoslav workers to foreign capitalists; rather than such a tack, the regime should assure employment within the country for all.

Such attitudes find a wide resonance in Yugoslavia, even for those who are unwilling to pay the political price that a commitment to domestic full employment currently involves. Thus Tito, who in the past has accused the new left of demagogy for insisting that all can find work in Yugoslavia, in 1973 associated himself with a position in favor of continued subsidization of the coal mines: "The coal mines employ large numbers of men—some of them having worked there for decades. We do not want these men now to go to some foreign country to work there."[54]

Finally, we can identify a dimension to the dialogue that might be termed the neo-capitalist critique of the outward migration of workers. This line of reasoning shares with the left a sense that the out-migration of workers and its internal ramifications represent a threat to core socialist values. It diverges from the mainline view and from the left in that it sees the remedy as greater, not less openness,[55] and sees greater openness and a willingness to further incorporate capitalist practices as a lesser threat to Yugoslav autonomy and the overall socialist orientation of Yugoslavia than the persistent outflow of Yugoslav labor to capitalist-owned factories abroad. This line of criticism deplores the continued restrictions on small private enterprises and the limits on the size of peasant ownings. Persons disposed to this view do not believe that the introduction of a socialist stock market would bring about the collapse of Yugoslav socialism.[56] Indeed, they see a socialist stock market as a vehicle for increasing the workers' marginal propensity to invest in Yugoslovia and to invest in plant and equipment rather than in consumer durables. They are, further, less resistant than others to encroachments on the law on joint enterprises, which requires that no more than 49 percent be held by a foreign partner.

FUTURE PATTERNS AND POLICIES

What is interesting about these critiques (with the exception of the Croatian nationalist viewpoint) is that there appears to be emerging a new prominent solution to the dilemmas posed by the out-migration of Yugoslav workers. Despite Tito's voiced concerns about three Yugoslav armies abroad and his willingness to employ federal subsidies to keep miners within the country; despite the demands that "all means including administrative measures" be employed to regulate the flow of workers; the regime seems to have shrunk from undertaking drastic measures to curb the outflow. The center and the left, even at a time when there has been "a step to the left," are of one mind that the out-migration of workers is dysfunctional to values they cherish—values like order and (scientific) socialism. But it seems to have been generally concluded that economic measures, as in the past, will continue to be the main regulatory mechanism. There has in practice been a reticence to employ the techniques that would succeed in curbing the outflow (and, one hastens to add, result in an enormous number of Yugoslavs already abroad simply remaining there), and would in fact entail "reverting . . . to the system of political absolutism." Despite the renewed demands for the mandatory teaching of Marxism, the emphasis on democratic centralism, and the guiding role of the party, there does not seem a proclivity to accept the advice of those who would insist that "'citizens going to work abroad should possess specific moral-political qualities'"—

which, as *Politika* wrote sarcastically, raised the issue of whether "members of the League of Communists would have priority with regard to work in capitalist enterprises" and brings us back "to the times when the obtaining of passports depended on janitors' statements."[57]

There remains, indeed, a body of influential thought committed to the posture, in Mijalko Todorovic's words at the Third Session of the Presidency, that migration "is in contemporary conditions a rational decision for those who go out and for the working class as a whole. It is the logical decision of an open society, such as ours, with democratic and human relationships and full trust in its citizens."[58] Or, in the words of Zeljko Brihta, editor of the Zagreb daily, *Vjesnik*, in May 1973: the "workers abroad have become a permanent phenomenon" and represent "a special kind and part of the European detente, a fact accompanying the process of transforming frontiers into bridges. They [the workers] are the best proof that 'the free exchange of people' has been realized in this part of the continent. . . . This is a kind of European integration, broader than that around the Common Market or in it."[59]

Moreover, there seems over the past few years to have emerged a partial acceptance of the neocapitalist critique; namely, that without fundamentally restructuring the political system, the only alternative in the long run to the outflow of manpower is the inflow of foreign capital. "The only distinguishing feature"—to quote Miljko Trifunovic, the editor of a major economic periodical—between foreign and domestic capital "is that domestic sources of capital are inadequate."[60]

Yugoslavia, by happenstance or design, seems to have learned the lesson Samuel P. Huntington claims for Thailand: "A government may . . . [grant] access to private, government, and international transnational organizations in such a way as to further its own objectives. . . . The widespread penetration of its society by transnational organizations will, obviously, have significant effects on that society. . . . In the process, [however, it may greatly strengthen] . . . itself as a government."[61] If this calculus is indeed operative, then nonalignment in the 1970s will entail the continued penetration of Yugoslavia by plural sources including major capital inflows from the Soviet Union, from private investors, especially in Germany and the United States, and from the IBRD.

Should this be so, and should the political preconditions for outmigration continue to obtain (as seemingly is to be the case), then we ought to be able to make some predictions about the nature of Yugoslav migration patterns during the next decade. Combining two different projections by Vinski, one dealing with income distribution across republics, the other with Yugoslav "gross social product,"[62] and accepting the idea that earnings of roughly $1,400 per capita (in 1970 dollars) represent an immigration-emigration equilibrium point, Slovene migration should never return to the rates of the early 1970s and migration from Croatia should also have peaked. It also flows logically from these projections that the migration from Serbia proper and Vojvodina should also have peaked by 1975. The steady growth of unemployment in these areas during the years 1972-74 suggest, however, a renewed upsurge in migration in response to the augmented demand stemming from an expected West European economic revival.

It appears, furthermore, that the out-migration rates from Macedonia will remain high throughout the decade, while those of Bosnia and Hercegovina, in particular the Muslim portion, and especially Kosovo and Montenegro, should increase throughout the decade. Furthermore, there is every reason to suspect that persons from the latter republics will migrate both to Europe and to the more developed, more European, parts of Yugoslavia.[63] The republics and regions of Yugoslavia that are now a highly integrated part of the general European labor market will be preoccupied in the last years of the coming decade far more with the consequences of the in-migration of workers from parts of the former Ottoman empire, within Yugoslavia and conceivably including persons from Turkey and Albania, than with the out-migration of their own workers to Western Europe.

NOTES

1. See, in this regard, James N. Rosenau, "Theorizing Across Systems: Linkage Politics Revisited," in *Conflict Behavior and Linkage Politics*, ed. Jonathan Wilkenfeld (New York: David McKay, 1973), pp. 25-58; and his "Pre-Theories and Theories of Foreign Policy," in *Approaches to Comparative and International Politics*, ed. R. Barry Farrell (Evanston, Ill.: Northwestern University Press, 1966), pp. 27-92.

2. Arnold Wolfers, *Discord and Collaboration* (Baltimore: Johns Hopkins Press, 1962).

3. Farrell, ed., *Approaches*, p. 7.

4. The term is, of course, Zbigniew Brzezinski's. See his *The Soviet Bloc* (Cambridge, Mass.: Harvard University Press, 1960).

5. For a discussion, see William Zimmerman, "Soviet Foreign Policy in the 1970s," *Survey* 19, no. 2 (Spring 1973): 188-98.

6. Zimmerman, *Soviet Perspectives on International Relations, 1956-1967* (Princeton: Princeton University Press, 1969).

7. For example, the essay by Vernon Aspaturian in Farrell, ed., *Approaches*, pp. 212-88.

8. Grey Hodnett and Peter Potichnij, *The Ukraine and Czechoslovak Crisis* (Canberra: Australian National University, Occasional Paper no. 6, 1970); Zvi Y. Gitelman, *The Diffusion of Political Innovation: From Eastern Europe to the Soviet Union* (Beverly Hills, Calif.: Sage Publications, 1972).

9. "Everyone knows that freedom and state socialism are incompatible," one Yugoslav economist told this author in 1968. For a more general essay relating economic decentralization and humanist values, see Branko Horvat, *An Essay on Yugoslav Society* (White Plains, N.Y.: IASP, 1969).

10. For evidence dating the origins of Titoism to World War II, see Paul Shoup, *Communism and the National Question* (New York: Columbia University Press, 1968); A. Ross Johnson, *The Transformation of Communist Ideology* (Cambridge, Mass.: MIT Press, 1972).

11. Shoup, *Communism*, pp. 249-60.

12. Vlado Benko, "Theses on European Security," *Review of International Affairs* 20, no. 471 (November 20, 1969): 4.

13. *Ekonomska Politika*, February 24, 1969, as translated by *Joint Translation Service*, no. 5267 (February 28, 1969): 38.

14. *Borba* (Belgrade), May 17, 1969, in *Joint Translation Service*, no. 5329 (May 21, 1969): 6.

15. Zvonimir Komarica, *Jugoslavija u savremenim Evropskim migracijama* (Zagreb: Ekonomski Institut, 1970), p. 104.

16. Ivo Vinski, "Zaposljavanje Jugoslavena u inozemstvu," *Ekonomski Pregled* 22, nos. 7-8 (July-August, 1971): 367.

17. *Nedeljne informativje novine (NIN)*, no. 1116 (May 28, 1972): 5.

18. Interview with Ivo Baucic. His findings will be reported in "Die beschaftigung ausladischer Arbeitnehmer in der Bundesrepublik Deutschland in Eihren Auswurkungen auf die internationalen Beziehungen," a paper prepared for the Forschungsinstitut der Deutschen Gesellschaft fur Aswartige Politik.

19. Komarica, *Jugoslavija*, pp. 5-6, contains a comparison of the five studies. Of the five, one—*SFRJ u Evropskim migracijama rada* (Zagreb, 1967)—has never been published, although many of its central findings have been reported publicly in several Yugoslav sources.

20. See, for instance, the detailed treatment in the article from *Ekonomska Politika*, February 24, 1969, as translated by *Joint Translation Service*, no. 5267 (February 28, 1969): 38.

21. See, for instance, Slobodan Stankovic, "Dolanc's Speech Indicates New Stage in Yugoslav Party," Radio Free Europe *Research*, September 20, 1972; R. Waring Herrick, "Soviet-Yugoslav Rapprochement Meeting Strengthens Opposition in Belgrade," Radio Liberty *Dispatch*, August 17, 1972; Slobodan Stankovic, "After Slovenian Central Committee Plenum," RFE *Research*, November 8, 1972; Robin Remington, "Nonalignment—On Whose Side," unpublished paper presented at the American Association for South Slavic Studies, New York, March 1973.

22. For a voice advocating such a tactic, see General Ivan Dolnicar's remarks at the joint session of the Yugoslav Presidency and the Presidium of the League of Communists as reported in *Borba*, February 6, 1973, and summarized in *NIN*, no. 1153 (February 11, 1973): 9.

23. In Velko Rus's words, "One of the general characteristics of an open system is that its parts or subsystems can be more intensively connected with their relevant sub-environment than with the other parts within the same system. . . . Individual republics or individual activities can be more intensively included in some processes or systems outside Yugoslavia than within Yugoslavia." "Questions for Discussion," *International Journal of Politics* 2, no. 1 (Spring 1972): 14.

24. Daniel Lerner, *The Passing of Traditional Society* (New York: Free Press, 1964).

25. *Savremene migracije*, p. 121. For a brief treatment of Yugoslav migration patterns, 1850-1960, see Institut drustvenih nauka (Centar za demografska istrazivanja), *Demografski i ekonomski aspekti pokretljivosti stanovnistva u Jugoslaviji posle drugog svetskog rata* (Belgrade: Savezni biro za poslove zaposljavanja, 1968), pp. 30-33.

26. Ivo Baucic, *Porijeklo i struktura radnika iz Jugoslavije u SR Njemackoj* (Zagreb: Institut za Geografiju, 1970), p. 70. A more general outline of a communication model is contained in ibid., pp. 68-73.

27. In 1969, some 60 percent found employment abroad through friends and acquaintances. *Ekonomska Politika*, February 24, 1969, as translated by *Joint Translation Service*, no. 5267 (February 28, 1969): 38.

28. M. Friganovic, M. Morokvasic, I. Baucic, *Iz Jugoslavije na rad u Francusku* (Zagreb: Institut za Geografiju, 1972).

29. Branko Horvat notes: "A sociologist who analyzes the motives of Croats who work abroad informed me that the... phrase ["Serbs rule in Croatia"] very often appears as one of the motives." "Nationalism and Nationality," *International Journal of Politics* 2, no. 1 (Spring 1972): 45.

30. Aleksa Milojevic and Vladimir Sultanovic, "Zaposljavanje u inostranstvu," *Pregled* (Sarajevo) 252, no. 1 (January 1972): 33-47, at p. 39.

31. Ivo Baucic and Zivko Maravic, *Vracanje i Zaposljavanje vansjkih migranata iz SR Hrvatske* (Zagreb: Institut za Geografiju, 1971), p. 80.

32. Ibid., p. 45.

33. T. Okun', "Inostrannye rabochie v Zapadnoi Germanii," *Mirovaia ekonomika i mezhdunarodnye otnosheniia*, no. 3 (March 1973): 137-38. See also "Foreign Workers in Western Europe," *World Marxist Review* 16, no. 7 (July 1973): 53-71, for a discussion by European Communists, East and West, of the general migration problem in West Europe. The one remark about Yugoslavia comes as a footnote to the observation, "The socialist countries are no longer, as they had been before the war, a reservoir of labor for the 'industrial West': The exception, so far, is Yugoslavia. There are over 460,000 Yugoslav workers in the FRG, where they make up the second biggest ethnic group" (p. 56).

34. See "Lov i na 'nasu divljac,'" *NIN*, no. 1135 (October 8, 1972): 39 for a scarcely disguised indication that proposals to require skilled persons to pay in order to go abroad are unacceptable because such proposals are reminiscent of Soviet regulations pertaining to Jewish emigrations.

35. Svetislav Polovina, "Migraciona kretania u Evropi i njihovo ekonomsko-drustveno znacenje," *Nase teme*, no. 12 (December 1969): 1949-50.

36. For a discussion, see Ivo Vinski, "Troskovi skolovanjadjece radnika na privremenom radu u inozemstvu," *Ekonomski pregled* 24, nos. 1-2 (January-February 1973): 43-54.

37. For a recent discussion of this prospect, see "Foreign Investment in Yugoslavia," RFE *Research*, May 10, 1973, pp. 1-5.

38. Farrell, ed., *Approaches*, p. 12.

39. Such was the charge directed primarily against Stane Kavcic by Edward Kardelj. See *Borba* (Belgrade), September 22, 1972. Slobodan Stankovic, in "Crisis Between 'Hardliners' and 'Soft-liners' in Yugoslav Party?" RFE *Research,* September 28, 1972, notes that Zagreb *Borba* carried Kardelj's attack on September 20. It is of note that Slovenia, Croatia, and Serbia all had direct ties with Munich in considerable measure because of the workers from the three republics working in Bavaria.

40. *Borba*, December 9, 1972, as cited in Slobodan Stankovic, "After the Third Party Conference in Belgrade," RFE *Research*, December 11, 1972. This concern, it should be stressed, appears to be overdone and fails to recognize how much women abroad affect the age structure of those abroad.

41. Edward Kardelj, "Social Differences and the Disposal of Social Capital," *Socialist Thought and Practice*, no. 45 (October-December 1971): 5-6.

42. Komarica, *Jugoslavija*, p. 45.

43. For figures and a brief discussion see Baucic, *Vracanje*, pp. 30-31 and Supplement 3.

44. Grecic, *Savremene migracije*, p. 180, reports *Ekonomska Politika*, no. 1067 (September 11, 1972) summarized a study of the Institut za socijalnu politiku to the effect that 40 percent of the children of workers abroad perform poorly in school and 28 percent of the marriages are not sustained. Just what one is to make of these figures in the absence of comparative data is unclear.

45. Dusan Kecmanovic, "Dusevni poremacaji ekonomskih emigranata," *Nase teme* 16, no. 1 (January 1972): 149-69.

46. *Politika*, April 18, 1971.

47. One Croatian nationalist in 1970 told me Belgrade was conducting a policy of "genocide." For less strident terminology but with much the same message, see Komarica, *Jugoslavija*, and Sime Djodan, "Regionalni ekonomski razvoj Jugoslavije," *Encyclopaedia moderna* 14, no. 10 (Fall 1969): 31-49.

48. "Zakljucci Harvatske pagvaske grupe o stanovnistvu, emigraciji i zaposlenosti u SR Hrvatskoj," *Encyclopaedia moderna* 6, no. 15 (Winter 1971): 107.

49. Ibid., p. 105.

50. F. Singleton, "The Roots of Discord in Yugoslavia," *World Today* 28, no. 4 (April 1972): 177-78.

51. Several English-language versions of Tito's speech exist. I have used the version translated from *Politika*, December 3, 1971, in the *International Journal of Politics* 2, no. 1 (Spring 1972): 86-93.

52. *Borba*, January 11, 1972, as translated by *Joint Translation Service*, no. 6135 (January 11, 1972): 13.

53. For one such example, see a *Borba* account (April 8, 1971) reporting that this idea was being mentioned in Slovenia. Note, too, "Lov i na 'nasu divljac,'" *NIN*, no. 1135 (October 8, 1972).

54. *Politika*, April 5, 1973.

55. For instance, Rus, "Questions," p. 13.

56. Kavcic was one such person. See Singleton, "The Roots," p. 175, for a report of a press interview by Kavcic in which the idea is discussed, and Kardelj's remark that such views constitute a "direct negation of our revolution." Scholarly discussions of the pros and cons of a socialist stock market include Miodrag Sukijasovic, "Neki nereseni problemi u Jugoslovenskom zakondavstvu o ulaganju stranog kapitala," *Meadjunarodni problemi* 22, no. 1 (1970): 31-42.

57. *Politika*, March 18, 1973.

58. As cited in Grecic's peroration (*Savremene migracije*, p. 298).

59. *Vjesnik*, May 8, 1973, and reported in Zdenko Antic, "Yugoslavia's Manpower Export Still Important," RFE *Research*, May 10, 1973.

60. Trifunovic, "The Yugoslav Economy and Direct Foreign Investment," *Review of International Affairs*, no. 532 (June 5, 1972): 30. For an observation that the 49:51 ratio does not affect the propensity to invest in Slovenia, see *Borba*, February 26, 1973.

61. "Transnational Organizations in World Politics," *World Politics* 25, no. 3 (April 1973): 364-65.

62. In "Drustveni proizvod Jugoslavije i zemalja istoka i zapada," *Ekonomski pregled*, no. 10-11 (October-November 1971): 27, Vinski projects Yugoslavia's gross social product (a concept slightly different from GNP) per capita for 1975 at $1,241, for 1980 at $1,655, and for 1985 at $2,202 (constant 1970 dollars). In "Kolektivna potrosnja u Jugoslaviji, 1970-1985," *Ekonomski pregled* nos. 11-12 (November-December 1972): 511, he estimates the average social product per republic in percentage terms (Yugoslavia = 100) for 1970 and 1985 as follows:

Republic	1970	1985
Slovenia	182	159
Croatia	123	119
Vojvodina	119	117
Serbia proper	100	107
Montenegro	73	81
Macedonia	68	78
Bosnia and Hercegovina	65	76
Kosovo	34	46

63. In fact, if we treat interrepublic and international migrations equally, Slovenia is already a net importer of labor. As Stipe Suvar remarked pointedly—"Drustvena pokretlji-

vost i razvojne perspektive Jugoslovenskog drustva," *Glediste* 12, nos. 11-12 (November-December 1971): 1489-1567 at 1567—"In Slovenia there already· work 130,000 workers from other republics. When that number of 'foreigners' is compared with the 1,700,000 Slovenes, then it turns out that 'the foreign' work force in Slovenia is greater than in West Germany (in West Germany there are 2,200,000 foreign workers for 60 million Germans)."

Jan F. Triska
Paul M. Cocks

In this volume we have tried to focus on and cope with what we consider to be the essential issues of political development and change in Eastern Europe. To get at those issues, we have employed modes of analysis which appeared to us, individually and collectively, the most appropriate for the respective problems studied. Have we succeeded?

Ours is the second full-fledged volume on the subject. The first, published in 1974, was *Politics of Modernization in Eastern Europe: Testing the Soviet Model*, edited by Charles Gati—a thought-provoking and insightful collection of perceptive essays. In a review of that study, the senior editor of this book said that expectations had been raised by that volume and that those who took on this matter in the future would have to do very well indeed. Have we done so?

There are two major problems, both critical, which this volume meets head on. The first is the easier one. It concerns the relationship between Communist studies and comparative politics. As Gabriel Almond points out in the preface, communism was studied as a new type of dictatorship in the 1920s and 1930s, and as a totalitarian dictatorship or "totalitarianism" in the 1950s. Comparative communism became a popular conceptualizing framework in the 1960s. In the 1970s the emphasis has increasingly shifted from comparative communism to comparative politics. The studies of communism have come in out of the cold, less because of any warm hospitality on the part of the discipline of comparative politics than because of the important strides and innovative thinking on the part of students of Communist politics. The studies of communism have a home now. Their gradual incorporation into comparative politics does signify an important phase "in the professional maturation of both fields." The process is far from over; but the guidelines are set, and the mutuality of interests is being recognized by scholars in both disciplines.

The second major critical problem is what appears to many of our generation as the perennial problem of modern studies of politics (although it is not more than thirty years old) which all students of politics share equally and in which students of communist politics are bogged down just as much as everyone else in the profession. This is the familiar horse-and-buggy argument between those who oppose "abstract theoretical approaches" and "quantitative analyses" of political behavior vs. those who criticize "non-cumulative, non-comparable, un-theoretical historical case studies." Two distinguished, sophisticated, and articulate advocates and critics of those respective approaches argued this one out at the conference which preceded this volume. Gordon Skilling emphasized "the need for concrete empirical case studies and for a historical approach in a field of study that is still underdeveloped and lacks the raw materials for sweeping theoretical generalizations." And he termed "misleading, and dangerous for conceptual clarity, the sweeping use of an ambiguous and culture-bound concept (modernization and political development) to Eastern Europe as a whole, ignoring the deep differences between the individual countries prior to communist rule."

David Finley, on the other hand, took to task historical case studies: "They are likely to be independent of any theory or to conceal implicit theory that should be explicit, to be non-cumulative, non-comparable, and to explain change in terms of voluntary responses to events. Because unique causal sequences are sought, patterns may be obscured. Ad hoc studies are also prone to focus on the 'high politics' of visible policy departures and in so doing to attribute insignificance to evolutionary change in the background conditions that may cumulatively produce a crisis situation."

Instead, Finely recommended that "we begin with the generalizing orientation of science, positing regular relationships among variables abstracted from the reality we want to explain and to which we give unambiguous definitions. To encompass development over time, we must take the effects of time seriously and make explicit allowance for the shifting nature of our variables. We must take advantage of theory, generated in contexts where aggregatable data such as afforded by accessible decision processes and survey research are available, to propose conceptual frameworks and specific hypotheses to explain behavior where the data are not available. Then . . . we should frankly turn to historical case studies of unique sequences of events with the aim of falsifying and modifying our hypotheses. . . . Such a strategy," Finley concluded, "promises to yield a product epistemologically superior to either social science or historical inquiry employed separately."

The debate goes on, and will go on; neither side has come forth with the definitive answer as yet. But both schools of thought agree on one thing: the need for more empirical studies, for more information, for greater accessibility of Communist countries to direct research. This, indeed, is our Achilles heel. This is the direction in which we must move. And in this effort, we hope, lies the major contribution of this volume. We are getting on with the job of doing the empirical research we say should be done, along the lines which we hope will contribute to our theoretical understanding of social reality.

NAME INDEX

Afanasyev, Viktor G., 74
Almond, Gabriel A., 34, 47
Apter, David E., 34
Armstrong, John A., 16

Barbic, Ana, 152, 153, 156
Baucic, Ivo, 345, 350
Beria, Lavrentii, 104, 317
Brezhnev, Leonid Ilich, 56, 76, 78
Brzezinski, Zbigniew, 3; *The Soviet Bloc*, 241, 320
Bukharin, Nikolai, 57

Campbell, John C., 318
Ceausescu, Nicolae, 76, 80, 217, 298
Churchill, Sir Winston, 316
Cojocaru, Constantin, 65
Conquest, Robert, 31
Croan, Melvin, 4, 74

Dahl, Robert, 178
Deutsch, Karl, 283, 335, 352
Dubcek, Alexander, 54

Easton, David, 34
Ellman, Michael, 63

Feld, Werner, 324
Fleron, Frederic J., 45
Friedrich, Carl J., 3; and Z. Brzezinski, 32

Gitelman, Zvi, 285
Gomulka, Wladyslaw, 54, 55
Grecic, Vladimir, 348
Griffiths, William, 12
Grossman, Gregory, 324

Hammond, Thomas, 181
Hewett, Edward A., 263
Hough, Jerry, 150
Huntington, Samuel P., 4, 7-14, 36, 122, 125, 147, 283, 301

Ionescu, Ghita, 7, 321

Jarosz, Maria, 129

Johnson, Chalmers, 119
Johnson, Lyndon B., 320
Johnson, Paul, economic reform scale, 44-45
Jowitt, Kenneth, 74, 80

Kadar, Janos, 5
Kanet, Roger E., 296
Kassof, Allen, 31
Kesselman, Mark, 124
Khrushchev, Nikita S., 5, 54, 55, 81, 104, 106
Komarica, Zvonimir, 339
Korbonski, Andrzej, 270, 330
Kautsky, John, 4

Lenin, Vladimir I., 283
Lerner, Daniel, 348
Little, Richard D., 150
Lodge, Milton, 45
Lowenthal, Richard, 17

Malenkov, Georgii, 317
Marx, Karl, 84, 188
McMillan, Carl H., 264
McNamara, Robert S., 105
Meyer, Alfred, 11, 31
Miller, Arthur, 325
Mil'ner, B., 71-72

Nelson, Daniel, 162, 163
Nelson, Joan, 147
Nie, Norman H., 120
Nixon, Raymond B., 46
Novotny, Antonin, 5, 54, 104, 248

Pryor, Frederic L., 68
Pye, Lucian, 35

Rakosi, Matyas, 5
Rankovic, Alexander, 337, 353
Roosevelt, Franklin D., 316
Rosenau, James, 277
Rush, Myron, 13
Rusk, Dean, 320

367

ABOUT THE EDITORS AND CONTRIBUTORS

JAN F. TRISKA is Professor of Political Science at Stanford University. Before coming to Stanford, he taught at Harvard, University of California at Berkeley, and Cornell University.

Dr. Triska has published widely on Soviet foreign policy, Soviet treaties and agreements, and East European politics. His most recent volume is Book 2, Volume 13, in the Monograph Series in World Affairs of the University of Denver, *Political Development and Political Change in Eastern Europe* (with Paul Johnson), 1976.

Professor Triska holds a J.U.D. from Charles University Law School in Prague, a J.S.D. from Yale Law School, and a Ph.D. in political science from Harvard.

PAUL COCKS is Research Fellow at the Hoover Institution and Lecturer in Political Science at Stanford University. Before coming to Stanford, he taught at Harvard University.

Specializing in Soviet domestic affairs, he is co-editor of *The Dynamics of Soviet Politics* (1976) and author of *The Scientific-Technological Revolution and Soviet Politics* (forthcoming). He also has written several book chapters and articles on comparative Communist systems.

Dr. Cocks holds an A.B. from Stanford as well as M.A. degrees in both Soviet and East Asian studies and a Ph.D. in political science from Harvard.

KENT BROWN received his A.B. in 1964 and M.A. in 1965 from the University of California at Davis. He did further graduate work at Berkeley and University of California at Los Angeles before entering the Foreign Service in 1966. His first overseas assignment was Panama, 1967-69, followed by a brief tour in Trinidad.

Mr. Brown spent the years 1970-73 as Consul and Political Officer at the American Embassy, Prague. After one year in the Department of State Operations Center in 1974, he was assigned to Stanford University as an advanced student in Soviet and East European Area Studies. At the same time he was extended an appointment as State Department Visiting Research Fellow by the Hoover Institution on War, Revolution and Peace. Mr. Brown is presently Officer in Charge of Czechoslovak Affairs at the Department of State in Washington.

LENARD J. COHEN is Assistant Professor of Political Science at Simon Fraser University. His main field of interest is East European politics, especially Yugoslavia. He is coeditor of *Communist Systems in Comparative Perspective* (1974) and is currently working on a study of East European parliamentary systems and electoral behavior. Professor Cohen received his A.B. and M.A. from the University of Illinois at Urbana. His Ph.D. in political science is pending from Columbia University.

MARY ELLEN FISCHER is Assistant Professor of Government at Skidmore College in New York. Working primarily in the field of East European politics, she is currently completing a study on political leadership in Romania since 1965. Professor Fischer holds an A.B. from Wellesley, an M.A. in Soviet studies, and Ph.D. in political science from Harvard.

CHARLES GATI is Professor and Chairman in the Department of Political Science at Union College. Since 1971 he has concurrently served as Visiting Professor of Political Science at Columbia University. Specializing in the international relations of Eastern Europe and Soviet foreign policy, he is editor and coauthor of *Caging the Bear: Containment and the Cold War, The Politics of Modernization in Eastern Europe: Testing the Soviet Model* (Praeger Publishers, second printing, 1976), and *The International Politics of Eastern Europe* (Praeger Publishers, 1976).

ZVI GITELMAN is Associate Professor of Political Science at the University of Michigan. He has published widely on Soviet and East European affairs. He is the author of *Jewish Nationality and Soviet Politics* (1972) and *The Diffusion of Political Innovation: From Eastern Europe to the Soviet Union* (1972). Prof. Gitelman holds an A.B., M.A., and Ph.D. in political science from Columbia University.

PAUL JOHNSON is Assistant Professor of Political Science at Yale University. Working primarily in the field of East European politics, he is coauthor with Jan F. Triska of *Political Development and Political Change in Eastern Europe* (1976). Professor Johnson received his A.B. from Rice University and both his M.A. and Ph.D. in political science from Stanford University.

KENNETH JOWITT is Associate Professor of Political Science at the University of California, Berkeley. He has published in *World Politics, American Political Science Review, Survey,* and *Studies in Comparative Communism.* His work *Revolutionary Breakthroughs and National Development* was published by the University of California Press in 1971. He is currently working on a theory of national development and continuing his work on patterns of political organization in Communist polities.

ANDRZEJ KORBONSKI is Professor of Political Science at the University of California, Los Angeles. He is author of *Politics of Socialist Agriculture in Poland 1945-1960,* and has written on various aspects of East European politics and economics. His articles have appeared in *Comparative Politics, International Organization, Journal of International Affairs, Slavic Review,* and *World Politics.*

Dr. Korbonski holds a B.Sc. in economics from the University of London, and an M.A. and Ph.D. in public law and government from Columbia University.

PAUL MARER is Associate Professor of Economics and Director of the East Europe Program at Indiana University. Before coming to Indiana, he taught at City University of New York. He is author of *Soviet and East European Foreign Trade, 1946-1969: Statistical Compendium and Guide* (1972) and *Postwar Pricing and Price Patterns in Socialist Foreign Trade (1946-1971)* (1972). He is coeditor of *Proceedings of the Conference on East-West Trade and Technology Transfer* (1974). In addition, he has written numerous chapters in books and articles in *The American Economic Review, Slavic Review, Soviet Studies, East Europe,* and *Studies in Comparative Communism*. Professor Marer received both his M.A. and Ph.D. in economics from the University of Pennsylvania.

SARAH MEIKLEJOHN TERRY is a Research Fellow of the Harvard Russian Research Center and an Associate Dean and Assistant Professor of Political Science at Tufts University. She has taught East European politics and comparative communism at Tufts University. She is currently working on a two-volume study of the Polish-German boundary question during and after World War II. Dr. Terry holds a B.A. from Cornell University, and an M.A. and Ph.D. in political science from Harvard. She also has studied at the Instytut Zachodni in Poznan, Poland.

WILLIAM ZIMMERMAN is Professor of Political Science and Director of the Center for Russian and East European Studies at the University of Michigan. Professor Zimmerman has published extensively on Soviet foreign policy, East European politics, and comparative foreign policies. He is the author of *Soviet Perspectives on International Relations* (1969) and of a forthcoming study on *Yugoslavia and the Consequences of Openness*. Professor Zimmerman received his A.B. from Swarthmore College, an M.A. from George Washington University, and Ph.D. in public law and government from Columbia University.

*THE INTERNATIONAL POLITICS OF EASTERN EUROPE
edited by
Charles Gati

CHANGE AND ADAPTATION IN SOVIET AND EAST
EUROPEAN POLITICS
edited by
Jane P. Shapiro
Peter J. Potichnyj

THE SOCIAL STRUCTURE OF EASTERN EUROPE:
Transition and Process in Czechoslovakia, Hungary, Poland,
Romania, and Yugoslavia
edited by
Bernard Lewis Faber

POLITICAL SOCIALIZATION IN EASTERN EUROPE:
A Comparative Framework
edited by
Ivan Volgyes

POLITICS IN THE GERMAN DEMOCRATIC REPUBLIC
John M. Starrels
Anita M. Mallinckrodt

*Also available in paperback as a PSS Student Edition